Handbook on Quality of Life for Human Service Practitioners

Robert L. Schalock
and
Miguel Angel Verdugo Alonso

David L. Braddock
AAMR Books and Research
Monographs Editor

Handbook on Quality of Life for Human Service Practitioners

Robert L. Schalock, PhD
Professor Emeritus
Hastings College

Miguel Angel Verdugo Alonso, PhD
Professor of Psychology of Disability
University of Salamanca

David L. Braddock, PhD
AAMR Books and Research
Monographs Editor

American Association on Mental Retardation

© 2002 by the American Association on Mental Retardation

Published by
American Association on Mental Retardation
444 North Capitol Street, NW
Suite 846
Washington, DC 20001-1512

The points of view expressed herein are those of the authors and do not necessarily represent the official policy or opinion of the American Association on Mental Retardation. Publication does not imply endorsement by the editor, the Association, or its individual members.

Printed in the United States of America

Library of Congress Cataloging-in-Publication Data

Schalock, Robert L.
    Handbook on quality of life for human service practitioners / Robert L. Schalock, Miguel Angel Verdugo Alonso.
       p. cm.
    Includes bibliographical references and index.
    ISBN 0-940898-77-2
       1. Human services — Evaluation — Handbooks, manuals, etc.   2. Quality of life — Evaluation — Handbooks, manuals, etc.   3. Evaluation reserach (Social action programs) — Handbooks, manuals, etc.   I. Verdugo, Miguel Angel.   II. Title.

HV35 .S33 2002
362.2'042--dc21   2002018380

Dedication

A life of quality is a shared life. To our students, wives (Sue and Teresa), and Miguel's daughter (Elisa), we say thank you for sharing ours.

Table of Contents

List of Tables vii

List of Figures ix

List of Appendixes ix

Acknowledgments xi

PART 1. An Overview of This Handbook and the Concept of Quality of Life 1

Chapter 1   About This Handbook 3

Chapter 2   The Concept of Quality of Life: Its Meaning, Importance, and Our Approach to It 11

PART 2. The Integration of Research on Quality of Life 31

Chapter 3   Education and Special Education 35

Chapter 4   Physical Health 51

Chapter 5   Mental Health and Behavioral Health 77

Chapter 6   Mental Retardation and Intellectual Disabilities 117

Chapter 7   Aging 143

Chapter 8   Family-Centered Quality of Life 165

Chapter 9   A Synthesis of Core Quality of Life Domains and Indicators ... 181

PART 3. The Measurement of Quality of Life 189

Chapter 10   Measurement Techniques Currently Used in Quality of Life Research 195

Chapter 11   A Systems Approach to Quality of Life Measurement 267

PART 4. The Application of the Concept of Quality of Life 287

Chapter 12   Individual-Level Application of the Concept of Quality of Life 291

Chapter 13   Organizational-Level Application of the Concept of Quality of Life 309

Chapter 14   Societal-Level Application of the Concept of Quality of Life 331

Chapter 15   Putting It All Together and Moving Ahead 347

References 371

Subject Index 425

List of Tables

Table 1.1.	Key contextual factors addressed in this handbook	7
Table 2.1.	Exemplary quality of life domains	16
Table 2.2.	Quality of life conceptualization principles	19
Table 2.3.	Quality of life application principles	20
Table 3.1.	Quality of life domains and indicators in education and special education	41
Table 4.1.	Quality of life domains and indicators in physical health	63
Table 5.1.	Quality of life domains and indicators in mental and behavioral health	88
Table 6.1.	Quality of life domains and indicators in mental retardation and intellectual disabilities	126
Table 7.1.	Quality of life domains and indicators in aging	150
Table 8.1.	Individual and family quality of life domains and indicators	171
Table 8.2.	Measurement and application principles of family quality of life	176
Table 8.3.	Quality-of-life-related caregiver guidelines	178
Table 9.1.	Rank order of quality of life domains and indicators by text's focus areas	182
Table 9.2.	Core indicators and descriptors per core quality of life domain	184
Table 10.1.	Quality of life measurement techniques used in education and special education	196
Table 10.2.	Quality of life measurement techniques used in physical health	202
Table 10.3.	Quality of life measurement techniques used in mental and behavioral health	210
Table 10.4.	Quality of life measurement techniques used in mental retardation and intellectual disabilities	218
Table 10.5.	Quality of life measurement techniques used in aging	224
Table 11.1.	Microsystem quality of life indicators	274
Table 11.2.	Mesosystem quality of life indicators	275
Table 12.1.	Component elements of self-determined behavior	296
Table 13.1.	Consumer satisfaction and organization-referenced outcomes	313
Table 13.2.	Important guidelines in selecting outcome measures	318
Table 13.3.	Support functions aggregated by quality of life core domains	321
Table 13.4.	Quality of life enhancement techniques	322

continued

Table 14.1.	Core concepts of disability policy	338
Table 15.1.	Quality of life conceptualization, measurement, and application principles	348
Table 15.2.	Core quality of life domain average (mean) rankings	350
Table 15.3.	Most commonly used core indicators per core quality of life domain	351
Table 15.4.	Core quality of life domains and potential motivation states	359
Table 15.5.	Suggested action steps for countries to apply the quality of life concept	361
Table 15.6.	Approaches to establishing reliability and validity	365

List of Figures

Figure 2.1.	Ecological approach: Exemplary quality of life indicators	18
Figure 2.2.	Heuristic model: Quality of life measurement, application, and evaluation	24
Figure 8.1.	Comparison of individual- and family-centered quality of life domains	170
Figure 8.2.	Individual and family outcomes-focused evaluation model	175
Figure 11.1.	Generic approach to quality of life measurement	268
Figure 11.2.	Quality of life measurement model	270
Figure 12.1.	An ecological model of quality enhancement	292
Figure 12.2.	Quality of life hierarchy	307
Figure 13.1.	Outcomes-based evaluation model	314
Figure 13.2.	Exemplary baseline and desired outcomes	316
Figure 15.1.	A quality of life integration model	360
Figure 15.2.	Major societal forces impacting a person	369

List of Appendixes

Appendix 3.1.	Education references corresponding to Table 3.1	47
Appendix 4.1.	Health references corresponding to Table 4.1	71
Appendix 5.1.	Mental and behavioral health references corresponding to Table 5.1	104
Appendix 6.1.	Mental retardation and intellectual disabilities references corresponding to Table 6.1	136
Appendix 7.1.	Aging references corresponding to Table 7.1	156
Appendix 10.1.	Numbered references corresponding to Table 10.1	234
Appendix 10.2.	Numbered references corresponding to Table 10.2	236
Appendix 10.3.	Numbered references corresponding to Table 10.3	243
Appendix 10.4.	Numbered references corresponding to Table 10.4	256
Appendix 10.5.	Numbered references corresponding to Table 10.5	261
Appendix 13.1.	Outcome planning inventory	330

Acknowledgments

An effort of this magnitude requires the contribution of many who have assisted us in development and production. First and foremost, a very special thank you to Darlene Buschow for her support and expert technical assistance. The extensive review of existing cross-cultural literature presented throughout the text was possible thanks to the dedicated, in-depth work of a group of doctoral students at the University of Salamanca, for whose exceptional collaboration we would like to express our deepest gratitude. María Gómez-Vela collaborated in the chapters about education and intellectual disabilities, Eliana Sabeh in health, Mónica Martín in mental health, Marta Rodriguez in aging, and Borja Jordán-de-Urries in intellectual disabilities. All of them also helped in the summary of assessment techniques. To each of these individuals plus our supportive wives, families, friends, and colleagues, we offer a profound and deeply felt "thank you."

> Robert L. Schalock, PhD
> Chewelah, Washington, USA
>
> Miguel A. Verdugo Alonso, PhD
> Salamanca, Spain

PART 1

An Overview of This Handbook and the Concept of Quality of Life

The concept of quality of life is not new, for a discussion of what constitutes well-being or happiness dates back to Plato and Aristotle. However, over the past three decades, the concept of quality of life has increasingly become a focus for research and application in the fields of education and special education, health care (physical and behavioral), social services (disabilities and aging), and families. To appreciate fully the importance of this concept, it is necessary to understand its semantic meaning and use throughout the world. In reference to its meaning, *quality* makes us think of the excellence or "exquisite standard" associated with human characteristics and positive values such as happiness, success, wealth, health, and satisfaction; *of life* indicates that the concept concerns the very essence or essential aspects of human existence. This semantic meaning explains why the concept is impacting the fields of education, health care, social services, and families as it is, because it makes us think about individuals, policies, and practices that change people's lives and their perception of a life of quality.

Our concept of a *Handbook on Quality of Life for Human Service Practitioners* is very simple: Provide the reader with a clear understanding of the concept of quality of life (QOL) and its importance to our readership, and then outline a model to guide the best practitioners in quality of life assessment, application, and evaluation. This needs to be done of course within the context of establishing one's credibility and basing the *Handbook's* contents on a thorough review and integration of the international QOL literature. Thus the purpose of part 1 is to establish our credibility, explain what this *Handbook* is all about, and sensitize the reader to the meaning and importance of the concept of quality of life.

There are two chapters in part 1. Chapter 1 ("About This Handbook") describes our involvement in the area of quality of life, the reasons why we have written this book, and the systems perspective that guides our work. Chapter 2 ("The Concept of Quality of Life: Its Meaning, Importance, and Our Approach to It") summarizes what is currently known about the meaning of *quality of life* and discusses the importance of this concept to people involved in the text's focus areas: education (regular and special), health care (physical and behavioral), social services (disabilities and aging), and families. In this second chapter we also introduce the reader to our QOL model, used throughout the *Handbook* to integrate the vast amount of information and provide the framework for the assessment, implementation, and evaluation of QOL principles and practices.

Throughout part 1 the reader is encouraged to keep the following three guiding principles and facts clearly in mind.

1. There is currently an increased concern for the social and psychological dynamics of perceived well-being, including factors related to social support, social integration, interpersonal trust, internal control, autonomy or independence, self-confidence, aspirations or expectations, and values having to do with family, job, and life in general.

2. Disability and change associated with impairments and aging are conditions that affect people's ability to make self-determined choices and live to the fullest. Living an ordinary life requires support beyond that normally needed by others at a similar age and stage of life. Such support may include a variety of forms such as specialist training, guidance, structured opportunities, or specially designed environmental or social arrangements. Providing these forms of support has been a major function of special education, health care, and rehabilitation programs. In this process, the concept of quality of life has become increasingly central in developing policy with respect to the best program practices as well as evaluating the impact that programs have on the lifestyles of their users.

3. Disabilities, health issues, and aging are often related to problems concerning participation in society; this means that such individuals and their families are in danger of being excluded from many situations and opportunities normally available to other people. The concept of quality of life has become central in social policy and in developing environments that allow access for all individuals to people, places, and resources.

CHAPTER 1

About This Handbook

A decade ago quality of life was predicted to become "the issue of the 1990s" (Schalock, 1990, p. x) in the field of intellectual disabilities and related areas. Research on this topic has expanded rapidly during the 1990s, resulting in more than 100 definitions (Cummins, 1997a), more than 1,400 references to quality of life in the psychological literature from 1992 to 1995 alone, and more than 1,000 individual measures of various aspects of quality of life (Hughes & Hwang, 1996). Researchers have responded to the challenge to address the issue of definition and measurement of the concept, and the notion has shown a degree of persistence and acceptance, although not without some reservations (Luckasson, 1990, 1997; Hatton, 1998; Wolfensberger, 1994).

Since its introduction into the fields of education, health care, and social services in the mid-1980s, we have learned a great deal about the concept of quality of life (QOL). The concept is not new, for the discussion of what constitutes well-being or happiness dates back to Plato and Aristotle. However, over the past few decades, the concept of quality of life has increasingly been applied to people with special needs and their families. Quality of life has been taken up as a challenge to respond to in terms of theory and applied research regarding social policy, the design of supports to individuals and groups, and program evaluation. Such interest is part of a wider view that quality of life is a relevant outcome for education, health care, and social service programs.

Our primary purpose in developing a QOL-referenced handbook for human service practitioners is to integrate the literature on the conceptualization, measurement, and application of quality of life in the areas of education (regular and special), physical health, mental and behavioral health, mental retardation and intellectual disabilities, aging, and families. These six areas are referred to throughout the text as "focus areas." In writing this *Handbook* for human service practitioners, we made every attempt to make the text user friendly and to accomplish the following six goals:

1. To explain the meaning and importance of the concept of quality of life, along with its measurement and application.

2. To outline an approach to the concept of quality of life (see Figure 2.2 in chap. 2) and suggest how others can use the heuristic model to access, apply, and evaluate the concept.

3. To identify core QOL domains and indicators for each of the text's focus areas. Throughout the text "QOL core domains" refers to the set of factors composing personal well-being; "QOL core indicators" refers to QOL domain-specific perceptions, behaviors, or conditions that reflect a person's well-being.

4. To demonstrate how core QOL indicators can be assessed through subjective (personal appraisal) and objective (functional assessment and social indicators) methods.

5. To summarize how the concept of quality of life can be understood and applied at the individual, organizational, and societal level.

6. To suggest evaluation strategies that can be used to determine personal and organizational-level quality outcomes.

Since 1985 more than 20,900 published articles have appeared containing the term *quality of life* in their titles. The text you are about to read is based on our initial reading of 9,749 abstracts. Of these, 2,455 articles or book chapters on the conceptualization, measurement, and application of the QOL concept were selected and read because they met the following four criteria: (a) there were multiple references in the article or book chapter; (b) the article or book chapter was empirically based, employing a reasonable number of participants; (c) the article or book chapter related to the conceptualization, measurement, or application of the concept of QOL; and (d) the article or book chapter related to one or more of the focus areas of our text. Of these 2,455 articles or book chapters, only 897 were used as the basis for the literature review in chapters 3 through 8, as only these articles or chapters specified particular QOL domains and/or indicators.

Understanding and applying the QOL concept is critically important for a number of reasons to today's human service practitioners, including policymakers, researchers, and consumers: (a) the QOL concept is impacting program development and service delivery in each of the text's focus areas; (b) the concept is being used as the criterion for assessing the effectiveness of services to program recipients in each of the text's focus areas; and (c) the pursuit of quality is apparent at three levels of today's education and social service programs: people who desire a life of quality, providers who want to deliver a quality product, and evaluators (including policymakers, funders, and consumers) who want quality outcomes. In addition, it has been our collective experience as people working actively in the field of quality of life for the past two decades that throughout the world the

QOL concept is being used as a:

- sensitizing notion that gives us a sense of reference and guidance from the individual's perspective, focusing on the core domains to a life of quality
- social construct that provides a model for assessing the core QOL domains
- unifying theme that provides a systematic framework to apply QOL-oriented policies and practices

To date, no text has integrated the literature on the conceptualization, measurement, and application of quality of life and related that literature to the six goals listed previously. As active researchers in both the area of quality of life and the international arena, we approach the QOL concept from a cross-cultural and systems perspective, striving to integrate both the emic (i.e., culture-bound) and etic (i.e., universal) aspects of the concept.

Our personal experiences in a number of countries in Europe, Asia, and the Americas support the universal appeal of the concept, which exists in a psychological environment that is increasingly cross-cultural (Keith, 1996; Keith & Schalock, 2000; Markus & Kitayama, 1991). There is no doubt but that cultural experience and assumptions play an important role in understanding and applying the QOL construct. Thus, without cross-cultural research and verification we cannot make broad generalizations about the conception, measurement, and application of the QOL construct.

In this regard, the authors have been involved in a number of cross-cultural studies confirming the concept's etic aspects. For example, Keith, Heal, and Schalock (1996) designed a study to investigate the meaning of 10 QOL concepts across seven cultures. Using a semantic differential technique, professionals working in the field of developmental disabilities were asked to rate the meaning of 10 concepts selected from the literature reflecting opinions of people with disabilities, accreditation standards, and the voluminous literature on QOL measurement: (a) rights, (b) relationships, (c) satisfaction, (d) environment, (e) economic security, (f) social inclusion, (g) individual control, (h) privacy, (i) health, and (j) growth and development. The 10 QOL concepts were rated on the dimensions of value, potency, and activity, using a variant of the rating scheme of Osgood, May, and Miron (1975), which they had developed to define meaning in 22 different languages. The study was conducted in Australia, England, Finland, Germany, Japan, Taiwan, and the United States. Results indicated a surprisingly high level of agreement in the rating of the 10 concepts across the seven countries. Thus these 10 QOL concepts were seen as sufficiently robust and universal to receive strong cross-cultural validation by professionals working in the field.

In a second study, Heal (1996) analyzed the contents of Goode's book on international perspectives and issues in quality of life (1994) and found that nearly all of the 10 concepts mentioned in the Keith et al. (1996) study were addressed in Goode's text. Based on this analysis, plus a meta-analysis of current QOL indicators (Cummins, 1997a, 1997b; Felce & Perry, 1996; Hughes & Hwang, 1996; Schalock, 1997, 2000b), it seemed reasonable to base the text's development and exposition on eight core QOL domains: (a) emotional well-being, (b) interpersonal relationships, (c) material well-being, (d) personal development, (e) physical well-being, (f) self-determination, (g) social inclusion, and (h) rights. There is also solid agreement that these eight core domains are valued by individuals differently and that the value attached to each domain varies across the life span (Elorriaga, Garcia, Martinez, & Unamunzaga, 2000; Flanagan, 1982; Stark & Goldsbury, 1990).

Our cross-cultural perspective is consistent with earlier work in which Schalock et al. (1990) administered the Quality of Life Questionnaire (Schalock & Keith, 1993) to 92 individuals with mental retardation in four countries (Australia, Federal Republic of Germany, Israel, and Republic of China) and compared their scores to the standardization sample of 522 people with mental retardation in the United States. Following appropriate translation and verification of the translations and data, two key results stood out: First, there was considerable consistency in the factor scores across the five countries; second, QOL scores increased in all countries with more normalized working and living environments.

In a more recent study, Schalock and Kelley (1999) asked colleagues in 14 countries in Europe, North America, and Asia to evaluate the influence of 10 values and 10 contextual variables on the development of integrated employment and community living programs in their countries. Two values (interpersonal relations and supports systems) and four contextual variables (public policies, academic or professional supports, teaching or rehabilitation staff availability, and attitudes toward people with disabilities) were rated the most influential. Once again, cross-cultural agreement on key aspects of quality of life was demonstrated. Thus we feel confident that we can approach our task in this text generally from a universal and cross-cultural perspective, but with considerable respect for cultural uniqueness and variability.

Respecting cultural uniqueness and variability requires an awareness of and sensitivity to the different "systems" and "contextual factors" that impact our lives. Thus throughout the *Handbook* we use an ecological (i.e., "systems") perspective that includes (Bronfenbrenner, 1979; Keith & Schalock, 2000):

- microsystem: the immediate social settings, such as family, home, peer group, and workplace, that directly affect the person's life
- mesosystem: the neighborhood, community, service agencies, and organizations that directly affect the functioning of the microsystem
- macrosystem: the overarching pattern of culture, social-political trends, eco-

nomic systems, and society-related factors that directly affect one's values, assumptions, and the meaning of words and concepts

In addition, each of the *Handbook's* six focus areas is being impacted by a number of culture-specific factors, which we refer to as "contextual factors." Most of these are related to the current reform movement's accountability and quality dimensions (Schalock, 2001). Key aspects of these contextual factors for each of the *Handbook's* focus areas are summarized in Table 1.1.

In our cross-cultural and systems-perspective work, we have found that one of the most significant impacts of the QOL concept is that it changes an individual's mind-set and the way he or she thinks about and approaches people at the margin

TABLE 1.1
Key Contextual Factors Addressed in This Handbook

Education and Special Education
1. A clear shift in educational policy from an emphasis on the process of education to concerns about the desired outcomes of schooling and standards against which schools and education-related outcomes can be judged.
2. The movement to include students with disabilities as full-time members of regular education.

Physical Health Care
1. A focus on the accountability dimension of the reform movement, with more emphasis currently being placed on efficiency and effectiveness as opposed to consumer satisfaction or quality of life.
2. The development of performance standards and practice guidelines to ensure adequate treatment and maximize potential person-referenced outcomes.

Mental and Behavioral Health
1. The development of a continuum-of-care habilitation concept in which different levels of support are provided to the person with mental illness.
2. A renewed emphasis on community support and rehabilitation programs.
3. An emphasis on adaptive behavior, personal well-being, quality of life, life activities, and community adjustment.
4. A focus on support needs and person-referenced outcomes.

(table continues)

TABLE 1.1. *(continued)*

Mental Retardation and Intellectual Disabilities

1. A transformed vision of what constitutes the life possibilities of people with mental retardation and intellectual disabilities.

2. A supports paradigm that underlies service delivery and focuses on supported living, employment, and inclusive education.

3. An interfacing of the concept of quality of life with quality enhancement, quality assurance, quality management, and outcome-based evaluation.

Aging

1. The emergence of a strong movement to protect the rights of older people.

2. An emphasis on successful aging that focuses attention on environmental factors that enhance the aging process.

3. A greater respect for: freedom, independence, and free exercise of individual initiative; an income in retirement to provide an adequate standard of living; an opportunity for employment free from discriminatory practices; an opportunity to participate in the widest range of meaningful civic, educational, recreational, and cultural activities; suitable housing; the needed level of physical and mental health services; ready access to effective social services; appropriate institutional care when required; and a life and death with dignity.

Families

1. Recently, families (especially families with one or more family members with a disability) have embraced the concept of quality of life as a sensitizing notion and a unifying theme for developing and implementing QOL-oriented policies and practices.

2. Although the area is just emerging in the international community and literature, a number of core family-centered quality of life domains and indicators are emerging in the literature including family interaction, daily family life, parenting, financial, emotional well-being, health, productivity, social well-being, physical environment (safety, space, comfort), and advocacy.

---

of society. Part of the change in attitude is to focus on the person, both as an individual and in relation to his or her environment; part is to shift the emphasis from a deficit orientation to an enhancement strategy; and part is to view the QOL concept as a change agent for the improvement of individuals' lives.

The authors realize that the concepts and models presented in this handbook may vary from country to country, and even from area to area within countries. The cross-cultural and systems-perspective understanding of quality of life is in its infancy, and we hope that the discourses resulting from this text will facilitate both increased understanding and collaborative work. We also realize that quality of life, like all concepts, has its critics. There are some who warn us about the dangers of its use, asserting that there are those who would use the concept to limit the lives of some individuals. We wish to be clear, however, in the view that one way to encourage positive use of the concept is to stress the centrality of the views and experiences of the individual. This handbook reflects current thought and research about the conceptualization, measurement, and application of the concept of quality of life and sets the stage for its continuing development. To that end, chapter 2 discusses further the concept of quality of life, including its meaning, importance, and our approach to it.

CHAPTER 2

The Concept of Quality of Life: Its Meaning, Importance, and Our Approach to It

Overview

Over the past few decades, the concept of quality of life (QOL) has increasingly become a focus for research and application in the fields of education and special education, health care (physical and behavioral), social services (mental retardation and intellectual disabilities and aging), and families. Although it might surprise the reader, we will not begin with a definition of *quality of life*. Rather, we will describe its meaning and importance in regard to what we will call (and define) as core domains and indicators. As stated in chapter 1, there are more than 100 definitions of the term, and the interested reader can find a summary and critique of these definitions in Cummins (1996) and Goode (1994). Our strong belief is that an operational description of the term and its meaning will be a better way to provide to our readership practical assessment, application, and evaluation information and strategies.

To appreciate fully the importance of the QOL concept, it is necessary to understand its semantic meaning and use throughout the world. In reference to its meaning, *quality* makes us think of the excellence or "exquisite standard" associated with human characteristics and positive values such as happiness, success, wealth, health, and satisfaction; *of life* indicates that the concept concerns the very essence or essential aspects of human existence (Lindstrom, 1992). This semantic meaning explains why the concept is impacting the *Handbook's* areas, because it makes us think about individuals, policies, and practices that change people's lives and their perception of a life of quality. Thus it has been our experience that throughout the world the QOL concept is being used as a:

- sensitizing notion that gives us a sense of reference and guidance from the individual's perspective, focusing on the core domains to a life of quality

- social construct that provides a model for assessing the core QOL domains
- unifying theme that provides a systematic framework to apply QOL-oriented policies and practices

Quality of life has been construed by some as an "inner sense" (Taylor & Bogdan, 1996), as a correlate of temperament or personality (Edgerton, 1996), as a construct sensitive to anthropological, sociological, and psychological influences (R. I. Brown, 2000a), or as a product of interaction between person and environment (Rapley, 2000). The nature of the QOL construct, as opposed to a simple definition, is important in the literature for a central compelling reason: If, as Edgerton (1996) has suggested, "features of a person's environment are less important in bringing about a sense of well-being than are aspects of that person's personality or temperament" (p. 88), the response of the field will be quite different than if Schalock (1997) is correct when, in identifying the best predictors of quality of life, he noted, "these are factors that programs can do something about" (p. 252). However, despite Edgerton's caution that environmental change may not change quality of life, he nevertheless identified a list of improvements (e.g., housing, health care, employment, recreation) that any society should provide — a list very much like the QOL predictors enumerated by Schalock (1997). Thus, while there may be disagreement on the relative weight of individual versus environmental contributors to quality of life, the importance of improving environmental situations for individuals is not in dispute.

In addition, the meaning and application of quality of life differ according to the discourse in which the QOL concept is expressed. Quality of life can be expressed, for example, in the context of program evaluation or evaluation research. Then its meaning will be "outcome" among other valued outcomes of services or programs. If we look at quality of life in the context of social policy, its meaning can be defined as a common target to guarantee a good life and equal opportunities for all citizens. In the context of disability, health care, and rehabilitation politics, the meaning of quality of life can be seen as enhancing or improving equality for all people, despite their condition. Quality of life in the context of individual preferences produces perhaps the most popular meaning of the concept, namely individually varying experiences of one's life. This discourse can be named "how to get all good things that a person appreciates" (L. Matikka, personal correspondence, 2000).

Thus discourses about the QOL concept need to be based on its conceptualization, plus a clear understanding of significant contextual factors that are driving its application to people in education, health, and social services environments. Contextual factors such as those summarized in Table 1.1 are very important, especially when we define disability, health impairments, and aging as problematic fits between a person and his or her environment. Additional contextual factors include (Schalock, 2000):

- a transformed vision of what constitutes the life possibilities of people who are disabled, of ill health, or aged
- a new way of thinking about such individuals that focuses on the person, the environmental variables that influence one's functioning, and the feasibility of change at both the individual and societal levels
- the current paradigm shift with its emphasis on inclusion, equity, empowerment, and community-based supports
- the quality revolution, with its emphasis on quality management, and valued person-referenced outcomes
- the evidence that individuals can be more independent, productive, community integrated, and satisfied when education, health care, and habilitation services and supports are based on QOL-oriented policies and practices

At its core the QOL concept makes us think differently about people at the margin of society and how we might bring about change at both the individual and societal level to enhance people's well-being and to reduce their exclusion from the mainstream of society. To that end, this chapter discusses three key aspects about the QOL concept: (a) its meaning from the perspective of core domains and indicators; (b) its importance as an overarching framework and set of principles and techniques to enhance a person's or family's sense of well-being; and (c) a heuristic model that explains our approach to its assessment, application, and evaluation. Throughout the chapter the reader is encouraged to think about his or her own quality of life and the factors that both define and enhance it. In that process we predict a number of questions will come to mind:

- What are the key descriptors of a life of quality?
- What are the major indicators of a life of quality?
- How do these descriptors and indicators vary across people, communities, and countries?
- How can one's quality of life be enhanced?.

The Meaning of Quality of Life

Defining and conceptualizing quality of life has been, and remains, a complex process that presents numerous technical and philosophical problems. This state of affairs has prompted us to suggest that we are better off not to define the term, but rather to agree about the core domains and indicators of a life of quality and a number of principles that define how quality of life should be conceptualized. Throughout the *Handbook,* core QOL domains are defined as "the set of factors composing personal well-being." Core QOL indicators are defined as "QOL domain-specific perceptions, behaviors, or conditions that reflect a person's well-being."

Quality of Life Domains and Indicators
Traditional belief has held that objective factors, such as the elimination of poverty, would enhance personal well-being. However, for general populations the correlation between income and sense of well-being is modest (Myers, 2000). Recognition of this fact led Campbell, Converse, and Rodgers (1976) to observe that "there is not much doubt that the central issue confronting any examination of the perceived quality of life involves the relationship between subjective and objective indicators of well-being" (p. 474). In distinction, Edgerton (1996) has questioned the nature of the relationship between objective and subjective factors and cautioned that, at least for some people, the subjective perception of well-being may not be closely linked to objective standards of quality. As noted by both Edgerton and Goode (1997a, 1997b), the nature of this relationship between the objective and the subjective is a difficult empirical question.

Parmenter and Donelly (1997) reviewed several studies that support Edgerton's view, revealing variable and often low correlation between objective and subject indicators of quality of life. There is currently no clear objective standard by which to assess quality of life, and researchers seem to agree that subjective assessment of individual perceptions of life experiences in areas such as relationships, community activity, physical and material well-being, personal development, satisfaction, and happiness needs to be considered. However, as pointed out by Hatton (1998), Edgerton (1990, 1996), and Stancliffe (2000), there are potentially some serious problems with assessing subjective quality of life: the difficulty in interviewing individuals who lack communication skills; the different meanings attributed to quality of life interviews by different individuals; and the concern that subjective well-being may be as much a product of individual disposition or personality as of discernible changes in life circumstances.

Felce (1997; Felce & Perry, 1996) has proposed a three-part model that attempts to integrate an objective description of life conditions and a subjective assessment of satisfaction with a third dimension: personal values and aspirations. The importance of personal values and the weighting of ratings of life experiences have been recognized and discussed by Campbell et al. (1976), Cummins (1997a, 1997b), and Renwick, Brown, and Raphael (2000). One could argue, however, that such influences as personal values are simply another feature of the subjective dimensions, just as Rapley (2000) asserted the contribution of social relationships to estimates of subjective well-being. The key point of consensus is that no current author fails to include a subjective dimension in any formulation of quality of life, and typical models (e.g., Cummins, 1996; Schalock & Keith, 1993) present subjective quality of life as their central outcome.

In an effort to move beyond this objective-subjective debate, Schalock (1996b) suggested a move to consensus on core QOL domains and indicators that might be measured at three levels: (a) personal, (b) functional or objective, and (c) social. This suggestion is consistent with Felce (1997), who proposed that the structure of QOL domains should meet two criteria: (a) in recognition of the complexity of life they must reflect the possibility of a multi-element, multiple-focus approach to assessment; and (b) they must generally reflect a broad knowledge of those things important to all of us.

The search for core QOL domains goes back to the pioneering work of Campbell et al. (1976). Subsequently, other investigators have suggested a number of core QOL domains that are quite similar (Hughes et al., 1996). This consistency is shown in Table 2.1. We feel that the eight core domains suggested by Schalock and listed at the end of Table 2.1 are quite consistent with those proposed by others, as well as being both empirical and experiential. These eight core domains lend themselves to multiple approaches to measurement, as each can be examined via multiple exemplary indicators. Such an approach also makes clear the artificial nature of the distinction between objective and subjective indicators of quality of life.

People live in a number of systems that influence the development of their values, beliefs, behaviors, and attitudes. This notion is probably best described in the work of Bronfenbrenner (1979), Cullen (1999), Dagnan, Ruddick, and Jones (1998), and Keith and Schalock (2000), who suggest an ecological perspective in describing the many contexts of human behavior. Throughout the *Handbook* we suggest that three levels of systems affect one's quality of life:

- the microsystem, or the immediate social settings, such as family, home, peer group, and workplace, that directly affect the person's life
- the mesosystem, or the neighborhood, community, service agencies, and organizations that directly affect the functioning of the microsystem
- the macrosytem, or the overarching patterns of culture, social-political trends, economic systems, and society-related factors that directly affect one's values, assumptions, and the meaning of words and concepts

This ecological approach makes a strong statement about including core QOL domains and indicators that reflect the multiple systems within which all people live: micro, meso, and macro. This concept is shown in Figure 2.1. Note that across the top one sees listed the eight core QOL domains; down the left side are listed the three levels of analysis, with the respective approaches to measurement

TABLE 2.1
Exemplary Quality of Life Domains

Investigator	Core Domains
Flanigan (1982)	Physical and material well-being Relations with other people Social, community, and civic activities Personal development and fulfillment Recreation
World Health Organization (1997)	Physical health Psychological Level of independence Social relations Environment Spirituality; religion; personal beliefs
Cummins (1996)	Material well-being Health Productivity Intimacy Safety Place in community Emotional well-being
Felce (1997)	Physical well-being Material well-being Social well-being Productive well-being Emotional well-being Rights or civic well-being
Schalock (1996b, 2000)	Emotional well-being Interpersonal relations Material well-being Personal development Physical well-being Self-determination Social inclusion Rights

that will be described in chapters 10 and 11; and within each cell are exemplary QOL indicators that are clarified further in chapters 3 through 8 for each of the *Handbook's* focus areas. As we will see in these chapters, although the core domains and indicators appear to be quite invariant across cultures, their importance varies according to one's life stage and whether one is focusing on the person, community, or larger society-culture.

Quality of Life Principles
The QOL principles that have guided us throughout this project have arisen not just from the QOL movement and literature but also from the "quality revolution." The quality revolution, with its emphasis on quality products and quality outcomes, emerged rapidly during the 1980s, when we were sensing the increased attention given to the QOL concept. One of the main products of the quality revolution was a "new way of thinking" about people at the margin of society that was guided significantly by the QOL concept. This new way of thinking stressed person-centered planning, the supports model, quality enhancement techniques, and person-referenced quality outcomes. More specifically, this new way of thinking allowed:

- service providers to reorganize resources around individuals rather than rearranging people in program slots
- consumers and service providers to embrace the supports paradigm
- program evaluation to shift its focus to person-referenced outcomes that could be used to improve organizational efficiency and enhance person-referenced services and supports
- management styles to focus on learning organizations, reengineered corporations, entrepreneurship, and continuous quality improvement

The QOL concept has had two significant impacts on the text's focus areas. First, embracing the concept has become a sensitizing notion, social construct, and unifying theme. Second, a number of principles have emerged that give additional meaning to the QOL concept and around which QOL application can be organized. The development of these principles has emerged from the international consensus work done by the Special Interest Research Group on Quality of Life of the International Association for the Scientific Study of Intellectual Disabilities. Table 2.2 summarizes five key QOL conceptualization principles (Schalock et al., in press).

In summary, the QOL concept is better understood today than it was yesterday, and its core domains and indicators are becoming well accepted. As we have just seen, the concept of quality of life cannot be separated from the context within which people with special needs live and interact. We have also seen that a

Level of Analysis / Core Quality of Life Domains

Level of Analysis	Emotional Well-Being	Interpersonal Relations	Material Well-Being	Personal Development	Physical Well-Being	Self-Determination	Social Inclusion	Rights
Macrosystem (Social Indicators)	Religious Freedom; Family Life Legislation	Public Safety	Economic Assistance (Social Insurance); Vocational Rehabilitation Legislation	Equal Opportunity Legislation; Education Rehabilitation Funding/Legislation; Social Economic Status	Housing Statistics; Health Insurance	Guardianship Laws; Consumer Empowerment	Zoning Laws (Opportunity)	Public Laws (e.g., IDEA, ADA, Civic Rights Act); Human Rights Legislation
Mesosystem (Functional Assessment)	Safety; Freedom from Stress; Freedom to Worship; Supports	Interactions; Family Life; Affection; Group membership; Social supports; Marital Status	Ownership; Employment Opportunities; Supported Employment; Shelter	Person-Centered Planning; Advancement Opportunities; Opportunity for Development; Education & Rehabilitation Programs; Augmentative Technology	Health Care; Physical Rehabilitation; Food & Nutrition; Recreational & Leisure	Opportunities for Choice Making/Decisions; Allowance for Choices/Personal Control; Person-Centered Planning	Community Access/Barrier Free Environments; Normalized & Integrated Environments; Community Participation Opportunities; Social Acceptance; Transportation; Role Status; Community Supports	Self-Control & Responsibility; Protection & Advocacy Policies; Due Process
Microsystem (Personal Appraisal)	Self-Concept; Happiness; Spirituality; Contentment; Satisfaction; Feeling of Well-Being; Mental Health Status	Friendships; Intimacy	Possessions; Income/Salary; Savings; Investments; Standard of Living	Educational Level; Adaptive Behavior Skills; Activities of Daily Living Skills; Instrumental Activities of Daily Living; Personal Competence	Health Status; Nutritional Status; Mobility	Autonomy; Self-Direction; Personal Control; Preferences; Choice	Community Participation/Activities; Circle of Friends; Access/Participation Opportunities; Natural Supports; Accepted Social Roles	Voting; Privacy; Self-Determination; Ownership; Personal Values; Sense of Dignity; Personal Freedom; Self-Advocacy Training & Development; Advocacy; Access

Figure 2.1. Ecological approach: Exemplary quality of life indicators.

TABLE 2.2
Quality of Life Conceptualization Principles

Quality of life:

1. is composed of those same factors and relationships for people in education or special education, physical health, mental and behavioral health, mental retardation and intellectual disabilities, aging, and families that are important to all people
2. is experienced when a person's needs are met and when one has the opportunity to pursue life enrichment in major life settings
3. has both subjective and objective components, but is primarily the perception of the individual that reflects the quality of life he or she experiences;
4. is based on individual needs, choices, and control
5. is a multidimensional construct influenced by personal and environmental factors such as intimate relationships, family life, friendships, work, neighborhood, city or town of residence, housing, education, health, standard of living, and the state of one's nation

complete understanding of the concept requires a systems perspective wherein one is sensitive to the micro-, meso-, and macrolevel influences on a life of quality — and one's perception of such. And we have also seen that our search has revealed eight core domains of a life of quality: emotional well-being, interpersonal relations, material well-being, personal development, physical well-being, self-determination, social inclusion, and rights. By embracing an ecological model such as that shown in Figure 2.1, one becomes sensitive to factors that affect life at different proximal levels to the person. At the same time, one glimpses the importance of the QOL concept — a topic to which we now turn.

The Importance of the Concept of Quality of Life

Although quality of life is critically important to each of us, its importance to education, health care, social services, and families has been most evident during the past two decades, which in turn were influenced by the quality revolution and the reform movement. Generally speaking, the importance of the QOL concept is that it provides an overarching person- or family-centered framework and set of principles to enhance people's psychological and subjective well-being. Five application principles, which are based on our work with the international consensus group (Schalock et al., in press), are summarized in Table 2.3.

TABLE 2.3
Quality of Life Application Principles

Quality of life application should:

1. enhance a person's well-being

2. be applied in light of the individual's cultural and ethnic heritage

3. collaborate for change at the personal, program, community, and national levels

4. enhance the degree of personal control and individual opportunity exerted by the individual in relation to his or her activities, interventions, and environments

5. occupy a prominent role in gathering evidence, especially in identifying the significant predictors of a life of quality and the impact of targeting resources to maximize positive effects

---

As shown clearly in Table 2.3, the importance and significance of the QOL concept is evident at the three systems levels: micro, meso, and macro. This section of the chapter sensitizes the reader to a number of important applications that will be described more fully in part 4. Each application reflects the concept's importance to those with whom we work and associate.

Microsystem: Personal Growth and Development Opportunities

There are currently four major thrusts at the microsystem level to enhance a person's perceived quality of life. First, there is strong advocacy for increased opportunities to participate in the mainstream of life, associated with increased inclusion, equity, choices, and self-determination (Wehmeyer & Schalock, 2001; Wehmeyer & Schwartz, 1998). Second, consumers are working jointly with researchers to determine the relative importance or value of the QOL core domains. Third, consumers are increasingly becoming involved in assessing their own quality of life (Schalock, Bonham, & Marchand, 2000). And fourth, the area of personal development and wellness training is becoming a major thrust in service and supports delivery (Schalock & Faulkner, 1997).

Mesosystem: Program and Environment Enhancement Techniques

We are also seeing service and support providers implementing quality enhancement techniques that focus on either the environment or the service and supports program (Schalock, 1994). Environmentally based enhancement techniques involve designing environments that are user friendly and reduce the mismatch between the person and the environment. Examples include (Ferguson, 1997): opportunity for involvement (e.g., meal preparation); easy access to the outdoor environment, modification to stairs, water taps, door knobs; safety (e.g., handrails, safety glass, nonslip walking surfaces); convenience (e.g., orientation aids such as color coding or universal pictographs); accessibility to home and community; sensory stimulation (e.g., windows, less formal furniture); prosthetics (e.g., personal computers, specialized assistive devices, high-technological environments); and opportunity for choice and control (e.g., lights, temperature, privacy, and personal space).

Program-based enhancement techniques are currently being built around the core domains of a life of quality. In reference to the eight core domains used in this handbook, for example, (a) emotional well-being can be enhanced by increased safety, stable and predictable environments, and positive feedback; (b) interpersonal relationships by fostering friendships, encouraging intimacy, and supporting families; (c) material well-being by supporting ownership, and employment; (d) personal development by fostering education and functional rehabilitation and by using augmentative technology; (e) physical well-being by ensuring adequate health care, mobility, wellness, and proper nutrition; (f) self-determination by encouraging choices, personal control, decisions, and personal goals; (g) social inclusion by emphasizing community roles, community integration, and volunteerism; and (h) rights by ensuring voting access, due process, and opportunities to assume civic responsibilities.

Macrosystem: Social Policies

There are currently more than 40 worldwide treaties or conventions of human rights. The 1990s witnessed a major initiative by the international community to improve the legal status and enhance the situation of people with special needs. Reflective of this initiative, the United Nations General Assembly adopted in 1993 the *United Nations Standard Rules on the Equalization of Opportunities for Persons with Disabilities* (United Nations, 1993). Eight of the 22 rules can be considered "enabler standards" that deal with issues such as international cooperation (technical and economic), information and research, policymaking and planning, coordination of work, personnel training, and monitoring and evaluation. Significantly, the 14 "outcome standards" are congruent with the eight proposed core QOL domains, as follows:

1. emotional well-being: reflected in the rule regarding religion
2. interpersonal relations: reflected in rules relating to family life and personal integrity
3. material well-being: employment, income maintenance, and social services
4. personal development: education and rehabilitation
5. physical well-being: medical care and recreation and sports

6. self-determination: self-advocacy organizations
7. social inclusion: support services
8. rights: awareness raising, accessibility, equal rights to participate

In summary, the importance of the QOL concept is both personal and societal. At the personal level, the concept makes us think about the excellence associated with human characteristics and positive values such as happiness, success, wealth, health, and satisfaction; at the societal level, the concept makes us sensitive to the needs of others and the potential discrepancy between what people need and what they have. Thus its importance to each reader is that it is both a sensitizing notion and a social construct that can be used as an overarching framework to make a significant difference in people's lives. The chapter's concluding section presents and discusses a heuristic QOL model that provides such a framework, which we use throughout the *Handbook* to explain further the assessment, application, and evaluation of QOL concepts, policies, and practices.

Our Heuristic Quality of Life Model

The 1990s and early 21st century have seen a significant change in how we view education, health care, and social service programs, including their values, purposes, character, responsibility, and intended outcomes. This change is referred to as the reform movement. Major characteristics include (Schalock, 2001) focusing on outputs rather than inputs; redefining clients as customers; decentralizing authority; using market rather than bureaucratic mechanisms; catalyzing public, private, and volunteer sectors; empowering citizens; and introducing private finance. Two aspects of the reform movement have a direct bearing on our heuristic model: its accountability dimension and its quality dimension.

Current accountability initiatives seek to improve management, increase efficiency and effectiveness, and improve public confidence in private and public programs. Throughout the world, governments are asking education, health care, and social service programs and providers to articulate goals and report results through the three processes of strategic plans, performance plans, and program performance reports. Analogously, public and private funding agencies are increasing their attention to the use of performance information in the budget process, moving toward full-scale implementation of results-based accountability and budgeting. These efforts are giving increased prominence to value for money, including the responsibility of managers at all levels to make the best use of resources and the need for good output and performance information, including consumer satisfaction and QOL-related outcomes.

In reference to the quality dimension, two phenomena are significantly influencing current education, health care, and social service programs: (a) the movement toward assessing the value and quality of respective programs on the basis of consumer satisfaction, and (b) the development of new models of service delivery that reflect quality enhancement, the devolution of government, the homogenization of services, and the community-based movement in human services. In this regard, contemporary discussions of quality outcomes are no longer grounded in the industrial-regulatory perspective wherein quality was defined as conformity with regulation and specification. In contrast, current definitions of quality are rooted in the postindustrial, knowledge-based society (Gardner, 1999). The worldwide growth of service economies and the information revolution have elevated the importance of customer service and the measurement of personal and consumer-referenced outcomes.

These two quality phenomena — the movement toward assessing the value and quality of respective programs on the basis of consumer satisfaction and person-referenced outcomes, and the development of new QOL-referenced models of intervention and service delivery — have impacted the area of quality of life in three significant ways.

1. They have provided a catalyst to develop methodological pluralism, which reflects the postmodernist's emphasis on responsive, constructive evaluation (Guba & Lincoln, 1989).

2. They emphasize the need to incorporate the systems perspective into one's QOL work, as people live in several systems (micro, meso, and macro) that influence the development of their values, beliefs, behaviors, and attitudes.

3. The concern for quality outcomes within a devolution environment has resulted in the development of practice guidelines that reflect quality programming and intervention.

These three impacts are reflected in our heuristic QOL model shown in Figure 2.2. As shown, the model has three major components: QOL domains (and indicators), a social systems perspective, and three potential foci (measurement, application, and evaluation). An overview of each component is presented next.

Quality of Life Domains and Indicators

A number of domains of personal well-being have been identified in the international QOL literature. Although the number varies slightly (see Table 2.1), the core domains (sometimes referred to as "dimensions") include the desired states of emotional well-being, interpersonal relations, material well-being, personal development, physical well-being, self-determination, social inclusion, and rights. Many QOL investigators suggest that the actual number of domains is perhaps

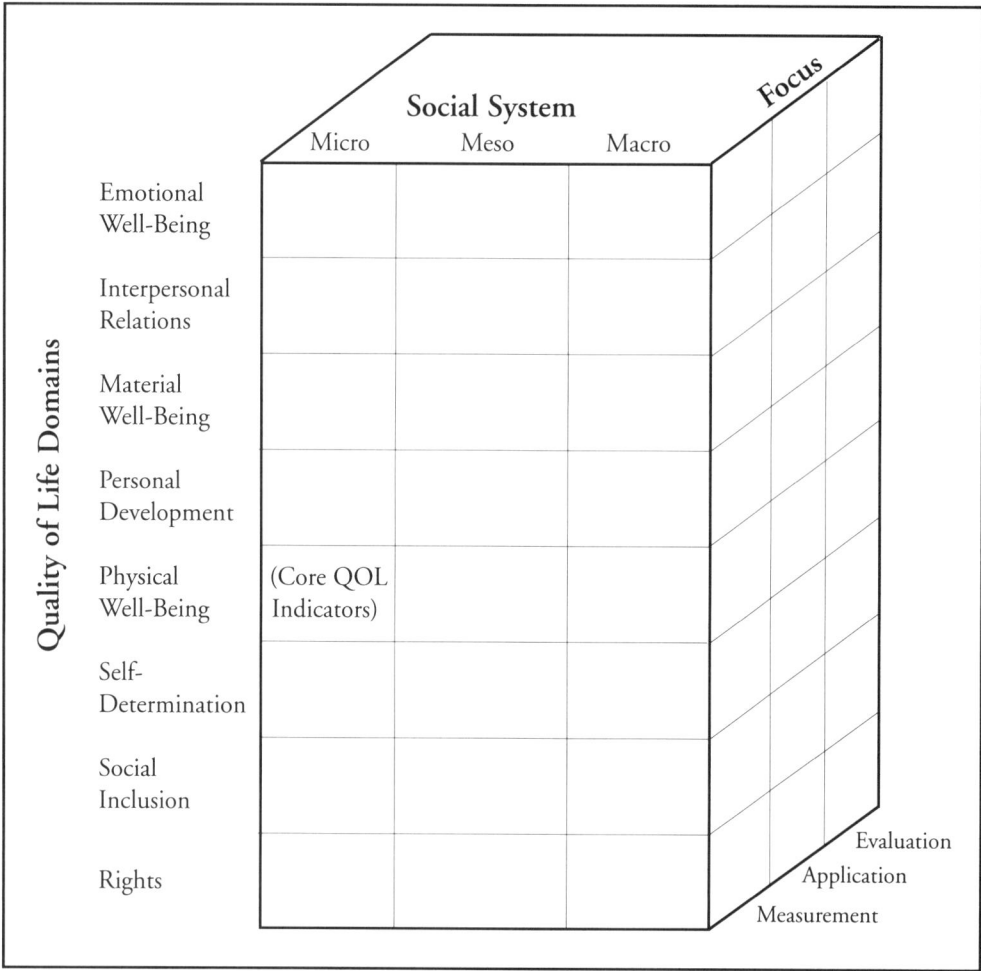

Figure 2.2. Heuristic model: Quality of life measurement, application, and evaluation.

less important than the recognition (a) that any proposed QOL model must recognize the need for a multi-element framework, (b) that people know what is important to them, and (c) that any set of domains must represent in aggregate the complete QOL construct. As noted above:

- Core QOL domains are: emotional well-being, interpersonal relations, material well-being, personal development, physical well-being, self-determination, social inclusion, and rights. These domains represent in aggregate the complete QOL construct presented throughout the *Handbook*.
- Core QOL indicators are: QOL domain-specific perceptions, behaviors, or conditions that reflect a person's perceived or real quality of life. Criteria for the

selection of an indicator are that it is functionally related to the respective QOL domain, measures what it is supposed to measure (validity), is consistent across people or raters (reliability), measures change (sensitivity), reflects changes only in the situation concerned (specificity), is affordable, timely, person-referenced, can be evaluated longitudinally, and is culturally sensitive.

Social Systems Perspective

By way of review, people live in several systems that influence the development of their values, beliefs, behaviors, and attitudes. As assumed throughout the *Handbook,* three system levels affect one's quality of life:

- the microsystem, or the immediate social settings, such as family, home, peer group, and workplace, that directly affect the person's life
- the mesosystem, or the neighborhood, community, service agencies, and organizations that directly affect the functioning of the microsystem;
- the macrosystem, or the overarching patterns of culture, social-political trends, economic systems, and society-related factors that directly affect one's values, assumptions, and the meaning of words and concepts

The systems perspective emphasizes the need to view quality of life from a broader perspective than just the individual. Indeed, as shown in Figure 2.2, core QOL domains and indicators can be defined and measured in reference to each system level. In addition, Figure 2.2 indicates that the application of the QOL concept in reference to measurement, application, and evaluation should also encompass each of the three system levels.

Foci

As QOL research and discussions have evolved, international consensus has moved away from thinking there is one definition or application of quality of life and toward describing and understanding its core domains and the conditions that promote and enhance a good life. Quality of life encompasses the basic conditions of life (e.g., adequate food, shelter, and safety) plus life enrichers (e.g., inclusive social, leisure, and community activities). These enrichers are based on the individual's values, beliefs, needs, and interests.

As we have seen, meanings of quality of life also differ according to the field of discourse. The QOL concept, for example, can be expressed in the context of its measurement as an outcome. It can also be expressed in the context of social policy as a common application target to guarantee a good life and equal opportunities for all citizens. Or it can be expressed in the context of individual preferences, which is perhaps its most popular meaning.

As the previous section of this chapter discussed a number of systems-level applications of the QOL concept and parts 3 and 4 focus in detail on its measurement and application, we discuss in the remainder of this chapter a concept pertinent to each of the three foci (measurement, application, evaluation): methodological pluralism. Our use of methodological pluralism is based on four premises:

1. Quality of life is a multidimensional construct in which culturally consensual values and shared attributes are reflected.

2. One's life of quality has both subjective and objective components.

3. People use QOL data for different purposes, including self-report, description, evidence, evaluation, and comparison.

4. The use of QOL data can be understood and applied within micro-, meso-, and/or macrosystems.

Measurement, application, and evaluation theory and strategies have undergone tremendous changes over the past 30 years. At least four stages can be identified (Shadish, Cook, & Leviton, 1991):

1. The 1960s, which stressed the assessment of program effectiveness at solving social problems.

2. The 1970s, which focused on how information is used in the design and modification of social programs.

3. The 1980s, wherein the major focus was to integrate work from the previous two stages.

4. The late 1980s and 1990s (called the postmodernist period) was characterized by minimizing the roles of science-based, quantitative research methodology and maximizing a social constructivist, qualitative, and pluralistic approach. Currently, this approach stresses that (Schalock, 2001): the pragmatic evaluation paradigm, ideographic research, context-specific knowledge, decision-oriented evaluation, and a combination of qualitative and quantitative research/evaluation designs.

In reference to our heuristic model (Figure 2.2), methodological pluralism is reflected primarily in the measurement and evaluation foci. Each approach, in its own way, recognizes the critical role that the person, those closest to the person, and the person's environments play on an individual's perceived quality of life. This notion is very consistent with the ecological approach to quality of life presented in this *Handbook* and necessitates the measurement and evaluation of QOL indicators across all systems levels proposed below.

Microsystem: Personal Appraisal

This measurement and evaluation level addresses the subjective nature of quality of life, typically asking the person how satisfied he or she is with the cell-specific exemplary indicator(s) (see Figure 2.2). For example, one might ask, "How satisfied are you with the skills and experiences you have gained or are gaining from your job?" or "How happy are you with your home or where you live?" Although the person's responses are subjective, responses need to be measured in psychometrically sound ways. A three-point Likert scale can be used both to indicate the level of expressed satisfaction and to demonstrate reliability and validity of measurement.

Increasingly, a person's measured level of satisfaction (i.e., personal appraisal) is a commonly used dependent measure in evaluating core QOL domains and indicators. It has several evaluative advantages: (a) satisfaction is a commonly used aggregate measure of individual life domains and demonstrates a trait-like stability over time (Andrews, 1974; Edgerton, 1996); (b) there is an extensive body of research on level of satisfaction across populations and service delivery recipients (Cummins, 1996); and (c) satisfaction as a dependent variable allows one to assess the relative importance of individual QOL domains and thereby assign value to the respective domain. The major disadvantages of using only satisfaction as a measure of quality of life include (a) the reported low or lack of correlation between subjective and objective measures of quality of life, (b) its limited utility for smaller group comparisons, (c) its tendency to provide only a global measure of perceived well-being, and (d) its discrepancy with the multidimensional nature of quality of life (Schalock, 2001). Because of these disadvantages, the general recommendation among QOL researchers is to include personal appraisal (i.e., subjective), functional assessment (i.e., objective), and social indicators as measures of the core QOL domains.

Mesosystem: Functional Assessment

This measurement and evaluation level addresses the objective nature of quality of life and reflects the person's interaction with neighborhood, community, or organization. The most typical formats used in functional assessment include rating scales, participant observation, and/or questionnaires. Each attempts to document a person's functioning across one or more core QOL domains. To accomplish this, most instruments employ an ordinal rating scale to yield a profile of the individual's functioning across major life activity areas such as home, work, school, or community.

There are advantages to using functional assessments to evaluate the core QOL domains: (a) objective measures can confirm results from the personal appraisal strategy; (b) adding objective measures to personal appraisal overcomes the commonly reported low correlation between subjective and objective measures of quality of life; (c) their use allows for the evaluation of outcomes across groups; and (d) objective measures provide important feedback to service providers, funders, and regulators as to how they can change or improve their services to enhance the recipient's functioning level.

There are also disadvantages to functional assessment: (a) it must be balanced with other considerations, such as the fact that not all outcomes related to one's perceived quality of life can be measured; (b) it can be costly, and one needs to be cautious that the functional assessment system does not consume in resources more than its information is worth; (c) it is useful to management or the decision-making process only to the extent that it answers the right questions; and (d) users of functional assessment data need to understand the role that many factors play in one's perceived quality of life and not focus exclusively on the service provider.

Macrosystem: Social Indicators
Social indicators generally refer to external, environmentally based conditions such as health, social welfare, friendships, standard of living, education, public safety, housing, neighborhood, and leisure. These indicators may be defined as a statistic of direct normative interest that facilitates concise, comprehensive, and balanced judgments about the conditions of major aspects of society (Andrews & Whithey, 1976). Such indicators are good for measuring the collective quality of community or national life; however, they are probably insufficient to measure either an individual's perceived quality of life or functional behavior(s). Campbell et al. (1976), for example, argue that social indicators reflect only an outsider's judgment of quality as suggested by external, environmentally based conditions. Thus "because we are accustomed to evaluating people's lives in terms of their material possessions, we tend to forget that satisfaction is a psychological experience and that the quality of this experience may not correspond very closely to these external conditions" (p. 3).

In summary, the methodological pluralism approach proposed in this *Handbook* combines personal appraisal, functional assessments, and social indicators. This approach to QOL measurement and evaluation has become a widely accepted strategy for three reasons. First, all activity focuses clearly on the multidimensional, core QOL domains and indicators. Thus one need not use different indicators for subjective versus objective measurement; rather, the core domains and indicators remain constant; what varies is whether one focuses on micro-, meso-, or macrolevel of measurement. Second, it allows one to incorporate multiple perspectives and systems-level analysis into the measurement, application, and evaluation of quality of life. And third, methodological pluralism allows researchers to meet the following objectives of using mixed-method evaluations: triangulation, or the determination of correspondence of results across personal appraisal and functional assessment strategies; complementarity, or the use of qualitative and quantitative methods to measure the overlapping but distinct facets of the QOL construct; and initiation, which allows one to recast questions or results from one strategy with questions or results from the contrasting strategy (Schalock, 2001).

Conclusion

In conclusion, a number of important ideas reflect the emerging framework for conceptualizing, measuring, applying, and evaluating quality of life. Quality of life is a rich and varied concept that draws on the resources of both science and art and is manifested not only in the data of research and measurement but also in a variety of personal expressions consistent with individual being, belonging, and becoming. It follows, therefore, that most conceptions of quality of life share common features and core ideas such as general feelings of well-being, feelings of positive social involvement, opportunities to achieve personal potential, choices and personal control, self-image, and a life-span perspective.

Our belief is that the meaning of quality of life is understood best in regard to its core domains and indicators that reflect a life of quality. We are seeing throughout the world its importance reflected in quality enhancement techniques being applied locally, nationally, and internationally on behalf of people with special needs and their families. As Renwick et al. (2000) remind us, a full picture of quality of life includes the interactions among factors at various degrees of immediacy to the person, and it is necessary to understand how factors at all levels affect a person's experienced quality of life. As stated so well by Rapley (2000), quality of life is "the product of interaction in community with others" (p. 157).

Throughout this first part, we have stressed the importance of approaching the QOL concept from an ecological perspective that results in both a better understanding of the factors that impact a person's perceived quality of life and the application of potential strategies to enhance one's life of quality. Our heuristic QOL model presented in Figure 2.2 incorporates our understanding of the QOL concept, the reform movement with its accountability and quality dimensions, methodological pluralism, and the key concepts discussed thus far: the core QOL domains and indicators, the systems perspective, and the foci for our collaborative work (measurement, application, and/or evaluation). We use this model throughout the rest of the *Handbook* to guide our efforts to provide effective techniques and strategies that the reader of a *Handbook on Quality of Life for Human Service Practitioners* should expect.

At this point, we need to share a word of caution with our readers: There is a lot of information included in parts 2 through 4. We have done our best to organize the key ideas and data into easy-to-read tabular and graphic formats. We have striven hard to ensure that the reader will neither get lost nor have the feeling that either we do not know where we are going in the *Handbook* or that the text is data rich and information poor. To that end, we have followed our own admonition to "know where you are going so you will end up in the right place." Part 2, "The Integration of Research on Quality of Life," presents our first major challenge and the reader's first opportunity to evaluate our clarity and organizational abilities. We trust we have succeeded.

PART 2

The Integration of Research on Quality of Life

Over the past two decades, research into quality of life has grown significantly, from both a qualitative and a quantitative point of view. Scientists, practitioners, service providers, administrators, and others involved in human services have paid special attention to the development and application of the concept of quality of life (QOL) in order to improve services. Published studies have helped to develop a better understanding of the concept, although the great range of disciplines involved has resulted in sometimes different approaches and research situations. Today we are able to reflect more globally and with a clearer understanding of the core quality of life domains and indicators based on the research summarized in part 2. This integration of QOL research has allowed us to propose and develop a unified model (see Figure 2.2) that is applicable to all human services and that allows professionals to use common language and share similar action criteria.

The research from 1985 to 1999 reviewed here in part 2 involves the fields of education and special education, physical health, mental health and behavioral health, mental retardation and intellectual disabilities, aging, and families. To be included in one of these six focus areas, the reference had to have the term *quality of life* in its title or as a keyword in its content. A computer search was carried out of MedLine, PsycLIT, ERIC (Educational Resources Information Center), Current Contents, SIIS (Centro de Documentación e Información del Real Patronato de Prevención y Atención a Personas con Minusvalía de España), DSSC (Disability Studies and Services Center), Whitakers, BIBSYS, TESEO, ISOC, and Psicodoc databases from 1985 through 1999 using 20 descriptors either singly (quality of life) or in combination: quality of life / health / mental health / education / aging / infancy / adolescence / disability / mental retardation / intellectual disabilities / physical disabilities / sensory impairment / blindness / deafness / family / employment / public policy / organizations / services / assessment. In addition we include a chapter (8) on "Family-Centered Quality of Life" based mainly on a Symposium on Family Quality of Life held in Seattle, Washington, in August 2000 in conjunction with the International Association for the Scientific Study of Intellectual Disabilities (IASSID) conference, and a book based on that conference (Turnbull, Turnbull, & Brown, in press).

As described in chapter 1, we found more than 20,900 published references. We then considered 9,749 of these, since they seemed appropriate to the objectives of the search. After reading the abstracts, we selected 2,455 references (book chapters and articles) for closer review because of their direct relevance. Finally, 897 complete articles and book chapters were used: 203 related to education, 166 to health (plus 62 related to infancy, mainly in this field), 142 to mental health, 223 to mental retardation and intellectual disability, and 101 to aging. The references found in chapter 8 ("Family-Centered Quality of Life") are not included in these numbers due to the recent emergence of work in this area and the fact that the core QOL domains and indicators presented in chapter 8 are thus based on work currently in progress.

Each of the following six chapters analyzes a different area of QOL research: education and special education, physical health, mental health and behavioral health, mental retardation and intellectual disabilities, aging, and families. Each section highlights the most often studied themes and research issues, with comments on purposes, core contents, and interfaces with professional work within the field. In addition, each chapter concludes with a section entitled "Domains and Indicators of Quality of Life." In each section, a table summarizes research conducted from 1985 to 1999 in the respective fields. Cited references are classified according to the domains and indicators of the proposed QOL model (see Figure 2.2), incorporating several new indicators and some expressions commonly used as synonyms. In the tables, domains and indicators are presented in decreasing order according to the number of appearances in the scientific literature reviewed. Consequently, it is possible to realize where the priorities of research lie and which areas still demand attention according to the model. Moreover, each reference includes a number that refers to the list of published articles at the end of the respective chapter. The numbered reference appears in plain font style when it is research based, and in bold when it is conceptual.

The reader will find this part of the text very helpful for at least four reasons: (a) it reflects the most comprehensive review of the international QOL literature in the text's focus areas; (b) each focus area's summary table is arranged from the highest to lowest number of domain-specific references, which indicates which domains have been researched the most extensively to date; (c) references are keyed to the respective domain or indicator, which will allow the reader to pursue individual areas of interest in more detail; and (d) the literature review found in each chapter results in a clear delineation of the most commonly used indicators for each of the core QOL domains.

It is important to note that the QOL concept is still emerging in the text's six focus areas and that currently there is considerable debate in the literature about its conceptualization, measurement, and application. There are a number of contextual issues around which this debate is occurring and within which future research and application issues will be resolved. Three of these issues concern (a) economic rationalism and the allocation of resources to people at the margin of society; (b) the disability, aging, patient, and family rights reform movements, including the rapid emergence of the self-advocacy movement; and (c) which outcomes best provide evidence that services and supports provided actually enhance the person's or family's well-being and changed societal behavior (Parmenter & Donnelly, 1997).

These three contextual variables and discourses (economic rationalism, the reform movements, and evidence outcomes) not only affect our approach to the QOL concept but also emphasize the need to be sensitive to the contextual issues summarized in Table 1.1 and the QOL conceptualization and application principles summarized in Tables 2.2 and 2.3. Additionally, they underscore the point that other areas need to be addressed, such as research, professional practice and education, and national and local policies. As mentioned in part 1, the QOL concept requires a change in our thinking, focusing on how to bring about change at the individual and societal level and how to reduce a person's exclusion from the mainstream of society.

As reflected in the research summarized here in part 2, the past two decades have seen considerable progress in understanding the significant role and impact that the QOL concept and discourses about it have played in the lives of people with special needs and the systems that affect those lives. Indeed, the QOL concept has extended beyond the person and has now influenced an entire service delivery system because of its power as a sensitizing notion, a social construct, and an unifying theme. At its core the QOL concept gives us a sense of reference and guidance from the individual's perspective, an overriding principle to enhance an individual's well-being and collaborate for change at the societal level, and a common language and systematic framework to guide our current and future endeavors. Such a framework for the analysis of QOL research and outcomes is presented in the following six chapters.

CHAPTER 3

Education and Special Education

Overview

During the past two decades, the concept of quality of life (QOL) and its application has attracted much interest and attention in the world of health and social services. However, its application in educational environments has only been recently proposed (R. I. Brown & Shearer, 1999; Echeita, 1997; Goode, 1997b; Hegarty, 1994; Raphael, 1999; Schalock, 1996b; Verdugo, 1995). One reason for this situation is that schooling is regarded throughout much of the world as a stage without a proper identity. Its main aim seems to be a transition period on the way to adult life. A second reason, stated by Hegarty (1994), is that the focus of recent educational reforms has concentrated more on structural and organizational factors in schools than on pupils' experiences. Both causes indicate that the QOL concept has been marginal and generally been given low priority within the educational system.

Despite the limited use of the QOL concept in schools, the changes in the conception of education worldwide, especially regarding students with special needs, have resulted recently in the promotion of student quality of life. Moreover, the evolution of the concepts that are serving as guidelines for the planning, management, and evaluation of educational services has followed a similar line. As a result, since the 1960s, the education of regular students and students with special needs has embarked on a questioning of its own normal procedures and responses in order to propose new QOL-oriented education models. Some authors share the belief that the traditional way of organizing special education does not contribute as expected to the improvement of quality of life of students with disabilities. They also think that it is a hindrance to the improvement of general educational systems and, more specifically, to the development of the ability to give appropriate responses to a broad range of students (Skrtic, 1991; Wang, 1995).

This debate sets the framework for this chapter, as the debate is still ongoing. We organize the chapter's material around three topics: (a) themes and research issues; (b) factors that facilitate the use of the QOL concept in school; and (c) domains and indicators of quality of life. The chapter concludes with a discussion of the current status of inclusive education and the need for schools to focus on the diverse dimensions of a student's life.

Themes and Research Issues

Normalization and Inclusion

Between the 1960s and 1990s, the world saw the dissemination of a new philosophy favoring diversity in schools and demanding (a) an end to segregation and (b) the development of normalization and integration policies (Álvarez, 1995; Bautista, 1991; Birch, 1974). The *Warnock Report* (Warnock, 1978) was a turning point in the segregationist movement and the spearhead of the new integration movement. The *Report* stated that the goals of education should be the same for every student. The *Report* also proposed that special-education programs offer the same supports and resources as the regular educational system to help students with special needs reach personal goals.

The Convention on the Rights of the Child (United Nations, 1989) affirmed the right of the child with a disability to have a complete and adequate life that would ensure dignity, promote self-confidence, encourage active participation in the community, and guarantee social and school inclusion. In 1993, in consultation with organizations representing people with disabilities, the United Nations adopted the *Standard Rules on the Equalization of Opportunities for Persons with Disabilities*. According to these guidelines, every country should recognize the principle of equal opportunities in the education of students with disabilities, ensure that special education is part of the educational system, and establish regulations with regard to inclusive education. Finally, *The Salamanca Statement and Framework for Action on Special Needs Education* (Salamanca Statement, 1994) established as the fundamental principle of inclusive education that children should learn together, if possible, and that ordinary schools should recognize and provide an answer to the varied needs of its students, with continuous supports and services regarding those needs.

Some of the most influential viewpoints in recent years concerning our understanding of multicultural education and inclusion have advanced alternative philosophies for structuring schools (Salend, 1998). Multicultural education and the inclusion movements seek equality and excellence through a global change in the educational system that would provide every student with the opportunity to obtain high-level education in general educational programs. These alternative approaches stress the need to design school environments with new teaching techniques that can stimulate and support the participation of all class members, promote social relations, and include academic and affective objectives in the curriculum (Ainscow, 1999). Another factor that these approaches emphasize is a focus on personal needs and experiences of students and the development of the acceptance of individual differences (Jones & Jones, 1995).

Quality of Life in School

Multicultural education and inclusion can be regarded as the result of progressive shifts in the attention paid to students with special needs: special education, mainstreaming, and inclusion. The main objective of this shift has been to change structural aspects of the system, mainly related to physical aspects of childcare (R. I. Brown & Shearer, 1999). Other objectives include a strong commitment to the incorporation of families and communities into the educational effort. However, the approaches have only recently begun to highlight the active role that students should play: hence the interest in evaluating students' quality of life both in regular education and special education programs (Schalock, 1996b).

Quality of life in general supports an inclusive framework (Halpern, 1994). Using the QOL concept in schools allows us to advance the "integral education" of the individual. Moreover, it can be useful as a base and conceptual guideline to many shifts and changes that the school has to undertake to fulfill students' needs. It may also contribute to the improvement of educational planning, the development of specific evaluation models of person-centered programs, and the expansion of the participation of education users or clients in every process and decision in which they are involved. Further reasons for the current interest in the concept include the need to evaluate the effect of integration in nonacademic areas, concern for student satisfaction, and the importance of their perceptions of class environment and quality of life in the school (Hegarty, 1994).

Reflective of this concept, Verdugo and Sabeth (2000) studied perceived quality of life in children between 8 and 12 years of age (and in children with learning disorders) in Spain and Argentina using open-ended questions about the children's experiences and their satisfaction, dissatisfaction, and wishes concerning change. Content analysis of the answers was categorized into the following dimensions: leisure and recreation, performance, interpersonal relations, physical and emotional well-being, collective well-being and values, and material well-being. The first three dimensions were more prevalent among the respondents. Wishes for change were focused mainly on collective well-being and values, together with interpersonal relationships and performance.

The QOL concept is especially important in secondary education and high school. Adolescence is an important period of transition from childhood to adulthood, and QOL models have successfully highlighted key issues that exceptional youth face (Raphael, 1999). Recently an initiative has been put forward to incorporate the QOL concept into schools in Spain in parallel with the implementation of the 1992 American Association on Mental Retardation system (FEAPS, 2000). This proposal focuses on students with intellectual disabilities and consists of a manual of "best practices" to provide guidelines for educational planning with specific objectives related to AAMR adaptive skills areas and the eight QOL domains listed in Figure 2.2. The proposal, together with the subsequent development of indicators, would extend the application of the QOL concept to many centers and programs in Spain. The success of this and similar proposals being made throughout the world depends on the factors described next, which facilitate the use of the QOL concept in schools.

Factors That Facilitate the Use of the QOL Concept in Schools

Since the beginning of the 1980s, the explanations of school problems have not been exclusively based on students' characteristics but refer explicitly to the responsibility of the school. As a consequence, there is a great deal of research into the "effects of school" and, more specifically, into factors linked to its efficiency. Research provides diverse efficiency and quality indicators, which begin to find a place in policies for educational change: positive motivational strategies; frequent opportunities for students to accept responsibilities and to participate in the organization of their school life and of the school itself; clear academic objectives that are recognized by everyone involved in education; good models of behavior; intellectually stimulating teaching; maximum communication between teachers and students; high expectations regarding student performance; shared norms; mutually agreed upon methods; joint planning; and self-tailored and functional education (Reynolds, 1992).

While changes at a political level took place in the 1980s, the 1990s witnessed their practical implementation. A remarkable aspect is the new professional criteria to evaluate the performance of students, especially those with special education needs (Brown & Lehr, 1993). There are doubts about the social validity of educational results (e.g., their relevance and social acceptability), the benefits they offer the individual and family, and how they affect the individual's quality of life. In practical terms this could mean, for example, that the level of participation of the students in community contexts should be evaluated whether or not significant relationships are promoted or there are more opportunities to take control of the situation or to make relevant choices.

Educational Resources

A crucial factor that facilitates the successful use of the QOL concept in schools is the development of curricular approaches that are open and flexible and make it easy to work in new areas of knowledge. Such new work is less academic than in traditional areas and linked more functionally to the integral development of the individual and the improvement of his or her quality of life. Examples include training in skills for life, especially those related to life in the community (Cronin,

1996; Verdugo, 1989a), and improvement in social competence and interpersonal relations (Snell & Vogtle, 1996; Verdugo, 1989b, 1997). The latter would be a crucial parameter for quality of life, as it allows us to work on other important factors for the individual's integrated development. It is a fundamental area for interaction and enriches the tapestry of life experience, especially when combined with rehabilitation that includes the gamut of technical aids and services that promote personal autonomy and community integration.

Other important educational resources include the growing numbers of longitudinal, developmentally sensitive, and comprehensive school-based approaches to primary prevention. Some examples include: *Choosing Options and Accommodations for Children (COACH): A Guide to Planning Inclusive Education* (Elias & Clabby, 1989; Giangreco, Cloninger, & Iverson, 1993), and *Child Development Project (CDP)* (Watson, Schaps, Battistich, Solomon, & Solomon, 1989). COACH was designed to help individual student-planning teams identify the content of educational programs for students with moderate to severe disabilities in general educational settings and activities. It is based on the principle that pursuing valued life outcomes is an important aspect of education. Those valued life outcomes include: having a safe, stable home in which to live, now and/or in the future; access to a variety of places and engaging in meaningful activities; a social network of personally meaningful relationships; a level of personal choice and control that matches one's age; and being safe and healthy. COACH and CDP regard children's social and emotional development as an educational goal that is as essential and important as their intellectual growth. These programs include issues related to positive interpersonal relationships, self-control, social awareness and group participation, decision-making and problem-solving strategies, and the knowledge and skills necessary for mutually beneficial and productive social relationships. Hence, the programs try to improve social competence of students and thereby to contribute to the enhancement of a life of quality.

Evaluation of Consumer Satisfaction

The evaluation of consumer satisfaction as a criterion of QOL enhancement has only begun to be implemented in the past decade. However, most studies conform to the family's perception about educational services and do not focus on students' satisfaction. For example, Ineichen and Rohde (1994) reviewed five recent surveys about satisfaction of families of students with chronic illness and/or disability regarding the availability and quality of education, health care, and day care (Dossertor & Nicol, 1990; Ineichen, 1993; Quine & Pahl, 1989; Todd et al., 1991) and presented the following indicators of service quality: information about possibilities at the end of the school period (future academic or professional guidance), coordination among the educational services and other community services, capacity to cope with specific disorders, availability of specific therapies, fluent communication with the family, availability of qualified staff, and involvement of the client in decision making.

Giangreco, Cloninger, Mueller, Yuan, and Ashworth (1991) have studied the perception within the families of students with disabilities of the meaning of a "good life" and how educational services can fulfill those perceptions. For parents, quality of life for their children involves: a safe, comfortable, and stable home; work valued by society that is meaningful, interesting, image enhancing, and preferred by the individual; access to multiple environments and activities so that their life is full and interesting; health and comfort; and social networks. Educational services may contribute to accomplishing those perceptions as long as they work in coordination with other professionals, open channels for a more fluent communication with families, and let families take a more active role in the process of definition and implementation of the educational program for their children.

Timmons (1993) studied the evaluation of satisfaction experienced by students with disabilities in schools. Timmons examined the quality of life of two groups of teenagers from 12 to 19 years of age: one group with special needs in a segregated class and, the second, their peers in regular education. The instrument employed covered four different areas (home, school, personal, and leisure). The results significantly favored students of the regular school in every area. The main differences involved independence, decision making and choice, opportunities, leisure pursuits, and friendships.

Domains and Indicators of Quality of Life

Based on our literature review, the most common QOL core domains considered in educational research and journals are related to emotional well-being and personal development (see Table 3.1). However, researchers also devoted much attention to the domains of interpersonal relations and social inclusion. Following these domains in frequency of citation (and amounting to about half of the references) are the domains of physical well-being, self-determination, and material well-being. Finally, the least amount of research was published in the rights domain.

It is noteworthy that the rights domain has received so little attention thus far, since many theoretical reflections, public policies, and educational practices in the past decade have been focused on this factor. Moreover, it is surprising that social inclusion is not a better-studied domain, given its importance in every process of school change in the past few years. This might be explained by the lack of current research about quality of life in the education of children and adolescents. Only 26 articles met the criteria described earlier in regard to literature search, article review, and data utilization.

TABLE 3.1
Quality of Life Domains and Indicators in Education and Special Education

DOMAIN	INDICATORS	REFERENCES
1. EMOTIONAL WELL-BEING	**CONTENTMENT**	**8, 15, 22, 25**
	With school	16, 17, 25
	With home	25
	Global life satisfaction	4, 12, 13, 24
	With supports	17
	Self-satisfaction	13
	EMOTIONAL WELL-BEING	**1, 4, 8, 26**
	Negative affect	1, 17, 19, 26
	Positive affect	1, 19
	SELF-CONCEPT	**21**
	Identity	1, 17, 26
	Personality	9
	Self-worth	**3, 11**
	Self-esteem	2
	SAFETY	
	Free from mortal danger	**11**
	Safe environment	**3**
	Stability	6
	SPIRITUALITY	**8**

(table continues)

Note. Domains and indicators are ordered from most frequent to least frequent based on the number of references found. Each reference is related to the same indicator in its line. Conceptual references are printed in boldface and applied research references in regular font. Numbered references are identified in Appendix 3.1.

TABLE 3.1. *(continued)*

DOMAIN	INDICATORS	REFERENCES
	TRUST	21
	HAPPINESS	22
	Optimism	21
2. PERSONAL DEVELOPMENT	EDUCATION	21, 25
	Educational activities	25
	Educational achievements	8, 9, 11, 17
	Educational status	10
	Satisfaction	13
		3
	PERSONAL DEVELOPMENT	3, 5, 7, 21, 23
	Opportunities	1, 26
	FULFILLMENT	5, 22
	Work	17
	Adult roles	7
	Educational	8, 16
	PERSONAL COMPETENCE	10, 15, 21
	Intellectual competencies	20
	Skills (academics and aesthetics)	23
	Advancement (opportunities for future life)	17
3. INTERPERSONAL RELATIONS	INTERPERSONAL RELATIONS	5, 6, 8, 10, 11, 21, 23, 25
	SUPPORTS	3, 6, 8, 14, 23

(table continues)

TABLE 3.1. *(continued)*

DOMAIN	INDICATORS	REFERENCES
	INTERACTIONS	9
	With teachers	19, 26
	With peers	19, 14
	FAMILY	
	Satisfaction	13
	Support	14
	Involvement	3, 25
	FRIENDSHIPS	25
	Satisfaction	13
	INTIMACY	4
	AFFECTION	23
4. SOCIAL INCLUSION	COMMUNITY INTEGRATION AND PARTICIPATION	3, 6, 10, 23
	Access	3, 6, 8
	STATUS	1, 4, 17, 26
	ACCEPTANCE	
	Social belonging	15, 23
	SUPPORTS	3, 21
	Services	10
	WORK ENVIRONMENT	3, 11
	ROLES	23

(table continues)

TABLE 3.1. *(continued)*

DOMAIN	INDICATORS	REFERENCES
	SOCIAL INCLUSION	25
	RESIDENTIAL ENVIRONMENT	13
5. PHYSICAL WELL-BEING	PHYSICAL WELL-BEING	5, 7, 9, 21
	Security	3, 4, 5, 8, 11
	LEISURE	25, 8, 2, 23
	HEALTH	4, 8, 9, 21, 23
	FITNESS	21
	RECREATION	5, 8, 23
	ACTIVITIES OF DAILY LIVING	10, 21, 25
6. SELF-DETERMINATION	SELF-DETERMINATION	2, 14, 25
	AUTONOMY	11
	Independence	10, 15
	CHOICES	6, 14
	PERSONAL GOALS/VALUES	9, 23
	PERSONAL CONTROL	6, 21
	SELF-DIRECTION	2, 21

(table continues)

TABLE 3.1. *(continued)*

DOMAIN	INDICATORS	REFERENCES
7. MATERIAL WELL-BEING	MATERIAL WELL-BEING	4, 5, 7
	FINANCIAL	
	Productivity	4
	Income	10
	Financial security	8
	EMPLOYMENT	10, 23
	SHELTER	8, 25
	FOOD	8
8. RIGHTS	RIGHTS	
	Dignity	3
	Respect	3
	Equality	18
	CIVIC RESPONSIBILITIES	8

Conclusion

In conclusion, it is our collective belief that efficient special education practices can be developed within inclusive settings. Although the research into the impact of inclusion and mainstreaming in children is inconclusive, a positive future change would be to advance the proposal of quality indicators in inclusive programs (Cole, Horvath, Sprague, Wilcox, & Pratt, 1999; Salend, 1998). The analysis of core QOL domains and indicators of success in instruction is also vital for adult success in community employment. Such indicators should clearly include students' needs and wishes and should focus explicitly on the quality of life of the student as a fundamental aspect in the evaluation of the success or failure of education.

The world of education has focused thus far on the setting as the main variable to explain the student's success or failure. Depending on the setting, it has offered different models and systems: integration at the outset, inclusion afterwards.

Inclusion models have tried to find an answer by studying variables that are connected to educational processes within the classroom, with a main role played by teachers. However, education is more than teaching within a classroom and involves other possibilities beyond the school context (Timmons & Brown, 1997). As a consequence, the school also needs to focus on the diverse dimensions of the student's life; and educational planning and evaluation should follow students' needs and wishes.

Appendix 3.1
Education References Corresponding to Table 3.1

1. Binkley, M., Rust, K., & Williams, T. (1992). *Reading literacy in an international perspective.* Washington, DC: National Center for Education Statistics.

2. Carpenter, D., Bloom, L., & Boat, M. (1999). Guidelines for special educators: Achieving socially valid outcomes. *Intervention in School and Clinic, 34*(3), 143–149.

3. Cole, C., Horvath, B., Sprague, J., Wilcox, B., & Pratt, C. (1999). *Quality indicators for inclusive schools: A template for including all students.* Bloomington: Indiana University, Center on Education and Lifelong Learning, Institute for the Study of Developmental Disabilities.

4. Cummins, R., & McCabe, M. (1994). The comprehensive quality of life scale (COMQOL): Instrument development and psychometric evaluation on college staff and students. *Educational and Psychological Measurement, 54*(2), 372.

5. Dew, T., & Huebner, S. (1994). Adolescents' perceived quality of life: An exploratory investigation. *Journal of School Psychology, 32*(2), 185–199.

6. Giangreco, M., Edelman, S., Dennis, R., & Cloninger, C. (1995). Use and impact of COACH with students who are deaf-blind. *Journal of The Association for Persons with Severe Handicaps, 20*(2), 121–135.

7. Halpern, A. (1993). Quality of life as a conceptual framework for evaluating transition outcomes. *Exceptional Children, 59*(6), 486–498.

8. Halpern, A. (1994). Quality of life for students with disabilities in transition from school to adulthood. *Social Indicators Research, 33,* 193–236.

9. Harju, B., & Bolen, L. (1998). The effects of optimism on coping and perceived quality of life of college students. *Journal of Social Behavior and Personality, 13*(2), 185–201.

10. Heal, L. W., Khoju, M., & Rusch, F. R. (1997). Predicting quality of life of youth after they leave special education high school program. *Journal of Special Education, 31*(3), 279–299.

11. Hegarty, S. (1994). Quality of life at school. In D. Goode (Ed.), *Quality of life for persons with disabilities: International perspectives and issues* (pp. 241–249). Cambridge: Brookline Books.

12. Huebner, E. (1994). Conjoint analyses of the students' life satisfaction scale and the Piers-Harris self-concept scale. *Psychology in the Schools, 31,* 273–277.

13. Huebner, S., Laughlin, J., Ash, C., & Gilman, R. (1998). Further validation of the multidimensional students' life satisfaction scale. *Journal of Psychoeducational Assessment, 16,* 118–134.

14. Karan, O., Lambour, G., & Greenspan, S. (1990). Persons in transition. In R. L. Schalock (Ed.), *Quality of life: Perspectives and issues* (pp. 85–92). Washington, DC: American Association on Mental Retardation.

15. Keith, K., Yamamoto, M., Okita, N., & Schalock, R. L. (1995). Cross-cultural quality of life: Japanese and American college students. *Social Behavior and Personality, 23*(2), 163–170.

16. Mendoza, R., Batista-Foguet, J. M., & Oliva, A. (1994). Lifestyles of European school children: Findings of the WHO cross-national study on health-related behaviour. In J. P. Dauwalder (Ed.), *Psychology and promotion of health* (pp. 8–19). Bern, Switzerland: Hogrefe and Huber.

17. Mok, M., & McDonald, R. (1994). Quality of school life: A scale to measure student experience or school climate? *Educational and Psychological Measurement, 54*(2), 483–495.

18. Ortiz, C. (2000). Hacia una educación inclusiva. La educación especial ayer, hoy y mañana. *Siglo Cero, 31*(1), 5–11.

19. Roberts, L., & Clifton, R. (1992). Measuring the affective quality of life of university students: The validation of an instrument. *Social Indicators Research, 27,* 113–137.

20. Roberts, L., & Clifton, R. (1992). Measuring the cognitive domain of the quality of student life: An instrument for faculties of education. *Canadian Journal of Education, 17*(2), 176–191.

21. Schalock, R. L. (1996). The quality of life of children's lives. In A. H. Fine & N. M. Fine (Eds.), *Therapeutic recreation for exceptional children* (pp. 83–94). Springfield, IL: Charles C. Thomas.

22. Shinn, D. (1986). Education and the quality of life in Korea and the United States: A cross-cultural perspective. *Public Opinion Quarterly, 50,* 360–370.

23. Stainback, S., & Stainback, W. (1999). *Aulas inclusivas.* Madrid: Narcea.

24. Terry, T., & Huebner, S. (1995). The relationship between self-concept and life satisfaction in children. *Social Indicators Research, 35,* 39–52.

25. Timmons, V. (1993). *Quality of life of teenagers with special needs.* Unpublished doctoral dissertation, University of Calgary, Alberta, Canada.

26. Wilson, M. (1988). Internal construct validity and reliability of a quality of school life instrument across national and school level. *Educational and Psychological Measurement, 48*(5), 995–1009.

CHAPTER 4

Physical Health

Overview

In the past century scientific and technological breakthroughs in the field of medicine have brought about a significant revolution in medical practices. Despite the benefits of such an improvement, some hold that "high tech" medicine dehumanizes patients and that, although technology can extend life, there are actually states of life that are worse than death. We are facing, therefore, a conflict between quantity and quality of life, from which complicated ethical dilemmas arise.

Until recently the state of a population's health and the benefits of health care were exclusively assessed in terms of mortality and morbidity. The interest in research about quality of life (QOL) began in the 1960s. In the mid-1970s researchers, faced with a growing demand from a more holistic approach toward health problems, started measuring the impact of health on general well-being (Woodend, Nair, & Tang, 1997).

To a certain extent, the interest in QOL assessment has grown due to the ascendance of chronic diseases, the impossibility of finding a direct connection between objective morbidity and medical condition, the need to take appropriate and justified budgetary decisions about the allocation of limited health resources, and a growing social awareness of patients' rights. Other aspects that have had a similar effect include the shifting role and responsibility of key health care decision makers and consumer movements that give patients a new voice in decisions regarding their care (Grégoire, 1995; Read, 1988).

Health care professionals are becoming increasingly aware that enhancing quality of life is one of the major goals of medical care and technology (Patrick & Erickson, 1988). This reflects an important change in the attitudes of clinical and health service researchers regarding the choice of methods to measure outcomes. Health-related quality of life (HRQOL) is an important concept in current research that tries to bring together the constructs of health and quality of life. I. Brown, Renwick, and Nagler (1996) state that quality of life is closely related to and has borrowed a great deal from the concept of health. Good health is a universally held QOL indicator, but having a good overall life is likely to result in people being more healthy as well. Both health and quality of life are social constructs, but quality of life may be a more abstract concept.

There is a general consensus that HRQOL is multidimensional and that any measure taken during treatment purporting to improve a person's quality of life must address the impact that disease and its treatment is having on a variety of domains. It is a patient-centered approach and is therefore a departure from the more traditional measurements of clinical outcomes (Abbott & Gee, 1998).

Although it has not often been clearly and explicitly defined, the concept of HRQOL has been used in several studies reviewed in this chapter, and many assessment instruments have been developed that focus on both physical factors and psychosocial issues of a patient's life. It is beyond the scope of this chapter to review or analyze the plethora of HRQOL instruments developed. However, here we do give clearer meaning to the concept of HRQOL and summarize the QOL literature in the field of physical health. To that end the chapter is divided into the following five sections: (a) the objectives of HRQOL studies; (b) concepts and measures; (c) principal diseases studied; (d) health and quality of life in infancy; and (e) QOL domains and indicators. The chapter concludes with a discussion of the shift in medical outcomes research from typical clinical outcomes to new QOL-related outcomes.

The Objectives of HRQOL Studies

With the aim of measuring health-related quality of life for the general population, researchers have attempted to gather information about health from the following perspectives:

- Epidemiological studies to identify trends in the health of the population.

- Evaluation of the effects of social and health policies. The adoption of HRQOL assessment into the policy and regulatory process requires a complex research methodology that is still in its formative stage. Results are affected by how, when, where, by whom, and from whom the data are gathered (Schuttinga, 1995).

- Resource allocation. Within the context of economic and medical cost-benefit analysis, the concept of quality-adjusted life years (QALY) has been proposed and has produced considerable debate. For example, Kaplan (1995) suggests that QOL studies must be at the core of any logical plan to allocate resources for health care.

- Clinical decision making. According to some authors (Albrecht & Fitzpatrick, 1994; Bucquet, 1993; Ebrahim, 1995; Patrick & Erickson, 1988; Robine, Mathers, & Bucquet, 1993), evaluations have been aimed at:

  1. *Monitoring and assessing patient status,* especially to describe, quantify, and evaluate the impact of disease on the wider aspects of the patient's life at different stages of the illness and within different groups of patients (e.g., cancer, diabetes).

  2. *Selecting treatments.* With chronic disease, a crucial requirement of any treatment should be a clear demonstration of its beneficial effects on daily activities and well-being.

  3. *Monitoring the effects of treatments* that have been selected, to demonstrate that an intervention improves HRQOL or that an intervention does not adversely affect HRQOL. A person may feel and function better following an intervention, but this may not be measurable by conventional measurements of clinical outcome. Consequently, patients' views are crucial.

  4. *Developing a shared view of the disease and of treatment outcomes* with patients. For example, by discussing the effects of a diagnosis, the doctor and patient can develop a shared understanding of the disease impact on the patient by assessing health and QOL outcomes.

  5. *Assessing the implications of diagnosis.*

  6. *Identifying patient's perception of satisfaction* with health services and planning services according to these results.

In addition, some scholars (e.g., Dropsy, 1993; Epstein & Lydick, 1995; Freeman, 1995) emphasize the interest of the pharmaceutical industry in developing research on quality of life, as such results may have economic implications for their companies. Such an area is not free from disputes and uncertainties over sponsors' motives, ethical tensions between researchers and the pharmaceutical industry in terms of dissemination of information about the efficacy of a given drug, the utility of a given QOL instrument developed under industry sponsorship, or problems with translation of the inventories from one culture to another, as the pharmaceutical industry is multinational.

Concept and Measures

Many researchers use the HRQOL concept in studies of the progress of chronic diseases and treatments, although there is unlikely to be universal agreement on what quality of life actually is. For example, Jacobson, Groot, and Samson (1995) hold that quality of life is defined as the individual's subjective perception of well-being as it relates to health status and comprises the following dimensions: physical functioning, pain, emotional status, satisfaction with treatment, and concerns about the future. Schipper, Clinch, and Powell (1990) consider that quality of life represents the functional effect of an illness and its therapy upon a patient, as perceived by the patient and taking into account four broad domains: physical and occupational function, psychological state, social interaction, and somatic sensation. Chwalow (1993) suggests that quality of life is related to the integration of the illness into the individual's daily life.

Definitions found in this review are consistent with the integral concept of "health" as defined by the World Health Organization (1997): not only nonexistence of illness but also physical, psychical, and social well-being. These three dimensions seem to have guided the choice in most studies of the domains for the evaluation of HRQOL. However, the definition of quality of life proposed by the World Health Organization is much more comprehensive (Kuyken, 1995):

> an individual's perception of their position in life in the context of the culture and value systems in which they live and in relation to their goals, expectations, standards and concerns. It is a broad-ranging concept affected in a complex way by the persons' physical health, psychological state, level of independence, social relationships, and their relationship to salient features of their environment. (p. 1405)

Most studies concerning HRQOL specifically focus on areas directly associated with illness, treatment, and immediate consequences. Moreno and Ximénez (1996) argue that including quality of life in the concept of health would be a mistake because interdependence does not imply indistinctness. They think that approaching quality of life exclusively from the point of view of health would be incorrect. Cummins (1997a) notes that there is confusion as to what might constitute a reasonable set of dependent variables to use in measuring medical outcomes and quality of life.

Current theoretical and methodological approaches agree on the multidimensional nature of the concept, but there is no clear consensus on the domains to be included. Scholars assess between three and six domains, which may include the following: physical well-being (physical status and symptoms, autonomy, physical capacity), psychological well-being, functional (occupational) ability, general health perception and well-being, and social activity (Aaronson, 1991; Abbott & Gee, 1998; Guillemin, 1993; Woodend et al., 1997).

Health-Related Quality of Life

In recent years the concept of health-related quality of life has become quite popular among researchers and professionals. HRQOL refers to the various aspects of a person's life that are affected strongly by changes in health status. Authors stress similar aspects: effects of illness and treatment upon physical, emotional, and social well-being (Cella et al., 1999) and/or level of well-being and satisfaction associated with events in a person's life as influenced by disease, accidents, or treatments (Patrick & Erickson, 1988). However, Cummins (1997a) argues that HRQOL introduces a reductionist perspective on well-being and frequently focuses exclusively on pathology.

Patrick and Erickson (1988) contend that social, economic, and cultural aspects of quality of life are important considerations for patients, families, medical practitioners, and society in general; but the focus for clinicians and for clinical trials is primarily on health-related quality of life. They warn of the danger of not making a distinction between the relative contributions of the medical illness and those of other factors, such as personal or family problems that are unrelated to the illness. If this distinction in quality of life is neglected, investigators may substantially overestimate the impact of health-related factors and may conversely undervalue seriously the effect of nonmedical phenomena. Wright (1994) maintains that although the majority of available scales are labeled as measures of health status or HRQOL, each of them, almost without exception, focuses exclusively on negative features. Consequently, existing indices are more appropriately labeled as measurements of disease-related quality of life. Fromm, Andrykowski, and Hunt (1996) hold a similar opinion when they show that standard QOL indices may not measure HRQOL dimensions, thus yielding a potentially incomplete picture of current quality of life, because we cannot forget that a life-threatening disease can trigger positive effects such as a greater appreciation for life or enhanced interpersonal relationships that can contribute to a life of quality.

In short, there are some who use the term *quality of life* not as a multidimensional concept but only in connection to health or illness. Conversely, others prefer to talk about HRQOL, and some recognize the fact that quality of life is an all-embracing concept, including not only health-related factors but also different facets other than medical. Sometimes other terms, such as *health status* or *functional status,* are confused with and used without distinction from *quality of life*.

Quality-Adjusted Life Years

Most controversy regarding the QOL concept has been generated in the area of resource allocation. Calls for a rational system for the allocation of health service resources have led to cost-utility analyses associated with measurements of quality of life. Cost-utility analysis is used to relate the cost of an intervention to the number of quality-adjusted life years gained through intervention (Cohen, 1996; Parmenter, 1994, 1996). A quality-adjusted life year is defined as the equivalent of a completely well year of life or a year free of any symptoms, problems, or health-related disabilities (Kaplan, 1995). The values of QALYs, then, represent the proportion of time, on average, that an individual spends functioning optimally over a given time period.

The use of the QALY measure has aroused criticism from clinical and academic circles. According to its critics, it focuses only on how resources are allocated and does not take into account individual rights and needs of different groups of patients. Nevertheless, Gudex (1986) qualifies this by saying that these choices have actually been made always, only not formally identified, and that decisions are now becoming more difficult with the increasingly limited resources within the health system. There have also been doubts about its supposed objectivity in calculation, combining quantity and quality of life, together with the conceptual and psychometric suppositions at the base of the measure. For example, many accept the view that people are prepared to sacrifice some constant proportion of their remaining years of life to achieve a given improvement in their health status, despite the years that remain (Cohen, 1996; Cummins, 1997a; Newport, 1996; Parmenter, 1994, 1996).

Principal Diseases Studied

Cancer

Fallowfield (1993), Mercier and Schraub (1993), and Montazeri, Gillis, and McEwen (1998) suggest that lack of information about some aspects of a life-threatening disease may have a negative effect on the individual's well-being, including uncertainty of prognosis, guilt about causality, fear of painful, and/or an undignified death. Other factors that play a crucial role in the individual's well-being include: anxiety in prediagnostic examinations; financial, professional, social, sexual, and family problems during and after the illness; and opportunities (or lack thereof) to ask questions about the disease and to participate in decisions about the treatment. Research has found that initial quality of life perception is a strong prognostic factor for survival. The extent to which treatments and their resultant side-effects affect quality of life depends partly on the site of the cancer, the stage of the disease, the tumor response, the type of treatment, and the likelihood of cure.

As far as type of treatment chosen is concerned, research results are not conclusive on the effects on quality of life. Although Aaronson (1991) maintains that QOL studies have demonstrated that less invasive surgery is better for patients (better body image, fewer sexual problems), Ganz and Coscarelli (1995) found few differences between two surgical groups (modified radical mastectomy versus segmental mastectomy and radiation therapy). Ganz and Coscarelli observe a positive relationship between age and measurements of psychosocial status and quality of life. Such a result coincides with the conclusions of Cordoba et al. (1995), who found, in a study of 55 patients with breast cancer, a positive relationship between posttraumatic stress disorders (PTSD) and younger age. Lower income and, to a lesser extent, inferior education were also associated with PTSD-like symptoms. These authors indicate that exposure to more prolonged, extensive, or aversive medical treatment might be associated with increased risk for PTSD or PTSD-like symptoms in survivors of a life-threatening illness and that poor social support is a risk factor for general poor adjustment. Conversely, Litwins and Rodriguez (1994) compared 32 bone marrow transplant and 22 conventional chemotherapy recipients and observed that quality of life was not significantly associated with age, socioeconomic status, time since diagnosis, or time since last treatment.

HIV

It is common to find descriptions in the HIV literature of markedly negative effects on patients' quality of life due to the stress developed as a result of this incurable illness, depending on the stage the patient is in: diagnosis, symptomatic stage, or terminal stage (Fallowfield, 1993; Lutgendorf, Antoni, Shneiderman, & Ironson, 1995; Siffert, Atoui, & Reynes, 1993). Measured HRQOL is affected by serious physical alterations, psychoemotional effects (e.g., negation, isolation, separation from partner, libido decrease, depression, guilt, self-concept and self-esteem problems), intellectual-neurological consequences, and financial problems (e.g., loss of job, cost of treatment). Moreover, the patient endures an immense psychological burden due to multifaceted social and moral pressures and stigmatization.

As far as potential interventions are concerned, Lutgendorf et al. (1995) observed that a cognitive behavioral intervention in HIV patients, the cognitive behavioral stress management (CBSM), can help improve the ability to cope. In addition, social support contributes to an improved quality of life in factors such as emotional functioning, social functioning, and sense of well-being for HIV-infected men during several phases of the HIV spectrum. They present important determinants of quality of life in HIV infection (e.g., coping ability, appraisal of stressors, self-efficacy, ability to elicit social support, and immune functioning) that have an impact on the emotional, social, and physical functioning of the person. The authors also describe how these factors can be modulated through psychosocial interventions.

Brain Injury

The significant deficits experienced by brain-damaged survivors at a cognitive, behavioral, and emotional level (Miller, 1992; Stambrook, Peters, & Moore, 1989; Veach, 1993) represent major hindrances for them to restart their normal lives and recover their professional lives and interpersonal relations within their families and personal relationships (Seaman, Roberts, Gilewski, & Nagai, 1993). The rehabilitation process is fundamental for the improvement of the quality of life of the patient and his or her family, including programs based on community integration and multilevel intervention: cognitive, behavioral, social, linguistic, and vocational.

Seaman et al. (1993) developed a seven-phase interdisciplinary, structured, and cognitively based community reintegration program, which attempted to improve patients' quality of life by working with the patient, the family, the treatment team, and the sociocultural network. The East Mountain Head Injury Center (EMHIC) has a program that is based on a medical model of acute rehabilitation for moderate and severe head trauma survivors and focuses on community integration (Huber & Edelberg, 1993). Veach (1993) introduces and discusses the importance of community-based rehabilitation programs that use the resources within the survivor's local community, such as health clubs, self-paced learning labs in a community college setting, art and craft courses, nature centers, volunteer worksites, and on-the-job training or educational curriculum funded through the state rehabilitation sector.

Although most efforts focus on the development of community integration programs, Burleigh, Farber, and Gillard (1998), in a study of 30 people with traumatic brain injury (TBI), found that their results did not support the hypothesis that there is a positive relationship between total community integration and life satisfaction of people with TBI. The relationship between life satisfaction and social integration showed a low, but significant, correlation between the two. Participants with greater social integration reported greater satisfaction with their lives. They also observed that there is a significant inverse relationship between years after injury and total community and social integration: the longer the time since injury, the lower the community social integration scores achieved. For life satisfaction, the older the patient was at the time of injury, the higher the life satisfaction scores.

Multiple Sclerosis

Several factors make multiple sclerosis (MS) a disease with important QOL implications. First, its unpredictable nature makes it difficult for patients to gain a sense of control over their illness. Second, MS typically affects young adults, thereby limiting their most productive years. Third, patients must rely on treatments that only alleviate symptoms. Finally, the disease, although limiting, may not in reality be apparent to others (Cella et al., 1999).

Aronson (1997), in a study on the quality of life of 697 individuals with MS and their caregivers, found that health received the lowest satisfaction rating among six components of quality of life; family relations received the highest satisfaction rating, followed closely by friendships and housing. Poorer quality of life among those with MS was associated with unemployment, moderate or worse MS symptoms, fatigue, mobility limitations on stairs, and a disease course other than stable. An attitude of acceptance toward MS was associated with increased satisfaction. The study also found that the impact of MS cannot be predicted solely on the basis of disease severity. The 345 caregivers also gave family relations, friendships, and housing the highest satisfaction ratings, with the lowest rating reserved for finances. Poorer quality of life as a whole was associated with being a spouse, longer duration of care giving, moderate or worse MS symptoms in the care recipient, and a disease course other than stable.

Jonsson, Dock, and Ravnborg (1996) evaluated quality of life and rehabilitation outcomes at two different time points: before admission and after leaving the hospital. Patients had received a standard multidisciplinary rehabilitation treatment (e.g., medical care, physiotherapy, occupational therapy, neuropsychological or psychological treatment). The Laman and Lankhorst Questionnaire (LLQ) used to assess quality of life correlated significantly with the total Beck Depression Inventory score (BDI), but not with gender, age, disease duration, type of MS, or disease severity. Patients had low-weighted QOL scores on the following items: fatigability, dependence on other people, concerns about deterioration, and walking. Likewise, the BDI showed high scores on fatigability, work difficulty, and somatic preoccupation.

Cardol, Elvers, Ostendorp, Brandsma, and Groot (1996) completed a study with 15 patients with amyotrophic lateral sclerosis and did not find a significant correlation between independence in carrying out day-to-day activities and quality of life, although they did find a significant relationship between sleeping and quality of life. An enhanced quality of life was also associated with purposeful and meaningful activity.

Other Illnesses

Because people with cardiovascular illnesses (e.g., angina or myocardial infarction) often require quite dramatic changes of lifestyle, this group has received attention from researchers interested in determining the illnesses' effects on family relations, work, leisure, psychological alterations, and sexual activity. Heart disease affects all these areas of daily life, and the assessment of its effects on a person's quality of life is just as important as other measures of physical functioning (Fallowfield, 1993).

Woodend, Nair, and Tang (1997) conducted a study in which a group of cardiac outpatients (27 rehabilitation patients and 31 pacemaker patients), staff members, and family members was asked what it considered important to the patients' quality of life. The staff rated exercise tolerance, general health status, symptom relief, chest pain, and perceived benefits of treatment as the most important physical elements. Both patients and family members agreed that among the psychological elements, self-esteem, satisfaction with life, and confidence were the most important aspects to a life of quality. The staff felt that depression and anxiety regarding health were the most important aspects. Staff also ranked fear of recurrence and death among the five most important psychological elements. According to the patient group, the five most important social elements were internal control over social life, family life, interpersonal relations, changes in marriage, and changes in family.

Several studies have analyzed the quality of life of patients with epilepsy and its correlation with other facets of personality (Trueman & Duthie, 1998; Zhu, Jin, Xie, & Xiao, 1998). Although findings do not present significant differences compared to other population groups without the disease, data show that patients with epilepsy tend to display higher levels of anxiety and depression (Trueman & Duthie, 1998). Patients' general well-being was not related to the duration of the disease, but rather to the frequency of their seizures. Higher scores of general well-being were associated with patients' higher educational level, extroversion, and objective support received (Zhu et al., 1998). Results suggest that personality characteristics are the main factors influencing general well-being. Thus, for these patients, psychological therapy and treatment should increase general well-being and quality of life.

Satisfaction with life has also been assessed in spinal cord injury (SCI) patients (Coyle, Lesnik-Emas, & Kinney, 1994; Fuhred, Rintala, Hart, Clearman, & Young, 1992). Levels of assessed satisfaction were lower than previously reported for the general population (Fuhred et al.) and also indicated that individuals with SCI are at an elevated risk of experiencing a significant depressive episode after discharge (Coyle et al.). From the standpoint of the World Health Organization model of disablement, the life satisfaction of people with SCI appears to be influenced, albeit indirectly, by selective aspects of their social role performance (handicap), but not by the degree of their impairment or disability. Leisure satisfaction was the most significant predictor of life satisfaction in a study of 91 adults with SCI. The challenge facing the rehabilitation community is facilitating ready access for adults with SCI to both employment and leisure opportunities (Coyle et al.).

Studies on quality of life have involved many other illnesses, including diabetes (Jacobson, Groot, & Samson, 1995), cystic fibrosis (Moorcroft, Dodd, & Webb, 1998), genetic skeletal dysplasias (Apajasalo, Sintonen, Rautonen, & Kaitila, 1998), neuromuscular disorders (Reid & Renwick, 1994), hypertension (Rosen & Kostis, 1995; Shapiro, Hui, Oakley, Jagoda, & Jammer, 1995), migraine (Dahlöf & Dimenás, 1995; Dahlöf & Solomon, 1998; Solomon, 1997), inflammatory bowel disease (MacPhee, Hoffenberg, & Feranchak, 1998), asthma (Blumenschein & Johannesson, 1998), amputation (Williamson & Walters, 1996), and stroke (O'Mahony, Rodgers, Thomson, Dobson, & James, 1998). The objective of other studies was to analyze lifestyles and general health, taking into account the effects on quality of life due to the consumption of drugs, alcohol, and tobacco (Davies, 1996; Fitzgerald, 1996; Lowe, 1996; Sherwood, 1996).

Health and Quality of Life in Infancy

Children with medical disorders face problems and limitations that challenge their general developmental tasks, adaptation, and life satisfaction (Gjaerum & Heyerdahl, 1998). The QOL concept has been important in adult medicine for decades, but it has only recently emerged as a relevant topic affecting ill children. Bullinger and Ravens-Sieberer (1995) remark that among studies published since the concept was first introduced in 1964, only 13% are devoted to children's quality of life. Gerharz (1997) presumes that the delay in the attempt to measure quality of life in children may have a simple reason: It is even more complex than in adults.

Methodological challenges facing child evaluations are related mainly to "age," which influences cognitive level, attention capacity, understanding, emotional state recognition, and communication (Juniper, Guyatt, Feeny, Griffith, & Ferrie, 1997; Manificat & Dazord, 1997). This has generated much debate about the reliability of respondent answers and consequently of the results. However, today there is a consensus about the importance of not extending the adult's vision onto the child's, because the child has his or her own perception of life events (Casas, 1992). Eiser (1997) analyzes why the understanding of quality of life in children will not be achieved by scaling down ideas developed through work with adults: Developmental changes in emotional and cognitive reactions to health and illness are unique and distinct from those of adults; children's diseases are different from those in adults; and the social implications also vary (e.g., there is a greater involvement of the family than when an adult is the patient). As a result, quality of life in infancy should be a specific and differential field of study.

Most studies on infancy and quality of life are mere theoretical reflections and developments from work with adults and cover a wide range of subjects (e.g., health, disability, family, prevention, education, home environment, and services). The QOL concept has only recently been approached as a holistic and multidimensional concept, together with the evaluation of the child's level of satisfaction or well-being from his or her viewpoint. To date, we do not have available a general approach for the different components of quality of life at the different stages of childhood. We can only highlight the following initial considerations:

- psychoemotional perceptions and effects of chronic illness on the child and family and limitations on daily life routines (Czyzewski, Mariotto, Bartholomew, LeCompte, & Sockrider, 1992; Garralda, 1994; Gjaerum & Heyerdahl, 1998; Juniper et al., 1997; Koegel, Stiebal, & Koegel, 1998; Obuchowska & Obuchowski, 1992; Schalock, 1996a)
- effects of treatment and their repercussions on well-being (Gritti, Vajro, Di Sarno, Comito, & De Vicenzo, 1998; Guyatt, Juniper, Griffith, Feeny, & Ferrie,

1997; Le Bidois, Vouhe, Tamisier, Sidi, & Cachaner, 1998; Masera et al., 1999)
- quality measures for assessing health care services, plans, providers, and systems (Lieu & Newton, 1998; Mangione-Smith & McGlynn, 1998)

Research has also examined some factors related to health prevention and mental health (Kramer, 1992), health-related behavior and lifestyle (Mendoza, Batista-Foguet, & Oliva, 1994), intercultural studies (Daniels & Hogg, 1991), educational opportunities and services for children with disabilities (Giangreco, Cloninger, Mueller, Yuan, & Ashworth, 1991; Koegel et al., 1998; Logan, 1999; Sloper, 1998; Wesley, 1994), ethical issues and legislation (Brotherson, Cook, & Cunconan-Lahr, 1995; Campbell & McHaffie, 1995), and longitudinal studies that attempt to isolate the effects of specific situations or childhood events on subsequent stages of the individual's life (Ford & Kidd, 1998).

In recent years scientific literature has attempted to design and validate multi-dimensional measurement instruments such as the KINDL Questionnaires (Ravens-Sieberer & Bullinger, 1998), the AUQUEI Questionnaire (Nicolas, Dazord, & Manificat, 1996; Manificat & Dazord, 1997; Manificat, Dazord, Cochat, & Nicolas, 1997), and the PedsQL: Pediatric Quality of Life inventory (Varni, Seid, & Rode, 1999) among others. However, there are still few studies that take into account the child's point of view, and quite often QOL evaluation has only been indirect (made by an external observer, parents, caregivers, etc.). Moreover, instruments have mainly been transposed from adult studies (Bullinger & Ravens-Sieberer, 1995).

In summary, infancy requires urgent research in order to define and bring the QOL concept into practice and to develop appropriate assessment instruments that take into account the child's point of view when determining his or her level of satisfaction.

Quality of Life Domains and Indicators

Although there is an extremely broad range of articles and chapters that refer to quality of life in health, there are actually very few studies suitable for inclusion in Table 4.1. In this field it is relatively common to use and abuse the term *quality of life* in the titles of publications. Inherent connotations and benefits from using the term (giving a positive expression, focusing on the user, etc.) are the most probable cause for its excessive use. Moreover, the term has been used frequently to refer to patient recovery from certain disorders. After a progressive refinement of the material, we have finally selected 55 references that actually focus on physical health from the perspective of our heuristic QOL model (Figure 2.2).

TABLE 4.1
Quality of Life Domains and Indicators in Physical Health

DOMAIN	INDICATORS	REFERENCES
1. PHYSICAL WELL-BEING	**HEALTH** Physical functioning and status Symptoms of disease (progression, severity, and frequency) Health/treatment satisfaction General perception of health Perceived physical appearance (satisfaction with one's looks) Physical discomfort (problems, limitations, and changes)	**1, 2,** 3, 4, 5, 6, 7, **8,** 9, 11, 12, 13, **14,** 15, 16, 18, 19, 20, **21, 22,** 23, 25, 26, **27,** 29, 31, 32, **34, 35,** 37, 38, 39, 40, **41,** 42, **43,** 44, 46, 47, **48,** 49, **50, 51,** 52, **53, 54,** 55
	ACTIVITIES OF DAILY LIVING Usual daily activities Outdoor (physical activity: walks, cycling, etc.) and indoor (housework tasks, TV, etc.)	4, 7, 13, 15, **21,** 23, 25, 26, **27, 35,** 40, **41, 43,** 44, **51,** 52, **54**
	LEISURE AND RECREATION ACTIVITIES Leisure satisfaction and enjoyment Recreational activities, hobbies/pastimes	4, 13, 17, **22,** 23, 24, 25, 31, 36, **41, 43,** 47
	MOBILITY Movement (ambulation) Transportation	4, 11, 12, **22,** 25, 31, **34, 35,** 40, **43,** 54

(table continues)

Note. Domains and indicators are ordered from most frequent to least frequent based on the number of references found. Conceptual references are printed in boldface and applied research references in regular font. Numbered references are identified in Appendix 4.1.

TABLE 4.1. *(continued)*

DOMAIN	INDICATORS	REFERENCES
	NUTRITION	4, 6, 7, **14**, **22**, 31, 40, 52
	HEALTH CARE	**1**, 7, 26, 30, 31, **34**, 37, 52
	PHYSICAL WELL-BEING (GLOBAL)	8, **28**, **33**, 37, **43**, 48, 51
2. EMOTIONAL WELL-BEING	CONTENTMENT Satisfaction (affective well-being) Emotional comfort, functioning (limitations/ problems), behavior, and performance Mental and mood functioning (displeasure, frustration, affliction) Psychological being, health, and status (psychosocial adjustment)	**1**, **2**, 3, 4, 7, **8**, 11, 12, **14**, 15, 16, 18, 19, 20, 25, 26, 30, **35**, 36, 37, 38, 40, **41**, 42, **43**, 44, 46, 47, 49, **51**, 52, **54**, 55
	STRESS Anxiety Distress/despair (psychological) Emotional reactions Fortitude/resignation	4, 7, 10, 11, 13, **21**, **22**, 23, 24, 25, 38, **41**, **43**, 48, 50, 51, 52, **54**, 55
	HAPPINESS Mood (optimistic) Depression/sadness Zest/apathy	4, 7, 10, 12, 16, **21**, **22**, 25, 32, 38, **43**, 46, 48, **51**, 52, 54
	SELF-CONCEPT	6, 8, 10, 16, 23, 25, 26, 27, **41**, 50, 53

(table continues)

TABLE 4.1. *(continued)*

DOMAIN	INDICATORS	REFERENCES
	SPIRITUALITY	14, 20, 25, **43**, 50
	EMOTIONAL WELL-BEING (GLOBAL)	8, 28, 37, **43**, 54
3. INTER-PERSONAL RELATIONS	INTERACTIONS Social relations/interactions/contacts/emotional ties Social belongings (being close to people in family, having a spouse or special person) Quality of relationships Medical interaction Neighborhood	4, 6, 7, 11, **14**, 19, 20 **21**, **22**, 24, 25, 26, 27, **33**, 36, 37, 38 39, **41**, **43**, 45, 46 **48**, 49, 50, **51**, **52** **53**, 54
	FAMILY Family life, relationships, problems Family satisfaction Household duties	5, 7, **8**, **14**, 16, **21**, **22**, 25, 29, 39, **43**, **48**, **53**
	FRIENDSHIPS	4, 5, **14**, **43**, **52**, **53**
	AFFECT	32, **43**, **48**, **51**
	INTIMACY	19, **43**
4. MATERIAL WELL-BEING	EMPLOYMENT Job/work/profession Vocational issues Occupational status/functioning	2, 5, 7, **8**, **14**, 19, **21** **22**, 24, 25, 31, 36 37, 40, **41**, **43**, 47, **48**, 50, **51**, **53**, 54
	HOUSING Type of residence/accommodation Home management	5, 7, 24, 25, 36, 40, **43**, **53**

(table continues)

TABLE 4.1. *(continued)*

DOMAIN	INDICATORS	REFERENCES
	FINANCES Money matters (expenditures, pocket money) Financial situation (disincentives)	5, 7, **8**, 25, **34**, 37, 40, **41**
	SOCIOECONOMIC STATUS	16, 29, **53**
	MATERIAL WELL-BEING (GLOBAL)	27, 28, 33
5. SOCIAL INCLUSION	**ROLE** Social/role functioning Social life Social performance	1, 3, 6, 18, 25, **28**, 35, **38**, 42, **43**, 44, **50**, **51**, 54
	COMMUNITY ACTIVITIES	2, 21, 22, 34, 35, 43, 53
	SUPPORT	38, **43**, 47, **51**, 55
	ACCEPTANCE	8, **51**, 54
	RESIDENTIAL ENVIRONMENT	7, 20
6. PERSONAL DEVELOPMENT	**PERFORMANCE** Cognitive performance Personal functioning Cognitive well-being (alertness, disorientation, problems in reasoning)	1, 6, 19, 24, 29, **34**, 36, 37, 40, **43**, 45, 49, **51**, 54

(table continues)

TABLE 4.1. *(continued)*

DOMAIN	INDICATORS	REFERENCES
	PERSONAL COMPETENCE Cognitive functioning	7, 15, 41, 50, 51, 52, 54
	EDUCATION	4, 8, 29, 40, 43, 50, 53
	SKILLS	2, 7, 22, 37, 41, 51, 54
	VOLUNTARY ACTIVITY	4
	PROGRESS	7
7. SELF-DETERMINATION	**GOALS/PERSONAL VALUES** Hopes/expectations/ beliefs/ desires/interests/own ideas or opinions	7, 10, 20, 22, 25, 37, 40, 41, 50, 51
	AUTONOMY	27, 37, 41, 48, 50
	PERSONAL CONTROL Self-control (behavioral, emotional, etc.)	37, 51, 55
8. RIGHTS	**LEGAL OBLIGATIONS OR RIGHTS** Guardianship Equality of opportunity	41, 43, 51
	ACCESS Opportunity	51

The comprehensive concept of health held by the World Health Organization (WHO), which takes a multidimensional view when dealing with physical, emotional, and social well-being, has facilitated considerable research. The WHO's concept takes on board other scientific and professional interests beyond the restricted concern for the patient's physical health. Health psychology has also made a significant contribution in this area. Furthermore, the study of lifestyles becomes more relevant and interesting when the evaluation concerns the impact of health on one's lifestyle.

Although there is a great interest in HRQOL, we cannot say that a multidimensional model of quality of life is being applied broadly. Conceptual research and theoretical model development are relatively rare when compared to other areas. However, different proposals in published articles and chapters do follow the model proposed in the present *Handbook,* as their dimensions and indicators correspond closely with our own. The only dimension barely substantiated by research was rights. Moreover, there are still few studies on self-determination, but this may well change in time, as we see later in the areas of mental behavioral health and mental retardation and intellectual disabilities.

Most reviewed studies focus on the evaluation of physical well-being and emotional well-being and on indicators from both dimensions. Interest in emotional well-being has significantly increased in recent years, whereas interest was previously almost exclusively reserved for physical well-being. Other important dimensions, such as personal development, self-determination, and rights, received scant attention from researchers, with 16, 13, and 4 references respectively. Interpersonal relationships, material well-being, and social inclusion received more attention (34, 27, and 24 respectively). The most interrelated dimensions are physical with emotional well-being, and interpersonal relations with social inclusion. However, connections are more often made between different indicators within each dimension.

It is logical that when dealing with health most attention has been directed toward evaluating physical and emotional well-being, because the short-term effects and symptoms that trigger somatic disorders affect many of the indicators found within them. Most researchers highlight the health indicator in studies classified in Table 4.1 (47 out of 55), which are mainly focused on the analysis of physical functioning. Different terms are used, such as *physical functioning, physical status, physical health, symptoms of disease progression,* and *severity and frequency of symptoms.* Other indicators frequently cited in physical well-being were activities of daily living (17), leisure and recreation activities (12), and mobility (10).

Within emotional well-being, special attention is directed toward the contentment indicator (33 references). This indicator is also related to indicators in other dimensions evaluating patient satisfaction. Such attention has increased in recent years, just as it has done in the fields of aging and mental health. Some synonyms are *satisfaction, affective well-being, emotional comfort, behavior and performance; mental and mood functioning,* and *psychological being.* Other relevant indicators of emotional well-being are stress (19), happiness (16), and self-concept (11).

As far as interpersonal relations and material well-being are concerned, the most cited indicators are interactions (29) and employment (22). Synonym terms referring to interactions include: *social relations, contacts, social belonging* (being close family members, having a spouse or special person), *quality of relationships, medical interaction, social communication, social separation, isolation, interpersonal functioning, sexual life,* and *marital interaction.* Within interpersonal relations, the family indicator was cited 13 times. In material well-being, far below the employment indicator are housing and finances.

Conclusion

The QOL concept as it relates to health is an interesting measure for economists, politicians, decision makers, administrators, managers, sociologists, psychologists, doctors, and other professionals. There is a straightforward explanation: Quality of life presents the results of the individual's efforts to achieve a high level of well-being and is a guiding principle for actions and interventions aimed at its enhancement.

Agreements and disagreements are apparent in the field of medicine. Medical ethics and the recognition of the individual's fundamental rights have opened the debate not only about quality of life but also about quality of death for individuals with chronic diseases. Scientific breakthroughs are being made that could lead in the near future to a scenario where chronic diseases and their maintenance become the medical world's greatest priority. Hence health psychology seems to have much to offer; specific coping styles, confrontation, personal well-being, avoidance, acceptance-resignation are fundamental issues that have been stressed when working with people with conditions such as cancer, HIV, diabetes, and cardiovascular disease. Practitioners have a major role to play, identifying indicators, accurate assessment techniques, intervention programs, and lifestyles linked to onset of disease. However, creating interdisciplinary work teams is a fundamental task if we want to approach the QOL concept holistically (Parmenter, 1994).

Researchers in the field of health are moving toward a more complex and multidimensional approach to the QOL concept. Interest has shifted from typical clinical outcomes (morbidity and mortality) to new QOL-related outcomes. The concept of HRQOL is a measurement that can be useful, albeit somehow reductionist. The best instruments are those that include a general evaluation for any type of illness or group and a specific one.

In the area of HRQOL more truly multidimensional studies should be conducted that provide an adequately operational QOL concept, such as the one proposed in Figure 2.2. We should evaluate more domains and indicators in the model, such as self-determination. It is also necessary to develop more domain-centered therapeutic programs. Furthermore, the well-known QALYs should be reconsidered on the grounds that they lack ethical and scientific foundations and produce unreliable results concerning the individual. The key factor is to develop a holistic view of health and illness, a view that focuses on the whole person's potential, not just the potentially debilitating effects of an illness.

APPENDIX 4.1
Health References Corresponding to Table 4.1

1. Aaronson, N. K. (1991). Methodologic issues in assessing the quality of life of cancer patients. *Cancer, 67*(3), 844–850.

2. Abbott, J., & Gee, L. (1998). Contemporary psychosocial issues in cystic fibrosis: Treatment adherence and quality of life. *Disability and Rehabilitation, 20*(6-7), 262–271.

3. Alonso, J., Prieto, L., & Antó, J. M. (1995). La versión española del SF-36 health survey: Un instrumento para la medida de los resultados clínicos. *Medicina Clinica, 104,* 771–776.

4. Apajasalo, M., Sintonen, H., Rautonen, J., & Kaitila, I. (1998). Health-related quality of life of patients with genetic skeletal dysplasias. *European Journal of Pediatrics, 157,* 114–121.

5. Aronson, K. J. (1997). Quality of life among multiple sclerosis patients and their caregivers. *Neurology, 48,* 74–80.

6. Bjordal, K., Ahlner-Elmqvist, M., Tollesson, E., Jensen, A. B., & Razavi, D. (1994). Development of a European Organization for Research and Treatment of Cancer (EORTC) questionnaire module to be used in quality of life assessments in head and neck cancer patients. *Acta Oncológica, 33*(8), 879–885.

7. Brown, I., & Renwick, R. (1999). *The quality of life profile: A generic measure of health and well-being.* [On-line]. Available: www.utoronto.ca/qol/profile.htm

8. Bucquet, D. (1993). Qualité de vie, santé perceptuelle: Définition, concept, évaluation. In C. Hérisson & L. Simon (Dir.), *Evaluation de la qualité de vie* (pp. 1–7). Paris: Masson.

9. Bullinger, M., & Ravens-Sieberer, U. (1995). Evaluation de la qualité de vie des enfants: Revue de la littérature. *Revue Européenne de Psychologie Appliquée, 45*(4), 245–254.

10. Burleigh, S. A., Farber, R. S., & Gillard, M. (1998). Community integration and life satisfaction after traumatic brain injury: Long-term findings. *American Journal of Occupational Therapy, 52*(1), 45–52.

11. Cardol, M., Elvers, J. W. H., Ostendorp, R. A. B., Brandsma, J. W., & Groot, I. J. M. (1996). Quality of life in patients with amyotrophic lateral sclerosis. *Journal of Rehabilitation Sciences, 9*(4), 99–103.

12. Cella, D. F., Diennen, K., Arnason, B., Reder, A., Webste, M., Karabastos, B., Chang, C., Lloyd, S., Mo, F., Stewart, J., & Stefoski, D. (1999). Validation of the functional assessment of multiple sclerosis quality of life instrument. *American Academy of Neurology, 47,* 129–139.

13. Christie, M. J., French, D., Sowden, A., & West, A. (1993). Development of child-centered disease-specific questionnaires for living with asthma. *Psychosomatic Medicine, 55,* 541–548.

14. Chwalow, J. (1993). Méthodologie de l'évaluation de la qualité de vie dans les essais cliniques. In C. Hérisson & L. Simon (Dir.), *Evaluation de la qualité de vie* (pp. 22–32). Paris: Masson.

15. Cleary, P. D., Wilson, I. B., & Fowler F. J., Jr. (1995). Health-related quality of life in HIV-infected persons: A conceptual model. In J. E. Dimsdale & A. Baum (Eds.), *Quality of life in behavioral medicine research* (pp. 191–204). Hillsdale, NJ: Lawrence Erlbaum.

16. Coyle, C. P., Lesnik-Emas, S., & Kinney. W. B. (1994). Predicting life satisfaction among adults with spinal cord injuries. *Rehabilitation Psychology, 39*(2), 95–112.

17. Dahlöf, C. G. H., & Dimenäs, E. (1995). Migraine patients experience poorer subjective well-being/quality of life even between attacks. *Cephalalgia, 15,* 31–36.

18. Dahlöf, C. G. H., & Solomon, G. D. (1998). The burden of migraine to the individual sufferer: A review. *European Journal of Neurology, 5*(6), 525–533.

19. Dazord, A., Mercier, C., Manificat, S., & Nicolas, J. (1995). Evaluation de la qualité de vie: Mise au point d'un instrument d'évaluation dans un contexte francophone. *Revue Européenne de Psychologie Appliquée, 45*(4), 271–278.

20. De Vries, J., & Van Heck, G. (1997). The World Health Organization quality of life. Assessment instrument (WHOQOL-100): Validation study with the Dutch version. *European Journal of Psychological Assessment, 13*(3), 164–178.

21. Dropsy, R. (1993). Qualité de vie: Le point de vue de l'industriel du médicament. In C. Hérisson & L. Simon (Dir.), *Evaluation de la qualité de vie* (pp. 49–58). Paris: Masson.

22. Fallowfield, L. (1993). *The quality of life: The missing measurement in health care* (3rd ed.). Great Britain: WBC Bridgend.

23. French, D. J., Christie, M. J., & Sowden, A. J. (1994). The reproducibility of the childhood asthma questionnaires: Measures of quality of life for children with asthma aged 4–16 years. *Quality of Life Research, 3,* 215–224.

24. Fromm, K., Andrykowski, M. A., & Hunt, J. (1996). Positive and negative psychosocial sequelae of bone marrow transplantation: Implications for quality of life assessment. *Journal of Behavioral Medicine, 19*(3), 221–240.

25. Fuhred, M., Rintala, D., Hart, K., Clearman, R., & Young, M. (1992). Relationship of life satisfaction to impairment, disability, and handicap among persons with spinal cord injury living in the community. *Archives of Physical Medicine and Rehabilitation, 73,* 552–557.

26. Ganz, P. A., & Coscarelli, A. (1995). Quality of life after breast cancer: A decade of research. In J. E. Dimsdale & A. Baum (Eds.), *Quality of life in behavioral medicine research* (pp. 97–113). Hillsdale, NJ: Lawrence Erlbaum.

27. Germán, C. (1996). Autocuidados y calidad de vida. *Index de Enfermeria, 5*(18), 7–8.

28. Grégoire, J. (1995). L'évaluation de la qualité de vie. *Revue Européenne de Psychologie Appliquée, 45*(4), 243–244.

29. Halmiová, O., & Potasová, A. (1995). Quality of life and the environment as a source of load for cognitive development of children. *Studia Psychologica, 37*(3), 206–208.

30. Jacobson, A. M., Groot, M., & Samson, J. (1995). Quality of life research in patients with diabetes mellitus. In J. E. Dimsdale & A. Baum (Eds.), *Quality of life in behavioral medicine research* (pp. 241–262). Hillsdale, NJ: Lawrence Erlbaum.

31. Jonsson, A., Dock, J., & Ravnborg, M. H. (1996). Quality of life as a measure of rehabilitation outcome in patients with multiple sclerosis. *Acta Neurologica Scandinávica, 93,* 229–235.

32. Juniper, E. F. (1997). How important is quality of life in pediatric asthma? *Pediatric Pulmonary, 15,* 17–21.

33. Kajandi, M. (1994). A psychiatric and interactional perspective on quality of life. In L. Nordenfelt (Ed.), *Concepts and measurement of quality of life in health care* (pp. 257–277). Dordrecht, The Netherlands: Kluwer Academic.

34. Kaplan, M. K. (1995). Quality of life, resource allocation, and the U.S. health-care crisis. In J. E. Dimsdale & A. Baum (Eds.), *Quality of life in behavioral medicine research* (pp. 3–30). Hillsdale, NJ: Lawrence Erlbaum.

35. Kaplan, R. M., Ganiats, T. G., Dieber, W. J., & Anderson, J. P. (1998). The quality of well-being scale: Critical similarities and differences with SF-36. *International Journal for Quality in Health Care, 10*(6), 509–520.

36. Litwins, N. M., & Rodriguez, J. R. (1994). Quality of life in adult recipients of bone marrow transplantation. *Psychological Reports, 75,* 323–328.

37. Llinás, J., García-Mas, A., & Rossiñol, A. (1999). Cambios en la calidad de vida en un grupo de pacientes epilépticos tratados con lamotrigina. *Mapfre Medicina, 10*(II), 106–111.

38. Lutgendorf, S., Antoni, M. H., Shneiderman, N., & Ironson, G. (1995). Psychosocial interventions and quality of life changes across the HIV spectrum. In J. E. Dimsdale & A. Baum (Eds.), *Quality of life in behavioral medicine research* (pp. 205–240). Hillsdale, NJ: Lawrence Erlbaum.

39. Manificat, S., & Dazord, A. (1997). Evaluation de la qualité de vie de l'enfant: Validation d'un questionnaire, premiers résultats. *Neuropsychiatrie de L'Enfance et de L'Adolescence, 45*(3), 106–114.

40. Mendoza, R., Batista-Foguet, J. M., & Oliva, A. (1994). Lifestyles of European school children: Findings of the WHO cross-national study on health-related behaviour. In J. P. Dauwalder (Ed.), *Psychology and promotion of health* (pp. 9–19). Bern, Switzerland: Hogrefe & Huber.

41. Miller, L. (1992). Back to the future: Legal, vocational, and quality-of-life issues in the long-term adjustment of the brain-injured patient. *Journal of Cognitive Rehabilitation, 10*(5), 14–20.

42. Moinpour, C. M., Savage, M., Hayden, K. A., Sawyers, J., & Upchurch, C. (1995). Quality of life assessment in cancer clinical trials. In J. E. Dimsdale & A. Baum (Eds.), *Quality of life in behavioral medicine research* (pp. 79–96). Hillsdale, NJ: Lawrence Erlbaum.

43. Patrick, D. L., & Erickson, P. (1988). Assessing health-related quality of life for clinical decision making. In R. S. Walker & R. M. Rosser (Eds.), *Quality of life: Assessment and application* (pp. 9–50). London: MTP Press Limited.

44. Ravens-Sieberer, U., & Bullinger, M. (1998). Assessing health-related quality of life in chronically ill children with the German KINDL: First psychometric and content analytical results. *Quality of Life Research, 7,* 339–407.

45. Reid, D. T., & Renwick, R. M. (1994). Preliminary validation of a new instrument to measure life satisfaction in adolescents with neuromuscular disorders. *International Journal of Rehabilitation Research, 17,* 184–188.

46. Rosen, R. C., & Kostis, J. B. (1995). Antihypertensive therapy and quality of life: Effects of drug and nondrug interventions on sleep, mood state, and sexual functioning. In J. E. Dimsdale & A. Baum (Eds.), *Quality of life in behavioral medicine research* (pp. 145–160). Hillsdale, NJ: Lawrence Erlbaum.

47. Ruiz, M. A., & Baca, E. (1993). Design and validation of the quality of life questionnaire: A generic health-related perceived quality of life instrument. *European Journal of Psychological Assessment, 9*(1), 19–32.

48. Schraub, S., & Mercier, M. (1993). Measure de la qualité de vie en cancérologie. In C. Hérisson & L. Simon (Dir.), *Evaluation de la qualité de vie* (pp. 59–64). Paris: Masson.

49. Shapiro, D., Hui, K. K., Oakley, M. E., Jagoda, P., & Jammer, L. D. (1995). Effectiveness of a combined behavioral-drug intervention for hypertension: Drug, personality, and quality of life effects. In J. E. Dimsdale & A. Baum (Eds.), *Quality of life in behavioral medicine research* (pp. 171–190). Hillsdale, NJ: Lawrence Erlbaum.

50. Siffert, M., Atoui, N., & Reynes, J. (1993). Retentissement de l'infection par le HIV sur la qualité de vie. In C. Hérisson & L. Simon (Dir.), *Evaluation de la qualité de vie* (pp. 244–250). Paris: Masson.

51. Testa, M. A., & Nackley, J. F. (1994). Methods for quality-of-life studies. *Annual Revue of Public Health, 15,* 535–559.

52. Varni, J. W., Seid, M., & Rode, C. A. (1999). The PedsQL: Measurement model for the pediatric quality of life inventory. *Medical Care, 37*(2), 126–139.

53. Ware, J. E. (1991). Conceptualizing and measuring generic health outcomes. *Cancer, 67*(3), 774–779.

54. Wright, S. J. (1994). Health-related quality of life: A critical review of the concept and its measurement. In J. P. Dauwalder (Ed.), *Psychology and promotion of health* (pp. 163–169). Bern, Switzerland: Hogrefe & Huber.

55. Zhu, D. T., Jin, L. J., Xie, G. J., & Xiao, B. (1998). Quality of life and personality in adults with epilepsy. *Epilepsia, 39*(11), 1208–1212.

CHAPTER 5

Mental Health and Behavioral Health

Overview

In the field of mental and behavioral health, quality of life is associated with approaches that strive to enhance personal development and living conditions for people with psychological problems. Research has been linked to the emergence of community approaches within care services for the general population. It has also focused on assessing the impact of different treatments on the individual's day-to-day social and emotional functioning as well as analyzing the incidence of social support during the evolution of the illnesses and deficits experienced by the individual. Moreover, research in the area of mental and behavioral health has been carried out through the analysis of services for the population and their efficacy, together with a measure of user satisfaction regarding those services.

Although the concept of quality of life (QOL) has attracted significant attention from the field of medicine in recent decades, research into mental and behavioral health issues was not common until the 1990s, when it increased significantly. This increase is related in large part to the four mental and behavioral contextual factors summarized in Table 1.1: the development of a continuum of habilitation care in which different levels of support are provided to the person with mental illness; a renewed emphasis in community support and rehabilitation programs; an increasing emphasis in psychiatric rehabilitation on adaptive behavior and life activities; and the use of person-referenced and person-valued outcomes to evaluate the effectiveness of the intervention and supports received.

Our understanding of the QOL concept in the mental and behavioral health focus area begins with an overview of deinstitutionalization and the recent community integration movement for people with psychiatric impairments. The chapter further discusses four key phenomena in this movement: (a) the progression in thinking from deinstitutionalization to self-determination, (b) the concept of social support and quality of life, (c) the focus on personal and social functioning among clinical subpopulations, and (d) the domains and indicators of quality of life. The chapter concludes with a discussion of the current emphasis in mental and behavioral health on community support services, self-advocacy, and self-determination.

From Deinstitutionalization to Self-Determination

Quality of life for people with chronic mental illnesses discharged from psychiatric hospitals has frequently been studied. These studies have outlined the influence of different types of environmental and personal variables on the patient's quality of life (Leff, 1997; Oliver, Huxley, Bridges, & Mohamad, 1996). The main aim of the studies has been to assess the effects of deinstitutionalization on day-to-day behavior, focusing on whether discharged people with mental illness attain normal living conditions and are integrated into the community (Jones, Robinson, & Golightley, 1986; Lamb, 1993).

The stimulus for these studies has come largely from the evaluation of psychosocial rehabilitation programs for people with chronic mental disorders. The best-known models of psychosocial rehabilitation have applied the principles of normalization, integration, deinstitutionalization, individualization, well-being, and quality of life (Linhorst, 1988; McClary, Lubin, Evans, Watt, & Lebedun, 1989; Thomson, 1992). Authors have studied changes in the individual's functional autonomy after treatment and social benefits from programs after their application (Lipsey & Pollard, 1989).

People discharged from psychiatric rehabilitation programs adapt to living within their communities and feel that lifestyle and well-being generally improve, although their symptoms often persist (Gerber, Coleman, Johnston, & Lafave, 1994; Pinkney, Gerber, & Lafave, 1991). Patients' reports about their community experiences and reports from relatives and caregivers agree on the fact that they have the necessary skills for a successful adaptation to community life and are able to participate in many activities, including work, education, or leisure. People with serious psychiatric disabilities remain within psychiatric hospitals, although it is generally felt that they would be able to live successfully within the community as long as they had the appropriate services and supports to suit their needs. Moreover, many studies show that these people prefer to live in the community rather than in psychiatric hospitals (Baker & Intagliata, 1982; Lehman, Possidente, & Hawker, 1986; Lehman, Ward, & Linn, 1982; Mercier, 1989; Mercier, Tempier, & Renaud, 1992; Tempier, Caron, Mercier, & Leouffre, 1998).

Studies have also focused on the effects of sociodemographic variables such as gender, age, or profession (Garg, Yates, Jones, Zhou, & Williams, 1999) and the influence of various residential settings (Roessler, Salize, Cucchiaro, Reinhard, & Kernig, 1999; Simpson, Hyde, & Faragher, 1989) on the quality of life of chronic psychiatric patients. The results of these studies generally support community mental health care versus long-term hospital care to enhance quality of life (Roessler et al.). Factors influencing quality of life seem to be more closely related to the domain of social support than to the features of the treatment location (Roessler et al.). The more unstructured a setting the greater the comfort, autonomy, subjective well-being, and patient satisfaction (Oliver & Mohamad, 1992). Studies have also dealt with the influence of treatment location on patients with problems of substance abuse in the months following treatment (Garg et al.).

Poverty and its relationship to the hospitalization of mental health patients is highlighted frequently in the research reviewed. Some studies have focused on the dimensions of material well-being and income level of the population with psychiatric disorders and their effects on deinstitutionalization and community integration (Lafave, de Souza, Prince, Atchison, & Gerber, 1995; Pinkney et al., 1991; Tempier et al., 1998). Lack of resources is related to a lack of individualized, coordinated services for people with serious mental disorders. As a result, patients are frequently hospitalized and definitive deinstitutionalization is impossible (Lafave et al., 1995). To improve this situation, a suggestion is made often that clients, their peers, mental health agencies, and volunteer associations create partnerships. The situation also improves with the active participation of people with mental health problems in decisions concerning their personal lives.

One of the first issues to be studied in this focus area was the comparison between traditional services and community-centered services (Oliver et al., 1996). More recently, researchers have analyzed to what extent services are client centered and promote active participation. Nikkel, Smith, and Edwards (1992), for example, assessed the differences in the results from service models managed by peers, paternalistic models, and traditional services. The authors found that it was not possible to develop alternative services managed and conducted by consumers due to the lack of mental health resources allocated for such an objective. However, advocates for consumer participation have increased and have proposed concepts such as "self-help," "empowerment," and "quality of life" as key factors in some of the most innovative rehabilitation models (Felton et al., 1995; McLenan, 1995; O'Donnell et al., 1999; Stastny & Amering, 1997).

Recently community integration projects for patients with chronic mental disorders have attempted to achieve higher levels of subjective well-being (López, 1994). They have also become more concerned with attaining the highest level of autonomy and social integration of the individual (Bengtsson-Tops & Hansson, 1999). From such a point of view, active participation by the person and his or her family is promoted as part of the process of choosing objectives and learning skills. In the last decade, many service evaluation studies have been conducted from a consumer standpoint. They propose services derived from empowerment principles and recommend the integration of ex-patients as service planners and researchers (Campbell & Schraiber, 1989; McCabe & Unzicker, 1995; Pinkney et al., 1991; Stastny & Amering, 1997).

Quality of life of chronic psychiatric patients (e.g., schizophrenia and senile dementia) who have been integrated into the community has been studied longitudinally from the point of view of self-determination by Jones et al. (1986), focusing on the following issues: autonomy, independence, decision making, and intimacy. The results show that patients outside the hospital are more satisfied with issues related to self-determination, but there was also a negative result reported in this study: health care, personal hygiene, and basic needs are more problematic than for hospitalized patients.

The self-determination theory (Ryan & Deci, 2000) has influenced research into the social-contextual conditions that foster natural processes of self-motivation and a healthy psychological development. The authors suggest that "competence," "autonomy," and "relatedness" are three innate psychological needs that, if satisfied, will have a positive effect on the individual's self-motivation and mental health. Other authors have also highlighted the importance of leisure opportunities to promote the self-determination of people with mental health problems (Iso, Seppo, & Park, 1996; MacNeil & Anderson, 1999).

Social Support and Quality of Life

Some authors point to a lack of social support as a crucial risk factor for recurrent hospitalization of people with prolonged mental disorders (Dayson, Gooch, & Thornicroft, 1992). These individuals require intensive, flexible, and long-term support within the community. Hence they need continuous social and health care as well as rehabilitation (Lamb, 1993). Social support is fundamental to an enhanced quality of life for patients with mental disorders and for their families. The strengthening of support networks improves community adjustment, stress tolerance, and the well-being of people with chronic mental disorders (Schalock, Nelson, Holtan, & Sheehan, 1997). Achat et al. (1998) have shown that women's social networks have a positive effect on their mental functioning (mental health, vitality, and role-emotional functioning), especially in the case of chronic stress.

Most studies link social support with the QOL domains concerned with "interpersonal relations" and "social integration." These studies have focused on type, quantity, and quality of support provided and on how the support is perceived by the individual and family (Oliver et al., 1996). Social support to families must be adapted to the needs of the person (Garralda, 1994). Schalock et al. (1997) found that social support has positive effects on personal functioning and community adjustment. The authors compared a sample of community patients with chronic mental disorders to a community sample with the same sociodemographic characteristics and found that there was a need to strengthen support networks for people with chronic mental illness, which would lead to community adjustment, stress tolerance, and well-being.

When there is a lack of natural social supports, it is essential to have a highly individualized and directive support service that can meet various support needs in different areas: medication, therapy, supervision, day activities, psychosocial treatment, and employment (Curtis, Millman, Struening, & Dércole, 1992; Ford, Young, Perez, Obermeyer, & Rohner, 1992; Wright, Heiman, Shupe, & Olvera, 1989). The experiences that have emerged in developing supported housing projects have taken on a variety of forms, but common characteristics include the use of integrated housing or accommodation, flexibility in service delivery, and consumer's choice (Carling, 1993). Although the content of a model of community support service is not clear due to a lack of uniformity, these models have generally contributed to the maintenance and enhancement of quality of life in areas such as finance, housing, leisure, medication, assistance, and peer support (Muijen, Marks, Connolly, & Audini, 1992).

Community support teams can supervise an individual's mental state and reduce the anxiety of relatives, neighbors, and other professionals before an unnecessary hospital internment is necessary. Caring for the needs and wishes of patients, the teams can promote patients' independence and quality of life (Oliver et al., 1996; Sayce, Craig, & Boardman, 1991). Professional behavior ("professional conduct, skills, or interest") sometimes plays a more important role in the results obtained in intervention satisfaction and success than other features, such as the activities organized by services, fixed objectives, physical-environmental conditions, and interaction with other users (Gavino, 1991; López, 1994).

It is crucial to incorporate the patients' point of view into mental health rehabilitation planning and decision making. Patients' perception of their quality of life and of the assistance and social support they receive may have a decisive effect on their adaptation and adjustment. Sainfort, Becker, and Diamond (1996) found that the opinions of patients and service providers may coincide in clinical issues such as symptoms, but not in physical health and social relations. As far as social support is concerned, both patients and providers agree that it is an important variable to be taken into account, but they differ as to the intensity and mode of support delivery. Slade, Leesea, Taylor, and Thornicroft (1999) found that patient ratings for unmet needs and quality of life were more reliable than ratings by others. Consequently, the patients' standpoint regarding their difficulties should always be considered.

Social support services that have a positive effect on patients' perceptions significantly enhance their quality of life (Rosenfield 1992, 1997; Rosenfield & Neese-Todd, 1993). Hence patients' subjective appraisal of their own reality is important at the onset of intervention and is fundamental in the improvement of their living standards, because it is a determining factor for achieving successful integration into the community (Skantze, 1998).

Personal and Social Functioning among Clinical Subpopulations

Most studies on quality of life in mental and behavioral health have focused on the individual's social functioning, examining interpersonal relations, social integration, and self-determination opportunities. Some studies have tried to analyze the effects of drugs on patients' quality of life. A smaller number of studies have analyzed the impact of chronic physical illness on quality of life and specifically on patients' physical functioning and mental health. Most published studies deal with chronic mental patients. Individuals with a diagnosis of schizophrenia or depression have attracted most attention, but dementia and anxiety disorders have also been studied. Each diagnostic subpopulation is considered below.

Schizophrenia

Individuals with a diagnosis of schizophrenia frequently display a very deteriorated quality of life and personal functioning, especially with regard to social factors (Patterson et al., 1996). Rodríguez, Jarne, Soler, Miarons, and Grau (1995) measured the deterioration of social functioning in a sample of 100 schizophrenic patients and found that, despite the apparent remission of symptoms, social dysfunction was prevalent. As a result, patients not only feel uncomfortable, but quite often they also experience difficulties with people around them. Different studies on the description of social deterioration focus mainly on the individual's functioning: lack of spontaneous social behavior and social skills, loss of sexual interest, loss of motivational interest in leisure activities, and a tendency toward social isolation (Davis, Zeiss, Shea, & Tinklenberg, 1998; Dunn, O'Driscoll, Dayson, Wills, & Leff, 1990; Leff, 1997; Leff, O'Driscoll, Dayson, Wills, & Anderson, 1990; Rodríguez et al., 1995; Sturt & Wykes, 1986). The same applies to patients with obsessive-compulsive disorders in which the impairment of social functioning is correlated positively with disorder severity (Koran, Thieneman, & Davenport, 1996).

There are contradictory results concerning the incidence of sociodemographic and clinical variables on schizophrenics' well-being and quality of life. Some authors have not found significant results regarding age, gender, or living standards (Baker & Intagliata, 1982; Bobes & González, 1996; Lehman, Rachuba, & Postrado, 1995; Skantze, Mald, Dencker, May, & Corrigan, 1992; Sullivan, Wells, & Leake, 1992), while others did find them (Meltzer, Burnett, Bastani, & Ramirez, 1990; Shtasel, Gur, Gallacher, Heimberg, & Gur, 1992). Other variables that have been taken into account are diagnostic subtype, age at onset, duration of illness, previous psychiatric hospitalization, and functional level. Although results are inconclusive, most studies agree that a lower quality of life is related to type of residual schizophrenia, prolonged duration of illness, and previous hospitalization (Barcia, Morcillo, & Borgoñós, 1995; Browne et al., 1996; Morcillo, Barcia, & Borgoñós, 1995).

Duration is a difficult variable to study. Skantze et al. (1992) found that quality of life is positively correlated with a prolonged period of survival within the community. Conversely, Browne et al. (1996) observed that quality of life is not influenced by total period of education or duration of the individual's employment. Other studies either do not find a significant correlation in the number of previous hospitalizations or in the duration of illness, or they show an inverse correlation between the number of previous hospitalizations and quality of life (Meltzer et al., 1990).

A significant number of studies have focused on the evaluation of the effects of "psychoeducational intervention" and have found that in the long run there are significant changes in social functioning in participants (Atkinson, Coia, Harper, & Harper, 1996; Warner, 1999). Changes are more significant if intervention is focused on the family (Fristad, Gavazzi, & Soldado, 1998) and if it is implemented within a multifamilial group instead of separate families (Fristad, Stephen, Gavazzi, & Soldado, 1996; Gavazzi, Fristad, & Law, 1997). It seems evident that QOL enhancement in people with a diagnosis of schizophrenia who are trained in social skills stems from their improvement in interpersonal relations and the extension of their social networks (Hayes, Halford, & Varghese, 1995).

Studies on social networks indicate that the quality of relations changes not by number of contacts but by type of contact. The relationship between social functioning and social networks is complex, and this could hinder attempts to discover whether greater social functioning leads to more extensive social networks or vice versa (Atkinson et al., 1996; DeJong, Giel, & Sloof, 1985). It is also obvious that changes in quality of life cannot be simply attributed to the social characteristics of the group or an increase in number of contacts or vice versa (Atkinson et al.). In groups receiving this type of intervention, patients are encouraged to think about how their illnesses affect their lives and how they can use their knowledge about their illnesses to gain more control over their lives. This may help patients to rethink, rebuild, or readapt some of their behaviors and to implement some of the learned skills.

Studies that have evaluated the influence of neuroleptic drugs on the individual's functioning and the enhancement of their quality of life have focused: (a) on the evaluation of the improvement in social functioning and interpersonal and intrapsychic factors (Browne et al., 1998; Meltzer et al., 1990; Naber, 1995), or (b) on the assessment of the general advance in various QOL areas (Barcia, Ayuso, Herraiz, & Fernández, 1996; Bobes, González, Bousoño, & Sáiz, 1997). The interest in quality of life has increased markedly after the importance gained by "second generation" psychotropic drugs, which have fewer collateral effects (e.g., problems in interpersonal interaction, physical appearance, motivational, cognitive, and affective deterioration) (Angermeyer & Katschnig, 1997; Awad, 1992). A fundamental problem in pharmacological treatment is that neuroleptics do not lead to an improvement in negative symptoms such as concentration and lack of motivation. On the contrary, sometimes those symptoms are intensified. Although neuroleptic drugs can improve the efficacy of the treatment of some symptoms (e.g., adaptation level, social functioning, identity, and self-confidence), psychosocial programs are still necessary to improve social functioning (Stewart et al., 1988), especially in family life and social relations (Agosti, Stewart, & Beattie, 1991). On the other hand, patients do not normally share their psychiatrists' opinion that a reduction in psychopathological symptoms using psychopharmacotherapy is desirable because it leads to the patient's increased well-being (Angermeyer & Katschnig, 1997).

The combination of pharmacology and occupational therapy has yielded positive results for improving quality of life within rehabilitation services (Cohi, 1990). Occupational therapy, especially if it is aimed at obtaining long-lasting effects, is usually set within the framework of integral rehabilitation programs (Dazord, Augier, Guisti, & Frot, 1996). This is especially important due to the current reduction of patients' stays in psychiatric hospitals.

Schizophrenia studies mirror those of other fields of research on quality of life, in that there is debate between those who prefer objective measures and those who prefer subjective ones (McKenna, 1997). Some authors (e.g., Browne et al., 1996, 1998; Katschnig & Angermeyer, 1997) emphasize the need for an objective clinical evaluation of psychiatric patients' quality of life, because self-report might be influenced by persistent psychotic symptoms, idiosyncratic perspectives, patients' values, and their adaptation to adverse circumstances (Lehman, 1993). In distinction, Skantze (1998) shows that patients feel, experience, and are able to inform reliably about their social deficits. This would support the argument that quality of life can be assessed only subjectively. The quality of life perceived by the individual merits more attention in order to enhance client satisfaction with mental health services and his or her psychological well-being (Schalock et al., 1997). In a study on the quality of mental health vocational services, Janikowski, Bordieri, and Musgrave (1991) indicate that there is a need to evaluate quality of life from multidimensional perspectives.

The convergent validity of the perception of quality of life among physicians and patients with chronic mental illness has been suggested by Lehman (1993). Sainfort et al. (1996) conducted an in-depth study of the validity of these perceptions and observed the existence of a minor agreement between well-being assessments made by professionals and patients in every dimension, except for symptoms. Hence, most authors think it is necessary to negotiate the objectives of the treatment and services between professionals and patients. As a result, patients would be involved in the process of their own recovery and social inclusion.

The stigma perceived by mental patients associated with the tendency to become labeled after psychiatric treatment has a negative effect on their satisfaction with life (Rosenfield, 1997; see also Finzen & Hoffmann-Richter, 1997). Thus many chronic mental patients with schizophrenia are not willing to attend psychiatric treatment services due to the stigma. However, subjective quality of life or patients' satisfaction can improve when the patients receive quality services, neutralizing the effects of stigma.

Depression
Studies on depression have focused on single dimensions relevant to human behavior. Only recently have these studies used multidimensional models. The ongoing discussion between subjective evaluation of patients' satisfaction with life and objective indicators of their living conditions indicates that it would be useful to incorporate other domains of QOL measurement together with the assessment of psychological well-being and satisfaction with life (Bech, 1994, 1996).

Although research is still too limited to support a model of quality of life for this population, Katschnig and Angermeyer (1997) proposed a framework with two psychological and two sociological dimensions. Psychological dimensions are cognitive (e.g., self-esteem and satisfaction) and affective (e.g., well-being). Sociological dimensions are functioning in daily life and environmental conditions. The authors link their model to pharmacological and cognitive intervention along with other kinds of environmental intervention. The Katschnig and Angermeyer proposal is consistent with the comprehensive, multidimensional model presented in Figure 2.2. The development of domains and their indicators within an ecological model and within system theory (with micro [subjective], meso [functional], and macro [functional] levels of analysis) allows one to employ a quantitative and qualitative methodological pluralism approach in the evaluation of a person's quality of life.

Most studies on depression focus on the analysis of quality of life in major depressive disorders, exploring antidepressant pharmacological treatment (Hirschfeld et al., 1998) and types of psychological therapies. Some of the QOL domains that have received significant attention in such disorders are related to physical and emotional well-being, although multidimensional approaches are also used based on the standpoint of health-related quality of life (HRQOL). In such studies, social dysfunction has received priority attention (Katschnig & Angermeyer, 1997).

In pharmacological therapy, a decrease in medication is considered to be an indicator of improvement in quality of life in patients with depression. This is very important, as there are still a few patients who receive suitable doses of antidepressant medication in primary health care (Wells, Katon, Rogers, & Camp, 1994). However, Revicki, Simon, Chan, Katon, and Heiligenstein (1998) have demonstrated that low doses may produce improvement in depressive symptoms and have a positive effect on the use of medical services. On the other hand, there is a significant problem in that a high percentage of people do not respond to medication, in contrast to those with other disorders such as anxiety, drug abuse, and personality disorders.

There are many studies about the efficacy of various psychotherapeutic interventions to enhance quality of life in people with depression. Most of them combine psychotherapeutic with pharmacological intervention to attain higher levels of efficiency. Studies support Beck's cognitive therapy using bibliotherapy to enhance general satisfaction and self-efficacy (Frisch, 1994; Frisch, Cornell, Vilanueva, & Retzlaff, 1992; Grant, Salcedo, Hynan, Frisch, & Puster, 1995), and psychoeducational intervention to modify dysfunctional beliefs (Brent, Poling, McKain, & Baugher, 1993) and to improve of the skills of families (Fristad et al., 1996).

Quality of life assessment in depression is carried out with both generic instruments, because of their greater applicability (Bech, 1996), and specific instruments that analyze symptoms and problems for people with depression (Hunt & McKenna, 1993; Leval, 1995). Treatment for depression attempts to enhance the patient's quality of life in facets such as state of mind, self-efficiency, or positive thinking and self-esteem (Cornes & Arrojo, 1999). A general suggestion found in the literature is that it is best to use a combination of both types of measurements.

Anxiety
Quality of life for many people with specific anxiety disorders can affect personal relations, job performance, and other important aspects of life. Anxiety disorders are very common among populations in developed countries. The types that have been studied most commonly in terms of quality of life are social phobias and panic disorders related to agoraphobia and stress.

Social phobia is a dominant form of anxiety disorder among the general population (Magee, Eaton, Wittchen, McGonagle, & Kessler, 1996; Regier, Narrow, & Rae, 1990; Wacker, Müllejans, Klein, & Battegay, 1992), but it is quite infrequently recognized and treated by either primary care providers (Cass, Volk, & Nease, 1999) or mental health professionals (Ross, 1993; Schneier, Johnson, Hornig, Liebowitz, & Weissman, 1992). Epidemiological studies suggest that the disorder normally starts in childhood and early adolescence, becoming a way of life for most people who suffer from it (Schneier, 1994; Wittchen & Beloch, 1996). The phobia may be responsible for poor school and work performance, unemployment, alcohol abuse, breakdowns in intimate and social relations, and other negative consequences for the individual's quality of life (Liebowitz, Gorman, Fyer, & Klein, 1985; Magee et al., 1996; Schneier, 1994). Assessed quality of life is lower in social phobia than in other anxiety disorders (Bech & Angst, 1996), especially when social fears are pervasive (Schneier). Moreover, the HRQOL is poorer in patients with mental health disorders that have been recognized by their health providers than in those patients whose disorders have not been recognized (Cass et al., 1999).

Panic disorders with agoraphobia are one of the most studied anxiety disorders. Physical and emotional health are the most chronic problems of the disorder, with poorer results than other psychiatric pathologies (Schneier, 1994). Social functioning in panic disorders also shows deterioration (Sherbourne, Wells, & Judd, 1996) analogous to full-blown depression (Markowitz, Weissman, Quellette, Lish, & Klerman, 1989).

Telch et al. (1995) used a multidimensional approach to examine the impact of cognitive-behavioral treatment on quality of life of patients who have panic disorders with agoraphobia. Patients experienced a significant improvement in indicators and areas related to employment, social activities, and family relations. QOL indicators were not associated with the frequency of anxiety episodes but were linked to anxiety before the episodes. The therapy was highly effective, especially in combination with medication. Recently some studies are focusing on recovery in social anxiety disorders in order to improve treatment and enhance quality of life of patients (Bobes, 1998).

Warshaw et al. (1993) carried out a longitudinal study to evaluate quality of life in patients with anxiety disorders. They examined the effects of trauma and of posttraumatic stress disorder (PTSD) on general well-being. They found that people with PTSD displayed deficits in every health and functioning area and that their dissociation levels were higher than in patients without trauma. High levels of depression, attempts or threats of suicide, and abuse of prohibited substances show that trauma has long-lasting, adverse, constant, and profound consequences on quality of life in every domain (Massion, Warshaw, & Keller, 1993).

Lenz and Demal's review (1997) of the impact of different psychotherapies on mental and behavioral disorders allows us to conclude that the QOL concept is indispensable in psychotherapeutic research, despite the fact that a QOL model is frequently incomplete or missing in current research studies. One of the most relevant problems is the lack of a model and clear definitions of the QOL concept, resulting in a certain confusion in the use of the term. Moreover, we have improved the accuracy of evaluation instruments, differentiating between psychopathological symptom analysis and QOL assessment.

Dimensions and Indicators of Quality of Life

The most important domains (in order of frequency) and indicators used in reviewed publications can be found in Table 5.1. As shown, the QOL model proposed in this handbook has been broadly supported by research in the field of mental health and behavioral health. The eight proposed domains and most indicators have received increased attention from researchers, yet with some differences in emphasis that will be explained below. Only a few domains were found in the literature that are not in the model (see Figure 2.2): social well-being, personal values, and productivity. However, social well-being refers to the macrosystem level, while the others can be found as indicators of several model domains (e.g., values in self-determination, and productivity in terms of material well-being).

Table 5.1
Quality of Life Domains and Indicators in Mental and Behavioral Health

DOMAIN	INDICATORS	REFERENCES
1. INTER-PERSONAL RELATIONS	INTERACTIONS Social life (contacts, meetings) Social behavior Isolation Loneliness Withdrawal/retirement Communication Social Networks Conflicts Hostility	3, 5, 8, **11**, 13, **15**, 16, 18, **19**, 20, 22, **23**, 25, 26, **28**, **29**, 30, **31**, **32**, 33, 34, **35**, **36**, 38, **39**, 42, 44, **45**, 46, 47, 49, 50, 51, 52, **53**, 54, 55, **56**, **58**, 59, 60, 61, 64, **67**, **68**, 69, 70, 71, 72, 73, 74, 75, 76, 77, **78**, **79**, 80, 81, 83, **84**, 85, **86**, 87, 88, **89**, 90, 91, 92, 93, 94, **95**, **96**, 97, 98, 99, 102, 103, 105, **106**, **107**, 108, **111**, **112**, 112, 110, 113, 116, 117, 118, 120, **121**, 122, 123, **124**, **126**, 127, 128, 129, 130, 133, **135**, 136, 137, 138, 139, **140**, 141, 142

(table continues)

Note. Domains and indicators are ordered from most frequent to least frequent based on the number of references found. Conceptual references are printed in boldface and applied research references in regular font. Numbered references are identified in Appendix 5.1.

Table 5.1. *(continued)*

DOMAIN	INDICATORS	REFERENCES
	FAMILY	5, 6, 7, 13, **15**, 16, **17, 18, 19,** 20, **23, 24,** 25, 26, **28,** 30, **31,** 33, 34, **35, 36,** 39, 42, 43, 44, 45, 46, 47, **48,** 50, 51, 52, **53,** 54, 55, **58,** 61, **62,** 64, 67, 69, 70, 73, 74, 75, 76, 77, **78, 79,** 80, 81, 83, **84,** 85, **86,** 87, 88, **89,** 90, 93, 94, **95, 96,** 98, 99, 102, 103, **106, 107,** 108, 110, **111, 112,** 116, 117, 118, 119, **121,** 123, 122, **124,** 127, 128, 129, 130, 133, **135,** 136, **140,** 141, 142
	SUPPORTS Helps/aids/assistance	**17, 19, 23,** 25, 27, **28, 29,** 33, 34, **35, 36,** 39, 41, 43, 45, 46, **48,** 51, 52, **56, 58,** 60, 61, **62,** 64, **67,** 69, **71,** 74, 75, 76, 77, **78, 79,** 80, 81, 83, **84,** 85, **86,** 87, 88, **89,** 90, 92, 93, 94, **95, 96,** 102, 105, **106, 107,** 108, 110, **111, 112,** 117, 118, 119, **121,** 122, 123, **124,** 128, 130, 133, **135,** 137, **140**

(table continues)

Table 5.1. *(continued)*

DOMAIN	INDICATORS	REFERENCES
	AFFECT (e.g., feelings, emotions, empathy, love)	2, 6, **10**, 13, 16, **18**, 20, 22, **24**, **35**, **36**, **39**, 43, 44, 45, **47**, 48, 54, **56**, 57, **58**, 60, 61, **67**, **68**, 70, 71, 72, 73, 74, 75, 77, **78**, **79**, 80, **84**, 85, **86**, 87, 88, 88, 90, 92, 97, 99, **106**, **107**, 110, 113, 116, 117, 118, **121**, 122, 123, **126**, 127, 128, 130, 132, 133, 136, 137, 138, 141, 142
	FRIENDLY RELATIONSHIPS	5, 8, 13, **23**, 25, **28**, 30, 33, 34, **35**, **36**, 38, 42, 44, **45**, 46, 47, 49, 51, **53**, 54, 55, **56**, **67**, 69, 73, 74, 75, 76, 77, **78**, **79**, 80, 81, **86**, 87, 88, 90, 93, 94, 102, 110, **111**, 117, 118, 122, 123, **124**, 128, 130, 133, **135**, 136, 142
	INTIMACY	29, **36**, **45**, 87, 90, 91, **135**, 141, 142
2. PERSONAL DEVELOP-MENT	EDUCATION	2, 5, 6, 7, **9**, 16, **17**, **18**, 27, 30, **32**, 33, 34, **36**, 42, 43, 44, **45**, 47, **48**, 50, 51, 52, **53**, 54, 55, **58**, 61, **62**, 63, 66, 69, 70, 71, 73, 74, 75, 77, **78**, 79, 80, 81, 83, **84**, 85, **86**, 87, 90, 93, 94, **95**, **96**, 98, 103, **106**, **107**, 108, 110, **111**, **112**, 117, 118, 121, 123, 127, 128, 129, 130, 133, 135, 137, **140**, 141, 142

(table continues)

Table 5.1. *(continued)*

DOMAIN	INDICATORS	REFERENCES
	SKILLS	5, **10**, 16, 17, **18**, **19**, 20, 25, **28**, **29**, 30, **32**, **35**, 38, **39**, 40, 44, 45, 46, 47, **48**, 51, **53**, 54, 55, **56**, **58**, 59, 61, 69, **71**, 73, 76, **79**, 80, 81, **84**, **86**, 87, 88, 90, 91, 92, 93, 94, **95**, **96**, 97, 98, 99, 102, **104**, **106**, **107**, 108, 110, **111**, **114**, **115**, 117, 118, **119**, 120, **121**, 122, **124**, **126**, 127, 128, 133, **135**, 136, 137, 138, **140**, 142
	VOLUNTARY ACTIVITY	2, **9**, **10**, 13, **15**, **18**, 22, **29**, 30, **31**, 33, **40**, 45, 46, 47, 49, 51, 55, **56**, 59, 60, 61, **65**, **66**, 69, 72, 73, 74, 75, 76, 80, 85, **86**, 88, 90, 92, 93, 97, 99, 102, **106**, 110, 113, **114**, **115**, 117, 118, 119, 120, 121, 123, **124**, **126**, 129, 130, 139, **140**, 141, 142
	PROGRESS Success/achievement/ solutions Productivity Improvement Evolution	**18**, 23, 25, **31**, **32**, 36, **45**, 47, 51, 52, 55, 57, **58**, **66**, 69, 70, 71, 80, 81, **84**, **86**, 88, 90, 92, 93, 94, **95**, 98, 103, **106**, **107**, 108, 110, **121**, **124**, **126**, 127, 133, 136, 137, 138, 141, 142

(table continues)

Table 5.1. *(continued)*

DOMAIN	INDICATORS	REFERENCES
	PERFORMANCE Personal/behavioral functioning Resolution/enforcement Fulfillment/execution	14, 17, 18, 19, 25, 30, 32, 36, 46, 47, 49, 61, 65, 70, 71, 72, 80, 90, 91, 92, 95, 99, 108, 115, 119, 121, 122, 126, 127, 128, 129, 132, 133, 135, 137, 138, 140, 141, 142
	PERSONAL COMPETENCE	18, 35, 36, 39, 40, 45, 53, 58, 63, 71, 73, 76, 80, 81, 86, 88, 91, 92, 95, 96, 99, 106, 110, 115, 119, 122, 124, 127, 128, 134, 135, 138
3. EMOTIONAL WELL-BEING	**CONTENTMENT** Satisfaction Pleasure/enjoyment Frustration Suicidal ideas/attempts Psychological distress	1, 2, 4, 6, 7, 8, 10, 11, 12, 13, 14, 15, 16, 17, 18, 19, 20, 22, 23, 25, 27, 28, 29, 30, 31, 32, 33, 34, 35, 36, 39, 40, 41, 42, 43, 44, 45, 46, 47, 49, 51, 52, 53, 54, 55, 56, 57, 58, 59, 60, 61, 63, 64, 65, 66, 67, 68, 69, 70, 71, 72, 73, 74, 75, 76, 77, 78, 79, 80, 81, 82, 83, 84, 85, 86, 87, 88, 89, 90, 91, 92, 93, 94, 95, 96, 97, 98, 99, 102, 103, 104, 105, 106, 107, 108, 110, 111, 113, 114, 115, 116, 117, 118, 119, 120, 121, 122, 123, 124, 126, 127, 128, 129, 130, 133, 134, 135, 136, 137, 138, 139, 140, 141, 142

(table continues)

Table 5.1. *(continued)*

DOMAIN	INDICATORS	REFERENCES
	ABSENCE/LACK OF STRESS Reaction to distressful situations Anxiety/nervousness/ restlessness/agitation Restiveness/relaxation Coping/management/ tolerance/resistance/ reduction of stress	6, 8, 13, **18**, 22, **23**, 27, **29**, 30, **31**, 34, **35**, **36**, 38, **39**, **40**, 44, 45, 47, **48**, 49, 52, **53**, 55, **58**, 59, 61, **62**, **65**, **68**, 69, 70, 72, 73, 74, 76, **78**, **79**, 80, 81, **86**, 88, **89**, 90, 92, **95**, **96**, 97, **107**, 108, 110, **111**, 113, **114**, **115**, 117, 118, 119, **126**, 127, 128, 129, **134**, **135**, 137, 138, 139, **140**, 142
	SELF-CONCEPT Self-awareness/ self-consciousness Self-esteem Corporal image/body image Identity Personal knowledge	8, **11**, 16, **19**, 20, **28**, **29**, 30, 33, **35**, **36**, 38, **40**, 44, 46, 52, **53**, 55, **58**, 61, 63, **65**, **68**, 69, **71**, **78**, 80, 81, **84**, 85, **86**, 87, 88, 98, 102, **107**, 108, **111**, 117, 118, **121**, 122, **135**, 136, 141
	SAFETY/SECURITY	9, 13, 16, **28**, 33, 34, **35**, 46, **48**, 54, **58**, 64, 74, 75, 76, 77, **78**, **79**, 80, 83, **84**, 85, 87, 88, 93, **96**, 102, **107**, 116, 123, 128, 133, 136
	HAPPINESS	**1**, **10**, 13, 16, **17**, 20, 22, **36**, 38, **40**, 47, 54, **56**, 64, 72, 73, 75, 80, **84**, 85, 87, 88, **96**, 97, 102, 113, **114**, 118, **126**, 128, **134**, 136

(table continues)

Table 5.1. *(continued)*

DOMAIN	INDICATORS	REFERENCES
	SPIRITUALITY	16, **28, 35,** 69, 75, 77, **78, 79,** 80, 81, 83, **84,** 85, 87, 88, **106, 107,** 116, 117, 118, **135,** 136
4. PHYSICAL WELL-BEING	HEALTH Symptoms of disease Physical functioning Fitness Pain Physical fatigue Energy/vitality Sleep Perception of health Physical dependence (on drugs) Medication/pharmacology	6, 8, **9, 10, 12, 13, 15,** 16, **17, 18, 19,** 20, 22, 25, 26, 27, **28, 29,** 30, **32,** 33, 34, **35, 36, 39, 40,** 42, 43, 44, **45,** 46, 47, **48,** 49, 50, 51, 52, **53,** 54, 55, **56, 58,** 59, 60, 61, **62, 65, 66, 67, 68,** 69, 70, 71, 72, 73, 74, 75, 76, 77, **78, 79,** 80, 81, **82,** 83, **84,** 85, **86,** 87, 88, **89,** 90, 91, 92, 93, 94, **95, 96,** 97, 98, 99, 102, 103, **104,** 105, **106, 107,** 108, 110, **111, 112,** 113, **114, 115,** 116, 117, 118, 119, 120, **121,** 122, 123, **124, 126,** 127, 128, 129, 130, 132, 133, **134, 135,** 136, 137, 138, 139, 140, 141, 142
	HEALTH CARE Medical care Medical attendance Intervention/treatment	17, 18, 19, 20, 24, 25, 29, 32, 33, 34, 36, 39, 47, 49, 51, 52, 53, 54, 56, 58, 60, 61, 62, 64, 66, 67, 69, 70, 71, 73, 74, 75, 77, 78, 81, 80, 82, 84, 85, 86, 88, 89, 90, 91, 92, 93, 95, 96, 103, 106, 107, 108, 111, 112, 116, 117, 118, 122, 123, 128, 130, 132, 133, 134, 135, 136, 137, 141, 142

(table continues)

Table 5.1. *(continued)*

DOMAIN	INDICATORS	REFERENCES
	ACTIVITIES OF DAILY LIVING Daily practice/functioning Self-care/hygiene	2, **3**, 13, **15**, **18**, **19**, 20, 30, 33, 34, **35**, **39**, 47, 49, 52, 54, **58**, **65**, **68**, 69, 73, 74, 77, **78**, **79**, 80, 85, **86**, 90, 91, **95**, 99, 102, 103, **104**, 105, **107**, 108, 110, **111**, **114**, **116**, 117, 120, **121**, 122, 123, **124**, **126**, 128, 130, 133, **135**, **140**, 141, 142
	LEISURE/RECREATION ACTIVITIES	7, **11**, 16, **18**, 20, 30, 33, 34, **39**, **40**, 42, 44, 45, 47, 51, 54, **56**, **65**, **68**, 69, 74, 75, 76, 77, **78**, **79**, 80, 81, 83, **84**, 85, **86**, 87, 88, 93, **96**, 98, 99, 102, 103, **107**, 110, **111**, **114**, 116, 117, 118, **121**, **124**, 129, 133, **135**, 136
	NUTRITION	9, **48**, 53, **58**, **65**, 69, 70, **86**, **96**, **107**, 111, 117, 118, 119, **121**, **124**, 130, 133, 137, 142
	MOBILITY	9, **18**, 20, **35**, 49, **56**, **58**, 69, 73, **84**, 90, 91, **95**, 103, 110, 117, 118, 123, 127

(table continues)

Table 5.1. *(continued)*

DOMAIN	INDICATORS	REFERENCES
5. SOCIAL INCLUSION	**ROLES** Social/role functioning Functional status Role performance	3, 4, 8, 13, 15, 16, 17, 18, 22, 25, 26, 27, **28**, **36**, **40**, 44, 47, 51, 54, **56**, 61, **67**, **68**, 69, 70, 71, 72, 75, 78, **79**, 80, **84**, **86**, **89**, 90, 91, 92, 94, **95**, 97, 99, 103, **106**, 107, 108, 110, **111**, 113, **114**, **115**, 117, 120, **121**, 122, 123, **124**, 127, 128, 129, 132, 133, **135**, 136, 137, 139, **140**, 141, 142
	SUPPORTS Resources of social support Social aids/social work Welfare	17, 19, 23, 25, 27, **28**, 33, **36**, 39, 46, 48, 51, 55, **56**, 58, 60, 61, **62**, 64, **67**, 69, 71, 74, 75, 76, **78**, **79**, 80, 81, 83, **84**, 85, **86**, 87, 88, **89**, 90, 92, 93, 94, **95**, **96**, 102, 105, **106**, **107**, 108, 110, **111**, **112**, 117, 118, 119, **121**, 122, 123, **124**, 128, 130, 133, **135**, 137
	RESIDENTIAL ENVIRONMENT Hospital environment Outpatient environment	17, 18, 19, 24, 25, 30, 32, 33, 34, **36**, 38, **39**, 41, 47, **48**, 51, 54, **56**, 58, 61, 64, **66**, **67**, 69, 70, **71**, 73, 74, 75, 76, 77, 80, 81, 83, **84**, 85, **86**, 87, 88, 93, **95**, 103, 108, **111**, 116, 117, 118, 123, **124**, 127, 128, 133, **135**, 139, 142

(table continues)

Table 5.1. *(continued)*

DOMAIN	INDICATORS	REFERENCES
	COMMUNITY ACTIVITIES Social activities/social training/ participation/ social behavior Community tasks/exercises	13, 22, **23**, 26, **31**, **32**, **35**, 42, 43, 44, **45**, 46, 47, 49, 50, 51, **56**, 59, 60, 61, 64, **66**, 69, 72, 73, 75, 76, 80, **84**, 85, **86**, 87, 91, 93, **96**, 97, 99, 102, 105, **107**, 110, **112**, 113, **114**, **121**, 123, **126**, 129, 130, 133, **140**
	ACCEPTANCE Admission/rejection Social adaptation/social inclusion/social belonging	**23**, 28, **29**, 35, **36**, 39, **45**, 53, **56**, **62**, 72, 80, **84**, 92, 93, 94, **96**, 99, 102, **106**, 111, 117, 118, **124**, **126**, **135**, **140**, 141
	WORK PLACE	33, **36**, 40, 46, **66**, 69, 92, 93, **114**, **126**, 129, 138
6. SELF-DETER-MINATION	**AUTONOMY** Independence Self-sufficiency Self-support Self-maintenance Self-care	2, 3, 9, 11, 13, 18, 19, 22, 25, **28**, 30, **35**, 39, **45**, 46, 47, 49, 51, 52, **56**, **58**, 64, 69, 72, 75, 76, 78, 80, 81, **86**, 87, 92, 93, 94, **95**, **96**, 97, **107**, 108, 110, **111**, 113, 117, 118, 120, **121**, 123, **124**, 128, 132, 133, **135**, 137, 139, 142

(table continues)

Table 5.1. *(continued)*

DOMAIN	INDICATORS	REFERENCES
	GOALS/PERSONAL VALUES Personal project of life Expectation/desires/ aspirations Hope Dreams/ambitions	6, 7, 8, **11**, **15**, 16, **17**, 25, **28**, **31**, **32**, 33, **35**, **40**, 46, 52, 55, **56**, **58**, 61, 63, **66**, 69, 71, 75, 79, 80, 81, **82**, **84**, **86**, 87, 88, 90, 92, 93, 94, **96**, 102, 105, **106**, **107**, 110, **111**, 117, 118, 119, 121, 123, **124**, **126**, 130, 133, 138, **140**
	PERSONAL CONTROL	13, **15**, 20, 25, **28**, **35**, 38, **40**, 44, 45, 52, **58**, **65**, **67**, 78, 80, **84**, 90, 92, 94, **96**, 102, **107**, 110, **114**, **115**, 117, **121**, **124**, **126**, 138, 142
	ENVIRONMENTAL CONTROL Advice/counseling	16, 25, 36, 80, 85, 87, 88, 90, 92, 94, **95**, 103, **106**, **107**, 110, **114**, 116, 117, **121**, 123, **124**, 128, 130, 133, 136, 137, 139
	DECISIONS	18, 20, **31**, **39**, **40**, 46, **58**, 61, 64, 71, 80, 83, 94, **96**, 102, 105, **106**, 110, **121**, **126**, 133, 136, 137, 138
	CHOICES	18, 25, **31**, **35**, 46, 60, 69, 71, 92, 94, **96**, 103, 110, **114**, **115**, **124**, **126**, 127, 128, **140**

(table continues)

Table 5.1. *(continued)*

DOMAIN	INDICATORS	REFERENCES
	SELF-MANAGEMENT	44, 52, 61, **66**, 69, 71, **86**, 92, 110, 116, **121**, 123, **126**
	ATTITUDES	8, 16, **71**, 76, 80, 85, 87, 88, 92, **106**, 116, 119, **121**, 123, **124**, **134**, 136, 141
7. MATERIAL WELL-BEING	EMPLOYMENT	3, 6, 7, 8, 13, 16, **17**, **18**, 20, 22, **23**, 26, **28**, 30, 33, 34, **35**, **36**, **39**, 40, 42, 47, 49, 51, 52, 54, 55, **56**, 61, 63, **66**, **67**, 69, 70, 72, 74, 75, 76, 77, **78**, **79**, 80, 81, 83, **84**, 85, **86**, 87, 88, 92, 93, 94, **96**, 97, 98, 99, 102, 103, 105, **106**, **107**, 108, 110, **111**, 113, **114**, 116, 117, 118, 119, 120, **121**, 122, 123, **124**, **126**, 127, 128, 129, 130, 133, 136, 137, 138, 139, **140**, 142
	HOUSING	6, 8, **9**, 16, **18**, 25, 27, **28**, 33, 34, **35**, **39**, 42, 51, 54, 55, **56**, **58**, 64, 69, 70, 73, 74, 75, 76, 77, **78**, **79**, 80, 83, 85, **84**, 87, **86**, 88, **89**, 90, 93, **95**, **96**, 103, **107**, 110, 116, 117, 118, 119, 122, 123, 128, 129, 130, 133, **135**, 136, **140**, 141

(table continues)

Table 5.1. *(continued)*

DOMAIN	INDICATORS	REFERENCES
	FINANCES	6, 7, 8, 13, 16, 25, 27, **28**, 30, **32**, 33, 34, **35**, 44, 51, 54, 55, **66**, 69, 74, 75, 76, 77, **78**, **79**, 80, 83, **84**, 85, **86**, 87, 88, 91, 93, **95**, **96**, 102, 103, 110, **112**, 116, 117, 118, **121**, 122, 123, **124**, 128, 129, 130, 133, 136, 137, 141, 142
	SOCIOECONOMIC STATUS	3, 7, **15**, 25, 33, 34, **39**, 46, 54, **68**, 69, 74, 75, 77, **78**, 80, 85, 93, 98, 103, **106**, **107**, 110, **111**, 116, 123, 127, 128, 130, 133, **135**, 137
	SAFETY/SECURITY	34, **35**, 46, 54, **56**, 58, 64, **66**, **67**, 74, 75, 76, 77, **78**, **79**, 80, 83, **84**, 85, 87, 88, 93, **96**, 102, 103, **107**, 136
	PROPERTY	59, **96**
8. RIGHTS	ACCESS	25, **36**, 46, **56**, **62**, **66**, 77, **78**, 80, **84**, 85, **86**, 87, 88, 94, **95**, **96**, 110, **112**, 117, 118, 133, **135**, 137
	CIVIC RESPONSIBILITY	46, **62**, **66**, 69, 71, 80, 92, 94, **106**, **107**, **112**, **114**, 117, **121**, **124**, 129, 133

(table continues)

Table 5.1. *(continued)*

DOMAIN	INDICATORS	REFERENCES
	OBLIGATIONS/RIGHTS	18, 41, 46, 56, 66, 69, 89, 84, 94, 96, 107, 110, 112, 121, 140
	PRIVACY	51, 56, 64, 76, 78, 83, 85, 87, 130

The dimension of interpersonal relationships has been the most studied domain in the mental and behavioral health literature, closely followed by personal development and emotional well-being. This may be because most studies focus on evaluating specific deficits in people with psychiatric disorders with the goal of planning subsequent intervention. Accordingly, the satisfaction (contentment) and interactions indicators, which belong to the emotional well-being and interpersonal relations dimensions respectively, have been used most often by researchers.

In the past five years, the self-determination domain has received considerable attention both in planning and developing person-centered programs and in QOL enhancement techniques (Hoffman, Leckman, Russo, & Knauf, 1999; Katschnig, 1997). However, there is still a long way to go. Consequently, we should promote the active participation of people with mental illnesses in order to enhance the process of psychosocial rehabilitation. Moreover, we should create more programs and services managed by the people with mental disorders themselves (and their relatives), because their knowledge and experience of these illnesses will help them enhance desired community integration.

Physical well-being and social inclusion have also received significant attention, although not as frequently as the aforementioned domains. The health indicator of physical well-being has been widely used. It is especially prevalent when researchers evaluate the effects of drugs on people's functioning and QOL enhancement (Bech, 1996; Hirschfeld et al., 1998; Katschnig & Angermeyer, 1997; Revicki et al., 1998). Research on social inclusion has focused primarily on deinstitutionalization and community integration of people with psychiatric disorders.

Material well-being has received some attention, mainly in recent research about treatment sites (Garg et al., 1999; Leff, 1997; Oliver & Mohamad, 1992; Oliver et al., 1996; Simpson et al., 1989) and poverty levels (Lafave et al., 1995; Pinkney et al., 1991; Tempier et al.,1998). Rights is the domain that has least been taken into account in recent research.

We would like to emphasize the lack of research into material well-being and rights and urge that more research be directed toward both areas. We need to define community programs aimed at alleviating the persons' precarious living conditions, employment, and housing; and it is important to defend the people's rights using empirical research and developing theoretical models that analyze and promote those rights that are potentially being violated.

Studies show that there is a stable relationship between the different parts of the model depending on their purposes. For example, rights and social integration are the most closely related domains, although the former receives more attention. Many studies analyzing quality and quantity of interactions also evaluate community roles and activities developed by people in the study. Emotional and physical well-being can both be found in studies evaluating psychosomatic disorders. Finally, studies focusing on social integration also tend to evaluate the autonomy and values and personal goals component of the self-determination domain.

The most frequently used domains and indicators vary depending on the age of the person studied. In samples of youths, the most studied indicators, based on frequency of mention, were the following: interpersonal relations (interactions, family, and affection), personal development (education and advancement), emotional well-being (contentment and self-concept), and social inclusion (roles and supports). However, in adult samples, the most used indicators were social inclusion (roles and work environment), physical well-being (health, health care, activities of daily living, leisure, nutrition, and mobility), and self-determination (autonomy, personal goals or values). In this case, personal development has also been evaluated, but indicators vary and focus on skills, fulfillment, and personal competence.

The analysis revealed some interesting gender differences in the evaluation of well-being. In reference to women, their emotional well-being (contentment and happiness) is more frequently evaluated. Meanwhile, men's material well-being (socioeconomic status, financial situation, and employment) and emotional well-being (contentment and freedom from stress) have also attracted the interest of researchers. The domain of interpersonal relations did not differ between men and women, but in the case of men the most studied indicators were interactions and friendships, while in women they were family and affection.

With regard to the QOL model presented in Figure 2.2, we would like to point out that research in the area proposes "attitudes" and "participation" as new indicators for the personal development domains. The former is considered independent from other indicators of this domain. However, the participation indicator's content is similar to "voluntary activity." Within the self-determination domain, some studies refer to a new indicator, "environmental control," closely related to personal control. Other studies use similar terms, such as *supervision, monitoring,* and *social control.*

Conclusion

Chronic mental illnesses have a significant negative effect on quality of life. Interpersonal relations, emotional well-being, physical and material well-being, and general development of the individual can be affected. The main concern of mental health services is personal and social functioning problems and the social and work status of the individual.

Community support services provide significant improvements in possibilities and opportunities for autonomy and satisfactory social relations. Consequently, they should be promoted actively. Social and personal supports should be organized in the person's natural environment. Personal satisfaction with this type of alternative is commonplace in people with severe psychological problems.

There are still many limitations and difficulties in developing services managed and directed by consumers, as a small percentage of mental health resources are being spent on these kinds of programs. In recent years we have witnessed an increase in studies from the consumer's perspective. These studies emphasize the large amounts of resources that are invested in long-term hospital stays. These stays have a negative impact on quality of life, and satisfaction is very low.

In the field of mental and behavioral health, there is an increase in advocacy for empowerment and QOL enhancement. Some think that these approaches initiate a general paradigm shift in the caring model of human services (Racino, 1994), which would be the fourth revolution in mental health, after deinstitutionalization, community mental health, and self-help (Stastny & Amering, 1997).

The participation of people with psychiatric problems in decision making and planning regarding their treatment is crucial, because it contributes significantly to their well-being and the efficacy of the action they undertake. Within the field of mental and behavioral health, it is common to consider the individual with psychiatric problems as a key element in the process or as a fundamental support resource in the rehabilitation process. Thus we anticipate an increase in research on integration and the self-determination of individuals with mental health problems.

APPENDIX 5.1
Mental and Behavioral Health References Corresponding to Table 5.1

1. Aggernaes, A. (1994). On general and need-related quality of life. A psychological theory for use in medical rehabilitation and psychiatry. In L. Nordenfelt (Ed.), *Concepts and measurement of quality of life in health care* (pp. 241–255). London: Kluwer Academic.

2. Albert, S. M., del Castillo, C., Sano, M., Jacobs, D. M., Marder, K., Bell, K., Bylsma, F., Lafleche, G., Brandt, J., Albert, M., & Stern, Y. (1996). Quality of life in patients with Alzheimer's disease as reported by patient proxies. *Journal of American Geriatric Society, 44*(11), 1342–1347.

3. Angermeyer, M. C., & Katschnig, H. (1997). Psychotropic medication and quality of life: A conceptual framework for assessing their relationship. In H. Katschnig, H. Freeman, & N. Sartorius (Eds.), *Quality of life in mental disorders* (pp. 215–225). Chichester, England: John Wiley.

4. Angermeyer, M. C., & Kilian, R. (1997). Theoretical models of quality of life for mental disorders. In H. Katschnig, H. Freeman, & N. Sartorius (Eds.), *Quality of life in mental disorders* (pp. 19–30). Chichester, England: John Wiley.

5. Atkinson, J. M., Coia, D. A., Harper, W., & Harper, J. P. (1996). The impact of education groups for people with schizophrenia on social functioning and quality of life. *British Journal of Psychiatry, 168,* 199–204.

6. Atkinson, M. J., & Caldwell, L. (1997). The differential effects of mood on patients' ratings of life quality and satisfaction with their care. *Journal of Affective Disorders, 44,* 169–175.

7. Atkinson, M. J., Zibin, S., & Chuang, H. (1997). Characterizing quality of life among patients with chronic mental illness: A critical examination of the self-report methodology. *American Journal of Psychiatry, 154*(1), 99–105.

8. Awad, A. G. (1992). Quality of life of schizophrenic patients on medications and implications for new drug trials. *Hospital and Community Psychiatry, 43,* 262–265.

9. Ballero, F., & Escobar, J. M. (1997). Rehabilitación y demencia: Realidades y límites. *Daño cerebral y calidad de vida: Demencias* (pp. 347–354). Madrid: Fundación MAPFRE Medicina.

10. Barge-Schaapveld, D., Nicolson, N. A., Delespaul, P., & de Vries, M. W. (1997). Assessing daily quality of life with the experience sampling method. In H. Katschnig, H. Freeman, & N. Sartorius (Eds.), *Quality of life in mental disorders* (pp. 95–107). Chichester, England: John Wiley.

11. Barry, M. M. (1997). Well-being and life satisfaction as components of quality of life in mental disorders. In H. Katschnig, H. Freeman, & N. Sartorius (Eds.), *Quality of life in mental disorders* (pp. 31–42). Chichester, England: John Wiley.

12. Bech, P. (1996). Quality of life measurements in major depression. *European Psychiatry, 11,* 123–126.

13. Bech, P., & Angst, J. (1996). Quality of life in anxiety and social phobia. *International Clinical Psychopharmacology, 11*(3), 97–100.

14. Bech, P., & Rylander, A. (1997). The European Community quality of life task force. *European Psychiatry, 12,* 161–162.

15. Becker, M., & Diamond, R. (1997). New developments in quality of life measurement in schizophrenia. In H. Katschnig, H. Freeman, & N. Sartorius (Eds.), *Quality of life in mental disorders* (pp. 119–133). Chichester, England: John Wiley.

16. Bengtsson-Tops, A., & Hansson, L. (1999). Subjective quality of life in schizophrenic patients living in the community. Relationship to clinical and social characteristics. *European Psychiatry, 14,* 256–263.

17. Bobes, J., & González, M. P. (1997). Quality of life in schizophrenia. In H. Katschnig, H. Freeman, & N. Sartorius (Eds.), *Quality of life in mental disorders* (pp. 165–178). Chichester, England: John Wiley.

18. Bobes, J. (1998). How is recovery from social anxiety disorder defined? *Journal of Clinical Psychiatry, 59,* 12–16.

19. Bond, J. (1999). Quality of life for people with dementia: Approaches to the challenge of measurement. *Aging and Society, 19,* 561–579.

20. Brod, M., Stewart, A. L., & Sands, L. (1999). Conceptualization and measurement of quality of life in dementia: The dementia quality of life instrument (DQOL). *The Gerontologist, 39*(1), 25–35.

21. Browne, S., Garavan, J., Gervin, M., Roe, M., Larkin, C., & O'Callaghan, E. (1998). Quality of life in schizophrenia: Insight and subjective response to neuroleptics. *Journal of Nervous Mental Disorders, 186*(2), 74–78.

22. Bullinger, M. (1997). Generic quality of life assessment in psychiatry: Potentials and limitations. *European Psychiatry, 12,* 203–209.

23. Butterworth, J., Hagner, D., Kiernan, W., & Schalock, R. (1996). Natural supports in the workplace: Defining an agenda for research and practice. *Journal of The Association for Persons with Severe Handicaps, 21*(3), 103–113.

24. Caballero, P. J., & Pérez, J. L. (1997). Papel del médico general en el diagnóstico y asistencia del demente senil: Implicaciones prácticas. In Fundación MAPFRE Medicina (Ed.), *Daño cerebral y calidad de vida: Demencias* (pp. 239–244). Madrid: Editor.

25. Clark, R., & Teage, G. (1998). Cost-effectiveness of assertive community treatment versus standard case management for persons with co-occurring severe mental illness and substance use disorders. *Health Services Research, 33*(5), 1285–1307.

26. Cohi, A. (1990). Estudio comparativo de la calidad de vida en pacientes esquizofrénicos según la condición de tratamiento. *Revista de Psiquiatría, 17*(5), 201–218.

27. Cordoba, M. J., Andrykowski, M. A., Kenady, D. E., McGrath, P. C., Sloan, D. A., & Redd, W. H. (1995). Frequency and correlates of post-traumatic-stress-disorder-like symptoms after treatment for breast cancer. *Journal of Consulting and Clinical Psychology, 63*(6), 981–986.

28. Cornes, J. M., & Arrojo, M. (1999). Calidad de vida y enfermedad mental. *Revista de Psiquiatría, 26*(1), 9–17.

29. Davies, H., Zeiss, A., Shea, E., & Tinklenberg, J. R. (1998). Sexuality and intimacy in Alzheimer's patients and their partners. *Sexuality and Disability, 16*(3), 193–203.

30. Dazord, A., Augier, F., Guisti, P., & Frot, E. (1996). Quality of life and socio-professional rehabilitation: Study on patients with chronic mental diseases. *European Psychiatry, 11,* 277–293.

31. Dickens, P. (1994). Tools and techniques of human service quality involving workers and consumers: Quality circles and consumer views. In P. Dickens (Ed.), *Quality and excellence in human services* (pp. 131–146). Chichester, England: John Wiley.

32. Dickens, P. (1994). Quality systems in human services. In P. Dickens (Ed.), *Quality and excellence in human services* (pp. 147–176). Chichester, England: John Wiley.

33. Ellison, M. L., Danley, K. S., Bromberg, C., & Palmer-Erbs, V. (1999). Longitudinal outcome of young adults who participated in a psychiatric vocational rehabilitation program. *Psychiatric Rehabilitation Journal, 22*(4), 51–58.

34. Fabian, E. (1992). Supported employment and the quality of life: Does a job make a difference? *Rehabilitation Counseling Bulletin, 36*(2), 84–97.

35. Felce, F., & Perry, J. (1997). Quality of life: The scope of the term and its breadth of measurement. In R. I. Brown (Ed.), *Quality of life for people with disabilities. Models, research, and practice* (2nd ed., pp. 56–71). Cheltenham, England: Stanley Thornes.

36. Finzen, A., & Hoffmann-Richter, U. (1997). Stigma and quality of life in mental disorders. In H. Katschnig, H. Freeman, & N. Sartorius (Eds.), *Quality of life in mental disorders* (pp. 69–76). Chichester, England: John Wiley.

37. Fisher, M. A., & Mitchell, G. J. (1998). Patients' views of quality of life: Transforming the knowledge base of nursing. *Clinical Nurse Specialist, 12*(3), 99–105.

38. Ford, J. D., & Kidd, P. (1998). Early childhood trauma and disorders of extreme stress as predictors of treatment outcome with chronic posttraumatic stress disorder. *Journal of Traumatic Stress, 11*(4), 743–761.

39. Franch, J. L., & Viaña, J. L. (1997). Afrontamiento comunitario de la demencia. Papel y necesidades de la familia. *Daño cerebral y calidad de vida: Demencias* (pp. 195–210). Madrid: Fundación MAPFRE Medicina.

40. Frankenhaeuser, M. (1996). Stress without distress in tomorrow's workplace. In D. M. Warburton & N. Sherwood (Eds.), *Pleasure and quality of life* (pp. 29–37). Chichester, England: John Wiley.

41. Freeman, H. L. (1997). "Standard of living" and environmental factors as a component of quality of life in mental disorders. In H. Katschnig, H. Freeman, & N. Sartorius (Eds.), *Quality of life in mental disorders* (pp. 55–68). Chichester, England: John Wiley.

42. Frisch, M., Cornell, J., Vilanueva, M., & Retzlaff, P. (1992). Clinical validation of the quality of life inventory: A measure of life satisfaction for use in treatment planning and outcome assessment. *Psychological Assessment, 4*(1), 92–101.

43. Fristad, M. A., Arnett, M. M., & Gavazzi, S. M. (1998). The impact of psychoeducational workshops on families of mood disordered children. *Family Therapy, 25*(3), 151–159.

44. Fristad, M. A., Gavazzi, S. M., & Soldado, K. W. (1998). Multifamily psychoeducation groups for childhood mood disorders: A program description and preliminary efficacy data. *Family Therapy, 20*(3), 385–402.

45. Fristad, M. A., Stephen, M., Gavazzi, S. M., & Soldado, K. W. (1996). Psychoeducation: A promising intervention strategy for families of children and adolescents with mood disorders. *Family Therapy, 18*(3), 371–383.

46. Gardner, J. F., Nudler, S., & Chapman, M. S. (1997). Personal outcomes as measures of quality. *Mental Retardation, 35*(4), 295–305.

47. Garg, N., Yates, W. R., Jones, R., Zhou, M., & Williams, S. (1999). Effect of gender, treatment site, and psychiatric comorbidity on quality of life outcome in substance dependence. *The American Journal on Addictions, 8,* 44–54.

48. Garralda, M. E. (1994). Chronic physical illness and emotional disorder in childhood. *British Journal of Psychiatry, 164,* 8–10.

49. Gater, R. A., Kind, P., & Gudex, C. (1995). Quality of life in liaison psychiatry. A comparison of patient and clinical assessment. *British Journal of Psychiatry, 166,* 515–520.

50. Gavazzi, S. M., Fristad, M. A., & Law, J. C. (1997). The understanding mood disorders questionnaire. *Psychological Reports, 81,* 172-174.

51. Gerber, G. J., & Coleman, G. E. (1994). Quality of life of people with psychiatric disabilities 1 and 3 years after discharge from hospital. *Quality of Life Research, 3,* 379–383.

52. Giner, J., Ibañez, E., Cervera, S., Leal, C., Baca, E., & Baca, B. J. (1999). El cuestionario sevilla de calidad de vida: Perspectiva histórica de su instauración. *Actas Españolas de Psiquiatría, 27*(1), 8–13.

53. Gjaerum, B., & Heyerdahl, S. (1998). Assessment of the mental state in medically ill children and adolescents. *Current Opinion in Psychiatry, 11,* 635–641.

54. Goodman, M., Hull, J. W., Terkelsen, K. G., Smith, T. E., & Anthony, D. (1997). Factor structure of quality of life: The Lehman interview. *Evaluation and Program Planning, 20*(4), 477–480.

55. Grant, G. M., Salcedo, V., Hynan, L. S., Frisch, M. B., & Puster, K. (1995). Effectiveness of quality of life therapy for depression. *Psychological Reports, 76,* 1203–1208.

56. Gravestock, S. (1994). Quality assurance for adults with mental retardation and mental health needs: Recent advances and practices. In N. Bouras (Ed.), *Mental health in mental retardation* (pp. 319–327). Cambridge: Cambridge University Press.

57. Grégoire, J., de Leval, N., & Mesters, P. (1995). Adaptation française et étude des propriétés métriques de la quality of life in depression scale. *Revue Européenne de Psychologie Appliquée, 25*(4), 291–286.

58. Gurland, B., & Katz, S. (1997). Quality of life in older persons. In H. Katsching, H. Freeman, & N. Sartorius, *Quality of life in mental disorders* (pp. 193–211). Chichester, England: John Wiley.

59. Hayes, R. L., Halford, W. K., & Varghese, F. T. (1995). Social skills training with chronic schizophrenic patients: Effects on negative symptoms and community functioning. *Behavior Therapy, 26,* 433–449.

60. Henry, M. E., & Capitman, J. A. (1995). Finding satisfaction in adult day care: Analysis of a national demonstration of dementia care and respite services. *Journal of Applied Gerontology, 14*(3), 302–320.

61. Hoffmann, F. L., Leckman, E., Russo, N., & Knauf, L. (1999). In it for the long haul: The integration of outcomes assessment, clinical services, and management decision-making. *Evaluation and Program Planning, 22,* 211–219.

62. Iberia, J. (1997). El papel y actividad de las asociaciones de familias y afectados. In Fundación MAPFRE Medicina (Ed.), *Daño cerebral y calidad de vida: Demencias* (pp. 211–217). Madrid: Editor.

63. Janikowski, T., Bordieri, J., & Musgrave, J. (1991). Dimensions of client satisfaction with vocational evaluation services. *Vocational Evaluation and Work Adjustment Bulletin, 24*(2), 43–48.

64. Jones, K., Robinson, M., & Golightley, M. (1986). Long-term psychiatric patients in the community. *British Journal of Psychiatry, 149,* 537–540.

65. Jung, K. (1996). Effective strategies for stress management in everyday life. In D. M. Warburton & N. Sherwood (Eds.), *Pleasure and quality of life* (pp. 59–66). Chichester, England: John Wiley.

66. Kamis-Gould, E., Brame, J., Campbell, J., Pascall, L., Schlosser, L., & Schlosser, B. R. (1991). A functional model of quality assurance for psychiatric hospitals and corresponding staffing requirements. *Evaluation and Program Planning, 14,* 147–155.

67. Katschnig, H. (1997). How useful is the concept of quality of life in psychiatry? In H. Katschnig, H. Freeman, & N. Sartorius (Eds.), *Quality of life in mental disorders* (pp. 3–16). Chichester, England: John Wiley.

68. Katschnig, H., & Angermeyer, M. C. (1997). Quality of life in depression. In H. Katschnig, H. Freeman, & N. Sartorius (Eds.), *Quality of life in mental disorders* (pp. 137–147). Chichester, England: John Wiley.

69. Kersten, E., Wilkinson, K., & Wright, S. (1999). Bringing staff on board: Creating an outcomes project tied to continuous quality improvement in an adult community residential service. *Evaluation and Program Planning, 22,* 221–232.

70. Klinkman, M. (1998). False positives, false negatives, and the validity of the diagnosis of major depression in primary care. *Archives of Family Medicine, 7,* 451–464.

71. Klinkman, M. S. (1997). Competing demands in psychosocial care: A model for the identification and treatment of depressive disorders in primary care. *General Hospital Psychiatry, 19,* 98–111.

72. Koran, L., Thieneman, M., & Davenport, R. (1996). Quality of life for patients with obsessive-compulsive disorder. *American Journal of Psychiatry, 153*(6), 783–788.

73. Kutner, N. (1999). Family members' perceptions of quality of life change in dementia SCU residents. *Journal of Applied Gerontology, 18*(4), 423–440.

74. Lafave, H. G., de Souza, H. R., Prince, P. N., Atchison, K. E., & Gerber, G. J. (1995). Partnerships for people with serious mental illness who live below the poverty line. *Psychiatric Services, 46*(10), 1071–1073.

75. Lauer, G. (1994). The quality of life issue in chronic mental illness. In J. P. Dauwalder (Ed.), *Psychology and promotion of health: Vol. 2* (pp. 28–33). Seattle, WA: Hogrefe & Huber.

76. Leff, J. P. (1997). Whose life is it anyway? Quality of life for long-stay patients discharged from psychiatric hospitals. In H. Katschnig, H. Freeman, & N. Sartorius (Eds.), *Quality of life in mental disorders* (pp. 241–260). Chichester, England: John Wiley.

77. Lehman, A. F., Rachuba, L. T., & Postrado, L. T. (1995). Demographic influences on quality of life among persons with chronic mental illnesses. *Evaluation and Program Planning, 18*(2), 155–164.

78. Lehman, A. F. (1997). Instruments for measuring quality of life in mental illnesses. In H. Katschnig, H. Freeman, & N. Sartorius (Eds.), *Quality of life in mental disorders* (pp. 79–94). Chichester, England: John Wiley.

79. Lenz, G., & Demal, U. (1997). Psychotherapy and quality of life. In H. Katschnig, H. Freeman, & N. Sartorius (Eds.), *Quality of life in mental disorders* (pp. 227–239). Chichester, England: John Wiley.

80. López, A. E. (1994). *Valoración de los efectos de la rehabilitación psicosocial.* Unpublished doctoral dissertation, Universidad de Málaga, Málaga, Spain.

81. Lucas, R., Salcedo, A., Susín, C., Roca, B., Moreno, M., Zimmer, M., Jordá, E., Guillén, A., Garrido, I., & Puche, J. (1997). Calidad de vida en pacientes esquizofrénicos y en parientes de esquizofrénicos. *Revista de Psiquiatría de la Facultad de Medicina de Barcelona, 24*(6), 143–155.

82. Mezzich, J. E., & Schmolke, M. M. (1997). Quality of life and comprehensive clinical diagnosis. In H. Katschnig, H. Freeman, & N. Sartorius (Eds.), *Quality of life in mental disorders* (pp. 109–117). Chichester, England: John Wiley.

83. Oliver, J., & Mohamad, H. (1992). The quality of life of chronically mentally ill: A comparison of public, private, and voluntary residential provisions. *British Journal of Social Work, 22,* 391–404.

84. Oliver, J., Huxley, P., Bridges, K., & Mohamad, H. (1996). Definitions and conceptual issues concerning quality of life. In J. Oliver, P. Huxley, K. Bridges, & H. Mohamad (Eds.), *Quality of life and mental health services* (pp. 15–47). London: Routledge.

85. Oliver, J., Huxley, P., Bridges, K., & Mohamad, H. (1996). The development of a quality of life profile for operational use. In J. Oliver, P. Huxley, K. Bridges, & H. Mohamad (Eds.), *Quality of life and mental health services* (pp. 48–64). London: Routledge.

86. Oliver, J., Huxley, P., Bridges, K., & Mohamad, H. (1996). Quality of life in the mental health service context. *Quality of life and mental health services* (pp. 84–107). London: Routledge.

87. Oliver, J., Huxley, P., Bridges, K., & Mohamad, H. (1996). The quality of care and the quality of life in independent-sector residential homes. *Quality of life and mental health services* (pp. 111–127). London: Routledge.

88. Oliver, J., Huxley, P., Bridges, K., & Mohamad, H. (1996). Community-based support and community mental health support teams. *Quality of life and mental health services* (pp. 152–178). London: Routledge.

89. Oliver, J., Huxley, P., Bridges, K., & Mohamad, H. (1996). Lessons learned from the experiences of applying quality of life to mental health services. *Quality of life and mental health services* (pp. 235–250). London: Routledge.

90. Orange, J. B., & Colton-Hudson, A. (1998). Enhancing communication in dementia of the Alzheimer's type. *Topics in Geriatric Rehabilitation, 14*(2), 56–75.

91. Patterson, T., Kaplan, R. M., Grant, I., Semple, S. J., Moscona, S., Koch, W. L., Harris, M. J., & Jeste, D. V. (1996). Quality of well being in late life psychosis. *Psychiatry Research, 63,* 169–181.

92. Petterson, I. L., & Arnetz, B. B. (1998). Psychosocial stressors and well-being in health care workers: The impact of an intervention program. *Social Science and Medicine, 47*(11), 1763–1772.

93. Pickney, A. A., Gerber, G. J., & Lafave, H. G. (1991). Quality of life after psychiatric rehabilitation: The clients' perspective. *Acta Psychiatrica Scandinavica, 83,* 86–91.

94. Prilleltensky, I., Peirson, L., Gould, J., &. Gould, N. G. (1997). Planning mental health services for children and youth: Part I. A value-based approach. *Evaluation and Program Planning, 20*(2), 163–172.

95. Ramsay, M., Winget, C., & Higginson, I. (1995). Review: Measures to determine the outcome of community services for people with dementia. *Age and Aging, 24,* 73–83.

96. Renwick, R., Brown, I., & Nagler, M. (1996). *Quality of life in health promotion and rehabilitation: Conceptual approaches, issues, and applications.* London: Sage.

97. Revicki, D. A., Simon, G. E., Chan, K., Katon, W., & Heiligenstein, J. (1998). Depression, health-related quality of life, and medical cost outcomes of receiving recommended levels of antidepressant treatment. *The Journal Family Practice, 47*(2), 446–452.

98. Robert, M., Hirschfeld, A., Russell, J. M., & Delgado, P. L. (1998). Predictors of response to acute treatment of chronic and double depression with sertraline or imipramine. *Journal of Clinical Psychiatry, 59*(12), 669–675.

99. Rodriguez, A., Jarne, A., Soler, R., Miarons, R., & Grau, A. (1995). Estudio factorial y adaptación de la escala de calidad de vida en la esquizofrenia (QLS). *Revista de Psicología General y Aplicada, 48*(3), 353–364.

100. Rodriguez, J. (1995). *Health psychology and quality of life research. Vol. 1.* Murcia, Spain: University of Alicante and Sociedad Valenciana de Psicología Social, Health Psychology Department.

101. Rodriguez, J. (1995). *Health psychology and quality of life research. Vol. 2.* Murcia, Spain: University of Alicante and Sociedad Valenciana de Psicología Social, Health Psychology Department.

102. Rosenfield, S. (1997). Labeling mental illness: The effects of received services and perceived stigma on life satisfaction. *American Sociological Review, 62*(4), 660–672.

103. Rosenheck, R., Cramer, J., & Xu, W. (1998). Multiple outcome assessment in a study of the cost-effectiveness of clozapine in the treatment of refractory schizophrenia. *Health Services Research, 33*(5), 1237–1261.

104. Russell, C. K. (1996). Passion and heretics: Meaning in life and quality of life of persons with dementia. *Journal of American Geriatrics Society, 44*(11), 1400–1402.

105. Sainfort, F., Becker, M., & Diamond, R. (1996). Judgments of quality of life of individuals with severe mental disorders: Patient self-report versus provider perspectives. *American Journal of Psychiatry, 153,* 497–502.

106. Sartorius, N. (1997). Quality of life and mental disorders: A global perspective. In H. Katschnig, H. Freeman, & N. Sartorius (Eds.), *Quality of life in mental disorders* (pp. 319–328). Chichester, England: John Wiley.

107. Sartorius, N., & Janca, A. (1996). Psychiatric assessment instruments developed by the World Health Organization. *Social Psychiatry and Psychiatric Epidemiology, 31,* 55–69.

108. Savorani, G., Vulcano, V., Boni, S., Sarti, G., & Ravaglia, G. (1998). Behavioral disorders in dementia patients and their impact on the stress of caregiving relatives: The ARAD questionnaire. *Archives of Gerontology and Geriatrics, 26*(10), 481–485.

109. Savorani, G., Zanetti, O., Metitieri, T., Bianchetti, A., & Trabucchi, M. (1998). Effectiveness of an educational program for demented persons' relatives. *Archives of Gerontology and Geriatrics, 26*(10), 531–538.

110. Schalock, R., Nelson, G., Sutton, S., Holtan, S., & Sheehan, M. (1997). Evaluación multidimensional del estado actual y la calidad de vida de los receptores de servicios de salud mental. *Siglo Cero, 28*(4), 5–12.

111. Schmeck, K., & Poustka, F. (1997). Quality of life and child psychiatric disorders. In H. Katschnig, H. Freeman, & N. Sartorius (Eds.), *Quality of life in mental disorders* (pp. 179–191). Chichester, England: John Wiley.

112. Selmes, J. (1997). Política de la Unión Europea en la salud pública. El caso de la enfermedad de Alzheimer. *Daño cerebral y calidad de vida: Demencias* (pp. 219–224). Madrid: Fundación MAPFRE Medicina.

113. Sherbourne, C. D., Wells, K. B., & Judd, L. L. (1996). Functioning and well-being of patients with panic disorder. *American Journal of Psychiatry, 153*(2), 213–218.

114. Sherwood, N. (1996). Pleasure, choice, and the quality of everyday life. In D. M. Warburton & N. Sherwood (Eds.), *Pleasure and quality of life* (pp. 275–280). Chichester, England: John Wiley.

115. Sherwood, N. (1996). Stressors, product use, and everyday skills. In D. M. Warburton & N. Sherwood (Eds.), *Pleasure and quality of life* (pp. 89–96). Chichester, England: John Wiley.

116. Simpson, C. J., Hyde, C. E., & Faragher, E. B. (1989). The chronically mentally ill in community facilities: A study of quality of life. *British Journal of Psychiatry, 154,* 77–82.

117. Skantze, K. (1998). Subjective quality of life and standard of living: A 10-year follow up of out-patients with schizophrenia. *Acta Psychiatrica. Scandinavica, 98,* 390–399.

118. Skantze, K., Mald, U., Dencker, S. J., May, P. R. A., & Corrigan, P. (1992). Comparison of quality of life with standard of living in schizophrenic outpatients. *British Journal of Psychiatry, 161,* 797–801.

119. Skrabski, A., & Kopp, M. (1994). Health behaviour, psychiatric symptoms, and psychosocial background factors. In J. P. Dauwalder (Ed.), *Psychology and promotion of health* (pp. 21–27). Seattle, WA: Hogrefe & Huber.

120. Small, G. W., Birkett, M., Meyers, B. S., Koran, L. M., Bystrisky, A., Nemeroff, C. B., & Flioxetine Collaborative Study Group. (1996). Impact of physical illness on quality of life and antidepressant response in geriatric major depression. *Journal of the American Geriatric Society, 44,* 1220–1225.

121. Smith, M. K. (1998). Empowerment evaluation: Theoretical and methodological considerations. *Evaluation and Program Planning, 21,* 255–261.

122. Smith, T. E., Hull, J. W., & Goodman, M. (1999). The relative influences of symptoms, insight, and neurocognition on social adjustment in schizophrenia and schizoaffective disorder. *Journal of Nervous and Mental Disease, 187*(2), 102–108.

123. Solomon, P., & Draine, J. (1995). One-year outcomes of a randomized trial of consumer case management. *Evaluation and Program Planning, 18*(2), 117–127.

124. Stastny, P., & Amering, M. (1997). Integrating consumer perspectives on quality of life in research and service planning. In H. Katschnig, H. Freeman, & N. Sartorius (Eds.), *Quality of life in mental disorders* (pp. 261–269). Chichester, England: John Wiley.

125. Steinwachs, D., Flynn, L., Norquist, G., & Skinner, E. (1996). *Using client outcomes information to improve mental health and substance abuse treatment.* San Francisco: Jossey-Bass.

126. Suiter, J. I., & Bonnsetter, B. (1996). Individual coping strategies and behavioural style. In D. M. Warburton & N. Sherwood (Eds.), *Pleasure and quality of life* (pp. 47–57). Chichester, England: John Wiley.

127. Swanson, C. L., Gur, R. C., Bilker, W., Petty, R. G., & Gur, R. E. (1998). Premorbid educational attainment in schizophrenia: Association with symptoms, functioning, and neurobehavioral measures. *Biological Psychiatry, 44,* 739–747.

128. Swanson, J., Swartz, M., Estroff, S., Borum, R., Wagner, R., & Hiday, V. (1998). Psychiatric impairment, social contact, and violent behavior: Evidence from a study of outpatient committed persons with severe mental disorder. *Social Psychiatry and Psychiatric Epidemiology, 33,* S86–S94.

129. Telch, M. J., Schmidt, N. B., Jaimez, T. L., Jacquin, K. M., & Harrington, P. J. (1995). Impact of cognitive-behavioral treatment on quality of life in panic disorder patients. *Journal of Consulting and Clinical Psychology, 63*(5), 823–830.

130. Tempier, R., Caron, J., Mercier, C., & Leouffre, P. (1998). Quality of life of severely mentally ill individuals: A comparative study. *Community Mental Health Journal, 34*(5), 477–485.

131. Thorpe, L. M., Klinkman, M. S., Schwenk, T. L., & Coyne, J. C. (1997). Depression in primary care: More like asthma than appendicitis: The Michigan depression project. *Canadian Journal of Psychiatry, 42,* 966–973.

132. Thorpe, L., Campbell, B., & Primeau, F. J. (1998). Discusión de un caso clínico: Paciente mayor con Psicosis. *Canadian Journal of Psychiatry, 43*(1), 10–14.

133. Trauer, T., Duckmanton, R. A., et al. (1998). A study of the quality of life of the severely mentally ill. *International Journal of Social Psychiatry, 44*(2), 79–92.

134. Tsimara-Papastamatiou, H. (1996). Stressors and cancer. In D. M. Warburton & N. Sherwood (Eds.), *Pleasure and quality of life* (pp. 39–46). Chichester, England: John Wiley.

135. Van Nieuwenhuizen, G., & Schene, A. H. (1997). Measuring the quality of life of clients with severe mental illness: A review of instruments. *Psychiatric Rehabilitation Journal, 20*(4), 33–42.

136. Vázquez-Barquero, J. L., Gaite, L., Ramírez, N., García, E., et al. (1997). Desarrollo de la versión española del perfil de calidad de vida de Lancashire LQOLP. *Archivos de Neurobiología, 60*(2), 125–139.

137. Walter, L. J., Schaefer, C., Albright, L., Parthasarathy, S., Hunkeler, E. M., Westphal, J., & Westphal, W. M. (1999). Role of a psychiatric outcome study in a large-scale quality improvement project. *Evaluation and Program Planning, 22,* 233–243.

138. Warburton, D. M., & Suiter, J. I. (1996). The costs of job dissatisfaction. In D. M. Warburton & N. Sherwood (Eds.), *Pleasure and quality of life* (pp. 13–28). Chichester, England: John Wiley.

139. Warshaw, M. G., Fierman, E., Pratt, L., Hunt, M., Yonkers, K. A., Massion, A. O., & Keller, M. B. (1993). Quality of life and dissociation in anxiety disorder patients with histories of trauma or PTSD. *American Journal of Psychiatry, 150*(10), 1512–1516.

140. Wiersma, D. (1997). Role functioning as a component of quality of life in mental disorders. In H. Katschnig, H. Freeman, & N. Sartorius (Eds.), *Quality of life in mental disorders* (pp. 43–54). Chichester, England: John Wiley.

141. Williams, G. M., & Walters, A. S. (1996). Perceived impact of limb amputation on sexual activity: A study of adult amputees. *Journal of Sex Research, 33*(3), 221–230.

142. Wittchen, H. U., & Beloch, E. (1996). The impact of social phobia on quality of life. *International Clinical Psychopharmacology, 11*(3), 15–23.

CHAPTER 6

Mental Retardation and Intellectual Disabilities

Overview

Research into quality of life in people with mental retardation or intellectual disabilities has significantly increased in the past decades and has now become a priority issue for many researchers. The recent changes in the conception of disability have resulted in a more comprehensive study of the needs of and supports for these individuals. Moreover, the trends of these changes have focused more on people than on the services or programs provided. Such a comprehensive approach to disability, together with the importance of considering the individual as a consumer of services, is fully integrated in the present conception of quality of life.

The concept of quality of life (QOL) has great potential as a synthesis of the purposes pursued in any domain and by any person. The concept is also very useful in service planning and evaluation. Furthermore, today the QOL concept is an innovative force transforming programs and activities for people with mental retardation or intellectual disabilities. To talk about quality of life means bringing people to the forefront. It also implies talking about the quality of what we do. The QOL concept focuses on organizational development of agencies and services; it can be a guideline and an indicator of the areas needing attention and action. The QOL concept advances the innovation of professional practices in the field of health, education, social services, and families toward more positive approaches concerning the individual regardless of personal limitations.

Numerous authors have studied quality of life in the field of mental retardation and intellectual disabilities since the mid-1980s including R. I. Brown (1988, 1997), Cummins (1993, 1996, 1997a), Goode (1988, 1994), Heal et al. (1985, 1995, 1997, 1999), Felce and Perry (1995, 1996, 1997), and Schalock (1990, 1996b, 1997; Keith & Schalock, 2000). This work has provided people with disabilities, their families, professionals, and supporting organizations an operative proposal that can be applied in different contexts with the aim of enhancing their living conditions and development. In fact, the QOL concept emerges as a principle that is applicable to the enhancement of our ever-changing society. As with the paradigm shift of the definition of mental retardation proposed by the American Association on Mental Retardation in 1992 — with its emphasis on self-determination, inclusion, equity, and community support — service providers and professionals are beginning to pay increasing attention to QOL enhancement in people with mental retardation or intellectual disabilities.

In this chapter we review a selection of theoretical and research publications about the quality of life for people with mental retardation or intellectual disabilities. We have excluded from this chapter publications about education, aging, and other areas that are specifically discussed in other chapters of part 2. Similarly, we have not included the analysis of assessment techniques, presented in part 3. Instead, we have placed a greater emphasis on research about community integration, deinstitutionalization, and employment. The chapter includes the following four sections: (a) the concept of quality of life, (b) community integration and deinstitutionalization, (c) employment, and (d) domains and indicators of quality of life. The chapter concludes with a brief overview of the trends in QOL-focused work in the area of mental retardation and intellectual disabilities. Throughout the chapter we use the terms *mental retardation* and *intellectual disabilities* as synonyms, although we are aware of their differential use among countries.

The Concept of Quality of Life

Quality of life is a global, holistic concept that does not refer to a single point in time (R. I. Brown, 1988; Timmons & R. Brown, 1997) and that, though based on an abstract idea (Borthwick-Duffy, 1992), has clearly evolved into a more operational definition in recent years. Today research focuses on its components and how to measure them, but it also discusses its applicability in a broad range of situations. Recently researchers arrived at a consensus document about the conceptualization, measurement, and application of the QOL concept (Schalock et al., in press). Although concepts and models vary from country to country, and even from area to area within countries, the consensus document proposed by the Special Interest Research Group on Quality of Life of the International Association for the Scientific Study of Intellectual Disabilities sets the stage for its continuing development.

Quality of life is a generic concept that is not exclusively related to a single group or population (Goode, 1997b). Most researchers agree that it is a multidimensional concept, which embraces the same components or domains in people with or without disability (Felce & Perry, 1997; Goode, 1990, 1994, 1997b; Keith & Schalock, 2000; Schalock, 1994, 1996b; Schalock, Keith, Hoffman, & Karan, 1989). However, we should not assume that people with disabilities exhibit the same characteristics as other population groups (Dennis, Williams, Giangreco, & Cloninger, 1993). We need to keep in mind the limits that disabilities present concerning health and cognitive development (Borthwick-Duffy, 1992; Flanagan, 1976), depending on the type of disability and age (R. I. Brown, 1988).

Traditionally, quality of life has been associated with a person's competencies and the performance of professional services. Some authors (Heal, Khoju, & Rusch, 1997; Heal, Khoju, Rusch, & Harnisch, 1999) still stress that personal competence is a key factor that determines an individual's quality of life. However, the efforts made recently in defining the QOL concept have stressed the relationships between individuals and their environments (R. I. Brown, 1988; Felce & Perry, 1995; Goode, 1994; Keith & Schalock, 2000; Velde, 1997; Verdugo, 1995; Vreeke, Janssen, Resnick, & Stolk, 1997).

Some authors (e.g., Emerson & Hatton, 1996) think that the process of transferring the rhetoric of quality of life into measurable outcomes for service-users is imperfect, as was the concept of normalization in earlier years. But the differences between the two concepts are absolutely clear, as research into quality of life has progressed to propose domains and indicators, while normalization referred to a more ambiguous general concept that was difficult to render operational. Consequently, the QOL concept may now be considered an international trend. This has happened because it allows us to answer a crucial question in the field of disabilities: to what extent the lives of people have been affected by the achievement of objectives pursued in programs and services (Renwick, Brown, & Raphael, 2000).

In spite of recognizing its subjective nature, the current emergence of an ecological approach to quality of life in the field of disability is moving ahead (Keith & Schalock, 2000; Mitchell & Winslade, 1997). The ecological model, which analyzes the microsystem, mesosystem, and macrosystem, enables us to focus on the needs of people within their environments and, subsequently, to develop more efficient support strategies. Over the following years, research will advance in the refinement of the different levels of the system and representative indicators. This is one of the aims of this *Handbook*.

Community Integration and Deinstitutionalization

There continues to be a need for us to be aware of the effects of deinstitutionalization and the outcomes of new residential alternatives as well as the establishment of guidelines for research on community integration. The approach for improving quality, adopted by human services in general and residential services in particular, and the development of the QOL concept as a principle of excellence for guiding best practices have contributed to the large number of studies reviewed for this chapter. The QOL concept has gone beyond assessing the optimal residential options, derived from the normalization principle, and currently takes into account socioenvironmental variables that promote the satisfaction and well-being of the individual (Reiter & Bendov, 1996). Thus objective indicators are incorporated, along with subjective factors related to the wishes and needs of the individual and people's beliefs and interpretations about themselves and their functioning in the world.

The review of studies about the effects of deinstitutionalization on people with developmental disabilities in the United Kingdom and Ireland between 1980 and 1994, with 46 different studies (71 publications) involving 2,350 individuals, allowed Emerson and Hatton (1996) to conclude that community-based residential services are generally related to an increased participation of individuals in daily activities and in the use of organizational services; more contact with caregivers, relatives, and friends; improvement in adaptive behavior; more opportunities for choice; and more community acceptance.

The process of placing people from institutions into community residential options requires individualized planning if it is to achieve significant life changes. Some studies have found barely significant changes; the cause of this may be that social inclusion means more than a simple relocation of individuals into more community-based residences (Allen, 1989; Fleming & Stenfert, 1990). When changes occur only in the physical-residential environment, their effect is often restricted to behaviors within the new setting. It is necessary to provide learning opportunities under the new conditions so that the person can become more competent in society and more independent. In the same way, challenging behaviors may be increased as a result of decreased environmental control over them (Mansell, 1994). However, most studies have not monitored community inclusion for an extended period of time.

In the 1990s the development of different longitudinal studies, which had been widely advocated (R. I. Brown, 2000b; Hatton, Emerson, Roberston, Henderson, & Cooper, 1995; Lord & Pedlar, 1991; Schalock & Genung, 1993), has allowed us to draw more categorical conclusions about the effects of deinstitutionalization. Generally speaking, the more time that has passed since the person left an institution, the better the results. For example, Schalock and Genung evaluated the status of housing and employment, quality of life, and daily living patterns of 85 individuals placed into independent housing and competitive employment 15 years before the organized study was conducted. Nineteen percent of the sample had returned to the program and received mental retardation/developmental disabilities services; 59% had not returned to the program and continued to live independently; and 70% had held a job for more than 11 years.

The study of well-being and perception of quality of life of the residents of the Johnstone Center was analyzed by Apgar, Cook, and Lerman (1998) 11 years after it was shut down. They analyzed adaptive and disruptive behavior, housing options, retrospective opinion about the care received in the center compared to the present, and quality of life in the seven domains proposed by Cummins (1991): material well-being, health, productivity, intimacy, emotional well-being, and position within the community (this domain was divided into two: integration in the community and personal autonomy). Out of the 155 former residents in the 1966 sample, 93 lived in other institutions while 62 lived in the wider community. The latter group exhibited higher levels of satisfaction with residential status, together with higher scores in material well-being, participation in community activities, daily and global autonomy, perceived safety, and emotional well-being. Neither this group nor those who were living in other institutions considered that the Johnstone Center was the most desired residential option.

Using a more objective perspective, Dagnan, Look, Ruddick, and Jones (1995) evaluated the change in quality of life experienced by 36 residents of community-based homes two years after leaving a hospital for people with learning disabilities. The authors, basing their work on Cragg and Harrison (1986), measured the physical details of the home, access to the community, leisure opportunities, community integration, routines within the home, resident education and training, staff behavior, and opportunities to express choices and make decisions. The results showed a significant improvement in every area.

Changes in lifestyles in different types of residential services have also been compared (Bellamy, Newton, LeBaron, & Horner, 1990; Burchard, Hasazi, Gordon & Yoe, 1991; Howe, Horner, & Newton, 1998). Howe et al. compared supported living and traditional residential support, examining lifestyles of participants in their social relations (number of people involved in activities and variety of activities) and in their participation in community activities (number of different activities and frequency). The results were clearly favorable to participants in supported living options. They improved their social relationships and participation in the community, and they increased their independence, with no difference in service costs. Burchard et al. compared 157 residents of group homes, supervised apartments, and family homes on multiple indexes of lifestyle (independent functioning, lifestyle normalization, physical and social integration, and employment) and adjustment (personal satisfaction with residence, work, social support, personal well-being, and behavioral problems). The authors found few differences between participants living at the family home and those with a previous history of institutionalization. However, degrees of autonomy and opportunities for the individual were greatest in supervised apartments, than in group homes, and finally in family homes. Nevertheless, every alternative involved significant difficulties for people to have access to competitive employment and to develop friendships and relationships with people without disabilities.

Che, Bruininks, Lakin, and Hayden (1993) examined personal competence and community participation of 336 people with mental retardation who were living in 181 small group homes and small foster homes. The authors found that personal competencies were not the decisive factor in differentiating between various residential options; it was the connection with housing or residence that determined the type of activity in which the person engaged. Consequently, lifestyle can be explained primarily by the place and the way life is lived.

Attention has also focused on comparing quality and costs of different types of housing and residences. But the great diversity of existing options, together with the dissimilar terminology used in various countries, makes it difficult to present a comparative analysis of these results. Nevertheless, in general there are no differences in cost of services, although there are extensive differences in type of segregated or community care (Conroy, 1996; Hatton et al., 1995; Howe et al., 1998; Verdugo, Canal, & Gutiérrez, 1997).

Hatton et al. (1995) evaluated quality and cost of four different service models for adults with mental retardation and associated sensory deficits. The four models were: specialized institution-based units; a specialized campus-style setting with further educational service; specialized community-based group homes; and "ordinary" community-based group homes. Measures of comparison included cost, staff-resident ratio, behavior, social atmosphere, acquired skills, quality of programmed activities, contact with professionals, and social life of residents. The specialized community-based group home was the model associated with a better service quality and a more satisfying lifestyle for residents. But it did not result in an increase in costs or staff-resident ratio. The authors concluded that it is the combination of structured environment with the orientation toward living in the community that is the basis of success.

Conroy (1996) compared results in small intermediate care facilities for mental retardation (ICF-MRs) with other community services. To that end, the author obtained information about behavior, health, choices, presence in the community, productivity, characteristics of residential services, activities, cost, environment, relationships between residents and staff, and other issues. The cost of both ICF-MRs and other residential services did not show significant differences, and the results were better in more flexible residential services versus more regulated services. The former obtained positive results in 10 of the 35 measured indicators.

Our analysis of the studies about deinstitutionalization and the development of community-based residences over the past decades suggest that the process of transforming institutions into community-based residences is associated with the following positive outcomes: (a) improvement in interpersonal relations (more contact with relatives, friends, and service staff); (b) enhanced material well-being, higher productivity, and better characteristics of home and residential setting; (c) improvement in adaptive behavior and competencies, with a higher number of educational, training, and leisure activities, and more involvement in activities; (d) increased independence and autonomy, with more opportunities to make choices and decisions, and control one's own life; (e) improvement of one's support network, including broader social network, lower staff-resident ratio, and thus more direct contact with staff; (f) easier access to the community, including more use of community services and participation in general; and (g) higher levels of general satisfaction. In addition, these positive results are not related to a higher cost of community services.

The limitations of the preceding conclusions are due to the fact that today the presence in the community of people with disabilities is still limited in most countries, and even more so when we consider individuals whose skills are severely impaired. In addition, interpersonal and social relations are often very limited and are frequently reduced to contacts with family and service staff, while interactions with peers are very restricted. Furthermore, the improvement in competence is often moderate and more focused on domestic routines rather than on social or employment areas. Improvement is dependent on training received and thus on quality of planned activities. Challenging behaviors are still a problem to be solved, since outcomes in community setting are very contradictory for this group (Mansell, 1994).

Employment

Employment and quality of life of people with disabilities is a crucial issue, although we do not have such an extensive body of literature as in other fields. The review in this section is based on publications from the late 1980s to 1999. During this period integrated and supported employment were the key issues in research (Fabian, 1991; Kiernan, Sanchez, & Schalock, 1989; Kiernan & Schalock, 1997; MacCraughrin, Ellis, Rusch, & Heal, 1993; Mank & Buckley, 1989; Sinott-Oswald, Gliner, & Spencer, 1991).

The relationship between quality (an important issue in companies) and quality of life, between quality of life and quality of professional life, and the strategies to foster change in organizations through the incorporation of these concepts has been approached in several studies (Albin, 1992; Goode, 1989; Kiernan & Schalock, 1997; Kiernan, Schalock, Butterworth, & Mank, 1997; Mank, 1997; Test, 1994). Goode (1989) indicates that we should modify directive style in order to increase quality of professional life, and we should put an emphasis on client participation in decision making. Albin (1992) proposes the use of the concept of total quality in supported employment services and community-based services. Together with the application of the principles derived from the concept of total quality, the authors stress the importance of clearly defining the client and of transforming facility-based services into community-based services. Following a similar trend, Test (1994) proposes a matrix that enables an analysis of social validity and of the type of consumers in studies about supported employment.

Some studies have tried to identify those variables that determine higher or lower work integration. Likewise, Bánfalvy (1996) examined the sociological characteristics of adults with intellectual disabilities and tried to understand their mode and quality of life. The author concludes that the educational and social levels of the parents are good predictors of professional integration and social activities of their children, even more than the level of learning difficulty of their children. Furthermore, Greenbaum, Graham, and Scales (1996) found that social-labor success is a function of IQ, severity of impairments, family support, and information about disability and its impact. The barriers hindering success are fear of discrimination, lack of adaptation, and lack of knowledge on labor rights.

There are numerous studies about supported employment and the QOL concept. Whereas there is no discussion about economic benefits of integrated employment versus segregated employment, some authors point out some limitations on possible changes in lifestyle due to limited salaries (Thompson, Powers, & Houchard, 1992) or limited social participation (Mank, 1997). The comparison between supported and sheltered employment, dealing with cost-benefit and cost-effectiveness in terms of quality of life, was done by MacCraughrin et al. (1993). The authors concluded that supported employment is more cost-effective than sheltered employment in the long run for people with mild, moderate, and severe mental retardation. An increased perceived quality of life was also more likely in supported employment, apart from the higher perceived loneliness of individuals in supported employment.

The perception of satisfaction with their situation in different jobs has been the focus of considerable research. The general conclusion is that results are more positive in integrated than in segregated work environments (Eggelton, Robertson, Ryan, & Kober, 1999; Fabian, 1991; Sinott-Oswald, Gliner, & Spencer (1991); Wehmeyer, 1994). Wehmeyer suggests, for example, that the perception of the locus of control is related to professional status; thus people with cognitive disabilities in competitive employment exhibit a higher level of internal control than others who are unemployed or in sheltered employment. Sinott-Oswald et al. found that people with mental retardation in supported employment present a higher perceived quality of life concerning environmental control, participation in the community, and perception of personal change than those who remain in sheltered employment. Such a perception is very similar in people without a disability. The results of the study by Eggelton et al. indicate that quality of life for people in integrated employment was much better than for unemployed people. In addition, there were no differences in perceived quality of life between people in sheltered employment and people at home.

One of the most efficient strategies proposed to achieve real inclusion of the individual in his labor environment is the development of natural supports (Butterworth, Hagner, Kiernan, & Schalock, 1996; Mank, 1996; Mank, Cioffi, & Yovanoff, 1997; Nisbet, 1992; Nisbet & Hagner, 1988). Nisbet (1992) coined this term to refer to supports received by the person in his or her work site. Butterworth et al. claim that natural supports include not only people but also the processes and culture of the work site and that natural supports are a key factor to increase the inclusion of the individual in the working environment, the person's satisfaction with self and coworkers, and the person's quality of life. Mank et al. (1997) found that to the extent that employment supports are more typical, there are higher salaries and better social integration. Coworkers play a crucial role in achieving this aim (Mank, Cioffi, & Yovanoff, 2000).

Other research-based findings indicating that employment is an important determining factor in enhancing quality of life include: the involvement of users in the choice and assessment of devices and assistive technology (Scherer, 1996); the achievement of an adequate match between the characteristics of the worker and the requirements of the position (Warburton & Suiter, 1996); the appropriate modifications of the environment together with the provision of individual supports (Cortina, Gómez, & Guell, 1998); and regular employment as the important quality outcome in supported employment. To promote integration, Mank and Buckley (1989) made a comprehensive proposal of three strategies: ecological analysis (of the settings where the individual pursues his or her activities, of the tasks carried out, and of relationships), environment modification (if it is not enriching or can be improved, without forgetting the role of coworkers), and individual support and training (systematically based on capacities and having the subject participate).

Domains and Indicators of Quality of Life

The research studies in the field of mental retardation and intellectual disabilities reviewed in this chapter follow closely the QOL model presented in Figure 2.2. Most studies use multidimensional perspectives, and the most widespread models coincide with the domains found in Figure 2.2. Table 6.1 presents a selection of existing scientific evidence in the area (71 references) based on our selection criteria discussed in chapter 1.

The domains that have been most extensively studied are social inclusion, physical well-being, interpersonal relations, and self-determination. An important number of references consider these domains essential. Next we find material well-being and emotional well-being, which also enjoy considerable attention from researchers, although with a lower number of references than the previous four. Finally, personal development and rights receive the least attention, especially the latter. However, both have a sufficient number of references to enable analysis of which indicators are studied the most.

The physical well-being domain is very important, especially because health (although nonspecific) is the most often cited indicator (48 out of 71 references). Studies that take this domain into account are often interested in the assessment

TABLE 6.1
Quality of Life Domains and Indicators in Mental Retardation and Intellectual Disabilities

DOMAIN	INDICATORS	REFERENCES
1. SOCIAL INCLUSION	**COMMUNITY INTEGRATION/ PARTICIPATION**	29, **38**, 41, 48
	Access	11, 16, 17, **28, 33**, 37, **49**
	Presence	12, 24
	Participation	3, 8, 10, **39**, 61, 62, **65**, 66, 68, 69, 70
	Using the community	7, **19**, 43
	SOCIAL INCLUSION	1, 2, 5, **6**, 13, 16, 17, 18, **22**, 26, **34, 36**, 37, 46, **48**, 50, 52, 53, 57, 58, 59, 70
	RESIDENTIAL ENVIRONMENT	3, 10, 21, **34**, 35, 46, **48**, 58, **64, 65**, 68
	Normalization	**34, 66**, 68
	Residential stability	3
	Satisfaction	**32**
	ROLE	11, 54, 60
	Lifestyle	5, **23**, 60, **63**
	Adaptative/problem behavior	10, **19**

(table continues)

Note. Domains and indicators are ordered from most frequent to least frequent based on the number of references found. Conceptual references are printed in boldface and applied research references in regular font. Numbered references are identified in Appendix 6.1. We have excluded the references to books by Schalock (1990, 1996, 1997), because they contain the quality of life model proposed in this handbook.

TABLE 6.1. *(continued)*

DOMAIN	INDICATORS	REFERENCES
	SUPPORTS Services and satisfaction with them	10, **34**, **36**, 41, **48**, 57
	ACCEPTANCE	19, 25, **34**, **48**, 55
	STATUS	1, 2, **15**
2. PHYSICAL WELL-BEING	**HEALTH**	1, 2, **6**, 10, 11, 12, **14**, 17, **21**, 23, 25, 26, 27, 28, 30, 31, 32, 40, **48**, 54, 58, **64**, 66, 69
	Physical safety	1, 2, **6**, 11, 25, 26, 27, 28, 31, 47, 54, 58, 66, 69
	Physical condition	10
	Healthy environment	29, 30
	Sleep	11
	Health and well-being	**23**, **27**, 63
	LEISURE	4, 10, 11, **21**, 28, 29, 32, 33, **34**, **36**, 38, 40, 45, **48**, **64**, 67, 70
	Satisfaction	33
	Sport	**20**, 33, 51
	Vacation behavior	**20**, 51
	Opportunities	16, 17, 37
	PHYSICAL WELL-BEING	13, **15**, **20**, 22, 28, **34**, **48**, 51, 70
	ACTIVITIES OF DAILY LIVING	4, **6**, 9, 19, 26, 32, 60, 70
	Activities at home	45

(table continues)

TABLE 6.1. *(continued)*

DOMAIN	INDICATORS	REFERENCES
	RECREATION	29, **31**, **33**, 54, 66
	NUTRITION	11, 28
	MOBILITY	11
	HEALTH CARE	47
3. INTER-PERSONAL RELATIONS	INTERACTIONS	34, 66, 71
	Work relations	20, 51
	Social relations	7, 8, **9**, 14, 19, 20, 21, 30, **32**, 38, 43, **48**, **49**, 50, 61, **64**, **65**, 69
	With staff	**9**, 16, 17, 37
	Quality of interpersonal relationships	3
	FAMILY	4, 10, 14, 21, 32, 40, 64, 65
	Marital relations	20, 21, 40, 51, **54**, **65**
	Parent-child relations	20, 22, 51
	Extended family relations	54
	INTERPERSONAL RELATIONS	13, 23, 24, **28**, 29, 39, 45, **63**, 68, 70
	Affiliation	27
	Loneliness	56
	FRIENDSHIPS	4, **9**, 10, 11, 21, 33, 54, **65**, 67
	SUPPORTS	60
	Social network	28, 54, 65, 68

(table continues)

TABLE 6.1. *(continued)*

DOMAIN	INDICATORS	REFERENCES
	INTIMACY	1, 2, 15
	Sexuality	66
	AFFECTION	11, 56
	Emotional relationships	64
4. MATERIAL WELL-BEING	EMPLOYMENT	4, 5, 6, 9, 14, 21, 29, 32, 34, 40, 48, 51, 54, 64, 65, 70
	Productivity	1, 4, 12, 15, 18, 22, 41, 57, 41, 48, 52 53, 59
	Job status	30
	Work life	45
	Work features	20
	Satisfaction	20
	FINANCIAL	6, 21, 26, 54, 58
	Income	11, 32, 47, 48, 66
	Financial security	54, 66
	MATERIAL WELL-BEING	1, 2, 13, 14, 15, 22, 28, 34, 51, 48, 49, 54, 70
	SHELTER	4, 21, 28, 65
	Physical details of the home	16, 17, 37, 50
	Comfort	21, 48, 49, 71
	SOCIAL ECONOMIC STATUS	21, 40, 65
	OWNERSHIP	69

(table continues)

TABLE 6.1. *(continued)*

DOMAIN	INDICATORS	REFERENCES
	SECURITY	28
	TRANSPORTATION	47
5. EMOTIONAL WELL-BEING	CONTENTMENT	11, 18, **23**, 28, **34**, 42, 44, **48**, 52, 53, 55, 56, 59, 60, **63**
	With work	5, 51
	With residence	5
	With supports	**4**, 5, 32
	Community satisfaction	42
	Satisfaction with services	42
	EMOTIONAL WELL-BEING	1, 2, **13**, **14**, **15**, 20, 22
	General well-being	**4**, 28
	Personal well-being	5, 62, **65**, 70
	Psychological well-being	**34**, **48**
	SELF-CONCEPT	
	Self-esteem	11, 40, **66**
	Personal perceptions	**48**
	Self	25, 27, **48**, **65**
	Self-image	**4**, 32
	SAFETY	**15**, 21
	Supports	11
	Stability	39, **66**

(table continues)

TABLE 6.1. *(continued)*

DOMAIN	INDICATORS	REFERENCES
	SPIRITUALITY	28
	Religion	21, 40, 47
	HAPPINESS	28, 30, 44
	Positive vision of life	44
	FREEDOM FROM STRESS	11, 56, 44
6. SELF-DETERMINATION	**AUTONOMY**	1, 2, 25, 27, 34, 50
	Independent functioning	5
	Independence/ interdependence	18, 41, 46, 48, 52, 53, 55, 57, 59, 68
	CHOICES	12, 24, 31, 34, 50, 58, 63, 66, 67
	Opportunities	6, 16, 17, 19, 37
	Options	23
	Preferences	45
	PERSONAL CONTROL	6, 11, 26, 35, 40, 58, 66
	Environmental control	7, 8, 31, 43, 61, 62, 65, 69
	Empowerment	66
	DECISIONS	6, 26, 58, 67
	Opportunities	16, 17, 37
	SELF-DIRECTION	29, 47
	Personal planning	54

(table continues)

TABLE 6.1. *(continued)*

DOMAIN	INDICATORS	REFERENCES
	SELF-DETERMINATION	13, 34
	RESIDENT INFLUENCE	71
	SELF-ADVOCACY	66
7. PERSONAL DEVELOPMENT	EDUCATION	16, 17, 21, 37, 47, 64, 65, 67, 70
	Culture	47
	Learning opportunities	9, 21, 68
	Attainment	25, 27, 28
	Intellectual development	54
	SKILLS	34, 48, 68
	Creativity and personal expression	20, 47, 51, 54
	Self-care	10
	For community life	10
	For home	16, 17, 37
	For employment	28
	PERSONAL DEVELOPMENT	13, 20, 34, 38, 48, 50, 51, 66, 71
	PERSONAL COMPETENCE	18, 24, 34, 52, 53, 55, 59
	FULFILLMENT	34, 50
	PURPOSEFUL ACTIVITY	20, 51

(table continues)

TABLE 6.1. *(continued)*

DOMAIN	INDICATORS	REFERENCES
8. RIGHTS	RIGHTS	4, 13, 23, 25, 27, 63
	Respect	24
	Basic human rights	66
	Freedom	66
	Citizenship	28
	CIVIC RESPONSIBILITIES	28, 34
	GUARDIANSHIP	47, 71
	ACTIVITIES (RELATING TO LOCAL AND NATIONAL GOVERNMENTS)	21, 40, 54
	DUE PROCESS	54

of many indicators; thus its presence is more significant. Such a high number of references about physical well-being is especially focused on the health and leisure indicators. The health indicator receives significant general attention, but it is also very specific regarding physical safety, which is important to everyone, but even more to individuals with more pervasive support needs. Leisure is stressed as a general indicator, which is consistent with leisure provision being cited as a compelling concern for individuals, families, and service providers. Another indicator included in the physical well-being domain is activities of daily living. The emphasis on this indicator embraces different types of activities related to community participation (Kennedy, Horner, Newton, & Kanda, 1990; Rapley & Hopgood, 1997).

The social inclusion dimension has received extensive attention from researchers since the 1980s. Deinstitutionalization and integration in the community fostered an important number of studies addressing the benefits of community versus institutional approaches. The aspects of inclusion versus segregation have become a determining factor for what was considered best practice. The social inclusion indicator that appears most often is community participation integration, followed by the assessment of the general dimension and residential environment. The community participation indicator is understood as related to presence, access, use, and participation in daily community activities. This indicator has been considered a key factor in comparing quality of life in different residential options (Dagnan et al., 1995), studying its relationship with personal characteristics (Che et al., 1993), and reflecting an individual's adjustment (Burchard et al., 1991). Residential environment has also been used to compare different residential options in order to analyze living conditions in specific centers of the population with more severe impairment (Dagnan, Ruddick, & Jones 1998; Kennedy et al., 1990). Other aspects that have been considered important in this dimension are the lifestyle, role, and status of the individual.

Within the dimension of interpersonal relations, the most mentioned indicators are interactions and family. The main interactions analyzed are social relations, although interaction at the work site and at home have also been studied. Freely chosen friendships and interpersonal relations are important aspects that have been analyzed. Within the family environment, research focuses on family relations; sometimes marital and parent-child relations are also mentioned. It is interesting to note that affective, sexual, and intimate relations have not received much attention in the research.

In self-determination the major indicator is autonomy, which is understood as personal independence, choices, and personal and environmental control. It has only been recently that the concept of self-determination has been related to the concept of quality of life, and we find that individuals with disability who present a better quality of life also enjoy higher levels of self-determination (Wehmeyer & Schalock, 2001; Wehmeyer & Schwartz, 1998).

Material well-being references concerned mainly employment and productivity. The relationship between employment and many other aspects of quality of life, such as financial independence, lifestyle, or community participation, have attracted the attention of many researchers. Research has also focused on financial issues, trying to identify factors related to income and financial security.

In terms of emotional well-being, contentment has been used as the major indicator. But many other aspects of emotional well-being are also taken into account, such as self-concept, spirituality, happiness, safety, and freedom from stress. In personal development the indicators of education and skills are especially important, although the general indicator of the dimension and personal competence is also present in research. Finally, in rights we find various indicators, although researchers have typically made a general analysis of this dimension.

Conclusion

In conclusion, since the 1960s, attention to people with mental retardation or intellectual disabilities has followed a progressive change from segregated to community environments. During the 1960s professionals and parents of people with disabilities demanded an improvement in the conditions of institutions, the deinstitutionalization of residents, and their inclusion in more community-based environments (Schalock, 2002). Then the dissemination of the principles of normalization significantly contributed to overcoming the conformism of satisfying basic individual needs, stressing the enhancement of quality of care giving. In recent decades there has been a proliferation of research specifically that addresses the assessment and enhancement of people's quality of life. Many of the articles reviewed in this chapter propose theoretical models and assessment instruments for this process as well as providing a driving force for new studies about the concept.

In the 1980s and 1990s the QOL concept was a landmark and to a certain extent became the criterion for assessing the success in the shift toward community models in housing and employment services. The main features of this research into quality of life for people with mental retardation or intellectual disabilities have included (Ionescu, 1995): the use of the QOL concept as an indicator of the effects of deinstitutionalization; the study of aging and its connection with quality of life; the increased importance given to subjective aspects of quality of life; the fact of having various objectives, including the point of view of the family; and the advancement toward more comprehensive models and those linked directly to intervention.

The review of literature about quality of life for people with mental retardation or intellectual disabilities in this chapter revealed the following trends: (a) the evaluation of the impact of different types of residences or housing in the quality of life of the individual, together with the changes derived from deinstitutionalization and the development of community approaches; (b) the evaluation of the impact of employment on one's quality of life; (c) the development of quality of life measurement procedures and instruments and the verification of their psychometric properties; and (d) the analysis of quality of life in specific disability groups, examining characteristics and differences according to age (specifically aging), type of disability, and cognitive level.

In addition to these trends, which are more objective and based on professional perspectives, other studies focused on analyzing the perceived quality of life and the relationships between quality of life and global satisfaction with life, on measuring consumer satisfaction with services, and on verifying changes in programs to improve the quality of organizations and services. More recently we have witnessed a merging of objective and subjective perspectives, especially with the emergence of person-centered approaches and ecological models of quality of life. We will continue to see these trends in the following chapter on aging.

APPENDIX 6.1
Mental Retardation and Intellectual Disabilities References Corresponding to Table 6.1

1. Apgar, D., Cook, S., & Lerman, P. (1998). *Life after Johnstone: Impacts on consumer competencies, behaviors and quality of life.* Research report. New Jersey Institute of Technology, Center for Architecture and Building Science Research.

2. Arostegi, I. (1998). *Evaluación de la calidad de vida en personas adultas con retraso mental en la comunidad autónoma del Pais Vasco.* Unpublished doctoral dissertation, Universidad de Deusto, Spain.

3. Borthwick-Duffy, S. A., Widaman, K. F., Little, T. D., & Eyman, R. K. (1992). *Foster family care for persons with mental retardation.* Washington, DC: American Association on Mental Retardation.

4. Brown, R., & Brown, P., & Bayer, M. (1994). A quality of life model: New challenges arising from a six-year study. In D. Goode (Ed.), *Quality of life for persons with disabilities: International perspectives and issues* (pp. 39–56). Cambridge, MA: Brookline.

5. Burchard, S., Hasazi, J., Gordon, L., & Yoe, J. (1991). An examination of lifestyle and adjustment in three community residential alternatives. *Research in Developmental Disabilities, 12,* 127–142.

6. Cabada, J. M. (1998). Calidad de vida de las personas con discapacidad. *Polibea, 48,* 18–27.

7. Campo, S., Sharpton, W., Thompson, B., & Sexton, D. (1996). Measurement characteristics of the quality of life index when used with adults who have severe mental retardation. *American Journal on Mental Retardation, 100*(5), 546–550.

8. Campo, S. F., Sharpton, W. R., Thompson, B., & Sexton, D. (1997). Correlates of the quality of life of adults with severe or profound mental retardation. *Mental Retardation, 35*(5), 329–337.

9. Carnaby, S. (1997). Une nouvelle évaluation de la vie en milieu ordinaire. Comparaison entre deus études de cas portant sur des services pour personnes avec un handicap mental, l'un situé à Milan et l'autre à Londres. *Revue Européenne du Handicap Mental, 4*(5), 22–39.

10. Che, T. H., Bruininks, R., Lakin, K., & Hayden, M. (1993). Personal competencies and community participation in small community residential programs: A multiple discriminant analysis. *American Journal on Mental Retardation, 98*(3), 390–399.

11. Chubon, R. A., Clayton, K. S., & Vandergriff, D. V. (1995). An exploratory study comparing the quality of life of South Carolinians with mental retardation and spinal cord injury. *Rehabilitation Counseling Bulletin, 39*(2), 107–118.

12. Conroy, J. (1996). The small ICF/MR program: Dimensions of quality and cost. *Mental Retardation, 34*(1), 13–26.

13. Cortina, A., Gómez, M., & Guell, M. (1998). Retraso mental: Integración laboral y calidad de vida. *Revista de Servicios Sociales y Política Social, 42,* 41–61.

14. Cummins, R. (1997). Assessing quality of life for people with disabilities. In R. I. Brown (Ed.), *Quality of life for people with disabilities: Models, research, and practice* (2nd ed., pp. 116–150). Cheltenham, England: Stanley Thornes.

15. Cummins, R. (1991). The comprehensive quality of life scale — intellectual disability: An initial report. *Australia and New Zealand Journal of Developmental Disabilities, 17*(2), 259–264.

16. Dagnan, D., Jones, J., & Ruddick, L. (1994). The psychometric properties of a scale for assessing quality of life of people with learning disabilities in residential care. *British Journal of Developmental Disabilities, 40,* 98–103.

17. Dagnan, D., Look, R., Ruddick, L., & Jones, J. (1995). Changes in the quality of life of people with learning disabilities who moved from hospital to live in community-based homes. *International Journal of Rehabilitation Research, 18,* 115–122.

18. Eggelton, I., Robertson, S., Ryan, J., & Kober, R. (1999). The impact of employment on the quality of life of people with an intellectual disability. *Journal of Vocational Rehabilitation, 13,* 95–107.

19. Emerson, E., & Hatton, C. (1996). Deinstitutionalization in the U.K. and Ireland: Outcome for service users. *Journal of Intellectual and Developmental Disability, 21*(1), 17–37.

20. Evans, D., Burns, J., Robinson, W., & Garret, O. (1985). The quality of life questionnaire: A multidimensional measure. *American Journal of Community Psychology, 13*(3), 305–322.

21. Felce, D., & Perry, J. (1995). Quality of life: Its definition and measurement. *Research in Developmental Disabilities, 16*(1), 51–74.

22. Felce, D., & Perry, J. (1997). Quality of life: The scope of the term and its breadth of measurement. In R. I. Brown (Ed.), *Quality of life for people with disabilities: Models, research, and practice* (2nd ed., pp. 56–71). Cheltenham, England: Stanley Thornes.

23. Fernandez, S., & Cobo, J. (1999). Calidad de vida, calidad del servicio. *Minusval, 121,* 35–37.

24. Fleming, I., & Stenfert, B. (1990). Evaluation of a community care project for people with learning difficulties. *Journal of Mental Deficiency Research, 34,* 451-464.

25. Gardner, J. F., Nudler, S., & Chapman, M. S. (1997). Personal outcomes as measures of quality. *Mental Retardation, 35*(4), 295–305.

26. Goode, D. (1997). Assessing the quality of life of adults with profound disabilities. In R. I. Brown (Ed.), *Quality of life for people with disabilities: Models, research, and practice* (2nd ed., pp. 72–90). Cheltenham, England: Stanley Thornes.

27. Gould, M. (1999). The council on quality and leadership in supports for people with disabilities. Personal outcomes chart book. [On-line]. Available: www.ncor.org/ncorchartbook/frame2.htm

28. Halpern, A. (1993). Quality of life as a conceptual framework for evaluating transition outcomes. *Exceptional Children, 59*(6), 486–498.

29. Harner, C., & Heal, L. (1993). *The multifaceted lifestyle satisfaction scale* (MLSS): Psychometric properties of an interview schedule for assessing personal satisfaction of adults with limited intelligence. *Research in Developmental Disabilities, 14,* 221–236.

30. Hawkins, B., Kim, K., & Eklund, S. (1995). Validity and reliability of a five-dimensional life satisfaction index. *Mental Retardation, 33*(5), 295–303.

31. Heal, L. W., Borthwick-Duffy, S. A., & Saunders, R. R. (1996). Assessment of quality of life. In J. W. Jacobson & J. A. Mulick (Eds.), *Manual of diagnosis and professional practice in mental retardation* (pp. 199–209). Washington, DC: American Psychological Association.

32. Hogg, J., & Lambe, L. (1997). An ecological perspective on the quality of life of people with intellectual disabilities as they age. In R. I. Brown (Ed.), *Quality of life for people with disabilities: Models, research, and practice* (2nd ed., pp. 201–227). Cheltenham, England: Stanley Thornes.

33. Hoover, J., Wheeler, J., & Reetz, L. (1992). Development of a leisure satisfaction scale for use with adolescents and adults with mental retardation: Initial findings. *Education and Training in Mental Retardation, 27,* 153–160.

34. Hughes, C., Hwang, B., Kim, J. H., Eisenman, L., & Killian, D. (1995). Quality of life in applied research: A review and analysis of empirical measures. *American Journal on Mental Retardation, 99*(6), 623–641.

35. Ionescu, S. (1995). La recherche dans le domaine de la qualité de vie des personnes présentant une déficience intellectuelle. *Revue Francophone de la Déficience Intellectuelle, 8*(1), 5–17.

36. Ittenbach, R., Bruininks, R., Thurlow, M., & McGrew, K. (1993). Community integration of young adults with mental retardation: A multivariate analysis of adjustment. *Research in Developmental Disabilities, 14,* 275–290.

37. Jones, J., Dagnan, D., Trower, P., & Ruddick, L. (1996). People with learning disabilities living in community-based homes: The relationship of quality of life with age and disability. *International Journal of Rehabilitation Research, 19,* 219–227.

38. Kennedy, C., Horner, R., Newton, J., & Kanda, E. (1990). Measuring the activity patterns of adults with severe disabilities using the resident lifestyle inventory. *Journal of The Association for Persons with Severe Handicaps, 15*(2), 79–85.

39. Kiernan, W. E., Sanchez, R., & Schalock, R. L. (1989). Epilogue. Economics, industry, and disability in the future. In W. E. Kiernan & R. L. Schalock (Eds.), *Economics, industry, and disability: A look ahead* (pp. 365–374). Baltimore: Paul H. Brookes.

40. Kinney, W., & Coyle, C. (1992). Predicting life satisfaction among adults with physical disabilities. *Archives of Physical Medicine and Rehabilitation, 73,* 863–869.

41. Kozleski, E., & Sands, D. (1992). The yardstick of social validity: Evaluating quality of life as perceived by adults without disabilities. *Education and Training in Mental Retardation, 27*(2), 119–131.

42. Lai Chun Yu, A., Jupp, J. J., & Taylor, A. (1996). The discriminate validity of the Lifestyle Satisfaction Scale for the assessment of Australian adults with intellectual disabilities. *Journal of Intellectual and Developmental Disability, 21*(1), 3–15.

43. Leibowitz, M., McClain, J., Evans, E., Ruma, P., & Rauner, T. (1994). Client perceptions of quality of life in accredited and nonaccredited community residential facilities. *Journal of Developmental and Physical Disabilities, 6*(4), 339–46.

44. Matikka, L. M. (1996). Effects of psychological factors on the perceived quality of life of people with intellectual disabilities. *Journal of Applied Research in Intellectual Disabilities, 9*(2), 115–128.

45. Neumayer, R., & Bleasdale, M. (1996). Personal lifestyle preferences of people with an intellectual disability. *Journal of Intellectual and Developmental Disability, 21*(2), 91–114.

46. Newton, J. S., Ard, W., Jr., Horner, R. H., & Toews, J. D. (1996). Focusing on values and lifestyle outcomes in an effort to improve the quality of residential services in Oregon. *Mental Retardation, 34*(1), 1–12.

47. Ouellette-Kuntz, H. (1990). A pilot study in the use of the Quality of Life Interview Schedule. *Social Indicators Research, 23,* 283–298.

48. Parmenter, T. (1992). Quality of life of people with developmental disabilities. *International Review of Research in Mental Retardation, 18,* 247–287.

49. Parmenter, T., & Donelly, M. (1997). An analysis of the dimensions of quality of life. In R. I. Brown (Ed.), *Quality of life for people with disabilities: Models, research, and practice* (2nd ed., pp. 201–227). Cheltenham, England: Stanley Thornes.

50. Perry, J., & Felce, D. (1995). Objective assessments of quality of life: How much do they agree with each other? *Journal of Community and Applied Social Psychology, 5,* 1–19.

51. Pilon, W., Arsenault, R., & Paré, C. (1997). La qualité de vie des personnes viellisantes présentant une déficience intellectuelle résidant dans la communauté comparée à celle des personnes viellisantes de la population générale. *Revue Francophone de la Déficience Intellectuelle, 8*(2), 115–127.

52. Rapley, M., & Beyer, M. (1996). Daily activity, community participation, and quality of life in an ordinary housing network. *Journal of Applied Research in Intellectual Disabilities, 9*(1), 31–39.

53. Rapley, M., & Beyer, S. (1998). Daily activity, community participation, and quality of life in an ordinary housing network: A two-year follow-up. *Journal of Applied Research in Intellectual Disabilities, 11*(1), 34–43.

54. Rasmussen, L. (1993). *Quality of life for parents of a child with a developmental disability.* Unpublished doctoral dissertation, University of Calgary, Alberta, Canada.

55. Reiter, S., & Bendov, D. (1996). The self-concept and quality of life of two groups of learning-disabled adults living at home and in group homes. *British Journal of Developmental Disabilities, 42,* 97–111.

56. Rosen, M., Simon, E. W., & McKinsey, L. (1995). Subjective measure of quality of life. *Mental Retardation, 33*(1), 31–34.

57. Sands, D., Kozleski, E., & Goodwin, L. (1991). Whose needs are we meeting? Results of a consumer satisfaction survey of persons with developmental disabilities in Colorado. *Research in Developmental Disabilities, 12,* 297–314.

58. Schalock, R. L. (1994). The concept of quality of life and its current applications in the field of mental retardation/developmental disabilities. In D. Goode (Ed.), *Quality of life for persons with disabilities: International perspectives and issues* (pp. 266–284). Cambridge, MA: Brookline.

59. Schalock, R., Bonham, G., & Marchand, C. (2000). Consumer-based quality of life assessment: A path model of perceived satisfaction. *Evaluation and Program Planning, 23*(1), 77–87.

60. Schalock, R., & Genung, T. (1993). Placement from a community-based mental retardation program: A 15-year follow-up. *American Journal on Mental Retardation, 98*(3), 400–407.

61. Schalock, R., Keith, K., Hoffman, K., & Karan, O. (1989). Quality of life: Its measurement and use. *Mental Retardation, 27*(1), 25–31.

62. Sinnott-Oswald, M., Gliner, J. A., & Spencer, K. C. (1991). Supported and sheltered employment: Quality of life issues among workers with disabilities. *Education and Training in Mental Retardation, 26*(4), 338–397.

63. Smull, M. (1999). *Essential lifestyle planning and other topics.* Paper presented at the annual meeting of the American Association of Mental Retardation, New Orleans, LA.

64. Stark, J., & Goldsbury, T. (1990). Quality of life from childhood to adulthood. In R. Schalock (Ed.), *Quality of life: Perspectives and issues* (pp. 71–84). Washington, DC: American Association on Mental Retardation.

65. Storey, K. (1997). Quality of life issues in social skills assessment of persons with disabilities. *Education and Training in Mental Retardation and Developmental Disabilities, 32*(3), 197–200.

66. Taylor, S. J. (1994). In support of research on quality of life, but against QOL. In D. Goode (Ed.), *Quality of life for persons with disabilities: International perspectives and issues* (pp. 260–265). Cambridge, MA: Brookline.

67. Timmons, V., & Brown, R. (1997). Quality of life issues for children with handicaps. In R. I. Brown (Ed.), *Quality of life for people with disabilities: Models, research, and practice* (2nd ed., pp. 183–200). Cheltenham, England: Stanley Thornes.

68. Van Gennep, A. (1997). Quality of community living in the Netherlands. *British Journal of Developmental Disabilities, 43,* 1–14.

69. Verdugo, M. A. (1994). El cambio de paradigma en la concepción del retraso mental: La nueva definición de la AAMR. *Siglo Cero, 25*(3), 5–24.

70. Vreeke, G. J., Janssen, C. G., Resnick, S., & Stolk, J. (1997). The quality of life of people with mental retardation: In research of an adequate approach. *International Journal of Rehabilitation Research, 20,* 289–301.

71. Wadsworth, J. S., & Harper, D. C. (1991). Increasing the reliability of self-report by adults with moderate mental retardation. *Journal of The Association for Persons with Severe Handicaps, 16*(4), 228–232.

CHAPTER 7

Aging

Overview

People of age often display a more fragile state of health, with different types of illness and deterioration linked to aging. However, this does not hinder elderly people from attaining acceptable levels of physical, psychological, and social well-being. The first trends in psychological studies aimed at enhancing the living conditions of people of age were focused on analyzing intellectual, memory, and learning skills. Research investigated individuals' adaptation to aging and retirement. Subsequently the level of activity and life satisfaction was examined. It was then that many studies about older people began to concentrate on the increase in life span and on quality of life.

Current quality of life (QOL) studies attempt to deepen our understanding of the objective factors that lead to individuals' well-being and the psychological processes that lessen deterioration and provide the individual with satisfaction and happiness. Together with this kind of research, studies have examined service delivery issues and social support for people of age. Efforts are made to "adding life to years rather than years to life" (Clark, 1995). Hence the QOL concept covers different factors that have also been termed "social determinants of health" (Raphael, 1996). Moreover, as we will see, there is an increased attention to the experience of the individual and his or her participation in the control over life, health, and the disease processes.

This chapter is written within the framework of the three contextual factors summarized in Table 1.1: the emergence of a strong movement to protect the rights of people of age; a focus on environmental factors that ameliorate the aging process; and an emphasis on providing programs and services to people of age based on principles such as freedom, independence, opportunity, and reducing the discrepancy between personalized needs and resources. The chapter includes the following three sections: (a) the variables that influence the quality of life of older individuals, (b) aging and intellectual disability, and (c) domains and indicators of quality of life. The chapter concludes with a discussion of the continued need to develop natural supports and person-centered programs for older people.

Variables That Influence the Quality of Life of Older Individuals

Quality of life depends on several environmental and personal factors that influence an individual's behavior. Quality of life for people of age is analyzed using several QOL indicators, including health, functional skills (ability to take care of oneself), financial situation (having a pension and/or income), social relations (family and friends), physical activity, social and health care services, comfort in one's home (and immediate surroundings), satisfaction with life, and cultural and learning opportunities.

Sociodemographic and personality variables are used frequently to evaluate subjective well-being. Differences in the gender, age, marital status, and place of residence seem to be determining factors. However, quality of life for older adults seems not to depend as much on the context (comparable whether living in their own homes or in nursing homes) as on other variables such as age (better in younger people than in older people), gender (better in men than in women), and social status (better in people of higher social status) (Moreno & Ximenez, 1996).

Urciuoli, Dello Buono, Padoani, and De Leo (1998) evaluated the differences in perception of quality of life (e.g., physical health, cognitive functions, depression and anxiety, sexual functioning, social functioning, and religiousness) among people over 85 years of age living in nursing homes or at home. The authors did not find differences between institutionalized oldest-old individuals and those living at home, although the former are less self-reliance and more dependent regarding basic functions of daily living. Similarly, Shatahmasebi, Davies, and Wenger (1992) did not find a correlation between people's longevity and quality of life.

The most remarkable characteristic of the research reviewed is the person's autonomy and independence in different contexts (Clark, 1991); the deterioration of functional skills has an extremely negative impact on other facets of life. In fact, it is loss of independence that determines greater support requirements and, very often, the separation from the natural family and community context. Newson and Shutz (1996) analyzed the relationship between physical functioning, social support, depressive symptoms, and satisfaction with life. The authors concluded that physical functioning is a predictor of social support and that the latter significantly predicts depressive symptoms and satisfaction with life.

Emotional aspects proved to be very interesting. Kempen, Jelicic, and Ormel (1997), in a sample of 5,279 older individuals, examined the effects of some personality characteristics in relation to chronic medical morbidity and health. The results indicated that personality characteristics, such as neuroticism and self-reliance, had a significant influence on health-related quality of life (HRQOL) levels and the individuals' perceptions of those levels.

Received and perceived social support is one of the determining variables of older people's quality of life. Functional deterioration, together with limitations of personal autonomy in aged people, makes it necessary to secure help from other people to enable the elderly to continue to live in their own homes without further problems. A lack of family or conjugal support reduces the motivation of the aged individual to take care of himself or herself and is detrimental to the state of health (Ors & Laguna, 1997). When there is not sufficient natural social support, elderly people need specific support services to avoid institutionalization. The broader the social support for the individual, the lower the probability of the individual becoming ill. Hence, there is a need to implement intervention programs aimed at families as well as self-help groups, neighbors, and volunteers (Fernández-Ballesteros, Zamarrón, & Maciá, 1996).

The role of professionals is crucial in the quality of life experienced by the elderly. Wolkenstein and Butler (1992) explored whether or not quality of life was a meaningful concept for the healthy elderly population and how this group expected physicians to contribute to enhancing their quality of life. Physicians were perceived in both the opinion survey and in the focus group as deficient in appreciating, understanding, and contributing positively to the participant's quality of life. Physicians and other professionals caring for this population have to be attentive to the development of comprehensive psychosocial assessment and not only an analysis of physical well-being.

Quality of life perception in people of age and patients with chronic illness is not linked closely to objective indicators such as demographic features and the use of health care services. Conversely, subjective indicators (patients' perception of their health, memory, intellectual deterioration, physical functioning, and financial issues) are correlated with overall quality of life (Pearlman, 1991).

Studies of the quality of life for people of age with serious disabilities, such as Alzheimer's disease, tend to focus on quality of institutional care in nursing home settings. In such cases, factors related to interactional aspects seem to be more relevant. Montoro (1999) proposes a model for institutional care and analyzes the influence of predictive factors in welfare quality. The model involves three levels: institutional (environment, type and number of professionals, institutional structure), relational (residents and relatives), and interactional. The author found that the most remarkable aspects of welfare quality in aged people with or without disability refer to the institutional level (e.g., whether the center is for profit, familial configuration, percentage of staff per bed, stress training, and turnover), followed by family involvement and participation, and indicators of relational level (e.g., participation and informal care giving of relatives). However, in contrast to what was expected, factors in the interactional level, such as communication skills and personal conflict, were not significant with regard to welfare quality.

Aging and Intellectual Disability

Older people with an intellectual disability frequently find themselves within a familial and social caring system that has not been adapted previously to their needs. And they have to face the challenges of retirement and aging essentially within the family environment and with a significant lack of support. However, adults with intellectual disability currently live longer than in the past, have better health and more experiences, and age with a higher level of dignity than in previous generations (Janicki, 1996). Despite the fact that community inclusion offers new opportunities for an improved quality of life for this group, it has also brought with it greater risks related to physical health, mental and behavioral health, and rights.

Physical Health

Older people with intellectual disability have needs in physical health depending on social and economic circumstances of daily living. As shown in a recent study by the World Health Organization (Evenhuis et al., 2000), the circumstances of these individuals in most of the world are related to undeveloped economic conditions in which their fundamental priority (just as for the rest of the population) is basic health welfare, adequate nutrition, a home, education, human rights, and stable economy and society. However, research has so far focused primarily on developed countries. Consequently, it is critical to foster immediate and proactive cross-cultural research. At the same time, it is also necessary to develop efficient strategies aimed at promoting specific actions in developing countries.

People with intellectual disability present a greater variety of health disorders than individuals without such disabilities. These problems become more significant when the individual ages, because of increasing physical deterioration and the development of secondary conditions related to their disabilities. Health conditions have been related to obesity, hypertension, epilepsy, cerebral palsy, poor dental health, higher level of psychiatric morbidity, coronary heart diseases, and stroke. These conditions are more common — and their deterioration is also more rapid — in some etiologies such as Down's syndrome (Hawkins, 1997, 1999).

Physical and functional decline in older age requires an in-depth evaluation, given its potential complexity. Sensory and motor problems and communication impairments in people with intellectual disabilities restrict evaluation of their health to an even greater extent (Evenhuis et al., 2000). This is why some authors put forward an evaluation approach using a comprehensive and interdisciplinary perspective (Henderson & Davidson, 2000).

The training and education of primary care professionals in prevention and treatment skills for health conditions in this population should be a priority in services and programs. People with intellectual disability and their caregivers should know and apply healthy practices in nutrition, hygiene, substance abuse reduction, and sexuality (Evenhuis et al., 2000). In addition, there are many challenges that still face research in its effort to raise awareness of the specific development of some disorders within this population and to analyze the efficacy of different interventions.

Mental and Behavioral Health

Epidemiological studies still have a long way to go regarding this population, because we do not yet know much about their aging process. However, most studies comparing them with the general population find that mental and behavioral disorders are more pervasive in people with intellectual disabilities throughout their life span (Dalton & Janicki, 1999; Moos, 1999; Thorpe, Davidson, & Janicki, 2000). Psychiatric disorders are less frequent than affective ones in these people (Thorpe et al.), but people have a higher risk of exhibiting a mental disorder when they age.

Mental disorders in older people with intellectual disability have a direct impact on their cognitive and affective functioning, with negative effects on their general functioning level and quality of life. The interaction between biological, psychological, and social factors in the aging process is fundamental and has to be accurately evaluated for each individual. The aging process is characterized by its constant change in different facets of the individual. Besides, individuals age at different rates (Moos, 1999). Generally speaking, people with intellectual disability play more restricted social roles and functions, with fewer opportunities for learning experiences (World Health Organization, 2000).

The needs of those with intellectual disabilities change as people age. The significant increase in life expectancy of the population with cognitive impairment highlights this fact. The examination of treatment and support for aging people with intellectual disability stresses the importance of focusing on two types of basic needs (Moos, 1999) to ensure a minimum level of quality of life and reduce risks in mental health conditions. Among the most useful preventive strategies are promoting positive lifestyles and planning for appropriate social supports, generally reducing institutional alternatives that lead to social and emotional decline (World Health Organization, 2000).

Although empirical data are sparse concerning normal psychological functioning and developmental processes throughout the life spans of people with intellectual disabilities, professionals should become aware of mental health needs in older members of this population (Thorpe et al., 2000). Together with a new awareness by everyone supporting individuals with intellectual disability, some professionals (e.g., mental health, psychiatric, neurological, psychogeriatric, and clinicians) should be trained fully in the evaluation of and intervention with people with intellectual disability (World Health Organization, 2000). The complexity of the evaluation process requires a holistic approach to the problems, and special attention is required to improve the reliability and validity of the process undertaken. All this would be of great value in the understanding and treatment of dementia and other mental conditions in adults with intellectual disability (Thorpe et al., 2000).

Rights
It is estimated that at least 60 million people worldwide have some degree of intellectual disability and that over the next few years their number will increase (World Health Organization, 2000). Like other people, older adults with intellectual disabilities have needs related to their daily living. Nevertheless, people of age with disabilities are one of the most vulnerable sections of world minorities. Those living in less developed countries, like anybody within the general population, should be assured primarily of basic health welfare, adequate nutrition, a home in which to live, education, and stable economy and society. These are the first and foremost human rights of every individual in any society.

Aged people, together with their close relatives or people in whichever place they choose to live, have endured traditional cutbacks in their rights to a decent life. The lack of adequate services and support planning has had a dramatically negative effect on their quality of life. This situation has grown more profoundly for people with intellectual disability, because they are especially vulnerable (Herr & Weber, 1999) and their life expectancy has increased in such a short time and at such a significant rate that it has created enormous challenges to service providers and policymakers (Schalock, DeVries, & Lebsack, 1999). Moreover, the widespread stereotype that in the past equated them with childish individuals has restricted others' expectations for them and has had a negative impact on their rights and social functioning.

Care for older people with intellectual disabilities must be viewed within the context of life span development. Approaches and policies conceived for an aged population should embrace people with intellectual disabilities, implementing additional supports required for the enjoyment of a healthy and fulfilled life (Hogg, Lucchino, Wang, & Janicki, 2000). The objective in developing services is to ensure respect for individuals and their families, the inclusion of needs and wishes of the individual in self-tailored planning, the development of support plans aimed at minimizing the restrictions to community participation, and promoting the individual's growth and autonomy (World Health Organization, 2000). Consequently, the lines of action to attain quality aging in this population should focus on fostering community inclusion, self-determination, and maximum family support. And these principles should be applied earlier in a person's life so that these individuals can reach a fully developed potential in their old age.

In the past decade we have witnessed the initiation of significant changes in welfare for people of age with intellectual disability, which reflects an improved recognition of their rights. Such changes need to be more widely available in the future. This will involve certain challenges, including the definition of (a) which life domains should be the focus of services and (b) what are the major outcomes resulting in an enhanced quality of life for service consumers (Schalock et al., 1999).

Nonetheless, we still have to prevent all forms of social discrimination experienced by these individuals, including all instances of abuse and neglect. It is fundamental, therefore, to create a vision to remove prejudices and negative attitudes about people with disability (Herr & Weber, 1999). Moreover, as many choices and opportunities as possible should be offered in every sphere of life. Only by having different opportunities and choices can the individual exercise his or her rights as any other citizen.

Domains and Indicators of Quality of Life

Research reviewed in this chapter also supports the QOL model proposed in Figure 2.2. The most common QOL domain in the literature has been physical well-being, present in 81 out of 101 studies reviewed for this chapter. The social inclusion domain is cited by almost half of the articles (46 times), and emotional well-being by 34. Personal development is mentioned in a quarter of the total references (24), and interpersonal relations in 18. Finally, rights, self-determination, and material well-being domains are referenced in only a tenth of the studies (10, 10, and 7 respectively).

The most often cited indicators of physical well-being are health, global physical well-being, and health care (45, 25, and 21 respectively), residential environment and supports in social inclusion (24 and 20), psychological well-being and contentment in emotional well-being (15 and 12), personal competence in personal development (10), supports in interpersonal relations (11), and rights (10). Especially outstanding, therefore, are indicators cited in the physical well-being and social inclusion categories, representing a quarter of the total reviewed studies, while the other five indicators were present in 10% of the studies. As far as rights were concerned, the indicator coincides with the domain because most articles agree to single out a cluster of individual's rights instead of analyzing them separately.

Concern about physical health, as the most cited domain in research into quality of life of aged people, shows an ordinary priority in welfare programs and services. Health conditions are so important in older people that it determines many other potential components of quality of life. This is due to the fact that the individual's perception is drastically modified when serious health problems arise. Consequently, it is essential to evaluate and plan support in this area. Synonyms related to the health indicator include *illness, fitness, status physical functioning, physical independence, activity, pain,* and *medication*.

TABLE 7.1
Quality of Life Domains and Indicators in Aging

DOMAIN	INDICATORS	REFERENCES
1. PHYSICAL WELL-BEING	HEALTH Physical health (illness, fitness) Status physical functioning Pain Morbidity Medication Physical independence activity	3, 5, 7, **12**, **18**, **19**, **20**, 21, 22, 25, 26, 27, 34, 35, 37, 41, 43, 46, 47, 51, 52, 54, 55, 63, 65, **66**, **67**, 69, 70, 72, **73**, 75, **78**, 79, 80, 84, 85, 87, **100**
	Sensory skills (visual, hearing)	5, **11**, 13, 64, **66**, 76, **95**
	PHYSICAL WELL-BEING (GLOBAL)	1, 4, 5, 7, 8, 10, **12**, 13, **16**, **18**, **19**, 22, 24, 30, 33, 47, 52, 65, **66**, 68, 72, 79, 84, 94, **99**
	HEALTH CARE Medical assistance Institutional care Care services	3, 17, **18**, **20**, 25, **31**, 35, 36, 50, 55, 62, 67, 71, 72, 76, 78, **86**, **89**, 90, 93, 98
	ACTIVITIES OF DAILY LIVING Self-care Leisure Recreation activities	13, 14, 15, **20**, 42, 46, 52, 81, **85**

(table continues)

Note. Domains and indicators are ordered from most frequent to least frequent based on the number of references found. Conceptual references are printed in boldface and applied research references in regular font. Numbered references are identified in Appendix 7.1.

Table 7.1. *(continued)*

DOMAIN	INDICATORS	REFERENCES
	LEISURE	**19**, 33
	NUTRITION	86
	MOBILITY	5
2. SOCIAL INCLUSION	RESIDENTIAL ENVIRONMENT Living environment Service provision Quality of services	1, 15, 17, 25, 27, 29, **38**, 43, 45, 48, 49, 53, 56, 61, 62, 73, 74, 86, 88, 91, 94, 96, 97, 98
	SUPPORTS	2, 6, 7, 10, **11**, 18, 25, 30, 35, **39**, 42, 60, 62, 65, 80, 82, **84**, **92**, 93, 94
	SOCIAL INCLUSION Community presence	48, 70, 80, 91, 96
	VOLUNTEER ACTIVITIES Participation Activity	14, **23**, 26, 43
	ROLES	80
3. EMOTIONAL WELL-BEING	PSYCHOLOGICAL WELL-BEING	3, 7, 21, 22, **24**, 44, 45, 47, 51, 54, **58**, 68, 69, **83**, 89
	CONTENTMENT Satisfaction Happiness Life satisfaction	4, 8, **12**, **16**, **24**, 28, 33, **37**, 57, 80, **89**, 93

(table continues)

Table 7.1. *(continued)*

DOMAIN	INDICATORS	REFERENCES
	MENTAL HEALTH	41, 43, 45, 51, 64, 70, 86
	SELF-CONCEPT Self-esteem	14, 15
4. PERSONAL DEVELOPMENT	PERSONAL COMPETENCE Functional capacity Deficits	2, 6, 9, 10, 11, 25, 37, 38, 39, 40, 42, 43, 77, 86, 91, 100
	EDUCATION	8, 17, 33, 43, 57, 82, 101
	SKILLS	16, 23
5. INTER PERSONAL RELATIONS	SUPPORTS	2, 10, 11, 28, 29, 42, 44, 59, 65, 68, 71
	INTERACTIONS Social life Social relations Meaningful activity Participation Relationship with physicians	44, 61, 68, 91, 99
	FRIENDSHIPS Friendly relationships Loneliness	22, 26, 46, 47, 86
6. RIGHTS	RIGHTS	2, 4, 25, 38, 40, 42, 77, 86, 91, 100

(table continues)

Table 7.1. *(continued)*

DOMAIN	INDICATORS	REFERENCES
7. MATERIAL WELL-BEING	EMPLOYMENT Work Incentives Retirement	4, 38, 49, 55
	SOCIAL ECONOMIC STATUS	28, 29
	HOUSING	90
	FINANCIAL	72
8. SELF-DETERMINATION	AUTONOMY	16, 40, 42, 86
	SELF-DIRECTION	37, 42, 47
	CHOICES	45, 86, 91
	PERSONAL GOALS/ VALUES	35

The place where the person lives and its characteristics are another vital component of quality of life in elderly people. Some studies compare different housing choices and their effects on quality of life perceived by older people; others evaluate quality of services in nursing homes and institutions in order to develop improvement plans. As more community-oriented models have been developed, research has shifted its interest toward supports. As a result, studies analyze existing social support resources, support networks, and the roles of families and service providers. Moreover, and from a different but supplementary perspective, supports are considered the most important indicator to establish appropriate interpersonal relations. Together with concern about physical well-being and the analysis of housing and support received, research has also focused on psychological and emotional functioning and the individual's satisfaction with life.

Conclusion

In conclusion, quality of life in older adults is considered an important factor in promoting health and optimizing the aging process and rehabilitation efforts (Raphael, 1996). Different conceptualizations of quality of life within the field have embraced a multidimensional approach that takes into account not only physical functioning, energy, and personal vitality but also psychological and emotional well-being, lack of behavioral problems, social and sexual functioning, perceived and received supports, together with satisfaction with one's life and health perceptions (R. I. Brown, 2000a; De Leo, René, & Diekstra, 1998; Schalock et al., 1999; Wolkenstein & Butler, 1992).

In geriatrics the attention of service providers and professionals to people of age has included a conceptual shift toward a different set of ethics based on the empowerment of the consumer and oriented by gerontology and the field of developmental disabilities (Clark, 1995). Accordingly, R. I. Brown (2000a) stresses the importance of maximizing independence, choices, and appropriate support, together with the individual's empowerment and self-perception. Schalock et al. (1999) propose that the challenge is to strive for equity, empowerment, and inclusion.

Throughout the literature reviewed in this chapter, one finds reference to the enhancement of practices based on the implications of the principles of quality of life (R. I. Brown, 2000a), natural inclusion into general infrastructures (Hogg et al., 2000), and the development of holistic evaluations of mental health problems (Thorpe et al., 2000). The literature also stresses that we should not overlook the fundamental role played by professionals in the enhancement of quality of life and in the need for improved professional training.

Despite the development of natural supports and person-centered programs, the number of older people in nursing homes is still growing at a high rate throughout much of the world. There is still a long way to go to convert the prevalent care model into a more person-enhancing approach. Older people living in nursing homes usually exhibit individual characteristics related to dependence in daily life. The institution itself often presents very negative structural and organizational characteristics (e.g., lack of contact with the outside world, lack of daily life activities within the center, and lack of personal decision making) influencing the quality of life for the residents.

From a policy and program planning point of view, people of age with intellectual disabilities should have access to general population health infrastructures, thus favoring natural inclusion (Hogg et al., 2000). In addition, a common theme in the literature is that services and supports should adjust to each individual in order to foster and promote participation in valued social roles (Conliffe & Walsh, 1999; Thorpe et al., 2000).

From an ecological point of view, it is proposed both in the literature reviewed and in this *Handbook* that we develop a wider concept of the lives of people of age with intellectual disability, relating to the family, neighbors, friends, service providers, informal community support, and the political and philosophical context in which they find themselves (R. I. Brown, 1997; Hogg et al., 2000). The ecological approach to quality of life underlines the nature of the interaction between each person and the larger environment and is thus more suitable for the analysis of physical, social, and psychological factors that affect the lives of the older people who are intellectually disabled. However, we should bear in mind the potential cultural differences within care models developed in different countries.

Adults with intellectual disability play an active role in their communities and feel more satisfied about themselves and their lives when they lead an independent life (Edgerton, 1996). In recent years research and attention in the field of aging and intellectual disability has emphasized the importance of the individual in developing choices, acting according to personal interests, and exhibiting self-determination (Hawkins, 1999). With all these, it is expected that the behavioral adaptation patterns and the individual's quality of life will improve.

APPENDIX 7.1
Aging References Corresponding to Table 7.1

1. Allen, P. (1995). Evaluating quality. In D. Pilling & G. Watson (Eds.), *Evaluating quality in services for disabled and older people* (pp. 107–113). London: Jessica Kingsley.

2. Ansello, E. F., & Janicki, M. (2000). The aging of nations. In M. Janicki & E. Ansello (Eds.), *Community support for aging adults with lifelong disabilities* (pp. 3–18). Baltimore: Paul H. Brookes.

3. Avis, N. E. (1998). Quality of life in older adults with HIV disease. *Research on Aging, 20*(6), 822–846.

4. Bearon, L. B. (1989). No great expectations: The underpinnings of life satisfaction for older women. *The Gerontologist, 29*(6), 772–778.

5. Bess, F. H., Lichtenstein, M. J., & Logan, S. A. (1990). Functional impact of hearing loss on the elderly. *American Speech-Language-Hearing Association, 19*, 144–149.

6. Bigby, C. (2000). Models of parental planning. In M. P. Janicki & E. F. Ansello (Eds.), *Community supports for aging adults with lifelong disabilities* (pp. 81–95). Baltimore: Paul H. Brookes.

7. Bowling, A., & Browne, P. D. (1991). Social networks, health and emotional well-being among the oldest old in London. *Journal of Gerontology, 46*(1), 20–32.

8. Brockett, R. G. (1985). The relationship between self-directed learning readiness and life satisfaction among older adults. *Adult Education Quarterly, 35*(4), 210–219.

9. Brown, R. I., Brown, P. M., & Bayer M. (1994). A quality of life model: New challenges arising from a six-year study. In D. Goode (Ed.), *Quality of life for persons with disabilities: International perspectives and issues* (pp. 39–55). Cambridge, MA: Brookline.

10. Brown, R. I. (1997). *Quality of life for people with disabilities: Models, research, and practice.* (2nd ed.). Cheltenham, England: Stanley Thornes.

11. Brown, R. I. (2000). Learning from quality of life models. In M. P. Janicki & E. F. Ansello (Eds.), *Community supports for aging adults with lifelong disabilities* (pp. 19–38). Baltimore: Paul H. Brookes.

12. Buela-Casal, G., Caballo, V., & Sierra, J. C. (1996). *Manual de evaluación en psicología clínica y de la salud.* Madrid: Siglo Veintiuno.

13. Carabellese, C. M., Apollonio, I. M., Rozzini, R. M., Bianchetti, A. M., Frisoni, G. B. M., Frattola, L. M., & Trabucchi, M. M. (1993). Sensory impairment and quality of life in a community elderly population. *Journal of the American Geriatrics Society, 41*(4), 401–407.

14. Castellón, A., & Rubio, R., & Rico A. (1999). Nivel de autoestima en los mayores tras un programa de ocio. *Revista Especial de Geriatría y Gerontología, 34*(4), 225–229.

15. Chowdhary, U. (1991). Clothing and self-esteem of the institutionalized elderly female: Two experiments. *Educational Gerontology, 17,* 527–541.

16. Clark, P. G. (1991). Ethical dimensions of quality of life in ageing: Autonomy vs. collectivism in the United States and Canada. *The Gerontologist, 31*(5), 631–639.

17. Clark, P. G. (1995). Quality of life, values, and teamwork in geriatric care: Do we communicate what we mean? *The Gerontologist, 35*(3), 402–411.

18. Clark, P. G. (1997). Values in health care professional socialization: Implications for geriatric education in interdisciplinary teamwork. *The Gerontologist, 37*(4), 441–451.

19. Clements, C. B. (1994). *The arts fitness quality of life activities program: Creative ideas for working with older adults in group settings.* Baltimore: Health Professions.

20. Coast, J., Peters, T. J., Richards, H., & Gunnell, D. (1998). Use of Euro-QOL among elderly acute care patients. *Quality of Life Research, 7,* 1–10.

21. De Gracia, M., Garre, J., & Marcó, M. (1999). Desarrollo y validación preliminar de la escala de percepción subjetiva del envejecimiento (EPSE). *Revista Especial de Geriatría y Gerontología, 34*(2), 92–100.

22. De Leo, M., René, F., & Diekstra, P. (1998). LEIPAD. An internationally applicable instrument to assess quality of life in the elderly. *Behavioral Medicine, 24,* 17–27.

23. Dengra, R., Mérida, C., Cobos, A., & Gálvez, M. C. (1996-1998). *Variables biopsicológicas que inciden en la participación de los mayores en programas comunitarios: Intervención en habilidades interpersonales y resolución de problemas. Necesidad, factibilidad, utilidad.* Unpublished document, University of Granada, Spain.

24. Eronen, M., Rankinen, T., Rauramaa, R., Sulkava, R., & Nissinen, A. (1997). Does ageing mean a better life for women? *Journal of the American Geriatrics Society, 45,* 594–597.

25. Evenhuis, H., Henderson, C. M., Beange, H., Lennox, N., Chicoine, B., & Working Group. (2000). *Healthy aging — adults with intellectual disabilities: Physical health issues.* Geneva, Switzerland: World Health Organization.

26. Everard, K. M. (1999). The relationship between reasons for activity and older adult well-being. *Journal of Applied Gerontology, 18*(3), 325–340.

27. Farré, R., & Frasque, P., & Romá, R. (1999). Estado de salud y calidad de vida de un colectivo de ancianos institucionalizados. *Revista Especial de Geriatría y Gerontología, 34*(1), 25–33.

28. Fernández-Ballesteros, R., Zamarrón, M. D., & Maciá, A. (1996). *Calidad de vida en la vejez en distintos contextos.* Madrid: Ministerio de Trabajo y Asuntos Exteriores, Instituto Nacional de Servicios Sociales.

29. Fernández-Ballesteros, R. (1997). Calidad de vida en la vejez: Condiciones diferenciales. *Anuario de Psicología, 73,* 89–104.

30. Fernández del Valle, J., & García, A. (1994). Redes de apoyo social en usuarios de ayuda a domicilio de la tercera edad. *Psicothema, 6*(1), 39–47.

31. Gillick, M. (1994). Doing the right thing: Quality assurance in the elderly. *Journal of the American Geriatrics Society, 42,* 1024–1026.

32. Glasgow, N. (2000). Rural/urban patterns of ageing and caregiving in the United States. *Journal of Family, 21*(5), 611–631.

33. Goff, K. (1993). Creativity and life satisfaction of older adults. *Educational Gerontology, 19,* 241–250.

34. Grégoire, J., de Leval, N., & Mesters, P. (1995). Adaptation française et étude des propriétés métriques de la quality of life in depression scale. *Revue Européenne de Psychologie Appliquée, 45*(4), 286–291.

35. Gustafson, D., Hawkins, R., Boberg, E., Pingree, S., & Serlin, R. (1998). Impact of a patient-centered, computer-based health information/support system. *American Journal of Preventive Medicine, 16*(1), 1–9.

36. Haas, B. (1999). A multidisciplinary concept analysis of quality of life. *Western Journal of Nursing Research, 21*(6), 728–743.

37. Hawkins, B. (1997). Health, fitness, and QOL for older adults with developmental disabilities and leisure. *Activities, Adaptation, and Aging, 21*(3), 29–35.

38. Hawkins, B. (1999). Rights, place of residence, and retirement: Lessons from case studies on aging. In S. S. Herr & G. Weber (Eds.), *Aging, rights, and quality of life: Prospects for older people with developmental disabilities* (pp. 93–107). Baltimore: Paul H. Brookes.

39. Henderson, C., & Davidson, P. (2000). Comprehensive adult and geriatric assessment. In M. Janicki & E. Ansello (Eds.), *Community supports for aging adults with lifelong disabilities* (pp. 373–386). New York: Brookes.

40. Herr, S. S., & Weber, G. (1999). Aging and developmental disabilities: Concepts and global perspectives. In S. S. Herr & G. Weber (Eds.), *Aging, rights, and quality of life: Prospects for older people with developmental disabilities* (pp. 1–16). Baltimore: Paul H. Brookes.

41. Higgs, P. (1999). Quality of life and changing parameters of old age. *Aging and Mental Health, 3,* 197–198.

42. Hogg, J., Lucchino, R., Wang, K., Janicki, M. P., & Working Group. (2000). *Healthy aging — adults with intellectual disabilities: Aging and social policy.* Geneva, Switzerland: World Health Organization.

43. Hughes, D. (1995). Aiming for objectivity and balance in the evaluation of the quality of life experienced by service users with learning disabilities. In D. Pilling & G. Watson (Eds.), *Evaluating quality in services for disabled and older people* (pp. 201–206). London: Jessica Kingsley.

44. Ishii-Kuntz, M. (1990). Social interaction and psychological well-being: Comparison across stages of adulthood. *International Journal of Aging and Human Development, 30*(1), 15.

45. Janicki, M. (1996). Quality of life for older persons with mental retardation. In R. L. Schalock (Ed.), *Quality of life: Vol. 2. Application to persons with disabilities* (pp. 105–115). Washington, DC: American Association on Mental Retardation.

46. Katz, S. (2000). Busy bodies: Activity, aging, and the management of everyday life. *Journal of Aging Studies, 14*(2), 135–153.

47. Kempen, G., Jelicic, M., & Ormel, J. (1997). Personality, chronic medical morbidity, and health-related quality of life among older persons. *Health Psychology, 16*(6), 539–546.

48. Kerruish, A. (1995). Quality for people — learning from service users about quality. In D. Pilling & G. Watson (Eds.), *Evaluating quality in services for disabled and older people* (pp. 158–163). London: Jessica Kingsley.

49. Kilbom, A. (1999). Evidence-based programs for the prevention of early exit from work. *Experimental Aging Research, 25*(4), 291–299.

50. Lachs, M. S., & Boyer, P. (1998). Caring for my dad: Can your parent live alone? *Prevention, 50*(10), 155–157.

51. Lawton, M., Winter, L., Kleban, M. H., & Ruckdesschel, K. (1999). Affect and quality of life. *Journal of Aging and Health, 11*(2), 169–199.

52. Lawton, M. (1991). Functional status and ageing well. *Generations, 15*(1), 31–34.

53. Leturia, F. (1998). Jubilación y calidad de vida. *Revista Española de Geriatría y Gerontología, 33*(1), 9–16.

54. Levin, J., & Chatters, L. (1998). Religion, health, and psychological well-being in older adults: Findings from three national surveys. *Journal of Aging and Health, 10*(4), 504–532.

55. Liao, Y., McGee, D., Guichan, C., & Cooper, R. (2000). Quality of the last year of life of older adults: 1986 vs. 1993. *Journal of the American Medical Association, 283*(4), 512.

56. Lindley, P., Band J., Gorf, B., Guerreo, M., Walker, D., & Gillespie, S. (1995). What do users think about quality? In D. Pilling & G. Watson (Eds.), *Evaluating quality in services for disabled and older people* (pp. 148–157). London: Jessica Kingsley.

57. Long, J., Anderson, J., & Williams, R. (1990). Life reflections by older kinsmen about critical life issues. *Educational Gerontology, 16,* 61–71.

58. Malaguarnera, M. (1995). The elderly and quality of life. *British Medical Journal, 311*(7013), 1136–1138.

59. Martorell, M. C., Gómez, O., & Cuenca, A. (1994). Calidad de vida y tercera edad. *Cuadernos de Medicina Psicosomática, 30,* 41–46.

60. Matsubayashi, K., & Okumiya, K. (1997). Quality of life of old people living in the community. *Journal of the American Medical Association, 350*(9090), 1521–1522.

61. Midgley, G. (1995). Evaluation and change in service systems for people with disabilities? In D. Pilling & G. Watson (Eds.), *Evaluating quality in services for disabled and older people* (pp. 33–49). London: Jessica Kingsley.

62. Montoro, J. (1999). Factores determinantes de la calidad del cuidado asistencial institucional a personas mayores y/o con discapacidad. *Papers, 57,* 89–112.

63. Moss, M. S., Lawton, M., & Glicksman, A. (1991). The role of pain in the last year of life of older persons. *Journal of Gerontology, 46*(2), 51–57.

64. Murlow, C., Aguilar, C., Endicott, J., Velez, R., Tuley, M., Charlip, W., & Hill, J. (1990). Association between hearing impairments and quality of life of elderly individuals. *Journal of the American Geriatrics Society, 38*(1), 45–50.

65. Newsom, J. T., & Schutz, R. (1996). Social support as a mediator in the relation between functional status and quality of life in older adults. *Psychology and Aging, 111*(1), 34–44.

66. Nieto, J., Abad, A., & Torres, A. (1998). Dimensiones psicosociales mediadoras de la conducta de enfermedad y la calidad de vida en población geriátrica. *Anales de Psicología, 14*(1), 75–81.

67. Nordenfelt, L. (1994). *Concepts and measurement of quality of life in health care.* London: Kluwer Academic.

68. O'Connor, B. (1995). Family and friend relationships among older and younger adults: Interaction motivation, mood, and quality. *International Journal of Aging and Human Development, 40*(1), 9–29.

69. Oldridge, N. (1998). Cardiac rehabilitation in the elderly. *Aging Clinical and Experimental Research, 10*(4), 273–283.

70. O'Mahony, P., Rodgers, H., Thomson, R., Dobson, R., & James, O. (1998). Is the SF-36 suitable for assessing health status of older stroke patients? *Age and Aging, 27,* 19–22.

71. Ors, A., & Laguna, A. (1997). Reflexiones sobre el envejecimiento y la calidad de vida. *Cultura de los Cuidados, 1*(2), 60–63.

72. Pearlman, R., & Uhlmann, R. (1991). Calidad de vida en personas mayores con enfermedad crónica no hospitalizados. *Journal of Gerontology: Medical Sciences, 46*(2), 31–38.

73. Pilling, D., & Watson, G. (Eds.). (1995). *Evaluating quality in services for disabled and older people.* London: Jessica Kingsley.

74. Pilling, S. (1995). QUARTZ, PASSING, and user involvement: Meeting points and departure points. In D. Pilling & G. Watson (Eds.), *Evaluating quality of services for disabled and older people* (pp. 135–147). London: Jessica Kingsley.

75. Ragnar, A. (1999). Sleep disorders in the elderly. *Drugs and Aging, 14*(2), 91–103.

76. Saravanabhavan, R., Martin, W., & Saravanabhavan, S. (1994). A model for assessing rehabilitation needs of the elderly American Indians who are visually impaired and living on reservations. *Journal of Applied Rehabilitation Counseling, 25*(2), 19–28.

77. Schalock, R., DeVries, D., & Lebsack, J. (1999). Rights, quality measures, and program changes. In S. Herr & G. Weber (Eds.), *Aging, rights, and quality of life: Prospects for older people with developmental disabilities* (pp. 81–92). Baltimore: Paul H. Brookes.

78. Scott, E., & Reuben, D. (1998). Measures of functional status in community-dwelling elders. *General International Medicine, 13,* 817–823.

79. Shatahmasebi, S. M., Davies, R. P., & Wenger, G. (1992). A longitudinal analysis of factors related to survival in old age. *The Gerontologist, 32*(3), 404–413.

80. Siebert, D. C., & Mutran, E. J. (1999). Friendship and social support: The importance of role identity to aging adults. *Social Work, 44*(6), 522–534.

81. Small, G. W., Birkett, M., Meyers, B. S., Koran, L. M., Bystrisky, A., Nemeroff, C. B., & Fluoxetine Collaborative Study Group. (1996). Impact of physical illness on quality of life and antidepressant response in geriatric major depression. *Journal of the American Geriatrics Society, 44*(10), 1220–1225.

82. Spence, S. A. (1997). Improving the quality of life for rural elderly African Americans through education: A nontraditional approach. *Educational Gerontology, 23,* 53–65.

83. Staats, S., & Stassen, M. (1987). Age and present and future perceived quality of life. *International Journal of Aging and Human Development, 25*(3), 167–177.

84. Steiner, A., Raube, K., Stuck, A., Aronow, H., Draper, D., Rubenstein, L., & Beck, J. (1996). Measuring psychosocial aspects of well-being in older community residents: Performance of four short scales. *The Gerontologist, 36*(1), 54–62.

85. Stewart, A., King, A., & Haskell, W. (1993). Endurance exercise and health-related quality of life in 50-65-year-old adults. *The Gerontologist, 33*(6), 782–789.

86. Thorpe, L., Davidson, P., & Janicki, M. P. (2000). *Healthy aging — adults with intellectual disabilities: Biobehavioural issues.* Geneva, Switzerland: World Health Organization.

87. Tyler, K. (2000). The effects of an acute stressor on depressive symptoms among older adults. *Research on Aging, 22*(2), 143–165.

88. Tyne, A. (1995). What have we been learning from PASS and PASSING in workshop and real evaluations? In D. Pilling & G. Watson (Eds.), *Evaluating quality in services for disabled and older people* (pp. 25–32). London: Jessica Kingsley.

89. Umoren, J. A. (1992). Maslow hierarchy of needs and OBRA 1987: Toward need satisfaction by nursing home residents. *Educational Gerontology, 18,* 657–670.

90. Urciuoli, O., Dello Buono, M., Padoani, W., & De Leo, D. (1998). Assessment of quality of life in the oldest-olds living in nursing homes and at home. *Archives of Gerontology and Geriatrics, 6,* 507–514.

91. Walker, A., Walker, C., & Gosling, V. (1999). Quality of life as a matter of human rights. In S. Herr & G. Weber (Eds.), *Aging, rights, and quality of life: Prospects for older people with developmental disabilities* (pp. 109–132). Baltimore: Paul H. Brookes.

92. Ward, R. A. (1985). Informal networks and well-being in later life: A research agenda. *The Gerontological Society of America, 25*(1), 55–61.

93. Waters, W., Heikkinen, E., & Dontas, A. (1989). *Health, lifestyles, and services for the elderly.* Copenhagen: World Health Organization Library Cataloguing in Publication Data.

94. Wells, L., & Singer, C. M. (1988). Quality of life in institutions for the elderly: Maximizing well-being. *The Gerontological Society of America, 28*(2), 41–60.

95. William, E., Keith, R., Saravanabhavan, R., & Kathy, C. (1993). Training programs for working with older American Indians who are visually impaired. *American Rehabilitation, 19*(1), 2–7.

96. Williams, P. (1995). The PASS and PASSING: Evaluation instruments. In D. Pilling & G. Watson (Eds.), *Evaluating quality in services for disabled and older people* (pp. 13–24). London: Jessica Kingsley.

97. Winter, M. (1999). Pathways to life quality. *Human Ecology Forum, 27*(2), 150–153.

98. Wolfson, P. (1995). ACE — An assessment of care environments. In D. Pilling & G. Watson (Eds.), *Evaluating quality in services for disabled and older people* (pp. 78–83). London: Jessica Kingsley.

99. Wolkenstein, A., & Butler, D. (1992). Quality of life among the elderly: Self-perspectives of some healthy elderly. *Gerontology and Geriatrics Education, 12*(4), 59–69.

100. World Health Organization. (2000). *Aging and intellectual disabilities. Improving longevity and promoting healthy aging: Summative report.* Geneva, Switzerland: Author.

101. Yamada, M. (1994). Adults' self-directed learning of the care of the elderly and communicative intergenerational relationships. *Educational Gerontology, 20,* 511–520.

CHAPTER 8

Family-Centered Quality of Life

Overview

The reader will find that this chapter is different in four ways from the preceding five chapters. First, the chapter does not analyze research data into the eight core domains encompassing the quality of life (QOL) model presented in Figure 2.2. There is a simple reason for this: The model's eight core domains stem from *person-centered* quality of life conceptualization and measurement, and at this point we do not know whether person-centered core QOL domains are the same as *family-centered* core domains. Therefore, a second difference is the use of those family-centered core QOL domains that potentially reflect a family's life of quality. As the reader will see, the two sets of core QOL domains appear to be very similar (see Figure 8.1), but only future factor and meta-analyses will clarify the relationship. A third difference is that the core domains are not ranked, because there is insufficient literature to do so in the area of family-centered quality of life. The good news is that this area is becoming a very rich and productive research endeavor. A final difference is that the content of this chapter is based primarily on a recent Symposium on Family Quality of Life held in Seattle, Washington, on August 1, 2000, and an in-depth reading of chapters 1 through 6 of the monograph from that conference (Turnbull, Turnbull, & Brown, in press). Throughout the conference and monograph, four common themes emerged that provide the context for this chapter:

1. It is important for families to have a clear understanding of the domain of well-being and the need for forward planning that links self-image and satisfaction. This importance is reflected in the current active and ongoing attempt to identify the core domains reflective of a family's quality of life.

2. Families with a member who has a disability are challenged not just by the disability and stigma associated therewith but also by the lack of services and the costs of services that do exist.

3. Family quality of life relates to specific domains of living, is currently linked closely to core individual QOL domains, and is impacted significantly by personal and social-cultural factors.

4. There is an implicit assumption in the current work in family-centered quality of life that our better understanding of the QOL concept will result in a positive theoretical and conceptual framework within which to understand and develop family-centered approaches to support.

This chapter contains three major sections. First, ongoing work on the conceptualization and measurement of family and individual quality of life is reviewed, suggesting considerable similarity between the "core domains" of a life of quality for individuals and for families. Second, four research strands are discussed that follow directly from the four common themes listed above. Third, the significant role that caregivers play in a person's life is discussed, followed by a listing of caregiver QOL guidelines. The chapter concludes with suggested research challenges posed by the concept of family-centered quality of life and a number of measurement and application principles to guide our future efforts.

Individual- and Family-Centered Quality of Life: A Brief Overview

We have learned much about the concept, measurement, and application of the QOL concept from the significant work on individual quality of life. Only relatively recently has a major effort been made to understand the domains of family quality of life and to identify core indicators for each. Because the emerging work on family quality of life is influenced and shaped significantly by the work done on individual quality of life, a brief discussion of the current status of each is advantageous.

Individual Quality of Life

One of the most exciting changes in recent years has been the emerging consensus of what constitutes the core domains of a life of quality. Interest in these domains goes back to the pioneering work of Thorndike (1939). Historically the social scientists' attempts to conceptualize the core QOL domains have fallen into the following three perspectives (Schalock, 1990): objective, subjective, and goodness of fit.

Objective Indicators
Objective indicators generally refer to external, environmentally based conditions such as health, social welfare, friendships, standard of living, education, public

safety, housing, neighborhood, and leisure. These indicators may be defined as a statistic of direct normative interest that facilitates concise, comprehensive, and balanced judgments about the conditions of major aspects of either society or one's life (Andrews & Whithey, 1976).

Subjective Indicators
Subjective indicators focus on a person's subjective reactions to life experiences and are usually measured from one of two perspectives: psychological well-being or personal satisfaction. An example of the first perspective is the work of Flanagan (1982), who identified five general domains of quality of life: physical and material well-being; relations with others; social, community, and civic activities; personal development and fulfillment; and recreation. The second perspective underlies the work of Heal and his associates (Heal, Rubin, & Park, 1995), who measured the individual's satisfaction with factors such as home and community, friends, leisure activities, self-control, and social support and safety.

The Goodness-of-Fit Perspective
The goodness-of-fit perspective proposes that quality of life is related to a match between a person's wants or needs and their fulfillment. For example, the goodness-of-fit model proposed by Murrell and Norris (1983) suggested that the characteristics of a given group interact with the resources and stressors of the environment, and that the quality of a person's life is a function of the discrepancy among resources, stressors, and needs. Similarly, Schalock and Jensen (1986) proposed that quality of life measurement should consider the congruence between environmental demands and a person's control of resources or skills to meet the demands.

Core Individual Quality of Life Domains
The past decade has seen significant work on identifying the core domains to a person's life of quality. As presented throughout this handbook, these core domains are emotional well-being, interpersonal relationships, material well-being, personal development, physical well-being, self-determination, social inclusion, and rights.

Family-Centered Quality of Life
There is a general agreement that a positive quality of life should be an appropriate outcome of public policy and services. By extension, a positive quality of life for families is regarded as "a useful indicator of outcomes of policy initiatives" (Bailey et al., 1998, p. 322). Indeed, improving quality of life for families may be the "only acceptable outcome" of policies and services (Osher, 1998, p. 232). Nevertheless, until recently, researchers and others have not been as successful in con-

ceptualizing, much less measuring, family quality of life as they have been in doing so for individual quality of life (Bailey et al.; Gardner & Nudler, 1997).

Overview of Family Quality of Life
Since the study of quality of life began in the 1970s (Andrews & Whithey, 1976; Campbell, Converse, & Rodgers, 1976), researchers have agreed on two fundamental concepts: (a) that quality of life is a multidimensional construct whose core domains are interrelated; and (b) that quality of life can include both subjective and objective aspects. The subjective aspect is usually tied to the importance of a particular domain to the family and to how the family members feel about life with respect to that domain. The value placed on a domain is also influenced by the family's experiences and culture. By contrast, the objective aspect is usually measured by income, housing, or health data. Although the subjective indicators of a specific domain do not necessarily correlate with the objective indicator, it is useful to compare populations on the objective as well as on the subjective indicators (Cummins, 1996, 1997b).

Intuitively, one would think that research on family quality of life in cases where family members have special needs would be the natural progression in improving our understanding of the concept and in developing tools to measure it. Unfortunately this step was not taken seriously until recently. The limited work on family QOL-related outcomes has focused on satisfaction, general family functioning, family stability, self-sufficiency, employment, reduction in stress, or increase in parenting skills (Anderson, Rivera, & Kutash, 1998; Bailey et al., 1998; Blacher, 2001; Flynt & Wood, 1989; Frey, Greenberg, & Fewell, 1989; Keogh, Bernheimer, Gallimore, & Weisner, 1998). The importance of the extension of that work to families with a member who has special needs is reflected in three principles: (a) the quality of life of an individual is intrinsically related to that of the family; (b) efforts to address the individual's quality of life must include considerations of the family's interpretation of quality of life; and (c) family-centered quality of life is integral to a number of core domains.

Family-Centered Core Quality of Life Domains
The above overview provides the context and framework for the emerging cross-national work (Turnbull et al., in press). For expository purposes, the core family-centered QOL domains that are currently being investigated in these cross-national studies are aggregated into the following eight domains: (a) emotional well-being, (b) physical health, (c) financial well-being, (d) family relations or functioning, (e) supports, (f) productivity, (g) community involvement and advocacy, and (h) recreation and leisure.

As discussed in the following section, the first proposed research strand involves comparing and potentially integrating the individual and family core QOL domains just discussed. This comparison and potential integration are important for at least three reasons. First, it will result in families having a clear understanding of the core QOL domains and how these domains can be the focus of efforts to enhance the family's functioning and perceived well-being. Second, it will move us closer to understanding the core QOL domains that we are researching, measuring, and applying. Third, it will allow us to develop a common language that can serve as a basis for QOL-oriented policies, programs, and procedures.

Future Family Quality of Life Research Strands

In this section four family QOL research strands are suggested that will facilitate establishing the empirical basis for the concept's application and evaluation. Each strand stems from the four common themes described at the beginning of the chapter. The four suggested future family QOL research strands are (a) to identify and validate family QOL domains, (b) to understand the linkages between the core concepts of disability policy and QOL domains, (c) to determine the significant factors influencing a family's life of quality, and (d) to begin answering the question, "How can family quality of life research make a difference?"

Identifying and Validating Family Quality of Life Core Domains

Based on work to date, it appears that the core domains of individual and family quality of life are quite similar. For example, as shown in Figure 8.1, there is considerable overlap in seven of the domain areas: material well-being with financial well-being; interpersonal relations with family relations and functioning; social inclusion with community involvement and advocacy; emotional well-being with emotional well-being; physical well-being with physical health; and personal development with productivity. A similar comparison is shown in Table 8.1, which summarizes some core indicators for each core domain, as found in the international literature summarized in the preceding five chapters.

Although it should be stressed that the family QOL domains summarized in Table 8.1 and Figure 8.1 should be considered as preliminary and still emerging, there are at least three reasons why this research strand is so important.[1] First, although it is a reasonable hypothesis that the definition of a life of quality will vary across families of different ages, geographic locations, and ethnicities, it is important to know how widely applicable the core domains are and whether or not they are the same for individuals and families. Second, policy development, applica-

---

[1] Results of the analysis of recent family quality of life surveys by the Beach Center have identified the following five factors: family interaction, parenting, general resources, health and safety, and support for family members with a disability (Turnbull, Poston, Park, Mannan, & Marquis, in press).

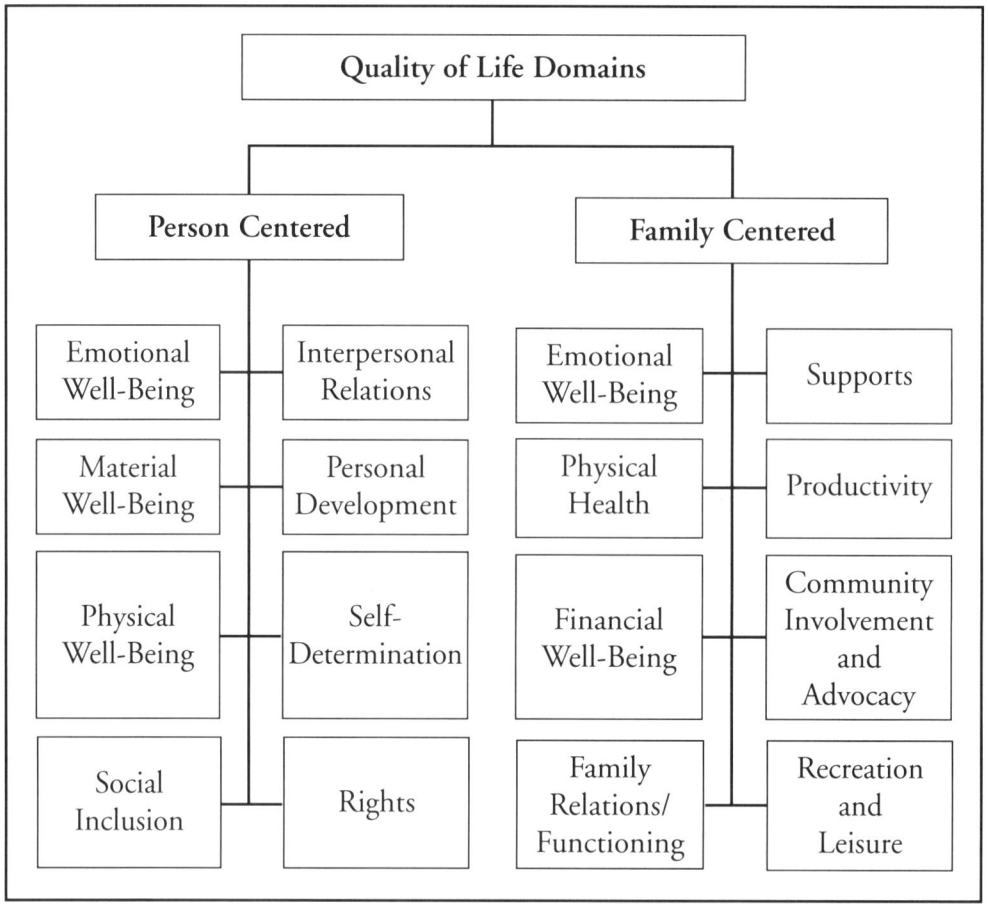

Figure 8.1. Comparison of individual- and family-centered quality of life domains.

tion, and evaluation require a common understanding of both the concept and its core domains, which will provide policymakers and evaluators with both a common conceptual model and a common language. Third, this research will also assist in determining whether family quality of life is a derivative of the quality of life of its members, or whether the quality of life of family members can be ascertained more easily from first examining family quality of life. The reader should be aware of two caveats regarding the statements just made. First, we are only beginning to work with core domains in family QOL research, and our understanding of these may change as research progresses over the next decade. Second, we need someplace to start, and the core domains and indicators listed in Figure 8.1 and Table 8.1 represent a reasonable beginning.

Table 8.1
Individual and Family Quality of Life Domains and Indicators

Person-Centered Domains	Exemplary Core Indicators				
Emotional well-being	Safety	Spirituality	Happiness	Freedom from stress	Self-concept
Interpersonal relations	Intimacy	Affection	Family	Interactions	Friendships
Material well-being	Ownership	Financial	Security	Food	Employment
Personal development	Education	Skills	Fulfillment	Personal competence	Purposeful activity
Physical well-being	Health	Nutrition	Recreation	Mobility	Health care
Self-determination	Autonomy	Choices	Decisions	Personal control	Self-direction
Social inclusion	Acceptance	Status	Supports	Work environment	Community integration
Rights	Privacy	Voting	Access	Due process	Ownership

Family-Centered Domains	Exemplary Core Indicators				
Emotional well-being	Control	Adaptability	Personal time	Spiritual and cultural well-being	
Supports	From others	From human services			
Physical health	Physical	Mental	Health care		
Productivity	Opportunities	Success	Career development	Employment	School
Financial well-being	Shelter	Transportation	Accommodations	Education	Health care
Community involvement and advocacy	Family involvement	Service system	Social belonging		
Family relations and functioning	Communication	Acceptance	Time together	Family relationships	Parenting roles
Recreation and leisure	Hobbies	Recreational sports and activities	Exercises	Spectator sports	

Understanding Linkages Between Policy Concepts and Domains

Recently we have seen significant progress in the development of two taxonomies. The first is the initial understanding of the core domains of individual and family quality of life. The second is the identification of the core concepts found within current United States public policy (Turnbull, Wilcox, Stowe, & Umbarger, 2001). These core concepts include civil rights, independence, empowerment, privacy, confidentiality, liberty, protection from harm, individualized and appropriate services, capacity-based services, priority-based services, productivity, inclusion, family integrity and unity, and family-centered coordination and accountability.

Studying these linkages is important for three reasons. First, the substance of public policy is typically based on those core concepts just listed. But these concepts are *processes* or standards, and thus relate to the *emphasis* within public policy rather that the *outcomes* of public policy. Second, a focus on public policy outcomes will allow investigators to focus on family QOL-referenced outcomes and evaluate the impact of certain policies on these outcomes. With the emerging consensus on the core family QOL domains, the evaluation of the impact of public policies can use changes in the family's subjective well-being, satisfaction, and perceived quality of life as dependent variables. This will also move policy analysis away from process to outcome evaluation (Schalock, 2001). Third, understanding these linkages will also allow for targeting of resources and quality enhancement techniques and determining whether some core concepts are more important than others on the family's perceived well-being. This understanding will require that researchers and evaluators use methodological pluralism that is described more fully in chapter 11.

Because of the critical importance of this research strand, in the future we need to determine further whether or not there are linkages between these core policy concepts and the core family QOL domains. Specific questions in this regard include:

- Is there any relationship between the two? If so, how do the core policy concepts such as liberty, equality, and community affect family QOL domains such as family interaction, physical environment, emotional well-being, health, productivity, and advocacy?
- What is the pathway for mapping quality of life pursuits from their genesis (policy) to their implementation, to the measurement of their effectiveness, and back again to policy?
- What is the relationship between the partnership domains of communication, trust, respect, commitment, equality, and skills to the core family-centered QOL domains?

Determining Factors That Influence Family Life of Quality

One of the biggest stumbling blocks in reference to QOL research has been overcome by shifting our mind set regarding the research and statistical design used to study quality of life. Specifically, we have seen a significant shift from a "between" to a "multivariate" or "within" approach. Historically the study of quality of life was approached from a between-groups (or conditions) perspective; hence, investigators sought to find factors such as socioeconomic status and large demographic population descriptors that could discriminate between those individuals or countries with a higher and those with a lower quality of life.

Shifting to a multivariate research design has a number of research and policy implications. First, it allows one to focus more on the correlates and predictors of a life of quality rather than comparing quality of life scores or status. More specifically, one can use multivariate research designs to determine the relationship among a number of measured predictor variables and perceived quality of life (e.g., Schalock, Lemanowicz, Conroy, & Feinstein, 1994; Schalock & Faulkner, 1997; Schalock, Bonham, & Marchand, 2000). Second, once these significant predictors are identified, policy and programmatic changes can be made to enhance the family's quality of life through techniques and strategies such as those described in chapters 12 through 14. Third, multivariate research designs help us understand better the complexity of the QOL concept and the role that a number of contextual variables play in the perception of a life of quality. Finally, multivariate designs shift the focus of our interventions from personal and/or family characteristics to environmental factors as major sources of quality of life enhancement.

How Can Family Quality of Life Research Make a Difference?

As discussed further in chapters 10 and 11, we are currently seeing a significant paradigm shift in how we conduct research and evaluation in the social sciences. The shift is referred to frequently as "social constructivism" that emphasizes the pragmatic evaluation design, ideographic research, context-specific knowledge, decision-oriented evaluation, and use of methodological pluralism that includes both quantitative and qualitative methodologies (Schalock, 2001). If the QOL concept is to make a demonstrable difference in the lives of families, the following three-step research strand will provide the framework for demonstrating that family QOL research makes a difference: (a) empower families to pursue a life of quality, (b) evaluate quality enhancement techniques, and (c) analyze quality outcomes.

Empower Families to Pursue a Life of Quality

Future research will need to reflect at least three major thrusts by families pursuing a life of quality. First, we will continue to see strong advocacy for increased opportunities to participate in the mainstream of life, associated with increased inclusion, equity, and choices. Related efforts will involve advocating for increased individualized supports within regular environments; inclusion in major activities such as decision making, person-centered planning, and participatory action research (Whitney-Thomas, 1997); and incorporating the concept of quality of life in international and national disability policies (Goode, 1997b).

Second, consumers will work jointly with researchers in determining the relative importance or value of the core domains suggested in Figure 8.1. For children and youth, for example, the most important dimensions may well be personal development, self-determination, interpersonal relationships, and social inclusion (Stark & Goldsbury, 1990); for families the most important dimensions may be physical and material well-being, interpersonal relationships, and emotional well-being (Schalock, DeVries, & Lebsack, 1999).

Third, consumers will increasingly become involved in assessing their own quality of life. In that regard, we (Schalock et al., 2000) have recently shown that consumers are excellent surveyors and can assess other consumers' quality of life with highly acceptable reliability and validity.

Evaluate Quality Enhancement Techniques

We will continue to see service providers implementing quality enhancement techniques that focus on what program personnel and services and/or supports can do to improve a family's perceived quality of life (Schalock, 1994). Specifically, implementation of two concepts will characterize the first decade of the 21st century. One is the belief that an enhanced quality of life is the result of a good match between a family's needs and their fulfillment (Cummins, 1996; Edgerton, 1996; Ferguson, 1997; Michalos, 1985; Murrell & Norris, 1983; Schalock, Keith, Hoffman, & Karan, 1989). The second is a corollary: that it is possible to assess the match between families and their environments (Schalock & Jensen, 1986). The importance of these two concepts is supported by data suggesting that reducing the discrepancy between people and their environments increases their assessed quality of life (Schalock et al., 1989). Therefore, once there is consensus on the core QOL domains, it will be possible both to implement and to evaluate the impact of a number of quality enhancement techniques that reduce the discrepancy between families and their environments.

Analyze Quality Outcomes

Human service organizations throughout the world are currently being challenged to provide quality services that result in quality outcomes. This is a challenging task because of two powerful, potentially conflicting forces: individual and family-centered values and economically based restructured services. The focus on individual and family-centered values stems from a number of sources, including the

QOL movement; the human rights and self-advocate movements' emphasis on equity, inclusion, empowerment, and respect; numerous public laws that stress opportunities and desired person- and family-referenced outcomes related to independence, productivity, community integration, and satisfaction; and research demonstrating that people and families can be more independent, productive, integrated within the community, and satisfied when QOL concepts are the basis of individual and family services and supports. Conversely, the focus on restructured services stems from economic restraints, an increased need for accountability, and the movement toward a market economy in health care and rehabilitation services.

How can service providers adapt to these two potentially conflicting forces and still accomplish two accountability goals: (a) to focus on valued, individual and family-referenced outcomes; and (b) to answer the ultimate question, "does it make any difference?" A heuristic model for doing so is presented in Figure 8.2. The model has three components: standard, focus, and critical outcomes. *Standards* reflect both subjective and objective components to a life of quality; *focus* represents the emphasis on the individual or the family; and *outcomes* indicate desired conditions from either the individual's or family's perspective.

The primary challenge to service providers and evaluators alike is to reach a balance in their evaluation efforts among the four types of outcomes summarized

	Standard	
	Objective	Subjective
Family	Self-sufficiency Home ownership Neighborhood & community involvement Increased parenting skills	Social relationships Social rapport Health and safety Reduction in stress Family relations
Individual	Health status Wellness indicators Activities/Instrumental activities of daily living Employment status	Decision making Self-esteem Independence Inclusion Social relations

Figure 8.2. Individual and family outcomes-focused evaluation model.

in Figure 8.2, recognizing that different constituents will emphasize their desired individual- or family-referenced outcomes. Thus, as we embark on the 21st century and undoubtedly continue to pursue these two accountability goals, what guidelines might assist our efforts to measure and enhance quality outcomes? The 10 principles summarized in Table 8.2, which are adapted from the work of the Special Interest Research Group on Quality of Life of the International Association for the Scientific Study of Intellectual Disabilities (IASSID) (Schalock et al., in press) should be very helpful.

Table 8.2
Measurement and Application Principles of Family Quality of Life

---

Measurement Principles

1. QOL measurement assesses the degree to which families have meaningful life experiences that they value.

2. QOL measurement enables families to move toward a meaningful life they enjoy and value.

3. QOL measurement assesses the degree to which life's domains contribute to a full and interconnected life.

4. QOL measurement is undertaken within the context of environments that are important to families: where they live, work, and play.

5. QOL measurement for families is based upon both common human experiences and unique, individual family experiences.

Application Principles

1. The primary purpose for applying the QOL concept is to enhance the family's well-being.

2. Quality of life needs to be applied in light of the family's cultural and ethnic heritage.

3. The aims of any QOL-oriented program should be to collaborate for change at the personal, family, program, community, and national levels.

4. QOL applications should enhance the degree of family control and opportunities exerted in relation to their activities, interventions, and environments.

5. Quality of life should occupy a prominent role in gathering evidence, especially in identifying the significant predictors of a life of quality and the impact of targeting resources to maximize positive effects.

Families as Caregivers

A person's quality of life cannot be separated from the care provided or the people providing the care. Across our text's focus areas, families are generally the primary caregivers, regardless of whether or not the recipient lives in a developed country (Fujiura, 1998, 2000) or a nondeveloped country (Goel, 2000; McConkey & O'Toole, 2000). Two recent examples from the fields of mental retardation and intellectual disabilities and mental and behavioral health reflect this trend.

In reference to individuals with mental retardation or intellectual disabilities, there is now widespread recognition of the central role that their families occupy throughout their lives, including their parents' continuing to care for the child at home well into adulthood. Key issues that Seltzer, Wyngaarden Krauss, Hong, and Orsmond (2001) and others (see Seltzer et al. for an extensive review of this literature) have investigated regarding this trend include the benefits and challenges to families of providing long-term care, the role of adult siblings in the caregiving context, and factors leading to a change in the living circumstances of the family member with mental retardation or intellectual disabilities. An additional issue is the importance to both the care provider and the care recipient of many of those family QOL domains referenced in Figure 8.1: emotional well-being, family relations or functioning, supports, and community involvement and advocacy.

Similar care-giver trends and issues relate to families or family members with mental or behavioral health needs (Bickman, Guthrie, Foster, & Lambert, 1995; Lehman, Rachuba, & Postrado, 1995; Schalock, Nelson, Sutton, Holtan, & Sheehan, 1997). Across these studies, families report the importance of QOL factors such as community inclusion, choices, the receipt of appropriate supports, independence, relationships, service coordination, health, respect or rights, and acceptance.

Thus it is important to consider a number of QOL-related guidelines that families can use to enhance the recipient's subjective well-being and quality of life. Based on the above literature and our initial work to date (Schalock et al., 1999), suggested care-giver QOL guidelines for each core QOL domain are summarized in Table 8.3.

Conclusion

In conclusion, the first decade of the 21st century will continue to see the concept of family-centered quality of life emerge in response to the need for a positive theoretical and conceptual framework within which to understand and develop family-centered approaches to support. Although there are challenges related to the uniqueness of the concept to each family and its differential use and operation, the promise of an enhanced family quality of life will continue to change the way

Table 8.3
Quality-of-Life-Related Caregiver Guidelines

Domain	Caregiver Guidelines
Emotional well-being	• Freedom from fear, harm, injury, neglect, or hurt • Opportunity to act on or pursue personal beliefs • Positive feedback about capabilities • Freedom from worry involving aspects of family, friends, where to live, financial situation
Interpersonal relations	• Involvement and relationships with family members • Involvement and relations with friends and acquaintances • Involvement and relationships with those providing organized activities such as church, recreation, leisure • Involvements and relationships with professional caregivers
Material well-being	• Money with which to buy things and do activities • Availability and use of furniture, pictures, radio and TV, and similar preferred items
Personal development	• Opportunities for developing new skills • Opportunities to engage in arts, crafts, and other personal enhancing activities
Physical well-being	• Allowing person to eat, dress, bathe, walk, and care for self • Receipt of appropriate health care • Nutritional well-being • Medication dosages • Opportunities for physical activity and exercise

(table continues)

Table 8.3. *(continued)*

Domain	Caregiver Guidelines
Self-determination	• Freedom to make choices or decisions about daily activities • Freedom to make choices or decisions about preferred food and clothing • Opportunities to express personal opinions and values • Opportunities to achieve personal goals
Social inclusion	• Being liked and accepted by cohabitants and having cohabitants involved with person's activities • Being liked and accepted by caregiver(s); having caregiver(s) involved in activities and conversations • Receiving help and support from cohabitants or caregivers
Rights	• Respect for person's privacy • Opportunities to give input regarding rules or schedules • Opportunities to own things • Opportunities to receive legal aid or advocacy assistance • Protection from negative or potentially harmful events or situations

people think and approach public policy and service delivery systems. Thus the 21st century will indeed be an exciting and active time as we jointly "pursue quality." This pursuit will involve families desiring and advocating for a life of quality, service and support providers producing quality products, and evaluators analyzing quality outcomes. However, despite the optimism expressed in the above predictions and guidelines, we should not forget that the first decade of the 21st century will probably continue to reflect the value clashes that we have experienced during the current decade. Thus much hard work, advocacy, and risk lie ahead. The 10 measurement and application principles presented in Table 8.2 should be of considerable value in those endeavors.

At its core the QOL concept gives us a sense of reference and guidance from the family's perspective, an overriding principle to enhance people's well-being and collaborate for change at the societal level, and a common language and systematic framework to guide our current and future endeavors. To accomplish this we need to focus on the following steps that are complementary to the four research strands suggested: (a) reach consensus on the core domains to a family-centered QOL, (b) align services and supports with the predictors of the core QOL domains, (3) align public policy with the concept of family-centered QOL, and (d) evaluate the evidence from QOL-oriented policy and practices. These steps will be discussed more fully in parts 3 and 4 (chap. 10 through 15).

Chapter 9

A Synthesis of Core Quality of Life Domains and Indicators

Overview

The reader was forewarned that this part of the *Handbook* would include considerable data and information regarding the interpretation of the international research literature on quality of life. At this point, we anticipate that the reader is wondering about general patterns and hoping for a brief synthesis and summary of this research. That is our purpose in this chapter. Although the chapter is very short, the reader will find it very useful.

The chapter contains two tables and one set of guidelines. Table 9.1 presents a rank ordering of the core quality of life (QOL) domains and indicators for each of the text's focus areas. This table will help investigators within specific areas, because it shows clearly which of the domains (and most frequently referenced indicators) have been used or proposed within each focus area. Table 9.2 presents the most frequently used indicators for all eight core QOL domains. For each indicator, there is also a listing of the descriptors obtained from the literature review. This table will be especially helpful to readers interested in the application of quality enhancement techniques and the evaluation of person-referenced outcomes. The chapter concludes with a brief discussion of six guidelines that one should keep in mind when using information contained in Tables 9.1 and 9.2. It is important to point out that the indicators and descriptors listed are person-referenced and reflect the microsystem level of analysis.

Synthesis of Core QOL Domains, Indicators, and Descriptors

Rank Order of Domains and Indicators

The rank order (1 = most frequently referenced) of each core QOL domain within each of the text's focus areas was based on the frequency of references associated with that domain in Tables 3.1 to 7.1. For example, for education and special education, the most frequently referenced domain was emotional well-being, followed by personal development, interpersonal relations, and so forth. The indicator(s) listed adjacent to each core domain in Table 9.1 is the indicator(s) reported most frequently for that core domain. As a further attempt to synthesize the core domain literature, an average ranking was computed for each domain, collapsing across the focus areas. Note that smaller mean rankings correspond to higher frequency of references in the literature. Independent of focus area, the most frequently referenced core QOL domain in the 897 articles and book chapters reviewed was physical well-being (M rank = 2.6), followed by emotional well-being (2.8), interpersonal relations (3.0), social inclusion (3.4), personal development (4.2), material well-being (5.8), self-determination (6.6), and rights (7.6). These rankings reflect only the published literature from 1985 to 1999 and may well change in the future.

TABLE 9.1
Rank Order of Quality of Life Domains and Indicators
by Text's Focus Areas

Focus Area	Domains	Indicators
Education and special education	1. Emotional well-being 2. Personal development 3. Interpersonal relations 4. Social inclusion 5. Physical well-being 6. Self-determination 7. Material well-being 8. Rights	Contentment and self-concept Education Interpersonal relations (teachers, family, peers) Community integration and participation Health and fitness Autonomy Financial status Dignity, respect, equality
Physical health	1. Physical well-being 2. Emotional well-being 3. Interpersonal relations 4. Material well-being 5. Social inclusion 6. Personal development 7. Self-determination 8. Rights	Health and activities of daily living Contentment and lack of stress Interactions (family, friends) Employment Community roles Performance Goals and personal values Guardianship and equality of opportunity

(table continues)

TABLE 9.1. *(continued)*

Focus Area	Domains	Indicators
Mental and behavioral health	1. Interpersonal relations 2. Personal development 3. Emotional well-being 4. Physical well-being 5. Social inclusion 6. Self-determination 7. Material well-being 8. Rights	Interactions (family, supports) Education and skills Contentment and lack of stress Health, health care, and activities of daily living Roles and supports Autonomy and goals and personal values Employment, housing, finances Access and civic responsibility
Mental retardation and intellectual disabilities	1. Social inclusion 2. Physical well-being 3. Interpersonal relations 4. Material well-being 5. Emotional well-being 6. Self-determination 7. Personal development 8. Rights	Community integration and participation Health and leisure Interactions and family Employment and financial status Contentment and self-concept Choices, autonomy, personal control Education and skills Basic human rights and respect
Aging	1. Physical well-being 2. Social inclusion 3. Emotional well-being 4. Personal development 5. Interpersonal relations 6. Rights 7. Material well-being 8. Self-determination	Health and health care Residential environment and supports Psychological well-being and contentment Personal competence Supports and interactions Human rights and equality Employment and social economic status Autonomy, self-direction, and choices
Families	(Insufficient data)	(Insufficient data)

Core Indicators and Descriptors

Table 9.2 lists the most frequently referenced core indicators for the eight core QOL domains, along with a number of descriptors for each. The authors were impressed that no indicator or descriptor appeared in more than one domain, with the exception of "supports," which was referenced frequently in both interpersonal relations and social inclusion. However, their descriptors are quite different. There was no attempt to rank order the core indicators and descriptors.

TABLE 9.2
Core Indicators and Descriptors per Core Quality of Life Domain

Domain	Indicators and Descriptors

1. Physical well-being	Health
	    Physical functioning
	    Disease symptoms
	    Physical discomfort/pain
	    Fitness
	    Energy/vitality
	    Nutritional status
	    Medication
	    Sensory skills

	Activities of daily living
	    Eating
	    Transfer
	    Mobility
	    Toileting
	    Dressing

	Health care
	    Availability
	    Effectiveness
	    Satisfaction

	Leisure
	    Recreation
	    Hobbies
	    Opportunities
	    Creativity

(table continues)

TABLE 9.2. *(continued)*

Core Domain	Indicators and Descriptors

2. Emotional well-being	Contentment
	    Satisfaction (across life activities)
	    Moods (e.g., frustration, happy, sad)
	    Mental and/or physical functioning
	    Pleasure, enjoyment

	Self-concept
	    Identity
	    Self-worth
	    Self-esteem
	    Body image

	Freedom from stress
	    Safe environment
	    Stable and predictable environment
	    Coping mechanisms/stress management

3. Interpersonal relations	Interactions
	    Social networks
	    Social contacts
	    Social life

	Relationships
	    Family
	    Friends
	    Peers

	Supports
	    Emotional
	    Physical
	    Financial
	    Feedback

4. Social inclusion	Community integration and participation
	    Access
	    Presence
	    Involvement
	    Acceptance

(table continues)

TABLE 9.2. *(continued)*

Core Domain	Indicators and Descriptors

	Community roles
	    Contributor
	    Lifestyle
	    Interdependence

	Social supports
	    Support network
	    Services

5. Personal development	Education
	    Activities
	    Achievements
	    Status
	    Satisfaction

	Personal competence
	    Cognitive
	    Social
	    Practical

	Performance
	    Success/achievement
	    Productivity
	    Improvement/personal development
	    Creativity/personal expression

6. Material well-being	Financial status
	    Income
	    Financial security
	    Benefits

	Employment
	    Occupational status
	    Employment status (full time, part time)
	    Work environment
	    Advancement opportunities

(table continues)

TABLE 9.2. *(continued)*

Core Domain	Indicators and Descriptors

	Housing
	    Type of residence
	    Ownership
	    Comfort

7. Self-determination	Autonomy/personal control
	    Independence
	    Self-direction
	    Self-sufficiency

	Goals and personal values
	    Hopes/desires/ambitions
	    Expectations
	    Beliefs
	    Interests

	Choices
	    Opportunities
	    Options
	    Preferences
	    Priorities

8. Rights	Human
	    Respect
	    Dignity
	    Equality

	Legal
	    Citizenship
	    Access
	    Due process

Guidelines

As we have shared the contents of Tables 9.1 and 9.2 with our colleagues for both their feedback and cross-validation, a number of guidelines have emerged that will benefit the reader. The six most important:

1. The core indicators and descriptors listed in Tables 9.1 and 9.2 are person centered and reflect the microsystem level of analysis. They will be expanded to the meso- and macrosystem level of analysis in chapters 11, 13, and 14.

2. Although most of the indicators and descriptors are appropriate for youth, few if any relate to infants and young children. As discussed in chapter 4 ("Physical Health"), developing core indicators and descriptors is sorely needed for these two groups.

3. Each core indicator and/or descriptor will need to be defined further (i.e., operationally) as we suggest in chapter 11 ("A Systems Approach to Quality of Life Measurement").

4. We do not evaluate the efficacy of one core domain indicator or descriptor over another. The rank ordering shown in Table 9.1 and the core indicators and descriptors summarized in Table 9.2 are those found in the literature reviewed. Although we do not recommend any one or any combination of indicators for each domain (a particular selection will depend on a number of factors such as purpose, resources, and expertise), we do encourage strongly the use of multiple indicators either to measure or to evaluate each core domain.

5. We also suggest strongly that investigators use both personal appraisal (subjective) and functional assessment (objective) strategies to measure and/or evaluate each domain. The concept of methodological pluralism was discussed in considerable detail in chapter 2 and will be further developed in chapter 11.

6. Domains other than the eight analyzed in chapters 3 through 7 might be of interest to various investigators. We make no claim that the eight core QOL domains referenced throughout the *Handbook* are either definitive or applicable to focus areas other than those included in the text. However, we do feel that they operationally define the QOL concept quite well and that their utility and face validity have been supported strongly in the literature reviewed in chapters 3 through 7. If other domains are used, we recommend only that they: (a) have a foundation in a thorough review of the respective area's literature, (b) be based on a comprehensive QOL model, and (c) include the concepts of person-referenced and holism; and (d) they embrace an ecological perspective.

PART 3

The Measurement of Quality of Life

Overview

Quality of life is a complex phenomenon to assess because it is elusive, multifaceted, and fraught with measurement problems. However, there is a history of its measurement that goes back at least to the time of Thorndike (1939). Over the past decade, efforts to assess quality of life have multiplied rapidly because of the great importance given to the concept of quality of life in personal and public policy. Historically, six approaches have been used in the area of quality of life measurement: (a) multidimensional scales, (b) ethnographic approaches, (c) discrepancy analysis, (d) direct behavioral measures, (e) social indicators, and (f) individuals assessing their own quality of life. A brief overview of each is found on the following pages.

Historical Approaches

Multidimensional Scales
Multidimensional scales focus on a person's subjective reactions to life experiences. Two different approaches can be used to measure these subjective evaluations: psychological well-being and personal satisfaction or happiness. The first perspective, psychological well-being, was first described in the work of Flanagan (1982), whose proposed QOL domains were summarized in Table 2.1. Measures of personal satisfaction or happiness indicate the extent to which people have positive feelings and attitudes about various aspects of their lives, such as marriage, family life, health, neighborhood, friendships, job, and standard of living (Campbell, Converse, & Rodgers, 1976). Following the lead of Flanagan and Campbell et al., more recent efforts at using multidimensional scales are represented in the work

of Heal and Chadsey-Rusch (1985), Cummins (1997a), and Schalock and Keith (1993).

Heal and Chadsey-Rusch (1985) produced an early multidimensional scale with four subscales: satisfaction with community, satisfaction with friends and free time, satisfaction with services, and general satisfaction. The scale was revised later and expanded to include the additional dimensions of satisfaction with job, with recreation and leisure, and with interpersonal interactions (Harner & Heal, 1993; Heal, Rubin, & Park, 1995).

Another early attempt to produce a multidimensional QOL scale was that of Cummins, who developed the Comprehensive Quality of Life Scale-Intellectual Disability (ComQoL-ID), an instrument with seven scales: material things, physical well-being, productivity, intimacy, safety, place in society, and emotional well-being. This instrument has also been revised several times (e.g., Cummins, 1991, 1993). Both the ComQoL-ID and the Quality of Life Questionnaire, discussed next, have been used widely in several countries by researchers investigating quality of life of people with intellectual disability, and efforts have been made to study the cross-cultural utility of these instruments (Keith, 1996; Keith, Yamamoto, Okita, & Schalock, 1995; Rapley & Lobley, 1995; Verri et al., 1999).

In the late 1980s Keith, Schalock, and Hoffman (1986) developed the Quality of Life Questionnaire (QOL.Q) that measured individual responses in three factors: environmental control, community involvement, and social relations. The QOL.Q was subsequently revised, with the most recent revision (Schalock & Keith, 1993) incorporating four scales: satisfaction, productivity, empowerment, and social belonging. This questionnaire has recently been modified for use by self-advocates to assess their own quality of life, with a fifth factor (dignity) added (Schalock, Bonham, & Marchand, 2000).

Ethnographic Approaches
Ethnographers such as Edgerton (1990, 1996; Edgerton & Gaston, 1991; Goode, 1990, 1994) suggest that the best way to assess one's quality of life is through longitudinal research that uses naturalistic, unobtrusive observation to understand people's lives within their natural contexts and through their own eyes. Similarly, Taylor and Bogdan (1996) have given intensive focus to individual lives, sometimes spending several days studying people's life circumstances and the perceptions of those around them. These approaches produce detailed personal accounts of the lives of individuals, often reported in the voices of the people themselves. Ethnographical approaches have been conducted by anthropologists and typically do not contain the kinds of psychometric or interview techniques found with the multidimensional scales just discussed.

Discrepancy Analysis

A critical aspect of a life of quality is the goodness of fit between individual needs and personal satisfaction of those needs as well as the nature of the fit between person and environment (Heal et al., 1995; Parmenter & Donelly, 1997; Schalock & Jensen, 1986). Earlier investigators (e.g., Land & Spilerman, 1975; Liu, 1976; Milbrath, 1979) suggested the potential utility of QOL measures in identifying unmet needs among various populations, with the implication that resource allocation might be influenced by such data. The assumption is that a better person-environmental fit indicates better quality of life (Schalock, Keith, Hoffman, & Karan, 1989).

More recently Heal et al. (1995) emphasized not only the goodness-of-fit criterion but also the role of personal competence, choice, and control as key aspects of satisfaction and quality of life. Thus while quality of life may be influenced by the person-environment fit, a key part of that fit may be the ability of the environment to support the skills and personal control required to minimize discrepancies between needs and aspirations (Heal et al.). This view is consistent with the findings of Wehmeyer and Schwartz (1998) of a positive correlation between QOL and self-determination.

The discrepancy analysis approach to QOL assessment proposes also that QOL is an important criterion for social policies. A number of analysts have recommended that QOL studies be used to identify unmet needs in different populations and that the information be used to weight differentially the importance of need areas that would then influence resource allocation decisions. For example, the goodness-of-fit model proposed by Murrell and Norris (1983) defined QOL as the criterion for establishing the goodness-of-fit between the person and the environment. In this model the characteristics of a given group interact with the resources and stressors of its environment. A central assumption is that a person's perceived quality of life is a function of the discrepancy between resources and stressors.

In sum, the importance of the goodness-of-fit approach is that it conceptualizes quality of life as both a process of quality enhancement and an outcome from education, health care, and social service programs. In addition, this perspective, if individual values and aspirations are truly honored, would seem to avoid the so-called "tyranny of QOL" (Keith, 2001; Taylor, 1994) and might have significant implications for social policy (Schalock et al., 1989).

Behavioral Measures

Some investigators have used behavioral measures as an indicator of quality of life. McGill, Emerson, and Mansell (1994), for example, reported changes in challenging behaviors as an indicator of improved quality of life for individuals moving from institutional to community settings. Investigators have reported that the direct observation of a number of behaviors, including engagement in activity, social interactions, personal freedom, and autonomy correlate significantly with assessed quality of life (Rapley & Hopgood, 1997).

In recognition of the importance of supports as contributors to lifestyles, Felce and Perry (1996) investigated the effects of staff training in active support within community housing. Active support involves staff members in a planning process directed at allocating their time and effort toward involving consumers in meaningful activities and in being responsive to the activity preferences of individuals. Such activity is subject to systematic observation and has been shown to contribute to quality of life of people with significant developmental disabilities (Felce, 2000), as have other programmatic changes associated with improved adaptive behavior (Felce, Lowe, & de Paiva, 1994).

Social Indicators

Social indicators generally refer to external, environmentally based conditions such as health, social welfare, friendships, standard of living, education, public safety, housing, neighborhood, and leisure. These indicators may be defined as a statistic of direct normative interest that facilitates concise, comprehensive, and balanced judgments about the conditions of major aspects of society (Andrews & Whithey, 1976). Such indicators are good for measuring the collective quality of community or national life; however, they are probably insufficient to measure either an individual's perceived quality of life or outcomes from education, health care, and/or social service programs. Campbell et al. (1976), for example, argued that social indicators reflect only an outsider's judgment of quality as suggested by external, environmentally based conditions. Thus "because we are accustomed to evaluating people's lives in terms of their material possessions, we tend to forget that satisfaction is a psychological experience, and that the quality of this experience may not correspond very closely to these external conditions" (p. 3).

Self-Assessment

One of the striking changes over the past 20 years is the development of a strong self-advocacy movement in which people across our text's focus areas are advocating for increased opportunities to participate in the mainstream of life (Heller, Pederson, & Miller, 1996). The impact of this change is obvious to most readers who are aware of consumers' advocating for increased individual supports within regular environments and inclusion in major activities such as decision making and person-centered planning. What might be less obvious is the increasing role that consumers are playing in assessment and evaluation activities — two areas that should serve as strong antidotes to the concerns expressed by Hatton (1998). To this end, there is every indication that we will continue to see the emergence and further development of what is typically referred to as participatory action research. As described by Whitney-Thomas (1997), participatory action research (PAR) is

> an emerging approach to problem solving and social change that is particularly suited to issues of quality of life. . . . [it is] described as the sine qua non when studying subjective outcomes. . . . PAR relies on the involvement of stakeholders who can either identify subjective elements of their own lives that warrant change or understand the social contexts in which change occurs. Individuals . . . can contribute to our collective understanding of how quality of life can be conceptualized, what a life of quality looks like, and ways to improve outcomes. (p. 181)

Participatory action research is rapidly becoming the method of choice among QOL researchers. For example, consumers are working jointly with researchers in determining the relative importance of the eight core QOL domains. Consumers are also being involved in assessing their own quality of life. For example, Schalock et al. (2000) showed recently that consumers are excellent surveyors and can assess other consumers' quality of life with highly acceptable reliability and validity. With adaptations to survey techniques and the language used in the survey, 81% of consumers were able to respond for themselves, despite having significant cognitive, physical, and language limitations.

Current Approach

As discussed in chapter 2, the current approach to the measurement of quality of life can be characterized by (a) its multidimensional nature involving core domains and indicators; (b) the use of methodological pluralism, which combines the use of personal appraisal, functional assessment, and social indicators; (c) the use of multivariate research designs to evaluate the ways that personal characteristics and environmental variables relate to a person's measured quality of life; (d) the incorporation of the systems perspective that captures the multiple worlds impacting people at the micro-, meso-, and macrosystems levels; and (e) the increasing involvement of customers in the design and implementation of QOL-oriented research and evaluation.

The two chapters in part 3 elaborate on these five characteristics in two significant ways. First, chapter 10 summarizes, based on the literature reviewed in chapters 3 through 7, the measurement techniques currently used in QOL research. In this chapter the reader will find five tables (one for each of the text's focus areas) and comprehensive references that summarize the measurement techniques used for each of the eight core QOL domains. Based on this extensive analysis, the chapter concludes with a discussion of five key measurement issues.

Chapter 11 outlines and discusses the parameters of a proposed "generic" measurement system. The proposed systems approach to quality of life measurement is based on a model that integrates the core QOL domains and indicators with the systems perspective and a number of measurement strategies related to personal appraisal, functional assessment, and social indicators. The chapter summarizes several measurement principles that resulted from an International QOL Consensus Workgroup sponsored by International Association for the Scientific Study of Intellectual Disabilities (IASSID) (Schalock et al., in press). The chapter also includes three helpful tables that list QOL indicators for each QOL domain for each of the three systems levels. The chapter concludes with a discussion of measurement guidelines, interpretation guidelines, and a number of cross-cultural issues.

CHAPTER 10

Measurement Techniques Currently Used in Quality of Life Research

This chapter presents a review of the most currently used techniques for measuring quality of life (QOL) in the fields of education and special education, physical health, mental and behavioral health, mental retardation and intellectual disability, and aging. Within each technique we have analyzed which domains relate to the model proposed in this handbook and developed a summary table for each of the text's focus areas (excluding families). As a result we have been able to determine the most commonly used measurement techniques and the domains more specifically treated in each focus area. Throughout the chapter we point out some of the methodological problems associated with QOL research.

Education and Special Education

Domains Studied and Techniques Used

Research into quality of life in education is very limited, as we saw in chapter 3. Serious discussion about the use of the concept in primary and secondary education has barely begun (R. I. Brown & Shearer, 1999; Goode, 1994; Hegarty, 1994; Raphael, 1999; Schalock, 1996b; Verdugo, 1995). Because the QOL concept is still not being employed in education as frequently as in our text's other focus areas, the number of techniques used is greatly limited and the areas of application within education are very diverse. Some techniques have been applied in infancy and in adolescence, some in higher education, and others in special education.

Table 10.1 summarizes the techniques and references related to studies about quality of life in educational settings, from an initial selection of 203 papers. Especially noteworthy is the fact that there is a large number of theoretical papers or chapters and very few empirical studies. Hence the number of references included in the table is only 16; the number of techniques totals 19. This does not allow us to draw any clear conclusions about techniques in education and special education. From the published literature analyzed, most techniques are multidimensional and quantitative. However, many researchers are suggesting the development of qualitative assessment techniques. Scales and questionnaires are the techniques used most commonly in this context. The following are the most suitable instruments for assessing the domains and indicators of the model proposed in this handbook: Quality of School Life Instrument (QSL) (Williams & Batten, 1981), Quality of Student Life Questionnaire (QSLQ) (Keith & Schalock, 1995), and Students' Life Satisfaction Scale (SLSS) (Huebner, 1991). Nevertheless, research in the future should provide us with new qualitative and quantitative techniques based on a multidimensional approach similar to the model we propose.

TABLE 10.1
Quality of Life Measurement Techniques Used in Education and Special Education

DOMAIN	TECHNIQUES[a]	REFERENCES[b]
EMOTIONAL WELL-BEING	Quality of School Life Instrument (QSL) (Williams & Batten, 1981)	1, 9, 13, 16
	Students' Life Satisfaction Scale (SLSS) (Huebner, 1991)	3, 6
	Quality of Student Life Questionnaire (QSLQ) (Keith & Schalock, 1995)	8, 15
	Comprehensive Quality of Life Scale (ComQoL) (Cummins, 1991)	2
	Perceived Life Satisfaction Scale (PLSS) (Adelman, Taylor, & Nelson, 1989; Smith, Adelman, Nelson, Taylor, & Phares, 1987)	3
	Self-Description Questionnaire (SDQ) (Marsh, 1990)	

(table continues)

[a] Original references for each technique are cited only on first appearance in this column and can be found in the general reference section.
[b] Full references for the numbered citations in this column can be found in Appendix 10.1.
Note. Domains and techniques are ordered from highest to lowest number of references found. All published techniques reviewed are included.

Table 10.1. *(continued)*

DOMAIN	TECHNIQUES	REFERENCES
	Life Orientation Test (LOT-R) (Scheier, Carver, & Bridges, 1994)	4
	The Six Domains Measure (Harju & Bolen, 1998)	4
	Piers-Harris Self-Concept Scale (Piers, 1984)	6
	Multidimensional Students' Life Satisfaction Scale (Huebner, 1994)	7
	Quality of Life of University Students Scale (based on Williams & Batten, 1981; Roberts & Clifton, 1992a)	10
	7-Point Rating Scale (Nationwide sample surveys on the quality of life) (Shinn, Ahn, Kim, & Lee, 1992)	12
	Parent Questionnaire and Child Questionnaire (Timmons, 1993)	14
PERSONAL DEVELOP-MENT	Quality of School Life Instrument (QSL)	1, 9, 13, 16
	Quality of Student Life Questionnaire (QSLQ)	8, 15
	Perceived Life Satisfaction Scale (PLSS)	3
	Students' Life Satisfaction Scale (SLSS)	

(table continues)

Table 10.1. *(continued)*

DOMAIN	TECHNIQUES	REFERENCES
	Life Orientation Test (LOT-R)	4
	The Original 48-Item COPE (Carver, Scheier, & Weintraub, 1989)	
	The 28-Item Brief COPE (Carver, 1997)	
	The Six Domains Measure	
	Quality of Life Composites — esteem, independence, and support (Heal, Khoju, & Rusch, 1997)	5
	The 25-Item Quality of Life Questionnaire (Roberts & Clifton, 1992b)	11
SOCIAL INCLUSION	Quality of School Life Instrument (QSL)	1, 9, 16
	Quality of Student Life Questionnaire (QSLQ)	8, 15
	Comprehensive Quality of Life Scale (ComQoL)	2
	Perceived Life Satisfaction Scale (PLSS)	3
	Students' Life Satisfaction Scale (SLSS)	
	Quality of Life Composites — esteem, independence, and support	5
	Multidimensional Students' Life Satisfaction Scale	7

(table continues)

Table 10.1. *(continued)*

DOMAIN	TECHNIQUES	REFERENCES
INTER-PERSONAL RELATIONS	Quality of School Life Instrument (QSL)	1, 9, 16
	Comprehensive Quality of Life Scale (ComQoL)	2
	Perceived Life Satisfaction Scale (PLSS)	3
	Students' Life Satisfaction Scale (SLSS)	
	The Six Domains Measure	4
	Quality of Life Composites — esteem, independence, and support	5
	Quality of Life of University Students Scale	10
PHYSICAL WELL-BEING	Comprehensive Quality of Life Scale (ComQoL)	2
	Perceived Life Satisfaction Scale (PLSS)- Students' Life Satisfaction Scale (SLSS)	3
	The Six Domains Measure	4
	Quality of Life Composites — esteem, independence, and support	5

(table continues)

Table 10.1. *(continued)*

DOMAIN	TECHNIQUES	REFERENCES
MATERIAL WELL-BEING	Comprehensive Quality of Life Scale (ComQoL)	2
	Perceived Life Satisfaction Scale (PLSS)	3
	Students' Life Satisfaction Scale (SLSS)	
	Nowicki-Strickland Locus of Control-Short Form (LOCS-SF) Nowicki & Strickland, 1973)	
	Quality of Life Composites — esteem, independence and support	5
SELF-DETERMI-NATION	Quality of Student Life Questionnaire (QSLQ)	8, 15
	Quality of Life Composites — esteem, independence, and support	5
RIGHTS	(Insufficient data)	(Insufficient data)

The techniques used in education normally assess an individual's satisfaction and personal development in the infant and adolescent stages, although some of them analyze other dimensions in the model, such as social integration and interpersonal relations. Another interesting technique is the Perceived Life Satisfaction Scale (PLSS) (Adelman, Taylor, & Nelson, 1989; Smith, Adelman, Nelson, Taylor, & Phares, 1987), which addresses pupils' satisfaction with their lives. Also Heal, Khoju, and Rusch (1997) developed three QOL composites — esteem, independence, and support — from 17 questionnaire variables, on which they based their examination of former special education students. Heal et al. found that competence is the main dimension affecting postschool success and proposed that the domain alone could justify the importance of quality of life in adolescents.

Methodological Problems

The measurement of quality of life in children and adolescents encounters problems concerning the age of the individual under assessment. Understanding, oral and written expression, and cognitive level are crucial limiting factors in the choice of tests (Juniper, Guyatt, & Jaeschke, 1995; Manificat & Dazord, 1997). Among other reasons, this may explain why we found few assessment instruments referenced in the literature.

Instruments should be multidimensional and should analyze how the child perceives his or her quality of life. Consequently, we need to examine indicators that are relevant to the child. And it is important to bear in mind the important changes that occur in a child's perception as he or she grows older. Approaches and methodology have to be very different in infancy and primary education compared to adolescence. And the QOL concept may have very different implications or usefulness for the two age groups. Some initial studies have been pursued in this idea (Verdugo & Gómez-Vela, 2000; Verdugo & Sabeh, 2000). Moreover, given the developmental age of the individual, it is also advisable to measure the opinions of relatives and professionals about the quality of life of their children and pupils.

Physical Health

Domains Studied and Techniques Used

Most techniques used in published studies about health assess the physical well-being and emotional well-being domains. The other domains involve a varied number of techniques, although significantly fewer than these two. In the rights domain we found no specific assessment technique.

In health, in contrast with mental and behavioral health discussed next, most studies only use a single assessment instrument. The number of studies using a single technique in the area is enormous, and most of them exhibit marginal psychometric properties. The reductionism of research in the area is common. And the general trend is that studies are focused exclusively on a functional assessment of the state of health in relation to a particular disease.

Table 10.2 presents the most commonly used techniques in the literature reviewed. We have not included many specific techniques on the grounds that they had been used only in a single study. The types of techniques applied are mainly scales, questionnaires, profiles, and inventories. Interviewees are both patients and professionals. Especially useful are those multidimensional and generic tests that focus on the measurement of the subjective health status and individuals' perception about their quality of life. Such tests are sometimes self-administered.

In the analysis of the most commonly used techniques, with different appli-

TABLE 10.2
Quality of Life Measurement Techniques Used in Physical Health

DOMAIN	TECHNIQUES[a]	REFERENCES[b]
PHYSICAL WELL-BEING	World Health Organization Quality of Life Assessment (WHOQOL-100) (WHOQOL Group, 1993, 1995a, 1995b)	19, 21, 45, 53, 57, 65, 73, 74, 75, 76
	Medical Outcomes Study 36 — Item Short-Form Health Survey (SF-36) (Ware et al., 1993, 1994)	3, 27, 38, 44, 46, 51, 52, 56, 65
	Nottingham Health Profile (NHP) (Hunt & McEwen, 1980)	2, 4, 13, 33, 34, 50, 55, 65, 70
	Sickness Impact Profile (SIP) (Bergner, Bobbit, Carter, & Gilson, 1981)	5, 8, 9, 16, 23, 47, 65, 70
	European Organization for Research and Treatment of Cancer Quality of Life Questionnaire (EORTC) (Aaronson, 1987)	1, 6, 22, 44, 60, 64, 65
	Pediatric Asthma Quality of Life Questionnaire (PAQLQ) (Townsend et al., 1991; Juniper, Guyatt, & Jaeschke, 1995)	30, 39, 40, 41, 42, 43, 65
	Diabetes Quality of Life Measure (DQOL) (Jacobson, Groot, & Samson, 1995)	20, 35, 36, 37, 65, 66
	Asthma Quality of Life Questionnaire (AQLQ) Juniper et al., 1992)	39, 40, 41, 48, 63, 65

(table continues)

[a] Original references for each technique are cited only on first appearance in this column and can be found in the general reference section.
[b] Full references for the numbered citations in this column can be found in Appendix 10.2.
Note. Domains and techniques are ordered from highest to lowest number of references found. Only techniques used in more than two studies are included.

Table 10.2. *(continued)*

DOMAIN	TECHNIQUES	REFERENCES
	Childhood Asthma Questionnaire (CAQ) (French, Christie, & Sowden, 1994)	15, 24, 42, 43, 65
	KINDL (Bullinger, 1994; Ravens-Sieberer & Bullinger, 1998)	10, 11, 58, 65
	Life Satisfaction Index-A (LSI-A) (Neugarten, Havighurst, & Tobin, 1961)	12, 25, 59, 65
	Quality-Adjusted Life Years Index (QALYs) (Williams, 1985; Gudex, 1986)	29, 44, 61, 65
	Pediatric Cancer Quality of Life Inventory (PCQL) (Varni et al., 1998)	65, 68, 69, 71
	Hamilton Rating Scale of Depression (Hamilton, 1967)	23, 28, 65
EMOTIONAL WELL-BEING	World Health Organization Quality of Life Assessment (WHOQOL-100)	19, 21, 45, 53, 57, 65, 73, 74, 75, 76
	Medical Outcomes Study 36-Item Short-Form Health Survey (SF-36)	3, 27, 38, 44, 46, 51, 52, 56, 65
	Nottingham Health Profile (NHP)	2, 4, 13, 33, 34, 50, 55, 65, 70
	Sickness Impact Profile (SIP)	5, 8, 9, 16, 23, 47, 65, 70
	European Organization for Research and Treatment of Cancer Quality of Life Questionnaire (EORTC)	1, 6, 22, 44, 60, 64, 65

(table continues)

Table 10.2. *(continued)*

DOMAIN	TECHNIQUES	REFERENCES
	Pediatric Asthma Quality of Life Questionnaire (PAQLQ)	30, 39, 40, 41, 42, 43, 65
	Diabetes Quality of Life Measure (DQOL)	20, 35, 36, 37, 65, 66
	Asthma Quality of Life Questionnaire (AQLQ)	39, 40, 41, 48, 63, 65
	Childhood Asthma Questionnaire (CAQ)	15, 24, 42, 43, 65
	KINDL	10, 11, 58, 65
	Life Satisfaction Index-A (LSI-A)	12, 25, 59, 65
	Quality of Well-Being Scale (QWB) Patrick, Bush, & Chen, 1973)	17, 44, 65, 70
	Pediatric Cancer Quality of Life Inventory (PCQL)	65, 68, 69, 71
	Hamilton Rating Scale of Depression (HAM-D, HDRS)	23, 28, 65
INTER-PERSONAL RELATIONS	World Health Organization Quality of Life Assessment (WHOQOL-100)	19, 21, 45, 53, 57, 65, 73, 74, 75, 76
	Nottingham Health Profile (NHP)	2, 4, 13, 33, 34, 50, 55, 65, 70
	Sickness Impact Profile (SIP)	5, 8, 9, 16, 23, 47, 65, 70
	European Organization for Research and Treatment of Cancer Quality of Life Questionnaire (EORTC)	1, 6, 22, 44, 60, 64, 65
	KINDL	10, 11, 58, 65

(table continues)

Table 10.2. *(continued)*

DOMAIN	TECHNIQUES	REFERENCES
	Life Satisfaction Index-A (LSI-A)	12, 25, 59, 65
	Pediatric Cancer Quality of Life Inventory (PCQL)	65, 68, 69, 71
SOCIAL INCLUSION	World Health Organization Quality of Life Assessment (WHOQOL-100)	19, 21, 45, 53, 57, 65, 73, 74, 75, 76
	Medical Outcomes Study 36-Item Short-Form Health Survey (SF-36)	3, 27, 38, 44, 46, 51, 52, 56, 65
	European Organization for Research and Treatment of Cancer Quality of Life Questionnaire (EORTC)	1, 6, 22, 44, 60, 64, 65
	Pediatric Asthma Quality of Life Questionnaire (PAQLQ)	30, 39, 40, 41, 42, 43, 65
	Childhood Asthma Questionnaire (CAQ)	15, 24, 42, 43, 65
	Asthma Quality of Life Questionnaire (AQLQ)	39, 40, 41, 48, 63
	Pedatric Cancer Quality of Life Inventory (PCQL)	65, 68, 69, 71
PERSONAL DEVELOPMENT	Nottingham Health Profile (NHP)	2, 4, 13, 33, 34, 50, 55, 65, 70
	Sickness Impact Profile (SIP)	5, 8, 9, 16, 23, 47, 65, 70
	European Organization for Research and Treatment of Cancer Quality of Life Questionnaire (EORTC)	1, 6, 22, 44, 60, 64, 65
	Pediatric Asthma Quality of Life Questionnaire (PAQLQ)	30, 39, 40, 41, 42, 43, 65

(table continues)

Table 10.2. (continued)

DOMAIN	TECHNIQUES	REFERENCES
	Asthma Quality of Life Questionnaire (AQLQ)	39, 40, 41, 48, 63
	Life Satisfaction Index-A (LSI-A)	12, 25, 59, 65
	Pediatric Cancer Quality of Life Inventory (PCQL)	65, 68, 69, 71
MATERIAL WELL-BEING	Sickness Impact Profile (SIP)	5, 8, 9, 16, 23, 47, 65, 70
	Diabetes Quality of Life Measure (DQOL)	20, 35, 36, 37, 65, 66
SELF-DETERMI-NATION	World Health Organization Quality of Life Assessment (QOL-100)	19, 21, 45, 53, 57, 65, 73, 74, 75, 76
	Sickness Impact Profile (SIP)	5, 8, 9, 16, 23, 47, 65, 70
	Life Satisfaction Index-A (LSI-A)	12, 25, 59, 65
RIGHTS	(Insufficient data)	(Insufficient data)

cations in the same domain and in different domains of the proposed model (see Figure 2.2), we limited the number of instruments to four: World Health Organization Quality of Life Assessment (WHOQOL-100) (World Health Organization Quality of Life Group, 1993, 1995a, 1995b), Medical Outcomes Study 36 — Item Short-Form Health Survey (SF-36) (Ware, Snow, Kosinski, & Gandek, 1993; Ware et al., 1994), Nottingham Health Profile (NHP) (Hunt & McEwen, 1980), and the Sickness Impact Profile (SIP) (Bergner, Bobbit, Carter, & Gilson, 1981).

There are several other assessment instruments with a high number of references in Table 10.2, but their content is focused on a specific item of research and thus of more limited value. Of these we mention the European Organization for Research and Treatment of Cancer Quality of Life Questionnaire (EORTC)

(Aaronson, 1987, 1991; European Organization for Research and Treatment of Cancer Quality of Life, 1993), and the Pediatric Asthma Quality of Life Questionnaire (PAQLQ) (Townsend et al., 1991; Juniper, Guyatt, & Jaeschke, 1995). As their titles suggest, both are related to specific diseases: cancer and asthma in children. There are many other content-specific tests that are too numerous to list in Table 10.2.

Methodological Problems

Health-related quality of life (HRQOL) measurement has used many different approaches and concepts and with different objectives suggested by researchers. Despite the wide range of instruments (e.g., Tamburini [1998] has described more than 800 in the areas of physical and mental health), the level of comparison among investigators remains limited (Patrick & Erickson, 1988). The following methodological problems arise regarding quality of life measurement in the area of health: standardized or nonstandardized assessment strategies, subjective or objective approaches and indicators, disease-specific or general measures, single instrument versus multiple instruments, total versus domain scoring, profile versus utility scoring, varied methods of administration, sources of information (health care providers, relatives, patient), methods of analysis and complexity of scoring, presentation of data and usefulness to decision making, content of questionnaires, translations, length and cost of administration, pertinence of instrument for setting, reliability, validity, stability, sensitivity, and so on (Aaronson, 1991; Bucquet, 1993; Chwalow, 1993; Evans, Dingus, & Haselkorn, 1993; Guillemin, 1993; Moinpour, Savage, Hayden, Sawyers, & Upchurch, 1995; Ware, 1991).

Quite often researchers have faced the choice between generic or specific-disease instruments (Bouvenot, 1993; Guillemin, 1993; Ware, 1991). Specific measurements have been devised for various specific groups of diseases, syndromes, or populations, such as diabetes, HIV, or cancer. However, they have the disadvantage that it is impossible to make comparisons among different disease groups, for results are not applicable to other groups for which tests have been developed and validated. Generic instruments are designed to analyze patients with diverse pathologies from different socioeconomic and cultural groups. Generic instruments that are widely used and cited in the research reviewed include SIP, SF-36, NHP, and WHOQOL-100. Tamburini (1998) presents more than 100 bibliographical references about the first three. They do provide comparisons among different illnesses or interventions and often evaluate more general aspects of the patient's health and global satisfaction. Their main limitations lie in the fact that they are not adequately sensitive to changes in health, and they are time consuming and costly.

Today there is a consensus about the best option: a combination of generic and specific measures. Criteria to choose an instrument involve (Shug, 1996): the level of observation chosen (individual patient, groups of patients, care systems), the aims of the research (describe, compare, or evaluate health outcomes), the context of interest (biomedical, sociological, humanistic), the sources of the information (patients, caregivers, doctors, or other care providers), and the users of the information (politicians, doctors, patient organizations, or patients).

Until a few years ago the measurement of quality of life in ill people had been a daily clinical practice characterized as formal, intuitive, and lacking rigor (Bouvenot, 1993). We have to bear in mind that systematic assessment, by itself, is far from simple since there is a wide range of meaning attributed to the term *quality of life* in research into health. Another problem is that the number of assessment tests keeps growing at an excessive rate, which can be explained best by the diverse purposes of researchers.

Methodological problems more frequently found in recent studies arise from the use of a single type of measurement. Researchers often resort to standardized assessment strategies or nonstandardized strategies strictly focused on objective or subjective indicators of our QOL model (see Figure 2.2), which are almost never assessed in combination. Most studies about health use only a single assessment instrument, and it can be specific or generic. In addition, studies normally present total scores or results without further specification about each domain.

Another methodological problem arises when we consider the value of the measures at an international level. Some of the instruments analyzed have been translated into other languages, reflecting the extent of their use. Kuyken (1995), on behalf of the WHOQOL Group, recognizes one limitation: these projects have tended to be concerned primarily with the languages of Europe and North America. He also thinks that there is a danger in translating an existing measurement, since a distortion in results can arise from the use of inappropriate HRQOL constructs, which are valid in the source language setting but not in the target language setting. Fitzpatrick (1995) also reflects on the need to reconsider whether the notions of well-being or of the value of life are universal or culture specific. Fox-Rushby and Parker (1995) suggest that even if there are universal dimensions to HRQOL, the methods used to develop these particular instruments have not been sufficiently sensitive to identify these domains. They consider that generic HRQOL instruments are not culture free but "culture full," reflecting in particular the beliefs and values of the researchers (mostly biomedical perceptions of health, well-being, and the quality of life) who contributed to their construction.

In summary, the fundamental problem with existing health-related measurement instruments is that they do not satisfy the clinical goal of indicating what clinicians and patients perceive as quality of life, because they generally have poor face validity. In addition, researchers often do not define what they conceptualize as quality of life, and they may not identify the domains of measurement that are supposed to denote quality of life rather than health status. Instead of measuring quality of life, many researchers are really measuring various aspects of health status. From an analogous point of view, the Division of Mental Health of the World Health Organization Group (Kuyken, 1995) considers that the SIP and the NHP, while beginning to provide a measure of the impact of disease, do not assess quality of life per se. Similarly Fox-Rushby and Parker (1995) reviewed nine instruments and found that the process of development has not involved the acquisition of a detailed understanding of the social, cultural, and economic contexts that influence the experience and articulation of health, illness, and the quality of life among populations in either group of instruments.

Mental and Behavioral Health

Domains Studied and Techniques Used

The published mental and behavioral health studies reviewed exhibit a great diversity of techniques, but most of them have been used only in one or two studies. This means that most instrumental technology already developed has not yet been used enough to verify its usefulness. The variety of techniques used in research is a common characteristic in all domains of the model, except for self-determination and rights, in which there is not yet a sufficient number of assessment techniques to permit generalizations. In these two domains, moreover, the few existing techniques are often focused only on certain indicators, and it is necessary to develop new techniques that reflect a broader approach to the domain. In the other domains, techniques very often measure a single dimension but include several indicators.

Most studies use more than one QOL assessment technique, employing up to five or six different instruments. Generally, their common aim is to establish correlations among scores. The variety of techniques is used also to determine whether hypotheses are confirmed and/or whether the results are contradictory.

Most QOL measurement techniques in mental and behavioral health are quantitative, but some qualitative techniques are also used. Scales and questionnaires are the most prevalent. Self-reports and interviews are second. Finally, one finds the use of inventories, checklists, indexes, and profiles.

This section of the chapter is based on the analysis of techniques employed in research into quality of life in mental and behavioral health summarized in chapter 5. Table 10.3 presents the techniques by categories following the domains of the proposed model. We also indicate references to studies where they have been used. Given the vast number of techniques employed, we have included only those that have been used in more than two studies. There is only one exception to this minimum number, and that is in reference to self-determination and rights domains, due to their infrequent mention.

Among the techniques used, the following six are the most adequate in our es-

TABLE 10.3
Quality of Life Measurement Techniques Used in Mental and Behavioral Health

DOMAIN	TECHNIQUES[a]	REFERENCES[b]
EMOTIONAL WELL-BEING	Quality of Life Interview (Lehman, 1988)	33, 34, 54, 74, 75, 77, 85, 103, 116, 122, 123, 128, 133
	Medical Outcomes Study 36 — Item Short-Form Health Survey (SF-36) (Ware et al., 1993, 1994)	13, 22, 47, 72, 97, 113, 120, 137, 139, 142
	Hamilton Rating Scale of Depression (HAM-D, HDRS) (Hamilton, 1967)	55, 70, 91, 97, 120, 127
	Quality of Life Scale (QLS) (Heinrichs, Hanlon, & Carpenter, 1984)	5, 26, 59, 99, 103, 127
	Satisfaction with Life Domains Scale (SLDS) (Baker & Intagliata, 1982)	6, 30, 75, 130, 133
	Lancashire Quality of Life Profile (LQOLP) (Oliver, 1991; Oliver & Mohamad, 1992)	16, 85, 87, 88, 136
	Quality of Life Uniscale (QLI) (Spitzer & Dobson 1981)	6, 85, 88, 105
	Affect Balance Scale (ABS) (Bradburn, 1969)	75, 85, 88, 136
	Cantril's Scale (Cantril, 1965)	16, 85, 88, 136

(table continues)

[a] Original references for each technique are cited only on first appearance in this column and can be found in the general reference section.
[b] Full references for the numbered citations in this column can be found in Appendix 10.3.
Note. Domains and techniques are ordered from highest to lowest number of references found. Only techniques used in more than two studies are included, except in the rights and self-determination dimension due to the paucity of total references.

Table 10.3. *(continued)*

DOMAIN	TECHNIQUES	REFERENCES
	Quality of Life Inventory (QOLI) (Frisch, 1994)	6, 38, 42, 55
	Quality of Life Index for Mental Health (QLI-MH) (Becker, Diamond, & Sainfort, 1993)	6, 7, 105
	Beck Depression Inventory (BDI) (Beck, Ward, & Mendelson, 1961; Beck & Beck, 1972)	38, 55, 119
	Rosenberg Self-Esteem Scale (RSES) (Rosenberg, 1965)	33, 85, 136
	Social Behaviour Schedule (SBS) (Sturt & Wykes, 1986)	76, 116, 122
PHYSICAL WELL-BEING	Quality of Life Interview	33, 34, 54, 74, 75, 77, 85, 103, 116, 122, 123, 128, 133
	Medical Outcomes Study 36-Item Short-Form Health Survey (SF-36)	13, 22, 47, 72, 97, 113, 120, 137, 139, 142
	Brief Psychiatric Rating Scale (BPRS) (Overall & Gorham, 1962; Kolakowska, 1976; Lukoff, Liberman, & Nuechterlein, 1986)	5, 16, 59, 122, 123, 127
	Quality of Life Scale (QLS)	5, 26, 59, 99, 103, 127
	Global Assessment of Functioning Scale: Symptoms (GAFS) (Awad, 1992)	8, 16, 69, 70, 117, 128
	Hamilton Depression Rating Scale (HAM-D)	55, 70, 91, 97, 120, 127

(table continues)

Table 10.3. *(continued)*

DOMAIN	TECHNIQUES	REFERENCES
	Satisfaction With Life Domains Scale (SLDS)	6, 30, 75, 130, 133
	Quality of Life Inventory (QOLI)	6, 38, 42, 55
	Quality of Life Uniscale (QLI)	6, 85, 88, 105
	Beck Depression Inventory (BDI)	38, 55, 119
	Quality of Life Index for Mental Health (QLI-MH)	6, 7, 105
	Social Behaviour Schedule (SBS)	76, 116, 122
	Scale for the Assessment of Negative Symptom (SANS) (Andreasen, 1983)	91, 122, 127
	Scale for the Assessment of Positive Symptoms (SAPS) (Andreasen, 1984)	91, 122, 127
INTER-PERSONAL RELATIONS	Quality of Life Interview	33, 34, 54, 74, 75, 77, 85, 103, 116, 122, 123, 128, 133
	Medical Outcomes Study 36-Item Short-Form Health Survey (SF-36)	13, 22, 47, 72, 97, 113, 120, 137, 139, 142
	Quality of Life Scale (QLS)	5, 26, 59, 99, 103, 127
	Global Assessment of Functioning Scale: Symptoms (GAFS)	8, 16, 69, 70, 117, 128
	Satisfaction With Life Domains Scale (SLDS)	6, 30, 75, 130, 133
	Lancashire Quality of Life Profile (LQOLP)	16, 85, 87, 88, 136
	Quality of Life Inventory (QOLI)	6, 38, 42, 55

(table continues)

Table 10.3. *(continued)*

DOMAIN	TECHNIQUES	REFERENCES
	Quality of Life Index Mental Health QLI-MH)	6, 7, 105
SOCIAL INCLUSION	Quality of Life Interview	33, 34, 54, 74, 75, 77, 85, 103, 116, 122, 123, 128, 133
	Medical Outcomes Study 36-Item Short-Form Health Survey (SF-36)	13, 22, 47, 72, 97, 113, 120, 137, 139, 142
	Global Assessment of Functioning Scale: Symptoms (GAFS)	8, 16, 69, 70, 117, 128
	Quality of Life Scale (QLS)	5, 26, 59, 99, 103, 127
	Satisfaction With Life Domains Scale (SLDS)	6, 30, 75, 130, 133
	Quality of Life Inventory (QOLI)	6, 38, 42, 55
	Pattison's Social Network Schedule (SNS) (Pattison, Difrancisco, Wood, Frazier, & Crowder, 1975; Llamas, Pattison, & Hunt, 1981; Pattison & Pattison, 1981)	5, 76, 123
MATERIAL WELL-BEING	Quality of Life Interview	33, 34, 54, 74, 75, 77, 85, 103, 116, 122, 123, 128, 133
	Medical Outcomes Study 36-Item Short-Form Health Survey (SF-36)	13, 22, 47, 72, 97, 113, 120, 137, 139, 142
	Quality of Life Scale (QLS)	5, 26, 59, 99, 103, 127

(table continues)

Table 10.3. *(continued)*

DOMAIN	TECHNIQUES	REFERENCES
	Satisfaction With Life Domains Scale (SLDS)	6, 30, 75, 130, 133
	Lancashire Quality of Life Profile (LQOLP)	16, 85, 87, 88, 136
	Quality of Life Inventory	6, 38, 42, 55
	Quality of Life Index Mental Health (QLI-MH)	6, 7, 105
PERSONAL DEVELOPMENT	Quality of Life Interview	33, 34, 54, 74, 75, 77, 85, 103, 116, 122, 123, 128, 133
	Medical Outcomes Study 36-Item Short-Form Health Survey (SF-36)	13, 22, 47, 72, 97, 113, 120, 137, 139, 142
	Quality of Life Scale (QLS)	5, 26, 59, 99, 103, 127
	Satisfaction With Life Domains Scale (SLDS)	6, 30, 75, 130, 133
	Quality of Life Inventory (QOLI)	6, 38, 42, 55
	Quality of Life Uniscale (QLI)	6, 85, 88, 105
	Quality of Life Index Mental Health (QLI-MH)	6, 7, 105
	Social Behaviour Schedule (SBS)	76, 116, 122
SELF-DETERMINATION	Medical Outcomes Study 36-Item Short-Form Health Survey (SF-36)	13, 22, 47, 72, 97, 113, 120, 137, 139, 142
	Quality of Life Uniscale (QLI)	6, 85, 88, 105
	Quality of Life Index for Mental Health (QLI-MH)	6, 7, 105

(table continues)

Table 10.3. *(continued)*

DOMAIN	TECHNIQUES	REFERENCES
	Patients' Attitudes Schedule (PAS) (Wykes, 1982)	49, 116
	Adapted Pleasant Events Schedule (APES) (Wilson, 1985) is a modification of the Pleasant Events Schedule (PES) (MacPhillamy & Lewinsohn, 1982)	2, 59
	Clients' Quality of Life (CQLI) (Mulkern & Manderscheid, 1984) and Uniform Client Data Instrument (UCDI) (Goldstrom & Manderscheid, 1982)	51, 93
	Morningside Rehabilitation Status Scale (Affleck & McGuire, 1984)	51, 93
	Subjective Quality of Life (Lehman, 1988)	25, 102
	The Quality of Life Self-Assessment Inventory (QLS-100) (Skantze et al., 1992)	117, 118
	The Standard of Living Interview (SOL I) (Skantze et al., 1992)	117, 118
RIGHTS	The Standard of Living Interview (SOLI)	117, 118
	Legal System Costs (Clark et al., 1994)	25

timation to assess the domains and indicators of the proposed model: Medical Outcomes Study 36 — Item Short-Form Health Survey (SF-36) (Ware et al., 1993, 1994), which measures every domain except rights; Quality of Life Index for Mental Health (QLI-MH) (Becker, Diamond, & Sainfort, 1993), which measures every domain except social inclusion and rights; Quality of Life Interview (Lehman, 1988); Satisfaction with Life Domains Scale (SLDS) (Baker & Intagliata, 1982); Quality of Life Inventory (QOLI) (Frisch, 1994); and Quality of Life Scale (QLS) (Heinrichs, Hanlon, & Carpenter, 1984), which measure every domain of the model except rights and self-determination. These techniques not only promote a multidimensional approach to the study of quality of life, they also demonstrate good psychometric features, including validity, reliability, and consistency (Bigelow, Brodsky, Steward, & Olson, 1982; Bobes et al., 1996; Bullinger, 1995, 1997; Bullinger, Anderson, Aaronson, & Cella, 1995; Goodman, Hull, Terkelsen, Smith, & Anthony, 1997; Jenkinson & Wright, 1993; Katz, Larson, & Phillips, 1992; Lehman, Postrado, & Rachuba, 1993; Long, 1983; Rodríguez, Jarne, Soler, Miarons, & Grau, 995; Schutt & Goldfinger, 1996; Sullivan, Karlsson, & Ware, 1994).

Table 10.3 also highlights another group of tests that measure some domains of the model, although not as many as those six listed above. These tests are Quality of Life Uniscale (QLI) (Spitzer & Dobson, 1981), which measures emotional well-being, physical well-being, personal development, and self-determination; Lancashire Quality of Life Profile (LQOLP) (Oliver, 1991; Oliver & Mohamad, 1992; Oliver, Huxley, Bridges, & Mohamad, 1996), which measures interpersonal relations, emotional well-being, and material well-being; Global Assessment of Functioning Scale: Symptoms (GAFS), which measures physical well-being and interpersonal relations; and Social Behaviour Schedule (SBS) (Sturt & Wykes, 1986), which measures emotional well-being, physical well-being, and personal development. Our review of the literature also indicates that there are other multidimensional tests that can be used to assess some dimensions of the model; they are not included in the table because they are not widely cited in the published literature.

Most tests referenced in recent studies are generic, such as those we have mentioned, and have been used with patients with chronic mental illness. However, in parallel with these, other disease-specific QOL instruments for psychiatric patient populations have been developed. Most of them focus on people diagnosed with depression and other mood disorders (Børup & Undén, 1994; Katschnig & Angermeyer, 1997; Thunedborg, Black, & Bech, 1995; Tuynman-Qua, De Jonghe, McKenna, & Hunt, 1992), and other specific psychotic disorders (Awad, Voruganti, & Heslegrave, 1997; Bigelow, Gareau, & Young, 1990; Lehman, 1988; McKenna, 1997; Skantze & Malm, 1994).

Our analysis of studies about quality of life in the mental and behavioral health focus area indicates that the domains that have attracted the most attention are emotional well-being, physical well-being, and interpersonal relations. The next most frequently considered are social inclusion, material well-being, and personal development. Finally, and with very few references, we found mention of self-determination and rights. The latter domain had an extremely low number of references. However, the self-determination dimension has received increased attention in the past five years.

Methodological Problems

Methodological problems in the measurement of quality of life in people with mental and behavioral health conditions are very significant, given the impact of the disorder on QOL indicators and on the individual's life satisfaction. Many studies include the impact of the state of health of the patient as a component in the research design. On the other hand, we also have to bear in mind the impact of doses and type of medication on patients' responses, as there can be alterations in early stages of treatment. Thus there is a need to refine instruments and methods and to make them more sensitive to changes in the course of an illness. Moreover, it is necessary to develop a deeper understanding of how and when the assessments of the results of treatments should be made (Atkinson, Zibin, & Chuang, 1997; Frisch, Cornell, Vilanueva, & Retzlaff, 1992; Lehman, 1983a, 1982b, 1988, 1997; Lehman et al., 1993).

The past few years have seen an increased interest in assessing the mental state of infants and adolescents, which had received almost no recent consideration, perhaps because no specific assessment techniques were available. Most QOL assessments have been applied only to adults, and their reliability and validity have been verified only for this type of participant. Today there is an increasing effort to adapt and validate most of these techniques to the infant and adolescent population.

Mental Retardation and Intellectual Disabilities

Domains Studied

The study of quality of life in people with mental retardation or intellectual disabilities benefits from a long history of intense activity that is reflected in the large number of references published over the past two decades. The number of techniques used is also very large. However, there is still a long way to go in research, and new techniques need to be developed as discussed in the following section on "measurement issues."

This section is based on the analysis of 51 research references that met our criteria. Given the considerable number of techniques that can be found only in one or two studies, Table 10.4 includes only those techniques that appear in at least three studies. The only exception is to be found in rights, which, due to its scarcity, includes reference to all the published studies we could find.

Many studies and techniques are based on multidimensional models. Thus they often examine different aspects of life for people with intellectual disabilities.

TABLE 10.4
Quality of Life Measurement Techniques Used in Mental Retardation and Intellectual Disabilities

DOMAIN	TECHNIQUES[a]	REFERENCES[b]
SOCIAL INCLUSION	Quality of Life Questionnaire (QOL.Q) (Schalock & Keith, 1993)	1, 11, 15, 30, 38, 9, 40, 43, 44, 45, 49
	Consumer Satisfaction Survey (Intellectual Disability) (Temple University, 1988)	3, 11, 25, 28, 42, 49
	Quality of Life Index (Schalock, Keith, Hoffman, & Karan, 1989; Campo, Sharpton, Thompson, & Sexton, 1996)	5, 6, 14, 25, 40, 46, 48
	Comprehensive Quality of Life Scale-Intellectual Disability (Cummins, 1991, 1993)	2, 3, 10, 11, 43
	Living in a Supervised Home: A Questionnaire on Quality of Life (Cragg & Harrison, 1986)	3, 11, 12, 13, 24
	Lifestyle Satisfaction Scale (LSS) (Heal & Chadsey-Rusch, 1985)	3, 11, 22, 29, 49
	Resident Lifestyle Inventory (RLI) (Bellamy, Newton, LeBaron, & Horner, 1990)	11, 25, 26, 31, 49
	Program Analysis of Service Systems (PASS) & Program Analysis of Service Systems' Implementation of Normalization Goals (PASSING) (Wolfensberger, 1975; Wolfensberger & Glenn, 1983)	9, 19, 35, 36

(table continues)

[a] Original references for each technique are cited only on first appearance in this column and can be found in the general reference section.
[b] Full references for the numbered citations in this column can be found in Appendix 10.4.
Note. Domains and techniques are ordered from highest to lowest number of references found. Only techniques used in more than two studies are included, except in the rights dimension due to the paucity of total references.

Table 10.4. *(continued)*

DOMAIN	TECHNIQUES	REFERENCES
	Multifaceted Lifestyle Satisfaction Scale (MLSS) (Harner & Heal, 1993)	3, 18, 43
	Resident Lifestyle Inventory (RLI) (Kennedy, Horner, Newton, & Kanda, 1990)	3, 23, 49
	Adaptative Behavior Scale (ABS) (Nihira, Foster, Shellhaas, & Leland, 1975)	9, 38, 39
INTER-PERSONAL RELATIONS	Quality of Life Index	5, 6, 14, 25, 40, 46, 48
	Comprehensive Quality of Life Scale-Intellectual Disability	2, 3, 10, 11, 43
	Lifestyle Satisfaction Scale (LSS)	3, 11, 22, 29, 49
	Resident Lifestyle Inventory (RLI)	3, 11, 23, 25, 26, 31, 49
	PALS (Rosen, Simon, & McKinsey, 1995)	3, 11, 41, 47
	PASS & PASSING	9, 19, 35, 36
	Multifaceted Lifestyle Satisfaction Scale (MLSS)	3, 18, 43
	Social Network Analysis Interview Form	6, 31, 49
SELF-DETERMI-NATION	Quality of Life Questionnaire (QOL.Q)	1, 11, 15, 30, 38, 39, 40, 43, 44, 45, 49
	Consumer Satisfaction Survey	3, 11, 25, 28, 42, 49

(table continues)

Table 10.4. *(continued)*

DOMAIN	TECHNIQUES	REFERENCES
	Quality of Life Index	5, 6, 14, 25, 40, 46, 48
	Living in a supervised home: A Questionnaire on Quality of Life	3, 11, 12, 13, 24
	PASS & PASSING	9, 19, 35, 36
	Adaptive Behavior Scale (ABS)	9, 36, 38, 39
	Multifaceted Lifestyle Satisfaction Scale (MLSS)	3, 18, 43
MATERIAL WELL-BEING	Quality of Life Questionnaire (QOL.Q)	1, 11, 15, 30, 38, 39, 40, 43, 44, 45, 49
	Quality of Life Index	5, 6, 14, 25, 40, 46, 48
	Consumer Satisfaction Survey	3, 11, 25, 28, 42, 49
	Comprehensive Quality of Life Scale-Intellectual Disability	2, 3, 10, 11, 43
	Living in a supervised home: A Questionnaire on Quality of Life	3, 11, 12, 13, 24
	Normalization Index (based on PASS-3, Wolfensberger, 1975)	9, 19, 35, 36
	Multifaceted Lifestyle Satisfaction Scale (MLSS)	3, 18, 43
PHYSICAL WELL-BEING	Comprehensive Quality of Life Scale-Intellectual Disability	2, 3, 10, 11, 43
	Resident Lifestyle Inventory (RLI)	11, 25, 26, 31, 49
	Living in a supervised home: A Questionnaire on Quality of Life	3, 11, 12, 24

(table continues)

Table 10.4. *(continued)*

DOMAIN	TECHNIQUES	REFERENCES
	PASS & PASSING	9, 19, 35, 36
	The Group Home Management Interview	9, 20, 35, 36
	Adaptive Behavior Scale (ABS)	9, 36, 38, 39
	Resident Lifestyle Inventory (RLI)	3, 23, 49
PERSONAL DEVELOPMENT	Quality of Life Questionnaire (QOL.Q)	1, 11, 15, 30, 38, 39, 40, 43, 44, 45, 49
	Quality of Life Index	5, 6, 14, 25, 40, 46, 48
	Living in a supervised home: A Questionnaire on Quality of Life	3, 11, 12, 13, 24
	Resident Lifestyle Inventory (RLI)	3, 11, 23, 25, 26, 31, 49
EMOTIONAL WELL-BEING	Quality of Life Questionnaire (QOL.Q)	1, 11, 15, 30, 38, 39, 40, 43, 44, 45, 49
	Comprehensive Quality of Life Scale-Intellectual Disability	2, 3, 10, 11, 43
	Lifestyle Satisfaction Scale (LSS)	3, 11, 22, 29, 49
	PALS	3, 11, 41
RIGHTS	PASS & PASSING	9, 19, 35

Every domain in the proposed model has received attention from researchers, but with different emphases. It seems logical that research reviewed would be consistent with the model proposed (see Figure 2.2), since the model has been developed from existing advances in this field of knowledge.

Social inclusion is the most studied domain in the model, with a broad use of techniques and extensive references (42 out of 51). Other domains present in the studies are interpersonal relations, self-determination, and material well-being (with 35 references each). Interpersonal relations is viewed in the research as a fundamental aspect that determines quality of life for people with intellectual limitations. It is quite common to find studies that assess social inclusion and interpersonal relations with the aim of confirming normalization (also deinstitutionalization) and integration of the individual in his or her own natural settings. But the most outstanding feature is attention devoted to self-determination. Unlike the other focus areas, with the exception of mental and behavioral health in recent publications, self-determination of people with intellectual disabilities already benefits from a significant number of studies and assessment techniques. It seems likely that research into this dimension will increase in the near future. The concepts of self-determination, together with quality of life, play a crucial role as guidelines for professional practices and for the planning of programs and services.

The domains of emotional well-being, personal development, and physical well-being are considered in a substantial number of studies. Emotional well-being is not as prevalent here as it was in the area of mental and behavioral health, where it was the most frequently researched domain. This seems reasonable, as problems are specific depending on each type of population. In the same way, physical well-being was more prevalent in the areas of health, mental and behavioral health, and aging, because in these contexts physical health is a priority.

The least often studied domain is rights (only five references). Despite the low number of studies about rights, this is the field of knowledge where we can find more explicit references to the domain. However, rights are more often present in theoretical approaches than in research studies. The reasons for this may be found in the difficulties of studying it. This domain may be based on approaches that differ from those of the other domains in three ways: (a) it may derive more from required environmental conditions than from identifiable behaviors; (b) it may involve an inherent difficulty in the investigation of indicators; or (c) it may reflect a lack of concern on the part of researchers, who are restricted by assumptions that relate to activities where the rights of the individual are not considered to be a crucial factor.

Techniques Used

Most QOL assessment techniques in mental retardation and intellectual disabilities are quantitative, but qualitative measurements are also used. Scales and questionnaires are predominant. However, interviews, inventories, and indexes are also used. Most tests demonstrate acceptable psychometric features with ample supporting research. In spite of the fact that some authors consider qualitative procedures as very important, analysis of the published literature shows that there is still very little published research using qualitative measures.

The two most frequently used tests in reviewed research are the Quality of Life Questionnaire (QOL.Q) (Schalock & Keith, 1990, 1993) and the Comprehensive Quality of Life Scale-Intellectual Disability (ComQol-ID) (Cummins, 1991, 1993). Although both tests have been designed with a multidimensional perspective in mind and include items about almost every domain in the proposed model, they are specifically focused on certain domains. The QOL.Q by Schalock and Keith has good psychometric properties (Rapley & Lobley, 1995; Rapley, Lobley, & Bozatzis, 1994; Verdugo, Caballo, Prieto, & Peláez, 2000). It focuses on social inclusion, self-determination, material well-being, personal development, and emotional well-being. The Cummins scale, which also has good psychometric properties (Cummins, 1993), analyzes social inclusion, interpersonal relations, material well-being, physical well-being, and emotional well-being.

Other tests that have been broadly applied and are noteworthy: Quality of Life Index (Campo, Sharpton, Thompson, & Sexton, 1996; Schalock, Keith, Hoffman, & Karan, 1989), Living in a Supervised Home: A Questionnaire on Quality of Life (Cragg & Harrison, 1986), Resident Lifestyle Inventory (RLI) (Bellamy, Newton, LeBaron, & Horner, 1990; Kennedy, Horner, Newton, & Kanda, 1990), Program Analysis of Service Systems (PASS) (Wolfensberger, 1975; Wolfensberger & Thomas, 1983), Lifestyle Satisfaction Scale (LSS) (Heal & Chadsey-Rusch, 1985), and Multifaceted Lifestyle Satisfaction Scale (MLSS) (Harner & Heal, 1993).

Aging

Domains Studied

Most techniques used in research into people of age focus on the well-being domain, with a predominance of studies based on physical health. We also find several techniques that assess emotional well-being and social inclusion. Next in prevalence are the techniques that explore the interpersonal relations, personal development, and material well-being domains. And finally, as we have already seen in the other focus areas, the rights domain does not have a specific measurement technique. Self-determination is measured by only two different techniques.

This section of the chapter is based on the analysis of techniques used in research into quality of life in aging people as discussed in chapter 7. Table 10.5 presents the techniques by categories following the domains of the proposed model. We also indicate references to studies where these techniques have been used. Although many other techniques have been used in studying older people, most are mentioned in only one or two studies. Consequently, the table includes only those techniques that have been used in at least three studies (out of the 74 reviewed).

TABLE 10.5 Quality of Life Measurement Techniques Used in Aging		
DOMAIN	TECHNIQUES[a]	REFERENCES[b]
PHYSICAL WELL-BEING	Medical Outcomes Study 36 — Item Short-Form Health Survey (SF-36) (Ware et al., 1993, 1994)	1, 11, 13, 25, 29, 40, 50, 60, 63, 71
	Instrumental Activities of Daily Living (IADL) (Katz, Ford, & Moskowitz, 1963; Lawton & Brody, 1969)	8, 20, 35, 56, 57
	The 15-Item Version of the Geriatric Depression Scale (SGDS) (Sheikh & Yesavage, 1986)	1, 46, 61, 66
	Activities of Daily Living (ADL) (Katz, Larson, & Phillips, 1992; Lawton, Moss, Fulcomer, & Kleban, 1982)	30, 35, 42, 64
	Self-Evaluation of Life Function Scale (SELF) (Linn & Linn, 1984)	1, 8, 46
	Hearing Handicap Inventory for the Elderly (HHIE) (Ventry & Weinstein, 1982; Weinstein, 1986; Weinstein, Spitzer, & Ventry, 1986)	1, 46, 61
	Quantified Denver Scale of Communication Function (QDS) (Alpiner, 1982)	
	A Short Portable Mental Status Questionnaire (SPMSQ) (Pfeiffer, 1975a)	

(table continues)

[a] Original references for each technique are cited only on first appearance in this column and can be found in the general reference section.
[b] Full references for the numbered citations in this column can be found in Appendix 10.5.
Note. Domains and techniques are ordered from highest to lowest number of references found. Only techniques used in more than two studies are included.

Table 10.2. *(continued)*

DOMAIN	TECHNIQUES	REFERENCES
EMOTIONAL WELL-BEING	Medical Outcomes Study 36-Item Short-Form Health Survey (SF-36)	1, 11, 13, 25, 29, 40, 50, 60, 63, 71
	Geriatric Depression Scale (GDS) (Yesavage & Brink, 1983)	1, 46, 60, 61
	Life Satisfaction Index-A (LSI-A) (Neugarten, Havighurst, & Tobin, 1961)	2, 4, 21, 49
	Hearing Handicap Inventory for the Elderly (HHIE)	1, 46, 61
	Quantified Denver Scale of Communication Function (QDS)	
	A Short Portable Mental Status Questionnaire (SPMSQ)	46, 61
	Rosenberg Self-Esteem Scale (Rosenberg, 1965)	9, 10, 26
	Philadelphia Geriatric Center Morale Scale (PGCMS) (Lawton, et al., 1982)	18, 21, 61
SOCIAL INCLUSION	Medical Outcomes Study 36-Item Short-Form Health Survey (SF-36)	1, 11, 13, 25, 29, 40, 50, 60, 63, 71
	Program Analysis of Service Systems (PASS) (Wolfensberger & Glenn, 1983)	32, 43, 44, 53, 69, 73
	Program Analysis of Service Systems' Implementation of Normalization Goals (PASSING) (Wolfensberger & Thomas, 1983)	

(table continues)

Table 10.2. *(continued)*

DOMAIN	TECHNIQUES	REFERENCES
	Hearing Handicap Inventory for the Elderly (HHIE) Quantified Denver Scale of Communication Function (QDS) A Short Portable Mental Status Questionnaire (SPMSQ)	16, 46, 61
	Philadelphia Geriatric Center Morale Scale (PGCMS)	18, 21, 61
PERSONAL DEVELOP-MENT	Medical Outcomes Study 36-Item Short-Form Health Survey (SF-36)	1, 11, 13, 25, 29, 40 50, 60, 63, 71
	Hearing Handicap Inventory for the Elderly (HHIE) Quantified Denver Scale of Communication Function (QDS) A Short Portable Mental Status uestionnaire (SPMSQ)	1, 46, 61
	EuroQoL	6, 7, 11
MATERIAL WELL-BEING	Medical Outcomes Study 36-Item Short-Form Health Survey (SF-36)	1, 11, 13, 25, 29, 40, 50, 60, 63, 71
INTER-PERSONAL RELATIONS	Medical Outcomes Study 36-Item Short-Form Health Survey (SF-36)	1, 11, 13, 25, 29, 40, 50, 60, 63, 71
	Geriatric Depression Scale (GDS)	1, 46, 60, 61
	Self-Evaluation of Life Function Scale (SELF)	1, 8, 46

(table continues)

Table 10.2. *(continued)*

DOMAIN	TECHNIQUES	REFERENCES
	Hearing Handicap Inventory for the Elderly (HHIE)	1, 46, 61
	Quantified Denver Scale of Communication Function (QDS)	
SELF-DETERMINATION	Medical Outcomes Study 36-Item Short-Form Health Survey (SF-36)	1, 11, 13, 25, 29, 40, 50, 60, 63, 71
RIGHTS	(Insufficient data)	(Insufficient data)

Techniques Used

The most commonly used techniques in the assessment of quality of life in older people are quantitative, although there are some descriptive studies and programs based on the analysis of data from clinical histories, longitudinal studies (e.g., the Groningen Longitudinal Aging Study [Ormel et al., 1992]), analytical data, and personal interviews (e.g., Farré, Frasque, & Romá, 1999). The most common type of technique used by researchers is scales, followed by questionnaires. Next in prevalence we find inventories and profiles. And finally, there are indexes, structured interviews, and surveys. Professionals and researchers often play a direct role in the application of the instruments, being responsible for providing individuals with information. Older people are generally confined to a passive role in providing information about their own quality of life. So there are very few self-reports.

The first questionnaires or inventories were created according to a single domain, with the aim being to analyze whether there were anomalies due to disease. The result was that, in many cases, only physical aspects of life were taken into account, without further attention to emotional, cognitive, and social areas. However, in recent research, instruments designed and used in QOL assessment are becoming more multidimensional. The most often analyzed domain is physical well-being, followed by emotional well-being, social inclusion, personal development, material well-being, and interpersonal relations. Self-determination appears in very few references, and rights does not appear at all in the published studies reviewed.

The most frequently used multidimensional instrument, and the one that assesses the highest number of domains proposed in the present *Handbook's* model, is the Medical Outcomes Study 36 — Item Short-Form Health Survey (SF-36) (Ware et al., 1993, 1994), which evaluates every domain except rights. Other techniques assessing more than one domain are the Mental Status Questionnaire (OARS) (Fillenbaum, 1988; Pfeiffer, 1975a, 1975b), which assesses physical well-being, emotional well-being, social inclusion, and material well-being; and the Philadelphia Geriatric Center Morale Scale (Lawton, Moss, Fulcomer, & Kleban, 1982), which assesses physical well-being, emotional well-being, social inclusion, and interpersonal relations.

Other techniques that have received researchers' attention are the Program Analysis of Service Systems (PASS) (Wolfensberger, 1975) and the Program Analysis of Service Systems' Implementation of Normalization Goals (PASSING) (Wolfensberger & Thomas, 1983). These two techniques were among the first to assess service quality, and their impact was very broad. They assess different features of programs and services, including items reflecting important aspects of one's quality of life. Nevertheless social inclusion features are specifically emphasized in these two techniques.

The techniques addressing only certain indicators in one domain include the Geriatric Depression Scale and its short version with 15 items (Sheikh & Yesavage, 1986; Yesavage & Brink, 1983), which assess depression; and the Life Satisfaction Index-A (LSI-A) (Neugarten, Havighurst, & Tobin, 1961). Both tests are related mainly to the emotional well-being domain. Many other specific scales focus on a single physical health issue. Examples include the assessment of health status (General Health Questionnaire [Goldberg, 1978]), the assessment of auditory and language disorders (Hearing Handicap Inventory for the Elderly [Ventry & Weinstein, 1982; Weinstein, 1986; Weinstein, Spitzer, & Ventry, 1986]), and the assessment of communication (Quantified Denver Scale of Communication Function [Alpiner, 1982]).

In summary, very few studies have approached QOL measurement in older people from different social or research perspectives. Our analysis also indicates that researchers frequently ignore what is being done in neighboring scientific areas. There is a clear need for developing common QOL assessment models and techniques that are person-centered and multidimensional.

Many techniques have been developed across the focus areas, with the exception of education, where there is still a lot of work to be done. There are diverse multidimensional assessment instruments, but the rights domain has received very little attention. As discussed in the following section on "measurement issues," we should develop techniques to help us in an appropriate measurement of the indicators involved. On the other hand, qualitative procedures can be useful for the development of programs and activities in the individual's natural setting. And finally, research must advance in the integration of perspectives from different existing scientific fields and from different disciplines interested in the assessment of quality of life.

In addition to the focus area and domain-specific issues, the analysis described in this chapter also identified the following six measurement issues that are worthy of the reader's consideration: (a) viability of measurement; (b) methodological decisions; (c) factors affecting responses; (d) the role of personal values; (e) the use of proxies; and (f) the emerging set of measurement principles. Each is discussed next.

Measurement Issues

Viability of Measurement

A distinction can be made between quality of life as a "sensitizing concept" and quality of life as a "definitive concept" (Taylor, 1994). Taylor quoted Blumer (1969) in pointing out that a sensitizing (unlike a definitive) concept offers general guidance or direction for study rather than providing merely a definition. In transforming *quality of life* to *QOL*, Taylor suggested that the concept may be reduced to precision at the expense of meaning and may produce a "tyranny of QOL" that prescribes lifestyles and limits personal freedom and satisfaction. "The good life," he concluded, should not "be reduced to the good life scale" (p. 264). Similarly, Edgerton (1990, 1996) fears that quality of life scales might result in measures that prompt imposition of specific life standards or expectations on the lives of individuals. These issues raise the kinds of moral questions about implications of QOL measurement that prompted Wolfensberger (1994) to suggest rejecting the concept of quality of life as a "hopeless term."

Hatton (1998) has articulated the inherent tension existing between QOL theory that focuses on the individualized nature of the concept and the need for measurement purposes to produce standardized measures of quality of life. Key aspects of this paradox were described by Antaki and Rapley (1996) regarding the inconsistency between specific, formal, "official" standardized QOL assessment and the more general, informal, nonpsychometric approaches that might be used more often simply to ask people whether they are happy with their lives.

Methodological Decisions

Heal and Sigelman (1996), in a seminal chapter on methodological issues in QOL assessment, discuss four fundamental methodological decisions that are made in the area of QOL measurement. First, measures can be objective or subjective, focusing on the objective circumstances of people's lives or assessing attitudinal phenomena such as perceived satisfaction. Second, a measure can be absolute or relative. That is, it can index directly people's perceived quality of life or it can compare their assessed quality of life to some standard. Third, quality of life can be reported directly by the respondents, or it can be assessed by someone else, such as an informant or a proxy. Fourth, the measure can be developed by the investigator or by the subjects of the investigation. Because any one of these methodological decisions can lead to different conclusions, investigators interested in measuring the QOL concept should take them seriously. A very helpful taxonomy and decision matrix is found in Heal and Sigelman (1996, p. 93).

Factors Affecting Reponses

In that same chapter Heal and Sigelman (1996) discuss a number of variables affecting responses in QOL survey research. The authors refer to earlier work (e.g., Sudman & Bradburn, 1982) to identify three broad classes of variables that can potentially alter or distort either objective or subjective survey data: (a) task variables such as question wording and question format; (b) interviewee variables involving characteristics such as age, sex, race, social class, and the extent to which the question implies a socially desired response; (c) respondent variables such as gender, age, or race.

The Role of Personal Values

A number of investigators (e.g., Cummins, 1997a, 1997b; Elorriaga, Garcia, Marinez, & Unamunzaga, 2000; Schalock, 2001) have highlighted the hierarchical nature of human needs, suggesting that QOL domains should be ordered in importance by each individual in a manner consistent with personal values. Renwick and Brown (1996) also stress the importance of taking into account the values (along with cognitions, beliefs, and interests) of the individual. Similarly Felce (1997) includes not only the subjective and objective domains in his QOL model but also a domain incorporating personal values and aspirations that produce overall well-being (i.e., quality of life) when added to the subjective and objective factors.

However, not all multidimensional measures of quality of life attempt to weight personal values in a systematic way. For example, the Quality of Life Questionnaire (Schalock & Keith, 1993) does not refer explicitly to the role of personal values, except to the extent that personal views are reflected in responses to subjective questions — a procedure different from the actual assignment of differential weights to domains based upon the individual's perception of their importance.

Use of Proxies

Stancliffe (2000), in a recent review of proxy respondents and quality of life, discusses a basic difficulty with proxy responding: proxies are usually called upon only when consumers are unable to respond for themselves. This frequently means that consumers who self-report have different characteristics from consumers for whom proxies are required. These differences often include communication skills, adaptive behavior, and level of impairment. Consequently, information source (self-report or proxy) and consumer characteristics are confounded. Thus "any difference between self-reports and proxy responses may be due to the discrepancy in the source of information or may be related to differences in the characteristics of the two consumer groups" (p. 5).

Both acquiescence and recency response biases have the potential to invalidate self-reported QOL data. Acquiescence is evident when the person replies yes to a yes/no question regardless of the content of the question; recency involves selecting the last alternative mentioned in either/or multiple-choice questions regardless of one's true opinion. Suggestions for overcoming response biases in QOL measurement include (Stancliffe, 2000):

- assessing the degree of response bias evident and taking appropriate action to reduce its effects;
- omitting participants with evident response bias or correcting statistically for response bias effects;
- identifying the characteristics on which proxies can provide valid and accurate information;
- specifying the type of information that proxies can (or cannot) validly supply and the aspects of that information that influence validity (e.g., subjectivity or objectivity, availability of written records, direct experience by the proxy);
- identifying factors that influence consumer to proxy concordance;
- examining the reliability of self-reports to determine when self-reports may appropriately be used as a yardstick for validating proxy data;
- using proxies for only those QOL surveys or questionnaires known to possess empirically well established consumer-to-proxy agreement.

Measurement Principles

QOL measurement reflects the unique blend of two meanings of quality: that which is commonly understood by people throughout the world, and that which has become valued by individuals as they live within their unique environments. Typically we measure the former by using indicators that can be observed reliably and appear to be universally held, such as material attainment, stability of human institutions, social connections, and life opportunities. Measuring quality of life as it is understood and valued from the individual perspective is usually carried out by identifying what specific things have come to be valued by individuals and by matching these to individuals' perceptions of personal satisfaction or happiness. Sometimes measurement of these two aspects of quality of life is referred to, respectively, as objective and subjective measurement. Both quantitative (i.e., objective) and qualitative (i.e., subjective) methods are useful in measuring quality of life, and both are necessary for a full measurement of a life of quality.

The consensus document on the conceptualization, measurement, and application of the QOL concept (Schalock et al., in press) proposes the following five QOL measurement principles.

1. QOL measurement assesses the degree to which people have meaningful life experiences that they value.

2. QOL measurement enables people to move toward a meaningful life they enjoy and value.

3. QOL measurement assesses the degree to which life's domains contribute to a full and interconnected life.

4. QOL measurement is undertaken within the context of environments that are important to the person: where he or she lives, works, and plays.

5. QOL measurement for individuals is based upon both common human experiences and unique, individual life experiences.

Conclusion

In conclusion, methodological pluralism and an ecological approach to the analysis of core QOL domains reflect the current approach to QOL measurement. Each of the measurement approaches summarized in this chapter has strengths and weaknesses, and each has the requirement to demonstrate psychometric robustness, discussed in more detail in chapter 11.

At the same time that we are continuing to focus on measurement issues and the resolution of measurement problems and concerns, the QOL movement is also becoming oriented toward application and policy. For example, one recent edited volume on quality of life (Schalock, 1997) contains major sections on organizational change, public policy, and culture. As Raphael (1996) noted, much work in the area of quality of life has been generally positivist in nature, focusing on relatively detached data collection procedures; however, recent examples suggest a movement toward naturalistic approaches, including personal narratives (e.g., Groulx, Dore, & Dore, 2000; Ward, 2000). Recent research also tends to be value-based, often explicitly addressing topics such as health promotion (I. Brown, Renwick, & Nagler, 1996), facilitating relationships and social integration (Snell & Vogtle, 1997). Additionally, researchers clearly intend that their work has implications for social policy (Goode, 1997b; Turnbull & Brunk, 1997). There are also important examples of interactive or participatory research (Schalock et al., 2000) and research with significant activist agenda (e.g., Antaki & Rapley, 1996). In short, research on the measurement of quality of life in the areas of education, health care, and social services is rich, diverse, multifaceted, and moving rapidly to the application phase. Before we focus in part 4 on the application of the QOL concept, we need to discuss a generic QOL measurement model. This we do in chapter 11.

Appendix 10.1
Numbered References Corresponding to Table 10.1

1. Binkley, M., Rust, K., & Williams, T. (1992). *Reading literacy in an international perspective.* Washington, DC: National Center for Education Statistics.

2. Cummins, R., & McCabe, M. (1994). The comprehensive quality of life scale (COMQOL): Instrument development and psychometric evaluation on college staff and students. *Educational and Psychological Measurement, 54*(2), 372.

3. Dew, T., & Huebner, S. (1994). Adolescents' perceived quality of life: An exploratory investigation. *Journal of School Psychology, 32*(2), 185–199.

4. Harju, B., & Bolen, L. (1998). The effects of optimism on coping and perceived quality of life of college students. *Journal of Social Behavior and Personality, 13*(2), 185.

5. Heal, L. W., Khoju, M., & Rusch, F. R. (1997). Predicting quality of life of youths after they leave special education high school program. *Journal of Special Education, 31*(3), 279–299.

6. Huebner, E. (1994). Conjoint analyses of the students' life satisfaction scale and the Piers-Harris self-concept scale. *Psychology in the Schools, 31,* 273–277.

7. Huebner, S., Laughlin, J., Ash, C., & Gilman, R. (1998). Further validation of the multidimensional students' life satisfaction scale. *Journal of Psychoeducational Assessment, 16,* 118–134.

8. Keith, K., Yamamoto, M., Okita, N., & Schalock, R. (1995). Cross-cultural quality of life: Japanese and American college students. *Social Behavior and Personality, 23*(2), 163–170.

9. Mok, M., & McDonald, R. (1994). Quality of school life: A scale to measure student experience or school climate? *Educational and Psychological Measurement, 54*(2), 483–495.

10. Roberts, L., & Clifton, R. (1992a). Measuring the affective quality of life of university students: The validation of an instrument. *Social Indicators Research, 27,* 113–137.

11. Roberts, L., & Clifton, R. (1992b). Measuring the cognitive domain of the quality of student life: An instrument for faculties of education. *Canadian Journal of Education, 17*(2), 176–191.

12. Shinn, D. (1986). Education and the quality of life in Korea and the United States: A cross-cultural perspective. *Public Opinion Quarterly, 50,* 360–370.

13. Terry, T., & Huebner, S. (1995). The relationship between self-concept and life satisfaction in children. *Social Indicators Research, 35,* 39–52.

14. Timmons, V. (1993). *Quality of life of teenagers with special needs.* Unpublished doctoral dissertation, University of Calgary, Alberta, Canada.

15. Verdugo, M. A., Caballo, C., Peláez, A., & Prieto, G. (2000). *Calidad de vida en personas con deficiencia visual* (Tech. Rep.). Salamanca, Spain: University of Salamanca, Instituto de Integración en la Comunidad.

16. Wilson, M. (1988). Internal construct validity and reliability of a quality of school life instrument across national and school level. *Educational and Psychological Measurement, 48,* 995–1009.

APPENDIX 10.2
Numbered References Corresponding to Table 10.2

1. Aaronson, N. K., Ahmezdai, S., & Bullinger, M. (1991). The European Organization for Research and Treatment of Cancer (EORTC) core quality of life questionnaire: Interim results of an international field study. In D. Osoba (Ed.), *Effect of cancer in quality of life* (pp. 185–203). Boston: CRC Press.

2. Alonso, J., Prieto, L., & Anto, J. M. (1994). The Spanish version of the Nottingham health profile: A review of adaptation and instrument characteristics. *Quality of Life Research, 3,* 385–393.

3. Alonso, J., Prieto, L., & Antó, J. M. (1995). La versión española del SF-36 health survey: Un instrumento para la medida de los resultados clínicos. *Medicina Clinica, 104,* 771–776.

4. Badia, X., Alonso, J., Brosa, M., & Lock, P. (1994). Reliability of the Spanish version of the Nottingham health profile in patients with stable end-stage renal disease. *Social Science and Medicine, 38,* 153–158.

5. Badia, X., & Alonso, J. (1995). Rescaling the Spanish version of the sickness impact profile: An opportunity for the assessment of cross-cultural equivalence. *Journal of Clinical Epidemiology, 48,* 949–957.

6. Bjordal, K., Ahlner-Elmqvist, M., Tollesson, E., Jensen, A. B., & Razavi, D. (1994). Development of a European Organization for Research and Treatment of Cancer (EORTC) questionnaire module to be used in quality of life assesments in head and neck cancer patients. *Acta Oncológica, 33*(8), 879–885.

7. Brown, I., & Renwick, R. (1999). *The quality of life profile: A generic measure of health and well-being.* [On-line]. Available: www.utoronto.ca/qol/profile.htm

8. Bruin, A. F. de., Buys, M., & de Witte, L. P. (1994). The sickness impact profile: SIP 68, a short generic version. First evaluation of the reliability and reproducibility. *Journal of Clinical Epidemiology, 47,* 863–871.

9. Bruin, A. F. de., de Witte, L. P., & Stevens, F. (1992). Sickness impact profile: The state-of-the-art of a generic functional status measure. *Social Science and Medicine, 35,* 1003–1014.

10. Bullinger, M., & Ravens-Siebener, U. (1995). Evaluation de la qualité de vie des enfants: Revue de la littérature. *Revue Européenne de Psychologie Appliquée, 45*(73), 255–256.

11. Bullinger, M., & Ravens-Sieberer, U. (1997). *KINDL children questionnaire (8–12 years).* Unpublished manuscript, University of Hamburg, Germany.

12. Burleigh, S. A., Farber, R. S., & Gillard, M. (1998). Community integration and life satisfaction after traumatic brain injury: Long-term findings. *American Journal of Occupational Therapy, 52*(1), 45–52.

13. Cardol, M., Elvers, J. W. H., Ostendorp, R. A. B., Brandsma, J. W., & Groot, I. J. M. (1996). Quality of life in patients with amyotrophic lateral sclerosis. *Journal of Rehabilitation Sciences, 9*(4), 99–103.

14. Cella, D. F., Diennen, K., Arnason, B., Reder, A., Webste, M., Karabastos, B., Chang, C., Lloyd, S., Mo, F., Stewart, J., & Stefoski, D. (1999). Validation of the functional assessment of multiple sclerosis quality of life instrument. *American Academy of Neurology, 47,* 129–139.

15. Christie, M. J., French, D., Sowden, A., & West, A. (1993). Development of child-centered disease-specific questionnaires for living with asthma. *Psychosomatic Medicine, 55,* 541–548.

16. Chwalow, A. J., Lurie, A., & Bean, K. (1992). A French version of the sickness impact profile (SIP): Stages in the cross-cultural validation of a generic quality of life scale. *Fundamental and Clinical Pharmacology, 6,* 319–326.

17. Czyzewski, D. I., Mariotto, M. J., Bartholomew, L. K., LeCompte, S. H., & Sockrider, M. M. (1992). *Measurement of quality of well-being in a child and adolescent cystic fibrosis population.* Presented at the Sixth Annual North American Cystic Fibrosis Conference, Washington, DC.

18. Dazord, A., Mercier, C., Manificat, S., & Nicolas, J. (1995). Evaluation de la qualité de vie: Mise au point d'un instrument d'évaluation dans un contexte francophone. *Revue Européenne de Psychologie Appliquée, 45*(4), 271–278.

19. De Vries, J., & Van Heck, G. (1997). The World Health Organization quality of life: Assessment instrument (WHOQOL-100): Validation study with the Dutch version. *European Journal of Psychological Assessment, 13*(3), 164–178.

20. Diabetes Control and Complications Trial (DCCT). (1988). Reliability and validity of a diabetes quality of life: Measure for the diabetes control and complications trial (DCCT). *Diabetes Care, 11,* 725–732.

21. Division of Mental Health, World Health Organization. (1998). Field trial WHOQOL-100: February 1998 [CD-ROM]. In M. Tamburini (Ed.), *Quality of life assessment in medicine.* Milano, Italy: Glamm Interactive. Also available: www.glamm.com/ql

22. European Organization for Research and Treatment of Cancer Study Group on Quality of Life. (1993). The European Organization for Research and Treatment of Cancer QLQ-C30: A quality-of-life instrument for use in international clinical trials in oncology. *Journal of the Netherlands Cancer Institute, 85,* 365–376.

23. Fallowfield, L. (1993). *The quality of life: The missing measurement in health care* (3rd ed.). London: WBC Bridgend.

24. French, D. J., Christie, M. J., & Sowden, A. J. (1994). The reproducibility of the childhood asthma questionnaires: Measures of quality of life for children with asthma aged 4–16 years. *Quality of Life Research, 3,* 215–224.

25. Fuhred, M., Rintala, D., Hart, K., Clearman, R., & Young, M. (1992). Relationship of life satisfaction to impairment, disability, and handicap among persons with spinal cord injury living in the community. *Archives of Physical Medicine and Rehabilitation, 73,* 552–557.

26. Ganz, P. A., & Coscarelli, A. (1995). Quality of life after breast cancer: A decade of research. In J. E. Dimsdale & A. Baum (Eds.), *Quality of life in behavioral medicine research* (pp. 97–113). Hillsdale, NJ: Lawrence Erlbaum.

27. Grégoire, J. (1995). L'évaluation de la qualité de vie. *Revue Européenne de Psychologie Appliquée, 25*(4), 243-244.

28. Grégoire, J., de Leval, N., & Mesters, P. (1995). Adaptation Française et étude des propriétés métriques de la quality of life in depression scale. *Revue Européenne de Psychologie Appliquée, 25*(4), 286–291.

29. Gudex, C. (1986). *QALYs and their use by the health service* (Discussion Paper No. 20). York, England: University of York, Centre for Health Economics.

30. Guyatt, G. H. (1997). Children and adult perceptions of childhood asthma. *Pediatrics, 99*(2), 165–168.

31. Henry, A. (1998). Quality of life and its assessment. *Student British Medical Journal, 6,* 280–283.

32. Heyland, D. K., Guyatt, G., Cook, D. J., Meade, M., Juniper. E., Cronin, L., & Gafni, A. (1998). Frequency and methodologic rigor of quality of life assessment in the critical care literature. *Critical Care Medicine, 26*(3), 591–598.

33. Hunt, S. M., & Wiklund, I. (1987). Cross-cultural variation in the weighting of health statements: A comparison of English and Swedish valuations. *Health Policy, 8,* 227–235.

34. Hunt, S. M., Alonso, J., & Bucquet, D. (1993). *European Guide to the Nottingham Health Profile.* Surrey, England: Brookwood Medical Publications.

35. Jacobson, A. M., Groot, M., & Samson, J. A. (1994). The evaluation of two measures of quality of life in patients with type I and type II diabetes mellitus. *Diabetes Care, 17,* 267–274.

36. Jacobson, A. M., & DCCT Research Group. (1994). The diabetes quality of life measure. In C. Bradley (Ed.), *Handbook of psychology and diabetes.* Boston: Harwood Academic.

37. Jacobson, A. M., Groot, M., & Samson, J. (1995). Quality of life research in patients with diabetes mellitus. In J. E. Dimsdale & A. Baum (Eds.), *Quality of life in behavioral medicine research* (pp. 241–262). Hillsdale, NJ: Lawrence Erlbaum.

38. Jenkinson, C., Wright, L., & Coulter, A. (1993). *Quality of life measurement in health care: A review of measures and population norms for the UK SF-36.* Oxford, England: Health Services Research Unit.

39. Juniper, E. F., Guyatt, G. H., & Epstein, R. S. (1992). Evaluation of impairment of health-related quality of life in asthma: Development of a questionnaire for use in clinical trials. *Thorax, 47,* 76–83.

40. Juniper, E. F., Guyatt, G. H., & Willam, A. (1994). Measuring quality of life in asthma. *American Revue of Respiratory Diseases, 147,* 832–838.

41. Juniper, E. F., Guyatt, G. H., & Feeny, D. H. (1995). Measuring quality of life in children with asthma. *Quality of Life Research, 5,* 35–46.

42. Juniper, E. F. (1997). How important is quality of life in pediatric asthma? *Pediatric Pulmonary, 15,* 17–21.

43. Juniper, E. F., Guyatt, G. H., Feeny, D. H., Griffith, L. E., & Ferrie, P. J. (1997). Minimum skills required by children to complete health-related quality of life instruments for asthma: Comparison of measurement properties. *European Respiratory Journal, 10,* 2285–2294.

44. Kaplan, R. M., Ganiats, T. G., Dieber, W. J., & Anderson, J. P. (1998). The quality of well-being scale: Critical similarities and differences with SF-36. *International Journal for Quality in Health Care, 10*(6), 509–520.

45. Kuyken, W. (1995). The World Health Organization quality of life assessment (WHOQOL): Position paper from the World Health Organization. *Social Science and Medicine, 41*(10), 1403–1409.

46. Leplège, A., Ecosse, E., Verdier, A., & Perneger, T. (1998). The French SF-36 health survey: Translation, cultural adaptation, and preliminary psychometric evaluation. *Journal of Clinical Epidemiology, 51*(11), 1013–1023.

47. Litwins, N. M., & Rodriguez, J. R. (1994). Quality of life in adult recipients of bone marrow transplantation. *Psychological Reports, 75,* 323–328.

48. Malo, J. L., Boulet, L. P., & Dewitte, J. D. (1993). Quality of life of subjects with occupational asthma. *Journal of Clinical Epidemiology, 91,* 1121–1127.

49. Manificat, S., & Dazord, A. (1997). Evaluation de la qualité de vie de l'enfant: Validation d'un questionnaire, premiers résultats. *Neuropsychiatrie de L'Enfance et de L'Adolescence, 45*(3), 106–114.

50. McEwan, J. (1993). The Nottingham health profile. In S. R. Walker & R. M. Rosser (Eds.), *Quality of life assessment: Key issues in the 1990s* (pp. 111–130). Dordrecht, The Netherlands: Kluwer.

51. McHorney, C. A., Kosinski, M., & Ware, J. E., Jr. (1994). Comparisons of the costs and quality of norms for the SF-36 health survey collected by mail versus telephone interview: Results from a national survey. *Medical Care, 32*(2), 551–567.

52. McHorney, C. A., Ware, J. E., & Raczek, A. E. (1993). The MOS 36-item short-form health survey (SF-36): II. Psychometric and clinical tests of validity in measuring physical and mental health constructs. *Medical Care, 31,* 247–263.

53. Mendoza, R., Batista-Foguet, J. M., & Oliva, A. (1994). Lifestyles of European school children: Findings of the WHO cross-national study on health-related behaviour. In J. P. Dauwalder (Ed.), *Psychology and promotion of health* (pp. 9–19). Bern, Switzerland: Hogrefe & Huber.

54. Moinpour, C. M., Savage, M., Hayden, K. A., Sawyers, J., & Upchurch, C. (1995). Quality of life assessment in cancer clinical trials. In J. E. Dimsdale & A. Baum (Eds.), *Quality of life in behavioral medicine research* (pp. 79–96). Hillsdale, NJ: Lawrence Erlbaum.

55. O'Brian, B. J., Banner, N. R., & Gibson, S. (1988). The Nottingham health profile as a measure of quality of life following combined heart and lung transplantation. *Journal of Epidemiology and Community Health, 42,* 232–234.

56. O'Mahony, P. G., Rodgers, H., Thomson, R. G., Dobson, R., & James, O. F. W. (1998). Is the SF-36 suitable for assessing health status of older stroke patients? *Age and Aging, 27,* 19–22.

57. Power, M., & Kuyken, W., on behalf of the WHOQOL Group. (1998). The World Health Organization quality of life assessment (WHOQOL): Development and general psychometric properties. *Social Science and Medicine, 46*(12), 1569–1585.

58. Ravens-Sieberer, U., & Bullinger, M. (1998). Assessing health-related quality of life in chronically ill children with the German KINDL: First psychometric and content analytical results. *Quality of Life Research, 7,* 339–407.

59. Reid, D. T., & Renwick, R. M. (1994). Preliminary validation of a new instrument to measure life satisfaction in adolescents with neuromuscular disorders. *International Journal of Rehabilitation Research, 17,* 184–188.

60. Ringdal, G. I., & Ringdal, K. (1993). Testing the European Organization for Research and Treatment of Cancer (EORTC) quality of life questionnaire on cancer patients with heterogeneous diagnoses. *Quality of Life Research, 2,* 129–140.

61. Rosser, R., Allison, R., Butler, C., Cottee, M., Rabin, R., & Selsi, C. (1993). The index of health-related quality of life (IHQL): A new tool for audit and cost-per-QALY analysis. In S. E. Walker & R. M. Rosser (Eds.), *Quality of life assessment: Key issues in the 1990s* (pp. 179–184). Dordrecht, The Netherlands: Kluwer.

62. Ruiz, M. A., & Baca, E. (1993). Design and validation of the quality of life questionnaire: A generic health-related perceived quality of life instrument. *European Journal of Psychological Assessment, 9*(1), 19–32.

63. Sanjuas, C., Alonso, J., & Sanchis, J. (1995). The quality of life questionnaire with asthma patients: The Spanish version of the asthma quality of life questionnaire. *Archives of Bronconeumologia, 31,* 219–226.

64. Sprangers, M. A., Cull, A., & Bjordal, A. (1993). The European Organization for Research and Treatment of Cancer approach to quality of life assessment: Guidelines for developing questionnaire modules. *Quality of Life Research, 2,* 287–295.

65. Tamburini, M. (1998). *Quality of life assessment in medicine* [CD-ROM]. Milano, Spain: Glamm Interactive.

66. The DCCT Research Group. (1987). Diabetes control and complications trial: Results of a feasibility study. *Diabetes Care, 10,* 1–19.

67. Trueman, P., & Duthie, T. (1998). Use of the hospital anxiety and depression scale (HADS) in a large general population study of epilepsy. *News Quality of Life Letter, 19,* 9–10.

68. Varni, J. W., Katz, E. R., Seid, M., Quiggins, D. J., Friedman-Bender, A., & Castro, C. M. (1998). *The pediatric cancer quality of life inventory* (PCQL). I. Instrument development, descriptive statistics, and cross-informant variance. *Journal of Behavioral Medicine, 21*(2), 179–199.

69. Varni, J. W., Seid, M., & Rode, C. A. (1999). The PedsQL: Measurement model for the pediatric quality of life inventory. *Medical Care, 37*(2), 126–139.

70. Visser, M. C., Fletcher, A. E., & Parr, G. (1994). A comparison of three quality of life instruments in subjects with angina pectoris: The sickness impact profile, the Nottingham health profile, and the quality of well-being scale. *Journal of Clinical Epidemiology, 47,* 157–163.

71. Ware, J. E. (1991). Conceptualizing and measuring generic health outcomes. *Cancer, 67*(3), 774–779.

72. Ware, J. E., & Sherbourne, C. D. (1992). The MOS 36-item short-form health survey (SF-36). I: Conceptual framework and item selection. *Medical Care, 30,* 473–483.

73. WHOQOL Group. (1993). Study protocol for the World Health Organization project to develop a quality of life assessment instrument. *Quality of Life Research, 2,* 153–159.

74. WHOQOL Group. (1994). Development of the WHOQOL: Rationale and current status. *International Journal of Mental Health, 23,* 24–56.

75. WHOQOL Group. (1994). The development of the World Health Organization quality of life assessment instrument (WHOQOL). In J. Orley & W. Kuyken (Eds.), *Quality of life assessment: International perspectives* (pp. 41–57). New York: Springer-Verlag.

76. WHOQOL Group, & Herrman, H. (1994). The development of the World Health Organization quality of life assessment instrument (WHOQOL). In J. Orley & W. Kuyken (Eds.), *Quality of life assessment in health care settings* (pp. 41–57). New York: Springer-Verlag.

APPENDIX 10.3
Numbered References Corresponding to Table 10.3

1. Aggernaes, A. (1994). On general and need-related quality of life: A psychological theory for use in medical rehabilitation and psychiatry. In L. Nordenfelt (Ed.), *Concepts and measurement of quality of life in health care* (pp. 241–255). London: Kluwer Academic.

2. Albert, S. M., del Castillo, C., Sano, M., Jacobs, D. M., Marder, K., Bell, K., Bylsma, F., Lafleche, G., Brandt, J., Albert, M., & Stern, Y. (1996). Quality of life in patients with Alzheimer's disease as reported by patient proxies. *Journal of American Geriatric Society, 44*(11), 1342–1347.

3. Angermeyer, M. C., & Katschnig, H. (1997). Psychotropic medication and quality of life: A conceptual framework for assessing their relationship. In H. Katschnig, H. Freeman, & N. Sartorius (Eds.), *Quality of life in mental disorders* (pp. 215–225). Chichester, England: John Wiley.

4. Angermeyer, M. C., & Kilian, R. (1997). Theoretical models of quality of life for mental disorders. In H. Katschnig, H. Freeman, & N. Sartorius (Eds.), *Quality of life in mental disorders* (pp. 19–30). Chichester, England: John Wiley.

5. Atkinson, J. M., Coia, D. A., & Harper, W., & Harper, J. P. (1996). The impact of education groups for people with schizophrenia on social functioning and quality of life. *British Journal of Psychiatry, 168,* 199–204.

6. Atkinson, M. J., & Caldwell, L. (1997). The differential effects of mood on patients' ratings of life quality and satisfaction with their care. *Journal of Affective Disorders, 44,* 169–175.

7. Atkinson, M. J., Zibin, S., & Chuang, H. (1997). Characterizing quality of life among patients with chronic mental illness: A critical examination of the self-report methodology. *American Journal of Psychiatry, 154*(1), 99–105.

8. Awad, A. G. (1992). Quality of life of schizophrenic patients on medications and implications for new drug trials. *Hospital and Community Psychiatry, 43,* 262–265.

9. Ballero, F., & Escobar, J. M. (1997). Rehabilitación y demencia: Realidades y límites. *Daño cerebral y calidad de vida: Demencias* (pp. 347–354). Madrid: Fundación MAPFRE Medicina.

10. Barge-Schaapveld, D., Nicolson, N. A., Delespaul, P., & de Vries, M. W. (1997). Assessing daily quality of life with the experience sampling method. In H. Katschnig, H. Freeman, & N. Sartorius (Eds.), *Quality of life in mental disorders* (pp. 95–107). Chichester, England: John Wiley.

11. Barry, M. M. (1997). Well-being and life satisfaction as components of quality of life in mental disorders. In H. Katschnig, H. Freeman, & N. Sartorius (Eds.), *Quality of life in mental disorders* (pp. 31–42). Chichester, England: John Wiley.

12. Bech, P. (1996). Quality of life measurements in major depression. *European Psychiatry, 11,* 123–126.

13. Bech, P., & Angst, J. (1996). Quality of life in anxiety and social phobia. *International Clinical Psychopharmacology, 11*(3), 97–100.

14. Bech, P., & Rylander, A. (1997). The ECST quality of life task force. *European Psychiatry, 12,* 161–162.

15. Becker, M., & Diamond, R. (1997). New developments in quality of life measurement in schizophrenia. In H. Katschnig, H. Freeman, & N. Sartorius (Eds.), *Quality of life in mental disorders* (pp. 119–133). Chichester, England: John Wiley.

16. Bengtsson-Tops, A., & Hansson, L. (1999). Subjective quality of life in schizophrenic patients living in the community. Relationship to clinical and social characteristics. *European Psychiatry, 14,* 256–263.

17. Bobes, J., & González, M. P. (1997). Quality of life in schizophrenia. In H. Katschnig, H. Freeman, & N. Sartorius (Eds.), *Quality of life in mental disorders* (pp. 165–178). Chichester, England: John Wiley.

18. Bobes, J. (1998). How is recovery from social anxiety disorder defined? *Journal of Clinical Psychiatry, 59,* 12–16.

19. Bond, J. (1999). Quality of life for people with dementia: Approaches to the challenge of measurement. *Aging and Society, 19,* 561–579.

20. Brod, M., Stewart, A. L., & Sands, L. (1999). Conceptualization and measurement of quality of life in dementia: The dementia quality of life instrument (DQoL). *The Gerontologist, 39*(1), 25–35.

21. Browne, S., Garavan, J., Gervin, M., Roe, M., Larkin, C., & O'Callaghan, E. (1998). Quality of life in schizophrenia: Insight and subjective response to neuroleptics. *Journal of Nervous Mental Disorders, 186*(2), 74–78.

22. Bullinger, M. (1997). Generic quality of life assessment in psychiatry. Potentials and limitations. *European Psychiatry, 12,* 203–209.

23. Butterworth, J., Hagner, D., Kiernan, W., & Schalock, R. (1996). Natural supports in the workplace: Defining an agenda for research and practice. *Journal of The Association for Persons with Severe Handicaps, 21*(3), 103–113.

24. Caballero, P. J., & Pérez, J. L. (1997). Papel del médico general en el diagnóstico y asistencia del demente senil: Implicaciones prácticas. *Daño cerebral y calidad de vida: Demencias* (pp. 239–244). Madrid: Fundación MAPFRE Medicina.

25. Clark, R., & Teage, G. (1998). Cost-effectiveness of assertive community treatment versus standard case management for persons with co-occurring severe mental illness and substance use disorders. *Health Services Research, 33*(5), 1285–1307.

26. Cohi, A. (1990). Estudio comparativo de la calidad de vida en pacientes esquizofrénicos según la condición de tratamiento. *Revista de Psiquiatría, 17*(5), 201–218.

27. Cordoba, M. J., Andrykowski, M. A., Kenady, D. E., McGrath, P. C., Sloan, D. A., & Redd, W. H. (1995). Frequency and correlates of posttraumatic-stress-disorder-like symptoms after treatment for breast cancer. *Journal of Consulting and Clinical Psychology, 63*(6), 981–986.

28. Cornes, J. M., & Arrojo, M. (1999). Calidad de vida y enfermedad mental. *Revista de Psiquiatría, 26*(1), 9–17.

29. Davies, H., Zeiss, A., Shea, E., & Tinklenberg, J. R. (1998). Sexuality and intimacy in Alzheimer's patients and their partners. *Sexuality and Disability, 16*(3), 193–203.

30. Dazord, A., Augier, F., Guisti, P., & Frot, E. (1996). Quality of life and socio-professional rehabilitation: Study on patients with chronic mental diseases. *European Psychiatry, 11,* 277–293.

31. Dickens, P. (1994). Tools and techniques of human service quality involving workers and consumers: Quality circles and consumer views. In P. Dickens (Ed.), *Quality and excellence in human services* (pp. 131–146). Chichester, England: John Wiley.

32. Dickens, P. (1994). Quality systems in human services. In P. Dickens (Ed.), *Quality and excellence in human services* (pp. 147–176). Chichester, England: John Wiley.

33. Ellison, M. L., Danley, K. S., Bromberg, C., & Palmer-Erbs, V. (1999). Longitudinal outcome of young adults who participated in a psychiatric vocational rehabilitation program. *Psychiatric Rehabilitation Journal, 22*(4), 51–58.

34. Fabian, E. (1992). Supported employment and the quality of life: Does a job make a difference? *Rehabilitation Counseling Bulletin, 36*(2), 84–97.

35. Felce, F., & Perry, J. (1997). Quality of life: The scope of the term and its breadth of measurement. In R. I. Brown (Ed.), *Quality of life for people with disabilities: Models, research, and practice* (2nd ed., pp. 56–71). Cheltenham, England: Stanley Thornes.

36. Finzen, A., & Hoffmann-Richter, U. (1997). Stigma and quality of life in mental disorders. In H. Katschnig, H. Freeman, & N. Sartorius (Eds.), *Quality of life in mental disorders* (pp. 69–76). Chichester, England: John Wiley.

37. Fisher, M. A., & Mitchell, G. J. (1998). Patients' views of quality of life: Transforming the knowledge base of nursing. *Clinical Nurse Specialist, 12*(3), 99–105.

38. Ford, J. D., & Kidd, P. (1998). Early childhood trauma and disorders of extreme stress as predictors of treatment outcome with chronic posttraumatic stress disorder. *Journal of Traumatic Stress, 11*(4), 743–761.

39. Franch, J. L., & Viaña, J. L. (1997). Afrontamiento comunitario de la demencia.papel y necesidades de la familia. *Daño cerebral y calidad de vida: Demencias* (pp. 195–210). Madrid: Fundación MAPFRE Medicina.

40. Frankenhaeuser, M. (1996). Stress without distress in tomorrow's workplace. In D. M. Warburton & N. Sherwood (Eds.), *Pleasure and quality of life* (pp. 29–37). Chichester, England: John Wiley.

41. Freeman, H. L. (1997). "Standard of living" and environmental factors as a component of quality of life in mental disorders. In H. Katschnig, H. Freeman, & N. Sartorius (Eds.), *Quality of life in mental disorders* (pp. 55–68). Chichester, England: John Wiley.

42. Frisch, M., Cornell, J., Vilanueva, M., & Retzlaff, P. (1992). Clinical validation of the quality of life inventory: A measure of life satisfaction for use in treatment planning and outcome assessment. *Psychological Assessment, 4*(1), 92–101.

43. Fristad, M. A., Arnett, M. M., & Gavazzi, S. M. (1998). The impact of psychoeducational workshops on families of mood disordered children. *Family Therapy, 25*(3), 151–159.

44. Fristad, M. A., Gavazzi, S. M., & Soldado, K. W. (1998). Multifamily psychoeducation groups for childhood mood disorders: A program description and preliminary efficacy data. *Family Therapy, 20*(3), 385–402.

45. Fristad, M. A., Stephen, M., Gavazzi, S. M., & Soldado, K. W. (1996). Psychoeducation: A promising intervention strategy for families of children and adolescents with mood disorders. *Family Therapy, 18*(3), 371–383.

46. Gardner, J. F., Nudler, S., & Chapman, M. S. (1997). Personal outcomes as measures of quality. *Mental Retardation, 35*(4), 295–305.

47. Garg, N., Yates, W. R., Jones, R., Zhou, M., & Williams, B. A. (1999). Effect of gender, treatment site, and psychiatric comorbidity on quality of life outcome in substance dependence. *American Journal on Addictions, 8,* 44–54.

48. Garralda, M. E. (1994). Chronic physical illness and emotional disorder in childhood. *British Journal of Psychiatry, 164,* 8–10.

49. Gater, R. A., Kind, P., & Gudex, C. (1995). Quality of life in liaison psychiatry. A comparison of patient and clinical assessment. *British Journal of Psychiatry, 166,* 515–520.

50. Gavazzi, S. M., Fristad, M. A., & Law, J. C. (1997). The understanding mood disorders questionnaire. *Psychological Reports, 81,* 172–174.

51. Gerber, G. J., & Coleman, G. E. (1994). Quality of life of people with psychiatric disabilities 1 and 3 years after discharge from hospital. *Quality of Life Research, 3,* 379–383.

52. Giner, J., Ibañez, E., Cervera, S., Leal, C., Baca, E., & Baca, B. J. (1999). El cuestionario sevilla de calidad de vida: Perspectiva histórica de su instauración. *Actas Españolas de Psiquiatría, 27*(1), 8–13.

53. Gjaerum, B., & Heyerdahl, S. (1998). Assessment of the mental state in medically ill children and adolescents. *Current Opinion in Psychiatry, 11,* 635–641.

54. Goodman, M., Hull, J. W., Terkelsen, K. G., Smith, T. E., & Anthony, D. (1997). Factor structure of quality of life: The Lehman interview. *Evaluation and Program Planning, 20*(4), 477–480.

55. Grant, G. M., Salcedo, V., Hynan, L. S., Frisch, M. B., & Puster, K. (1995). Effectiveness of quality of life therapy for depression. *Psychological Reports, 76,* 1203–1208.

56. Gravestock, S. (1994). Quality assurance for adults with mental retardation and mental health needs: Recent advances and practices. In N. Bouras (Ed.), *Mental health in mental retardation* (pp. 319–327). Cambridge: Cambridge University Press.

57. Grégoire, J., de Leval, N., & Mesters, P. (1995). Adaptation Française et étude des propriétés métriques de la quality of life in depression scale. *Revue Européenne de Psychologie Appliquée, 25*(4), 286–291.

58. Gurland, B., & Katz, S. (1997). Quality of life in older persons. In H. Katschnig, H. Freeman, & N. Sartorius (Eds.), *Quality of life in mental disorders* (pp. 193–211). Chichester, England: John Wiley.

59. Hayes, R. L., Halford, W. K., & Varghese, F. T. (1995). Social skills training with chronic schizophrenic patients: Effects on negative symptoms and community functioning. *Behavior Therapy, 26,* 433–449.

60. Henry, M. E., & Capitman, J. A. (1995). Finding satisfaction in adult day care: Analysis of a national demonstration of dementia care and respite services. *Journal of Applied Gerontology, 14*(3), 302–320.

61. Hoffmann, F. L., Leckman, E., Russo, N., & Knauf, L. (1999). In it for the long haul: The integration of outcomes assessment, clinical services, and management decision-making. *Evaluation and Program Planning, 22,* 211–219.

62. Iberia, J. (1997). El papel y actividad de las asociaciones de familias y afectados. *Daño cerebral y calidad de vida: Demencias* (pp. 211–217). Madrid: Fundación MAPFRE Medicina.

63. Janikowski, T., Bordieri, J., & Musgrave, J. (1991). Dimensions of client satisfaction with vocational evaluation services. *Vocational Evaluation and Work Adjustment Bulletin, 24*(2), 43–48.

64. Jones, K., Robinson, M., & Golightley, M. (1986). Long-term psychiatric patients in the community. *British Journal of Psychiatry, 149,* 537–540.

65. Jung, K. (1996). Effective strategies for stress management in everyday life. In D. M. Warburton & N. Sherwood (Eds.), *Pleasure and quality of life* (pp. 59–66). Chichester, England: John Wiley.

66. Kamis-Gould, E., Brame, J., Campbell, J., Pascall, L., Schlosser, L., & Schlosser, B. R. (1991). A functional model of quality assurance for psychiatric hospitals and corresponding staffing requirements. *Evaluation and Program Planning, 14,* 147–155.

67. Katschnig, H. (1997). How useful is the concept of quality of life in psychiatry? In H. Katschnig, H. Freeman, & N. Sartorius (Eds.), *Quality of life in mental disorders* (pp. 3–16). Chichester, England: John Wiley.

68. Katschnig, H., & Angermeyer, M. C. (1997). Quality of life in depression. In H. Katschnig, H. Freeman, & N. Sartorius (Eds.), *Quality of life in mental disorders* (pp. 137–147). Chichester, England: John Wiley.

69. Kersten, E., Wilkinson, K., & Wright, S. (1999). Bringing staff on board: Creating an outcomes project tied to continuous quality improvement in an adult community residential service. *Evaluation and Program Planning, 22,* 221–232.

70. Klinkman, M. (1998). False positives, false negatives, and the validity of the diagnosis of major depression in primary care. *Archives of Family Medicine, 7,* 451–464.

71. Klinkman, M. S. (1997). Competing demands in psychosocial care: A model for the identification and treatment of depressive disorders in primary care. *General Hospital Psychiatry, 19,* 98–111.

72. Koran, L., Thieneman, M., & Davenport, R. (1996). Quality of life for patients with obsessive-compulsive disorder. *American Journal of Psychiatry, 153*(6), 783–788.

73. Kutner, N. (1999). Family members' perceptions of quality of life change in dementia SCU residents. *Journal of Applied Gerontology, 18*(4), 423–440.

74. Lafave, H. G., de Souza, H. R., Prince, P. N., Atchison, K. E., & Gerber, G. J. (1995). Partnerships for people with serious mental illness who live below the poverty line. *Psychiatric Services, 46*(10), 1071–1073.

75. Lauer, G. (1994). The quality of life issue in chronic mental illness. In J. P. Dauwalder (Ed.), *Psychology and promotion of health: Vol. 2* (pp. 28–33). Seattle, WA: Hogrefe & Huber.

76. Leff, J. P. (1997). Whose life is it anyway? Quality of life for long-stay patients discharged from psychiatric hospitals. In H. Katschnig, H. Freeman, & N. Sartorius (Eds.), *Quality of life in mental disorders* (pp. 241–260). Chichester, England: John Wiley.

77. Lehman, A. F., Rachuba, L. T., & Postrado, L. T. (1995). Demographic influences on quality of life among persons with chronic mental illnesses. *Evaluation and Program Planning, 18*(2), 155–164.

78. Lehman, A. F. (1997). Instruments for measuring quality of life in mental illnesses. In H. Katschnig, H. Freeman, & N. Sartorius (Eds.), *Quality of life in mental disorders* (pp. 79–94). Chichester, England: John Wiley.

79. Lenz, G., & Demal, U. (1997). Psychotherapy and quality of life. In H. Katschnig, H. Freeman, & N. Sartorius (Eds.), *Quality of life in mental disorders* (pp. 227–239). Chichester, England: John Wiley.

80. López, A. E. (1994). *Valoración de los efectos de la rehabilitación psicosocial.* Unpublished doctoral dissertation, Universidad de Málaga, Málaga, Spain.

81. Lucas, R., Salcedo, A., Susín, C., Roca, B., Moreno, M., Zimmer, M., Jordá, E., Guillén, A., Garrido, I., & Puche, J. (1997). Calidad de vida en pacientes esquizofrénicos y en parientes de esquizofrénicos. *Revista de Psiquiatría de la Facultad de Medicina de Barcelona, 24*(6), 143–155.

82. Mezzich, J. E., & Schmolke, M. M. (1997). Quality of life and comprehensive clinical diagnosis. In H. Katschnig, H. Freeman, & N. Sartorius (Eds.), *Quality of life in mental disorders* (pp. 109–117). Chichester, England: John Wiley.

83. Oliver, J., & Mohamad, H. (1992). The quality of life of chronically mentally ill: A comparison of public, private, and voluntary residential provisions. *British Journal of Social Work, 22,* 391–404.

84. Oliver, J., Huxley, P., Bridges, K., & Mohamad, H. (1996). Definitions and conceptual issues concerning quality of life. In J. Oliver, P. Huxley, K. Bridges, & H. Mohamad (Eds.), *Quality of life and mental health services* (pp. 15–47). London: Routledge.

85. Oliver, J., Huxley, P., Bridges, K., & Mohamad, H. (1996). The development of a quality of life profile for operational use. In J. Oliver, P. Huxley, K. Bridges, & H. Mohamad (Eds.), *Quality of life and mental health services* (pp. 48–64). London: Routledge.

86. Oliver, J., Huxley, P., Bridges, K., & Mohamad, H. (1996). Quality of life in the mental health service context. In J. Oliver, P. Huxley, K. Bridges, & H. Mohamad (Eds.), *Quality of life and mental health services* (pp. 84–107). London: Routledge.

87. Oliver, J., Huxley, P., Bridges, K., & Mohamad, H. (1996). The quality of care and the quality of life in independent-sector residential homes. In J. Oliver, P. Huxley, K. Bridges, & H. Mohamad (Eds.), *Quality of life and mental health services* (pp. 111–127). London: Routledge.

88. Oliver, J., Huxley, P., Bridges, K., & Mohamad, H. (1996). Community-based support and community mental health support teams. In J. Oliver, P. Huxley, K. Bridges, & H. Mohamad (Eds.), *Quality of life and mental health services* (pp. 152–178). London: Routledge.

89. Oliver, J., Huxley, P., Bridges, K., & Mohamad, H. (1996). Lessons learned from the experiences of applying quality of life to mental health services. In J. Oliver, P. Huxley, K. Bridges, & H. Mohamad (Eds.), *Quality of life and mental health services* (pp. 235–250). London: Routledge.

90. Orange, J. B., & Colton-Hudson, A. (1998). Enhancing communication in dementia of the Alzheimer's type. *Topics in Geriatric Rehabilitation, 14*(2), 56–75.

91. Patterson, T., Kaplan, R. M., Grant, I., Semple, S. J., Moscona, S., Koch, W. L., Harris, M. J., & Jeste, D. V. (1996). Quality of well-being in late life psychosis. *Psychiatry Research, 63,* 169–181.

92. Petterson, I. L., & Arnetz, B. B. (1998). Psychosocial stressors and well-being in health care workers: The impact of an intervention program. *Social Science and Medicine, 47*(11), 1763–1772.

93. Pickney, A. A., Gerber, G. J., & Lafave, H. G. (1991). Quality of life after psychiatric rehabilitation: The clients' perspective. *Acta Psychiatrica Scandinavica, 83,* 86–91.

94. Prilleltensky, I., Peirson, L., Gould, J., & Gould, N. G. (1997). Planning mental health services for children and youth. Part I: A value-based approach. *Evaluation and Program Planning, 20*(2), 163–172.

95. Ramsay, M., Winget, C., & Higginson, I. (1995). Review: Measures to determine the outcome of community services for people with dementia. *Age and Aging, 24,* 73–83.

96. Renwick, R., Brown, I., & Nagler, M. (1996). *Quality of life in health promotion and rehabilitation: Conceptual approaches, issues, and applications.* London: Sage.

97. Revicki, D. A., Simon, G. E., Chan, K., Katon, W., & Heiligenstein, J. (1998). Depression, health-related quality of life, and medical cost outcomes of receiving recommended levels of antidepressant treatment. *Journal Family Practice, 47*(2), 446–452.

98. Robert, M., Hirschfeld, A., Russell, J. M., & Delgado, P. L. (1998). Predictors of response to acute treatment of chronic and double depression with sertraline or imipramine. *Journal of Clinical Psychiatry, 59*(12), 669–675.

99. Rodriguez, A., Jarne, A., Soler, R., Miarons, R., & Grau, A. (1995). Estudio factorial y adaptación de la escala de calidad de vida en la esquizofrenia (QLS). *Revista de Psicología General y Aplicada, 48*(3), 353–364.

100. Rodriguez, J. (1995). *Health psychology and quality of life research: Vol. 2.* Murcia, Spain: University of Alicante, Health Psychology Department, and Sociedad Valenciana de Psicología Social.

101. Rodriguez Marín, J. (1995). *Health psychology and quality of life research: Vol. 1*. Murcia, Spain: University of Alicante, Health Psychology Department, and Sociedad Valenciana de Psicología Social.

102. Rosenfield, S. (1997). Labeling mental illness: The effects of received services and perceived stigma on life satisfaction. *American Sociological Review, 62*(4), 660–672.

103. Rosenheck, R., Cramer, J., & Xu, W. (1998). Multiple outcome assessment in a study of the cost-effectiveness of clozapine in the treatment of refractory schizophrenia. *Health Services Research, 33*(5), 1237–1261.

104. Russell, C. K. (1996). Passion and heretics: Meaning in life and quality of life of persons with dementia. *Journal of American Geriatrics Society, 44*(11), 1400–1402.

105. Sainfort, F., Becker, M., & Diamond, R. (1996). Judgments of quality of life of individuals with severe mental disorders: Patient self-report versus provider perspectives. *American Journal of Psychiatry, 153,* 497–502.

106. Sartorius, N. (1997). Quality of life and mental disorders: A global perspective. In H. Katschnig, H. Freeman, & N. Sartorius (Eds.), *Quality of life in mental disorders* (pp. 319–328). Chichester, England: John Wiley.

107. Sartorius, N., & Janca, A. (1996). Psychiatric assessment instruments developed by the World Health Organization. *Social Psychiatry and Psychiatric Epidemiology, 31,* 55–69.

108. Savorani, G., Vulcano, V., Boni, S., Sarti, G., & Ravaglia, G. (1998). Behavioral disorders in dementia patients and their impact on the stress of caregiving relatives: The ARAD questionnaire. *Archives of Gerontology and Geriatrics, 26*(1001), 481–485.

109. Savorani, G., Zanetti, O., Metitieri, T., Bianchetti, A., & Trabucchi, M. (1998). Effectiveness of an educational program for demented persons' relatives. *Archives of Gerontology and Geriatrics, 26*(1001), 531–538.

110. Schalock, R., Nelson, G., Sutton, S., Holtan, S., & Sheehan, M. (1997). Evaluación multidimensional del estado actual y la calidad de vida de los receptores de servicios de salud mental. *Siglo Cero, 28*(4), 5–12.

111. Schmeck, K., & Poustka, F. (1997). Quality of life and child psychiatric disorders. In H. Katschnig, H. Freeman, & N. Sartorius (Eds.), *Quality of life in mental disorders* (pp. 179–191). Chichester, England: John Wiley.

112. Selmes, J. (1997). Política de la Unión Europea en la salud pública. El caso de la enfermedad de Alzheimer. *Daño cerebral y calidad de vida: Demencias* (pp. 219–224). Madrid: Fundación MAPFRE Medicina.

113. Sherbourne, C. D., Wells, K. B., & Judd, L. L. (1996). Functioning and well-being of patients with panic disorder. *American Journal of Psychiatry, 153*(2), 213–218.

114. Sherwood, N. (1996). Pleasure, choice, and the quality of everyday life. In D. M. Warburton & N. Sherwood (Eds.), *Pleasure and quality of life* (pp. 275–280). Chichester, England: John Wiley.

115. Sherwood, N. (1996). Stressors, product use, and everyday skills. In D. M. Warburton & N. Sherwood (Eds.), *Pleasure and quality of life* (pp. 89–96). Chichester, England: John Wiley.

116. Simpson, C. J., Hyde, C. E., & Faragher, E. B. (1989). The chronically mentally ill in community facilities: A study of quality of life. *British Journal of Psychiatry, 154,* 77–82.

117. Skantze, K. (1998). Subjective quality of life and standard of living: A 10-year follow-up of outpatients with schizophrenia. *Acta Psychiatrica Scandinavica, 98,* 390–399.

118. Skantze, K., Malm, U., Dencker, S. J., May, P. R. A., & Corrigan, P. (1992). Comparison of quality of life with standard of living in schizophrenic outpatients. *British Journal of Psychiatry, 161,* 797–801.

119. Skrabski, A., & Kopp, M. (1994). Health behaviour, psychiatric symptoms, and psychosocial background factors. In J. P. Dauwalder (Ed.), *Psychology and promotion of health Vol. 2* (pp. 21–27). Seattle, WA: Hogrefe & Huber.

120. Small, G. W., Birkett, M., Meyers, B. S., Koran, L. M., Bystrisky, A., Nemeroff, C. B., & Flioxetine Collaborative Study Group (1996). Impact of physical illness on quality of life and antidepressant response in geriatric major depression. *American Geriatric Society, 44,* 1220–1225.

121. Smith, M. K. (1998). Empowerment evaluation: Theoretical and methodological considerations. *Evaluation and Program Planning, 21,* 255–261.

122. Smith, T. E., Hull, J. W., & Goodman, M. (1999). The relative influences of symptoms, insight, and neurocognition on social adjustment in schizophrenia and schizoaffective disorder. *Journal of Nervous and Mental Disease, 187*(2), 102–108.

123. Solomon, P., & Draine, J. (1995). One-year outcomes of a randomized trial of consumer case management. *Evaluation and Program Planning, 18*(2), 117–127.

124. Stastny, P., & Amering, M. (1997). Integrating consumer perspectives on quality of life in research and service planning. In H. Katschnig, H. Freeman, & N. Sartorius (Eds.), *Quality of life in mental disorders* (pp. 261–269). Chichester, England: John Wiley.

125. Steinwachs, D., Flynn, L., Norquist, G., & Skinner, E. (1996). *Using client outcomes information to improve mental health and substance abuse treatment.* San Francisco: Jossey-Bass.

126. Suiter, J. I., & Bonnsetter, B. (1996). Individual coping strategies and behavioural style. In D. M. Warburton & N. Sherwood (Eds.), *Pleasure and quality of life* (pp. 47–57). Chichester, England: John Wiley.

127. Swanson, C. L., Gur, R. C., Bilker, W., Petty, R. G., & Gur, R. E. (1998). Premorbid educational attainment in schizophrenia: Association with symptoms, functioning, and neurobehavioral measures. *Biological Psychiatry, 44*, 739–747.

128. Swanson, J., Swartz, M., Estroff, S., Borum, R., Wagner, R., & Hiday, V. (1998). Psychiatric impairment, social contact, and violent behavior: Evidence from a study of outpatient committed persons with severe mental disorder. *Social Psychiatry and Psychiatric Epidemiology, 33*, S86–S94.

129. Telch, M. J., Schmidt, N. B., Jaimez, T. L., Jacquin, K. M., & Harrington, P. J. (1995). Impact of cognitive-behavioral treatment on quality of life in panic disorder patients. *Journal of Consulting and Clinical Psychology, 63*(5), 823–830.

130. Tempier, R., Caron, J., Mercier, C., & Leouffre, P. (1998). Quality of life of severely mentally ill individuals: A comparative study. *Community Mental Health Journal, 34*(5), 477–485.

131. Thorpe, L. M., Klinkman, M. S., Schwenk, T. L., & Coyne, J. C. (1997). Depression in primary care — More like asthma than appendicitis: The Michigan depression project. *Canadian Journal of Psychiatry, 42*, 966–973.

132. Thorpe, L., Campbell, B., & Primeau, F. J. (1998). Discusión de un caso clínico: Paciente mayor con psicosis. *Canadian Journal of Psychiatry, 43*(1), 10–14.

133. Trauer, T., Duckmanton, R. A., et al. (1998). A study of the quality of life of the severely mentally ill. *International Journal of Social Psychiatry, 44*(2), 79–92.

134. Tsimara-Papastamatiou, H. (1996). Stressors and cancer. In D. M. Warburton & N. Sherwood (Eds.), *Pleasure and quality of life* (pp. 39–46). Chichester, England: John Wiley.

135. Van Nieuwenhuizen, G., & Schene, A. H. (1997). Measuring the quality of life of clients with severe mental illness: A review of instruments. *Psychiatric Rehabilitation Journal, 20*(4), 33–42.

136. Vázquez-Barquero, J. L., Gaite, L., Ramírez, N., García, E., et al. (1997). Desarrollo de la versión española del perfil de calidad de vida de Lancashire — LQOLP. *Archivos de Neurobiología, 60*(2), 125–139.

137. Walter, L. J., Schaefer, C., Albright, L., Parthasarathy, S., Hunkeler, E. M., & Westphal, J. (1999). Role of a psychiatric outcome study in a large-scale quality improvement project. *Evaluation and Program Planning, 22,* 233–243.

138. Warburton, D. M., & Suiter, J. I. (1996). The costs of job dissatisfaction. In D. M. Warburton & N. Sherwood (Eds.), *Pleasure and quality of life* (pp. 13–28). Chichester, England: John Wiley.

139. Warshaw, M. G., Fierman, E., Pratt, L., Hunt, M., Yonkers, K. A., Massion, A. O., & Keller, M. B. (1993). Quality of life and dissociation in anxiety disorder patients with histories of trauma or PTSD. *American Journal of Psychiatry, 150*(10), 1512–1516.

140. Wiersma, D. (1997). Role functioning as a component of quality of life in mental disorders. In H. Katschnig, H. Freeman, & N. Sartorius (Eds.), *Quality of life in mental disorders* (pp. 43–54). Chichester, England: John Wiley.

141. Williams, G. M., & Walters, A. S. (1996). Perceived impact of limb amputation on sexual activity: A study of adult amputees. *Journal of Sex Research, 33*(3), 221–230.

142. Wittchen, H. U., & Beloch, E. (1996). The impact of social phobia on quality of life. *International Clinical Psychopharmacology, 11*(3), 15–23.

APPENDIX 10.4
Numbered References Corresponding to Table 10.4

1. Antaki, C., & Rapley, M. (1996). Questions and answers to psychological assessment schedules: Hidden troubles in quality of life interviews. *Journal of Intellectual Disability Research, 40*(5), 421–437.

2. Apgar, D., Cook, S., & Lerman, P. (1998). *Life after Johnstone: Impacts on consumer competencies, behaviors, and quality of life.* Research report. New Jersey Institute of Technology, Center for Architecture and Building Science Research.

3. Arostegi, I. (1998). *Evaluación de la calidad de vida en personas adultas con retraso mental en la comunidad autónoma del Pais Vasco.* Unpublished doctoral dissertation, Universidad de Deusto, Spain.

4. Burchard, S., Hasazi, J., Gordon, L., & Yoe, J. (1991). An examination of lifestyle and adjustment in three community residential alternatives. *Research in Developmental Disabilities, 12,* 127–142.

5. Campo, S., Sharpton, W., Thompson, B., & Sexton, D. (1996). Measurement characteristics of the quality of life index when used with adults who have severe mental retardation. *American Journal on Mental Retardation, 100*(5), 546-550.

6. Campo, S. F., Sharpton, W. R., Thompson, B., & Sexton, D. (1997). Correlates of the quality of life of adults with severe or profound mental retardation. *Mental Retardation, 35*(5), 329–337.

7. Che, T. H., Bruininks, R., Lakin, K., & Hayden, M. (1993). Personal competencies and community participation in small community residential programs: A multiple discriminant analysis. *American Journal on Mental Retardation, 98*(3), 390–399.

8. Chubon, R. A., Clayton, K. S., & Vandergriff, D. V. (1995). An exploratory study comparing the quality of life of South Carolinians with mental retardation and spinal cord injury. *Rehabilitation Counseling Bulletin, 39*(2), 107–118.

9. Conroy, J. (1996). The small ICF/MR program: Dimensions of quality and cost. *Mental Retardation, 34*(1), 13–26.

10. Cummins, R. (1991). The comprehensive quality of life scale — intellectual disability: An initial report. *Australia and New Zealand Journal of Developmental Disabilities, 17*(2), 259–264.

11. Cummins, R. (1997). Assessing quality of life for people with disabilities. In R. I. Brown (Ed.), *Quality of life for people with disabilities: Models, research, and practice* (2nd ed., pp. 116–150). Cheltenham, England: Stanley Thornes.

12. Dagnan, D., Jones, J., & Ruddick, L. (1994). The psychometric properties of a scale for assessing quality of life of people with learning disabilities in residential care. *British Journal of Developmental Disabilities, 40,* 98–103.

13. Dagnan, D., Look, R., Ruddick, L., & Jones, J. (1995). Changes in the quality of life of people with learning disabilities who moved from hospital to live in community-based homes. *International Journal of Rehabilitation Research, 18,* 115–122.

14. DeLaGarza, D. V., & Erin, J. N. (1993). Employment status and quality of life of graduates of a state residential school. *Journal of Visual Impairment and Blindness, 87*(6) [Special issue: Residential schools: Past, present, future], 229–233.

15. Eggelton, I., Robertson, S., Ryan, J., & Kober, R. (1999). The impact of employment on the quality of life of people with an intellectual disability. *Journal of Vocational Rehabilitation, 13,* 95–107.

16. Evans, D., Burns, J., Robinson, W., & Garret, O. (1985). The quality of life questionnaire: A multidimensional measure. *American Journal of Community Psychology, 13*(3), 305–322.

17. Fleming, I., & Stenfert, B. (1990). Evaluation of a community care project for people with learning difficulties. *Journal of Mental Deficiency Research, 34,* 451–464.

18. Harner, C., & Heal, L. (1993). The multifaceted lifestyle satisfaction scale (MLSS): Psychometric properties of an interview schedule for assessing personal satisfaction of adults with limited intelligence. *Research in Developmental Disabilities, 14,* 221–236.

19. Harper, D. (1994). Evaluating a training package for staff working with people with learning disabilities prior to hospital closure. *British Journal of Developmental Disabilities, 40,* 45–53.

20. Hatton, C., Emerson, E., Roberston, J., Henderson, D., & Cooper, J. (1995). The quality and cost of residential services for adults with multiple disabilities: A comparative evaluation. *Research in Developmental Disabilities, 16*(6), 439–460.

21. Hawkins, B., Kim, K., & Eklund, S. (1995). Validity and reliability of a five-dimensional life satisfaction index. *Mental Retardation, 33*(5), 295–303.

22. Heal, L., & Chadsey-Rusch, J. (1985). The lifestyle satisfaction scale (LSS): Assessing individuals' satisfaction with residence, community setting, and associated services. *Applied Research in Mental Retardation, 6,* 475–490.

23. Howe, J., Horner, R. H., & Stephen, N. J. (1998). Comparison of supported living and traditional residential services in the state of Oregon. *Mental Retardation, 36*(1), 1–11.

24. Jones, J., Dagnan, D., Trower, P., & Ruddick, L. (1996). People with learning disabilities living in community-based homes: The relationship of quality of life with age and disability. *International Journal of Rehabilitation Research, 19,* 219–227.

25. Kearney, C. A., & MacKnight, T. (1997). Preference, choice, and persons with disabilities: A synopsis of assessments, interventions, and future direction. *Clinical Psychology Review, 17*(2), 217–238.

26. Kennedy, C., Horner, R., Newton, J., & Kanda, E. (1990). Measuring the activity patterns of adults with severe disabilities using the resident lifestyle inventory. *Journal of The Association for Persons with Severe Handicaps, 15*(2), 79–85.

27. Kinney, W., & Coyle, C. (1992). Predicting life satisfaction among adults with physical disabilities. *Archives of Physical Medicine and Rehabilitation, 73,* 863–869.

28. Kozleski, E., & Sands, D. (1992). The yardstick of social validity: Evaluating quality of life as perceived by adults without disabilities. *Education and Training in Mental Retardation, 27*(2), 119–131.

29. Lai Chun Yu, A., Jupp, J. J., & Taylor, A. (1996). The discriminate validity of the lifestyle satisfaction scale for the assessment of Australian adults with intellectual disabilities. *Journal of Intellectual and Developmental Disability, 21*(1), 3–15.

30. Leibowitz, M., McClain, J., Evans, E., Ruma, P., & Rauner, T. (1994). Client perceptions of quality of life in accredited and nonaccredited community residential facilities. *Journal of Developmental and Physical Disabilities, 6*(4), 339–346.

31. Malette, P., Mirenda, P., Jones, P., Bunz, T., & Rogow, S. (1992). Application of a lifestyle development process for persons with severe intellectual disabilities: A case study report. *Journal of The Association for Persons with Severe Handicaps, 17*(3), 179–191.

32. Matikka, L. M. (1996). Effects of psychological factors on the perceived quality of life of people with intellectual disabilities. *Journal of Applied Research in Intellectual Disabilities, 9*(2), 115–128.

33. Neumayer, R., & Bleasdale, M. (1996). Personal lifestyle preferences of people with an intellectual disability. *Journal of Intellectual and Developmental Disability, 21*(2), 91–114.

34. Ouellette-Kuntz, H. (1990). A pilot study in the use of the quality of life interview schedule. *Social Indicators Research, 23,* 283–298.

35. Perry, J., & Felce, D. (1995). Living under the strategy: Do outcomes for users of Welsh community residential services live up to the all Wales strategy's underlying principles? *British Journal of Learning Disabilities, 41,* 102–105.

36. Perry, J., & Felce, D. (1995). Objective assessments of quality of life: How much do they agree with each other? *Journal of Community and Applied Social Psychology, 5,* 1–19.

37. Pilon, W., Arsenault, R., & Paré, C. (1997). La qualité de vie des personnes viellisantes présentant une déficience intellectuelle résidant dans la communauté comparée à celle des personnes viellisantes de la population générale. *Revue Francophone de la Déficience Intellectuelle, 8*(2), 115–127.

38. Rapley, M., & Beyer, M. (1996). Daily activity, community participation, and quality of life in an ordinary housing network. *Journal of Applied Research in Intellectual Disabilities, 9*(1), 31–39.

39. Rapley, M., & Beyer, S. (1998). Daily activity, community participation, and quality of life in an ordinary housing network: A two-year follow-up. *Journal of Applied Research in Intellectual Disabilities, 11*(1), 34–43.

40. Reiter, S., & Bendov, D. (1996). The self-concept and quality of life of two groups of learning-disabled adults living at home and in group homes. *British Journal of Developmental Disabilities, 42,* 97–111.

41. Rosen, M., Simon, E. W., & McKinsey, L. (1995). Subjective measure of quality of life. *Mental Retardation, 33*(1), 31–34.

42. Sands, D., Kozleski, E., & Goodwin, L. (1991). Whose needs are we meeting? Results of a consumer satisfaction survey of persons with developmental disabilities in Colorado. *Research in Developmental Disabilities, 12,* 297–314.

43. Schalock, R. (1994). Quality of life, quality enhancement, and quality assurance: Implications for program planning and evaluation in the field of mental retardation and developmental disabilities. *Evaluation and Program Planning, 17*(2), 121–131.

44. Schalock, R., Bonham, G., & Marchand, C. (2000). Consumer-based quality of life assessment: A path model of perceived satisfaction. *Evaluation and Program Planning, 23*(1), 77–87.

45. Schalock, R., & Genung, T. (1993). Placement from a community-based mental retardation program: A 15-year follow-up. *American Journal on Mental Retardation, 98*(3), 400–407.

46. Schalock, R., Keith, K., Hoffman, K., & Karan, O. (1989). Quality of life: Its measurement and use. *Mental Retardation, 27*(1), 25–31.

47. Simon, E. W., Rosen, M., Grossman, E., & Pratowski, E. (1994). The relationships among facial emotion recognition, social skills, and quality of life. *Research in Developmental Disabilities, 16*(5), 47–58.

48. Sinnott-Oswald, M., Gliner, J. A., & Spencer, K. C. (1991). Supported and sheltered employment: Quality of life issues among workers with disabilities. *Education and Training in Mental Retardation, 26*(4), 338–397.

49. Smull, M. (1999). *Essential lifestyle planning and other topics.* Paper presented at the annual meeting of the American Association of Mental Retardation, New Orleans, LA.

50. Van Gennep, A. (1997). Quality of community living in the Netherlands. *British Journal of Developmental Disabilities, 43,* 1–14.

51. Verdugo, M. A. (1994). El cambio de paradigma en la concepción del retraso mental: La nueva definición de la AAMR. *Siglo Cero, 25*(3), 5–24.

Appendix 10.5
Numbered References Corresponding to Table 10.5

1. Avis, N. E. (1998). Quality of life in older adults with HIV disease. *Research on Aging, 20*(6), 822–846.

2. Bearon, L. B. (1989). No great expectations: The underpinnings of life satisfaction for older women. *The Gerontologist, 29*(6), 772–778.

3. Bess, F. H., Lichtenstein, M. J., & Logan, S. A. (1990). Functional impact of hearing loss on the elderly. *American Speech-Language-Hearing Association, 19,* 144–149.

4. Bowling, A., & Browne, P. D. (1991). Social networks, health, and emotional well-being among the oldest old in London. *Journal of Gerontology, 46*(1), 20–32.

5. Brockett, R. G. (1985). The relationship between self-directed learning readiness and life satisfaction among older adults. *Adult Education Quarterly, 35*(4), 210–219.

6. Brooks, R., & EuroQoL Group. (1996). EuroQoL: The current state of play. *Health Policy, 37,* 53–72.

7. Brown, R. I. (1997). *Quality of life for people with disabilities. Models, research, and practice* (2nd ed.). Cheltenham, England: Stanley Thornes.

8. Carabellese, C. M., Apollonio, I. M., Rozzini, R. M., Bianchetti, A. M., Frisoni, G. B. M., Frattola, L. M., & Trabucchi, M. M. (1993). Sensory impairment and quality of life in a community elderly population. *Journal of the American Geriatrics Society, 41*(4), 401–407.

9. Castellón, A., Rubio, R., & Rico, A. (1999). Nivel de autoestima en los mayores tras un programa de ocio. *Revista Especial de Geriatría y Gerontología, 34*(4), 225–229.

10. Chowdhary, U. (1991). Clothing and self-esteem of the institutionalized elderly female: Two experiments. *Educational Gerontology, 17,* 527–541.

11. Coast, J., Peters, T. J., Richards, H., & Gunnell, D. (1998). Use of EuroQoL among elderly acute care patients. *Quality of Life Research, 7,* 1–10.

12. De Gracia, M., Garre, J., & Marcó, M. (1999). Desarrollo y validación preliminar de la escala de percepción subjetiva del envejecimiento (EPSE). *Revista Especial de Geriatría y Gerontología, 34*(2), 92–100.

13. De Leo, M., René, F., & Diekstra, P. (1998). LEIPAD. An internationally applicable instrument to assess quality of life in the elderly. *Behavioral Medicine, 24,* 17–27.

14. Dennis, R. E., Williams, W., Giangreco, M. F., & Cloninger C. J. (1993). Quality of life as a context for planning and evaluation of services for planning and evaluation of services for people with disabilities. *Exceptional Children, 59*(6), 499–512.

15. Everard, K. M. (1999). The relationship between reasons for activity and older adult well-being. *Journal of Applied Gerontology, 18*(3), 325–340.

16. Farré, R., Frasque, P., & Romá, R. (1999). Estado de salud y calidad de vida de un colectivo de ancianos institucionalizados. *Revista Especial de Geriatría y Gerontología, 34*(1), 25–33.

17. Fernández-Ballesteros, R., Zamarrón, M. D., & Maciá, A. (1996). *Calidad de vida en la vejez en distintos contextos.* Madrid: Ministerio de Trabajo y Asuntos Exteriores, Instituto Nacional de Servicios Sociales.

18. Fernández-Ballesteros, R. (1997). Calidad de vida en la vejez: Condiciones diferenciales. *Anuario de Psicología, 73,* 89–104.

19. Fernández del Valle, J., & García, A. (1994). Redes de apoyo social en usuarios de ayuda a domicilio de la tercera edad. *Psicothema, 6*(1), 39–47.

20. Fillenbaum, G. G. (1987). Activities of daily living. In G. L. Maddox (Ed.), *The Encyclopedia of Aging* (pp. 3–4). New York: Springer.

21. Goff, K. (1993). Creativity and life satisfaction of older adults. *Educational Gerontology, 19,* 241–250.

22. Grégoire, J., de Leval, N., & Mesters, P. (1995). Adaptation française et étude des propriétés métriques de la quality of life in depression scale. *Revue Européenne de Psychologie Appliquée, 45*(4), 286–291.

23. Gustafson, D., Hawkins, R., Boberg, E., Pingree, S., & Serlin, R. (1998). Impact of a patient-centered, computer-based health information/support system. *American Journal of Preventive Medicine, 16*(1), 1–9.

24. Haas, B. (1999). A multidisciplinary concept analysis of quality of life. *Western Journal of Nursing Research, 21*(6), 728–743.

25. Hayes, V., Morris, J., Wolfe, C., & Morgan, M. (1995). The SF-36 health survey questionnaire: Is it suitable for use with older adults? *Age and Aging, 24,* 120–126.

26. Hughes, D. (1995). Aiming for objectivity and balance in the evaluation of the quality of life experienced by service users with learning disabilities. In D. Pilling & G. Watson (Eds.), *Evaluating quality in services for disabled and older people* (pp. 201–206). London: Jessica Kingsley.

27. Ishii-Kuntz, M. (1990). Social interaction and psychological well-being: Comparison across stages of adulthood. *International Journal of Aging and Human Development, 30*(1), 15.

28. Janicki, M. (1996). Quality of life for older persons with mental retardation. In R. Schalock (Ed.), *Quality of life: Vol. 2. Application to persons with disabilities* (pp. 105–115). Washington, DC: American Association on Mental Retardation.

29. Jenkinson, C., Coulter, A., & Wright, L. (1993). Short-form 36 (SF-36) health survey questionnaire: Normative data for adults of working age. *British Medical Journal, 306,* 1437–1440.

30. Katz, S. (2000). Busy bodies: Activity, aging, and the management of everyday life. *Journal of Aging Studies, 14*(2), 135–153.

31. Kempen, G., Jelicic, M., & Ormel, J. (1997). Personality, chronic medical morbidity, and health-related quality of life among older persons. *Health Psychology, 16*(6), 539–546.

32. Kerruish, A. (1995). Quality for people — learning from service users about quality. In D. Pilling & G. Watson (Eds.), *Evaluating quality in services for disabled and older people* (pp. 158–163). London: Jessica Kingsley.

33. Kilbom, A. (1999). Evidence-based programs for the prevention of early exit from work. *Experimental Aging Research, 25*(4), 291–299.

34. Lachs, M. S., & Boyer, P. (1998). Caring for my dad: Can your parent live alone? *Prevention, 50*(10), 155–157.

35. Lawton, M. (1991). Functional status and aging well. *Generations, 15*(1), 31–34.

36. Lawton, M., Winter, L., Kleban, M. H., & Ruckdesschel, K. (1999). Affect and quality of life. *Journal of Aging and Health, 11*(2), 169–199.

37. Levin, J., & Chatters, L. (1998). Religion, health, and psychological well-being in older adults: Findings from three national surveys. *Journal of Aging and Health, 10*(4), 504–532.

38. Liao, Y., McGee, D., Guichan, C., & Cooper, R. (2000). Quality of the last year of life of older adults: 1986 vs. 1993. *Journal of the American Medical Association, 283*(4), 512.

39. Long, J., Anderson, J., & Williams, R. (1990). Life reflections by older kinsmen about critical life issues. *Educational Gerontology, 16,* 61–71.

40. MacHorney, C. A., Kosinski, M., & Ware, J. E. (1994). Comparisons of the costs and quality of norms for the SF-36 health survey collected by mail versus telephone interview: Results from a national survey. *Medical Care, 32,* 40–66.

41. Martorell, M. C., Gómez, O., & Cuenca, A. (1994). Calidad de vida y tercera edad. *Cuadernos de Medicina Psicosomática, 30,* 41–46.

42. Matsubayashi, K., & Okumiya, K. (1997). Quality of life of old people living in the community. *Journal of the American Medical Association, 350*(9090), 1521–1522.

43. Midgley, G. (1995). Evaluation and change in service systems for people with disabilities? In D. Pilling & G. Watson (Eds.), *Evaluating quality in services for disabled and older people* (pp. 33–49). London: Jessica Kingsley.

44. Montoro, J. (1999). Factores determinantes de la calidad del cuidado asistencial institucional a personas mayores y/o con discapacidad. *Papers, 57,* 89–112.

45. Moss, M. S., Lawton, M., & Glicksman, A. (1991). The role of pain in the last year of life of older persons. *Journal of Gerontology, 46*(2), 51–57.

46. Murlow, C., Aguilar, C., Endicott, J., Velez, R., Tuley, M., Charlip, W., & Hill, J. (1990). Association between hearing impairments and quality of life of elderly individuals. *Journal of the American Geriatrics Society, 38*(1), 45–50.

47. Newsom, J. T., & Schulz, R. (1996). Social support as a mediator in the relation between functional status and quality of life in older adults. *Psychology and Aging, 111*(1), 34–44.

48. Nieto, J., Abad, A., & Torres, A. (1998). Dimensiones psicosociales mediadoras de la conducta de enfermedad y la calidad de vida en población geriátrica. *Anales de Psicología, 14*(1), 75–81.

49. O'Connor, B. (1995). Family and friend relationships among older and younger adults: Interaction motivation, mood, and quality. *International Journal of Aging and Human Development, 40*(1), 9–29.

50. Oldridge, N. (1998). Cardiac rehabilitation in the elderly. *Aging Clinical and Experimental Research, 10*(4), 273–283.

51. O'Mahony, P., Rodgers, H., Thomson, R., Dobson, R., & James, O. (1998). Is the SF-36 suitable for assessing health status of older stroke patients? *Age and Aging, 27,* 19–22.

52. Pearlman, R., & Uhlmann, R. (1991). Calidad de vida en personas mayores con enfermedad crónica no hospitalizados. *Journal of Gerontology: Medical Sciences, 46*(2), 31–38.

53. Pilling, D., & Watson, G. (1995). *Evaluating quality in services for disabled and older people.* London: Jessica Kingsley.

54. Pilling, S. (1995). QUARTZ, PASSING, and user involvement: Meeting points and departure points. In D. Pilling & G. Watson (Eds.), *Evaluating quality of services for disabled and older people* (pp. 135–147). London: Jessica Kingsley.

55. Reuben, D. B., Valle, L. A., Hays, E. D., & Siu, A. L. (1995). Measuring physical function in community-dwelling older persons: A comparison of self-administered, interviewer-administered, and performance-based measures. *Journal of the American Geriatrics Society, 43,* 17–23.

56. Rodgers, W., & Miller, B. (1997). A comparative analysis of ADL questions in surveys of older people. *Journals of Gerontology: Psychological and Social Sciences,* (52B), 21–36.

57. Rozzini, R., Frisoni, G. B., Bianchetti, A., Zanetti, O., & Trabucchi, M. (1993). Physical performance test and activities of daily living scales in the assessment of health status in elderly people. *Journal of the American Geriatrics Society, 41,* 1109–1113.

58. Saravanabhavan, R., Martin, W., & Saravanabhavan, S. (1994). A model for assessing rehabilitation needs of the elderly American Indians who are visually impaired and living on reservations. *Journal of Applied Rehabilitation Counseling, 25*(2), 19–28.

59. Schalock, R., DeVries, D., & Lebsack, J. (1999). Rights, quality measures, and program changes. In S. Herr & G. Weber (Eds.), *Aging, rights, and quality of life: Prospects for older people with developmental disabilities* (pp. 81–92). Baltimore: Paul H. Brookes.

60. Scott, E., & Reuben, D. (1998). Measures of functional status in community-dwelling elders. *General International Medicine, 13,* 817–823.

61. Shatahmasebi, S. M., Davies, R. P., & Wenger, G. (1992). A longitudinal analysis of factors related to survival in old age. *The Gerontologist, 32*(3), 404–413.

62. Siebert, D. C., & Mutran, E. J. (1999). Friendship and social support: The importance of role identity to aging adults. *Social Work, 44*(6), 522–534.

63. Singleton, N., & Turner, A. (1994). SF-36 is suitable for elderly patients. *British Medical Journal, 307,* 126–127.

64. Sinoff, G., & Ore, L. (1997). The Barthel activities of daily living index: Self-reporting versus actual performance in the old. *Journal of the American Geriatrics Society, 45*(7), 832–836.

65. Small, G. W., Birkett, M., Meyers, B. S., Koran, L. M., Bystrisky, A., Nemeroff, C. B., & the Fluoxetine Collaborative Study Group (1996). Impact of physical illness on quality of life and antidepressant response in geriatric major depression. *Journal of the American Geriatrics Society, 44*(10), 1220–1225.

66. Steiner, A., Raube, K., Stuck, A., Aronow, H., Draper, D., Rubenstein, L., & Beck, J. (1996). Measuring psychosocial aspects of well-being in older community residents: Performance of four short scales. *The Gerontologist, 36*(1), 54–62.

67. Stewart, A., King, A., & Haskell, W. (1993). Endurance exercise and health-related quality of life in 50–65-year-old adults. *The Gerontologist, 33*(6), 782–789.

68. Tyler, K. (2000). The effects of an acute stressor on depressive symptoms among older adults. *Research on Aging, 22*(2), 143–165.

69. Tyne, A. (1995). What have we been learning from PASS and PASSING in workshop and real evaluations? In D. Pilling & G. Watson (Eds.), *Evaluating quality in services for disabled and older people* (pp. 25–32). London: Jessica Kingsley.

70. Urciuoli, O., Dello Buono, M., Padoani, W., & De Leo, D. (1998). Assessment of quality of life in the oldest-olds living in nursing homes and at home. *Archives of Gerontology and Geriatric, 6,* 507–514.

71. Ware, J. E., & Sherbourne, C. D. (1992). The MOS 36-Item short-form health survey (SF-36): Conceptual framework and item selection. *Medical Care, 30,* 473–483.

72. Waters, W., Heikkinen, E., & Dontas, A. (1989). *Health, lifestyles, and services for the elderly.* Copenhagen: World Health Organization Library Cataloguing in Publication Data.

73. Williams, P. (1995). The PASS and PASSING: Evaluation instruments. In D. Pilling & G. Watson (Eds.), *Evaluating quality in services for disabled and older people* (pp. 13–24). London: Jessica Kingsley.

74. Wolfson, P. (1995). ACE — An assessment of care environments. In D. Pilling & G. Watson (Eds.), *Evaluating quality in services for disabled and older people* (pp. 78–83). London: Jessica Kingsley.

CHAPTER 11

A Systems Approach to Quality of Life Measurement

Overview

The reader might be wondering, "Why should I read this chapter?" The answer lies in our observations and experiences with quality of life (QOL) measurement. Specifically, it has been our observation that numerous people have assessed and are attempting to assess a person's "quality of life" with little regard to the principles, practices, and procedures that reflect current understanding and best practices. To help overcome this situation, the present chapter is based on information regarding the measurement of quality of life that has been gleaned from the extrinsic QOL literature summarized in chapters 3 through 9, our own QOL research conducted over the past 20 years, and our involvement over the past 5 years in an international consensus project on the measurement of the QOL concept.

Quality of life is important to all people and should be thought of in the same way for all people. Assessing quality of life is required to understand the degree to which people experience a good life. It also implies that we value quality within people's lives and that we want to maintain and enhance the things that already, or could, add quality to people's lives. Measuring quality of life should never support maintaining or encouraging a low quality of life for anyone.

When assessing quality of life, we adopt the point of view that all people share the human experience together and that every human being is entitled to live a good life within his or her society. This central belief is the principal criterion to be used for assessing the ethics of measuring quality of life and reporting its measurement results.

The point that we make strongly in the chapter is that our best efforts and thinking should go into the measurement of one's perceived quality of life, for the stakes are too high if the resulting information is either incorrect or based on erroneous principles, practices, or procedures. To overcome the potential abuses resulting from incorrect or misguided conceptualization and measurement, we have developed this chapter around the following four key components to quality of life measurement: (a) a QOL measurement model that integrates our current understanding of the core QOL domains, the systems perspective, and our best practices in regard to measurement principles and methodological pluralism; (b) a number of domain and systems-level QOL indicators and the criteria that should guide their selection and use; (c) a number of measurement strategies, along with their desired psychometric properties, which can be used across the three systems levels; and (d) a step-wise procedure that we recommend for anyone seriously interested in the measurement of someone's quality of life.

Throughout the chapter we stress a general (i.e., generic) approach to QOL measurement that combines the systems perspective (i.e., micro-, meso-, and macrolevels) with the key core QOL domains and indicators, and three different measurement strategies. The generic approach is depicted in Figure 11.1, which summarizes the four primary parameters of QOL assessment: (a) the core QOL domains being investigated; (b) the selection of specific indicators for each domain considered; (c) the systems level of analysis (micro, meso, and/or macro); and (d) the assessment strategy used (personal appraisal, functional assessment, and/or social indicators). The chapter concludes with a discussion of cautions and guidelines regarding the measurement of quality of life. This discussion provides the transition to part 4 of the *Handbook,* on the application of the QOL concept.

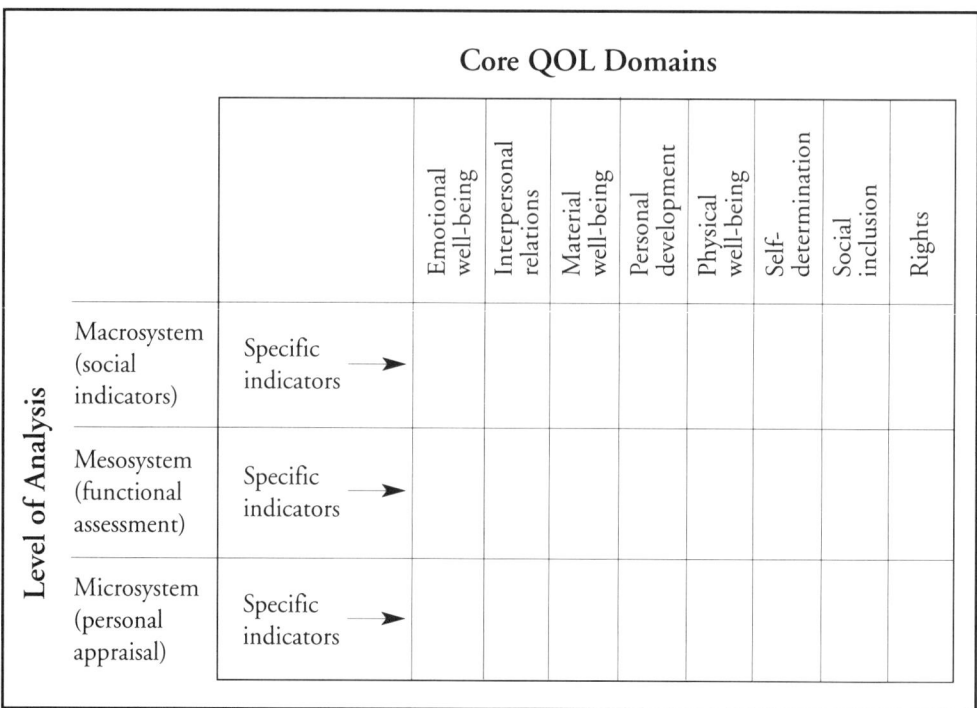

Figure 11.1. Generic approach to quality of life measurement.

Quality of Life Measurement Model

Figure 11.2 illustrates our QOL measurement model. This model integrates the key concepts that have already been discussed: core QOL domains, core indicators, the systems perspective, and measurement strategies (i.e., measures) related to personal appraisal, functional assessment, and social indicators. The eight domains that are listed around the figure represent in aggregate the complete QOL construct as we understand it. Thus these eight domains meet the criteria of being theory-based, literature-based, and multidimensional. Depending on the level of analysis, each domain can be defined operationally on the basis of three to four core domain and system-specific indicators discussed in the following section.

Measurement Overview

Measuring quality of life reflects the unique blend of two meanings of quality: that which is commonly understood by people throughout the world, and that which has become valued by individuals as they live within their unique environments. Typically we measure the former by using social indicators (i.e., macrosystem) that can be reliably observed and that appear to be universally held, such as material attainment, stability of human institutions, social connections, and life opportunities. Measuring quality of life, as it is understood and valued from the individual perspective, is usually carried out by either identifying what specific things have come to be valued by individuals and matching these to the individuals' perceptions of personal satisfaction or happiness (i.e., microsystem), or identifying overt behavior or status indicators measuring the degree to which specific role performance indicators are achieved (i.e., mesosystem). As discussed previously, quantitative and qualitative methods (i.e., methodological pluralism) are essential in measuring quality of life. All are necessary for a full understanding of a life of quality.

Measurement Principles and Guidelines

At the end of chapter 10 (p. 232) we summarized five QOL measurement principles stemming from the International Association for the Scientific Study of Intellectual Disabilities (IASSID) consensus document (Schalock et al., in press). On subsequent pages we list some guidelines for assessing quality of life for each of these five core principles.

Principle 1

QOL measurement assesses the degree to which people have meaningful life experiences that they value. Guidelines include:

- The measurement framework is based on well-established theory of broad life concepts.

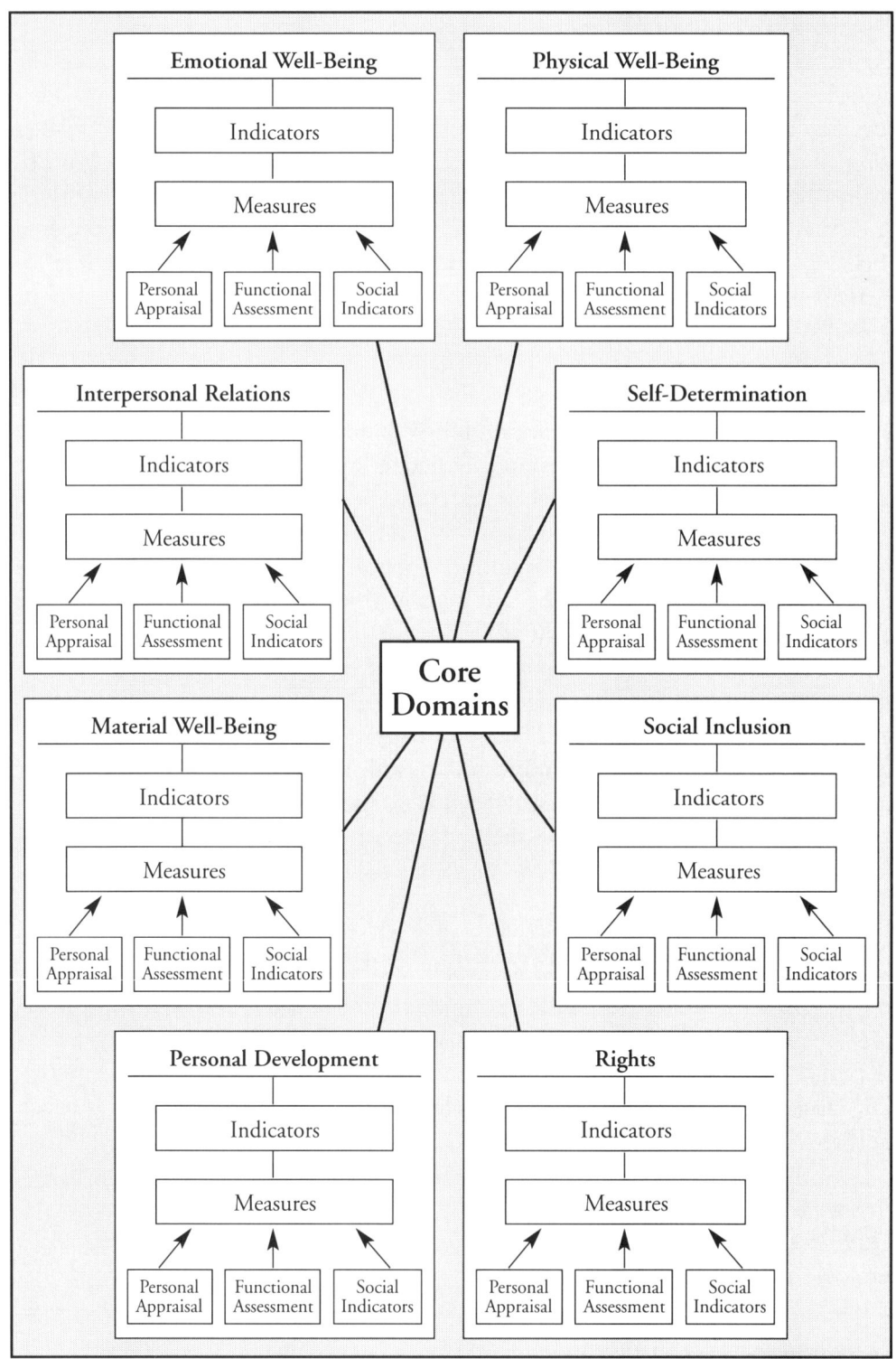

Figure 11.2. Quality of life measurement model.

- It is recognized that the meaning of life experiences that are positively valued varies across time and among cultures.
- The measurement framework provides a clear way to demonstrate the positive values of life.
- Measurement of quality of life represents placement on a continuum between the "best" and the "worst."

Principle 2
QOL measurement enables people to move toward a meaningful life they enjoy and value. Guidelines include:

- Measurement focuses on key aspects of life that can be improved.
- Measurement is carried out for a clear, practical purpose that supports people moving toward better lives.
- Measurement is described within a framework that is potentially positive, neutral, and negative — suggesting that it is possible to move toward the very positive.
- Measurement is interpreted within the context of an overall life-span approach.

Principle 3
QOL measurement assesses the degree to which life's domains contribute to a full and interconnected life. Guidelines include:

- Measurement uses a broad range of life domains, which are widely accepted as key indicators of the fullness and interconnectedness of life.
- Quantitative measurement uses key indicators of the fullness and interconnectedness of life within specific domains.
- Qualitative measurement procedures explore and describe a range of aspects within each domain.

Principle 4
QOL measurement is undertaken within the context of environments that are important to the person: where he or she lives, works, and plays. Guidelines include:

- Measuring quality of life from the perspective of people who are not able to speak for themselves should use methods such as observation and participant observation that are most applicable to such people.
- Measurement of one person's quality of life from another person's perspective might be useful in some instances, such as where people are not able to speak for themselves and others make life decisions on their behalf, but such measurement should be clearly identified as another person's perspective.

- Measurement takes an ecological approach, viewing the person in interaction with his or her living environments.
- Interpretation is carried out within the context of the person's environment.

Principle 5

QOL measurement for individuals is based upon both common human experiences and unique, individual life experiences. Guidelines include:

- Measurement uses both objective and subjective (perceptual) measurement.
- Measurement uses either qualitative or quantitative methods or both.
- Objective measurement uses quantitative instrumentation that reports frequencies and quantities of observable indicators. Subjective (i.e., perceptual) measurement uses degrees of expressed satisfaction with aspects of life or other kinds of subjective evaluations or descriptions about lives.
- Subjective measurement has both cognitive and affective components.
- A suggested *minimum* acceptable quantitative measurement standard of quality of life is the domain aggregate score, within either the objective or subjective dimension, and within two standard deviations of the national average.
- Measurement allows for weighting of domains and key indicators according to individual or group significance or value.
- Measurement allows for weighting of domains and key indicators to reflect individual or group cultural life experiences.
- In most cases, domain scores and descriptions are more useful and expressive than the total scores or descriptions that are aggregated from separate domain data.

Domain and Systems-Level Indicators

We have previously defined indicators as "QOL domain-specific perceptions, behaviors, or conditions that reflect a person's well-being." Criteria for the selection and use of an indicator are that it:

- is functionally related to the respective QOL domain
- measures what it is supposed to measure (i.e., validity)
- is consistent across people or raters (i.e., reliability)
- measures change (i.e., sensitivity)
- reflects changes only in the situation concerned (i.e., specificity)
- is affordable, timely, person-referenced, can be evaluated longitudinally, and is culturally sensitive

A list of potential domain and microsystem indicators has been developed based primarily on the synthesis of the international QOL literature presented in chapters 3 through 8 and summarized succinctly in chapter 9 (see Tables 9.1 and 9.2). These microsystem QOL indicators are listed in Table 11.1. The suggested mesosystem indicators listed in Table 11.2 are not based exclusively on our literature search, but also on the work of Andrews and Whitey (1976), The Beach Center (Turnbull, Turnbull, & Brown, in press), Campbell, Converse, & Rodgers (1976), Flanagan (1982), Gardner and Nudler (1997), Gettings and Bradley (1997), and Schalock (1999). We realize that the indicators listed in Table 11.2 need further development and confirmation through ongoing cross-cultural research, which is also true of the macrosystem indicators discussed later in this chapter and in chapter 14.

Measurement Strategies

We are proposing five different strategies that can be used to measure the core indicators listed in Tables 11.1 and 11.2 and that also encompass the three system levels: (a) rating scales; (b) attitude scales; and (c) questionnaires (microsystem); (d) functional measures (mesosystem); and (e) social or national indicators (macrosystem).

Microsystem or Personal Appraisal Level

Rating Scales

Rating scales are a series of ordered steps at fixed intervals used to rank people's judgments of objects, events, or other people from low to high or from poor to good. Examples include (Sommer & Sommer, 1997):

- Graphic rating scales, wherein the person places a check mark somewhere along the scale to indicate his or her evaluation (e.g., "terrible" to "excellent").
- Step scales, which require the rater to select one of a graded series of levels (e.g., "How would you rate the quality of _____? ['excellent' through 'terrible']").
- Comparative rating scales, wherein the person is asked to compare one or more phenomena (e.g., "Compared to your condition before admission, would you say that your condition is: much better, somewhat better, no different, worse, much worse?").

Although easy to construct and answer, the major problem with rating scales is that they may be neither reliable nor valid. Hence, if one chooses to use a rating scale, it is incumbent upon the administrator to demonstrate at least test-retest reliability and either content or construct validity. A related problem is not to realize that rating scales tend to be at the ordinal level of measurement; they should not be used in statistical analyses as though they were either interval- or ratio-based.

TABLE 11.1
Microsystem Quality of Life Indicators

Domain	Indicators
Emotional well-being	Contentment Self-concept Freedom from stress
Interpersonal relations	Interactions Relationships Supports
Material well-being	Financial status Employment Housing
Personal development	Education Personal competence Performance
Physical well-being	Health status Leisure Activities of daily living (eating, transfer, mobility, toileting, dressing)
Self-determination	Autonomy/personal control Goals and personal values Choices
Social inclusion	Community integration and participation Community roles Social supports
Rights	Human (respect, dignity, equality) Legal (citizenship, access, due process)

TABLE 11.2
Mesosystem Quality of Life Indicators

Domain	Indicators
Emotional well-being	Health & safety Freedom from stress Supports Respect Free of abuse and neglect Support families Consumer satisfaction Reduced family burden
Interpersonal relations	Interactions Family life Affection Group membership Social supports Marital status
Material well-being	Ownership indicators Employment status Shelter Welfare Economic status Financial stability
Personal development	Person-centered planning Advancement opportunities Education/planning opportunities Rehabilitation status Continuing education Augmentative technology — physical/environmental accommodation Engagement/activities time Educational status Academic and functional literacy Age-appropriate materials and tasks

(table continues)

TABLE 11.2. *(continued)*

Domain	Indicators
Physical well-being	Health care Physical rehabilitation Diet Leisure & recreation opportunities Pain management Physical accommodation
Self-determination	Opportunities for choice & decision making Personal control Participating action research (PAR) Personal goals in individual program plan (IPP) Money management Telephone usage
Social inclusion	Normalized & integrated environments Work environment Relations with neighbors Community access School or work status Role options (marital, familial, occupations, interpersonal) Presence and participation Social status Integrated activities Community participation opportunities Living status Transportation Role status Community supports

(table continues)

TABLE 11.2. *(continued)*

Domain	Indicators
Rights	Self-control and responsibility Protection & advocacy policies & procedures Contribution & citizenship Respect for cultural & individual differences Accommodation & adaptations Legal status (e.g., guardianship) Accessibility to services Privacy Voting access Legal assistance Preferences acted on in individual service plan or IPP Due process Advocacy Self-advocacy training & development Dignity & respect Service coordination

Attitude Scales

Attitude scales are designed to produce scores indicating the intensity and direction of (for or against) a person's feelings about an object or event. There are several types of attitude scales, but the two most frequently used are the Likert-type and the semantic differential.

Likert-type scales present a list of statements on an issue to which the respondent indicates degree of agreement, using categories such as strongly agree, agree, undecided, disagree, strongly disagree. A Likert scale contains only statements that are clearly favorable, neutral, or clearly unfavorable, and generally uses either a 3-, 5-, or 7-point scale. The major advantage of the Likert scale is that one can score items as 5, 4, 3, 2, or 1 (if using a 5-point scale) and thus be able to analyze the data.

The semantic differential is a procedure for measuring the meaning of concepts, wherein the person is asked to rate an object or concept along a series of scales with opposed adjectives at either end (e.g., quiet–noisy, dangerous–safe, sad–happy). This procedure is good for measuring the meaning (i.e., "connotative meaning") of things (Keith, Heal, & Schalock, 1996; Osgood, May, & Miron, 1975). In research on the semantic differential, three major categories of connotative meanings have been found: value (e.g., good–bad, ugly–beautiful, friendly–unfriendly, wise–foolish), activity (e.g., fast–slow, active–passive, energetic–inert, fast–slow, excitable–calm), and strength (e.g., weak–strong, large–small, hard–soft, heavy–light).

Attitude scales pose the same advantages and disadvantages as rating scales. In addition, they reflect the fact that people's opinions on a topic are complex and multidimensional. Thus, users of attitude scales, as of rating scales, need to report the basis on which the items were generated, the field test of the items, and their demonstrated reliability and validity.

Questionnaires

Questionnaires are a series of written questions on a topic about which the respondent's opinions are sought. They are a frequently used measurement strategy used to gather information about people's beliefs, attitudes, and values. There are two general aspects to a questionnaire: content (i.e., the subject matter) and format (i.e., its structure and appearance).

The items (i.e., outcome indicators) of a questionnaire can be generated from a number of sources and via a number of techniques such as focus groups or empowerment evaluation (Whitney-Thomas, 1997). It is critical that items are referenced to the domain-specific indicator being evaluated.

The format can include either opened-ended or closed questions. With open-ended questions, the respondent is asked questions such as "What do you like (or dislike) about _____?" Open-ended questions are desirable to use when (a) the evaluator does not know all the possible answers to a question, (b) the range of possible answers is so large that the question would become unwieldy in multiple-choice format, (c) the evaluator wants to avoid suggesting answers to the respondents, and (d) the evaluator wants answers in the respondent's own words. With closed-ended questions (also known as multiple-choice questions), the respondent is asked to choose among alternatives provided by the evaluator. Potential answers can then be scaled using a Likert-type scale such as described above. Closed-ended questions are desirable when: (a) there is a large number of respondents and questions; (b) the answers are to be scored by machine for further analyses; and (c) responses from several groups are to be compared (Sommer & Sommer, 1997).

Questionnaires have many of the same advantages and disadvantages as rating and attitude scales. In addition to the need to demonstrate test-retest reliability and content validity, the potential user should also be sensitive to the following limitations: (a) questionnaires may be of little use with respondents who are limited in either receptive or expressive language; (b) the responses offered may be superficial and biased toward a positive or socially desirable response; (c) questionnaires strike many respondents as impersonal, mechanical, and demeaning, and the response categories as limited, artificial, and constraining; and (d) questionnaires are not suitable for examining deeper levels of motivation or opinions on complex issues (an interview might be better).

With these limitations in mind, one needs to consider a number of factors for evaluating questionnaire items (Sommer & Sommer, 1997): (a) Is the question necessary and how useful will the answers be? (b) Is the item clear and unambiguous? (c) Is the respondent able to answer the question? (d) Will the respondent be willing to answer the questions asked? (e) Is the item as short as possible, while remaining clear and concise? (f) Do the response options provide a comprehensive choice of responses, such as very negative to very positive? (g) Is the answer likely to be affected by the social desirability? If so, can the question be altered to reduce this bias? (h) Are the questions balanced so that the number of favorable items equals the number of unfavorable items?

Mesosystem or Functional Measures Level

Functional measures represent a type of rating scale that typically uses a 3- to 5-point Likert-type rating scale with behavioral-based anchor points that depict the person's functional status or social involvement. Examples include:

- a rating of the person's health status (healthy, some impairments, considerable impairments)
- a rating of the person's activities of daily living (independent, semi-independent, dependent)
- a rating of the person's expressed level of satisfaction with _____ (high, somewhat, not satisfied)
- a rating of the person's social relations (considerable number of friends, some friends, few if any friends)
- a rating of family involvement with the program or service (considerable, some, none)
- a rating of the person's educational status (postsecondary, high school graduate or equivalent, grade school or below)
- a rating of the person's performance (top 30% of productivity rate, 40 to 69%, 39% or below)
- a rating of the person's employment status (full time, part time, unemployed)
- a rating of the person's self-direction or autonomy (makes own decisions, is associated with decisions or makes some, makes few if any decisions)
- a rating of the person's legal status (independent/own guardian, partial guardianship, full guardianship)

Advantages of functional measures include their being based on overt or behavioral indicators, which increase the reliability of the measurement, because these indicators are related to objective conditions experienced by the person. In addition, they can be used for mesolevel measurement that involves opportunities reflective of the various roles that people play within their communities. And finally, they are usable across a wide range of environments, including intervention programs, schools, work, the neighborhood, and organizations. Their major disadvantage is that, because they are based on observation, they are sensitive to the observer's opinions and prejudices.

Macrosystem Indicator Level

There is increasing evidence that macro- or societal-level factors have a significant impact on one's perceived quality of life. In a recent volume on cross-cultural perspectives on quality of life (Keith & Schalock, 2001), the following macrosocietal factors were emphasized as important to one's quality of life: social relationships and a sense of community (Rapley, 2000); cultural values and personal identity (Pengra, 2000); human rights and public consciousness (Smith-Davis, 2000); population, science and technology, education, and public attitudes (Goel, 2000); spirituality, citizenship, politics, and economy (Russo-Watson, 2000); rights and social inclusion (Castanon & Bujan, 2000; Walsh, 2000).

Despite widespread national and cultural differences in the availability and/or expression of these factors, a number of QOL-related trends are also apparent in the cross-cultural QOL literature summarized in this text, including making changes in service delivery philosophy and techniques; basing services and supports on the QOL concept; understanding quality of life in reference to social, political, and economic factors; approaching QOL application and evaluation from multiple levels, including international, local, and personal; and recognizing value and contextual variables in the conceptualization, measurement, and application of the QOL concept. It is too soon to evaluate the impact on one's perceived quality of life of these macrosocietal trends, because of the lack of fully recognized and accepted national and potential cross-cultural QOL indicators. However, it is not too soon to begin developing national indicators for each of the core QOL domains.

The development of national QOL indicators could be based on the concept of *social indicators* that are used frequently in social science research and evaluation to measure the collective quality of community life. To be useful, national QOL indicators would need to meet three criteria: (a) be objective and measured in psychometrically sound ways, (b) be based minimally on a national cross-sectional sample, and (c) be comparable across nations and cultures. The development of these national quality of life indicators should reflect: (a) current social indicators; (b) developments in social well-being (SWB) research; and (c) international covenants.

Current Social Indicators Research

Social indicators generally refer to external, environmentally based conditions such as health, social welfare, friendships, standard of living, education, public safety, housing, neighborhood, and leisure. These indicators can be defined as a normative statistic that facilitates concise, comprehensive, and balanced judgments about the conditions of major aspects of one's society (Andrews & Whithey, 1976). Currently there are a number of social indicators that can be viewed potentially as national QOL indicators in reference to the following core QOL domains: (a) material well-being: socioeconomic status, employment rates, poverty rates, standard of living; (b) personal development: literacy rates, graduation rates; (c) physical well-being: infant mortality rates, life expectancy, mortality rates.

However, to the authors' knowledge, there are currently no widely accepted social or national indicators for the QOL core domains of emotional well-being, interpersonal relations, self-determination, social inclusion, or rights. Future work in developing national QOL indicators for these domains could well be modeled after recent development in SWB research and international covenants.

Social Well-Being Research

A national SWB index could potentially become an index for the core QOL domain of emotional well-being. For example, Diener (2000) has called recently for a national index of SWB, which is based on people's cognitive and affective evaluations of their lives. As discussed by Diener, cultural and social factors influence SWB in several ways, including (a) some countries are better able to meet people's basic needs such as for food, clean water, and health, and these nations evidence higher levels of SWB, (b) culture alters the correlates of SWB by influencing people's goals and values, and (c) variations in cultural influences on mean levels of SWB appear to result from variations in optimism, social support, coping patterns, and the degree of regulation of individual desires. Ideally, the national SWB or QOL indicator would include various components of SWB, such as pleasant affect, unpleasant affect, life satisfaction, fulfillment, and specific states such as stress, affection, trust, and job.

If a national indicator of SWB were available, policies could be judged partly by how they influence happiness. In addition, the Eurobarometer surveys conducted in European nations could serve as a model for such an index (Diener, 2000).

International Covenants

In 1993 the United Nations General Assembly adopted the *Standard Rules on the Equalization of Opportunities for Persons with Disabilities.* These rules, while not legally binding, seek to provide guidelines for efforts by governments to further opportunities for equal participation of people with disabilities in all aspects of society. The following rules might also provide the basis for future work in developing national QOL indicators related to interpersonal relations, self-determination, social inclusion, and rights:

- awareness raising: about people with disabilities and other limiting conditions, including their rights and responsibilities, their needs, their potential, and their contributions;
- support services: including assistive devices that help people increase their independence and exercise their rights;
- accessibility: to the physical environment (e.g., housing, buildings, transportation, streets) and to information and communication;
- family life and personal integrity: full participation in family life, sexual relationships, marriage, and parenthood;
- recreation and sport: equal opportunities to participate in recreation and sports.

In summary, efforts to understand and measure the quality of life of those individuals represented in the text's focus areas at the macrosystem level exist in an increasingly culturally divergent environment that makes cultural exchange and cross-cultural understanding and research essential. As stated by Kuehn and McClainm (1994):

> The challenge is to develop an awareness and knowledge of the diverse cultural beliefs and behaviors . . . and to develop an understanding of the "good life" as perceived by different racial/ethnic/cultural groups. Without such knowledge, any quantitative or qualitative analyses of quality of life will be imprecise and will limit the ability of researchers to develop a universal theory of quality of life for the purpose of research or program planning. (p. 191)

Step-Wise Measurement Procedure

Once one has selected the desired systems level of measurement (i.e., micro, meso, and/or macro), core QOL domain(s) to measure, core indicators to assess the domain(s), and specific measurement strategies, and has determined the intended use of the resulting data, then it is useful to follow up with a six-step process that should ensure reliable, valid, and useful data. This six-step process is based on Figures 11.1 and 11.2.

- Step 1. Reaffirm the purpose of your investigation and the intended use of the resulting QOL measures.
- Step 2. Confirm the core QOL domains that will answer the question and provide the information that is necessary to fulfill the purpose of one's investigation.
- Step 3. Confirm the core QOL indicators.

- Step 4. Reaffirm the specific measurement strategy (i.e., measures) that will best provide the data needed, depending on the systems level being analyzed and the questions being asked. Keep in mind the issues of time, expertise, group composition, and need for demonstrated reliability and validity.
- Step 5. Demonstrate acceptable reliability and validity of your measures.
- Step 6. Interpret the results cautiously (see following section).

Cautions Regarding Quality of Life Measurement

QOL measurement is relatively new, but increasingly voluminous, as we showed in chapter 10. Despite the best of attentions and the implementation of the procedures presented in this chapter, there are cautions about QOL measurement that we want to address. We have collapsed these cautions into two sets of guidelines (one for measurement and one for interpretation) and a number of relevant cross-cultural issues.

Measurement Guidelines

Measurements should:

- be developed for the population under study
- be related to a QOL model
- include personal appraisal, functional assessment, and social indicators depending on the questions being asked and the anticipated use of the data
- have demonstrated reliability and validity
- have a clearly articulated use at the micro-, meso-, or macrosystem level
- be a guide for personal, service, or policy enhancement rather than a classification of individuals or of services or systems

Interpretation Guidelines

- QOL scores should be considered as relative and not absolute.
- Watch gain scores, for one's subjective evaluation of life conditions may reflect a trait more than a changing external condition.
- The potential ceiling effect may preclude longitudinal comparisons.
- Do not use grouped data, recognizing that the standard of comparison is the person.
- Realize that one's perceived quality of life changes over time, and therefore one should expect only incremental change.

- Understand that the relative importance of the core QOL domains will vary across the life span of the person and among cultures.
- Commit oneself to longitudinal measurement and evaluation.

Cross-Cultural Issues

As we attempt to bring together the various issues involved in the cross-cultural understanding of the concept of quality of life and its measurement, several central themes emerge that are likely to guide our future work (Keith, 1996; Magana, 2000).

- Culture is not a clearly defined term. It is not defined by biology or by nationality; rather, it is a construct involving shared values, beliefs, behaviors, and attitudes.
- Although sensitivity to culture is essential, it is necessary to recognize that in the measurement of quality of life, it is the individual (and his or her perceptions) who must remain the focus.
- Comparative cross-cultural studies of quality of life, if their emphasis is only to evaluate and compare, are likely to do little to advance our understanding of individual needs and wishes. However, comparative studies that illuminate key characteristics of cultures and the quality of life of people within them are likely to contribute to cross-cultural understanding and communication in important ways.
- We must recognize and overcome our proclivity to project our own norms on people of other cultures.
- In investigating the concept of quality of life, the emphasis should be on our common humanity.

Conclusion

In summary, we have attempted in this chapter to outline the parameters and guidelines for a generic approach to QOL measurement. The process begins with a clear focus on the intended purpose of measurement and the addressed systems level. Once those questions are answered, the process continues by selecting core QOL domains and indicators. Once the indicators are selected, a number of measurement strategies can be used to assess these perceptual or behaviorally based QOL indicators. In addition to the use of a variety of methods, the current approach to QOL measurement can be characterized as using a multidimensional perspective, multivariate research designs, the systems perspective, and participatory action research. We also feel strongly about the need to integrate the criteria, principles, and guidelines presented throughout the chapter.

In conclusion, there is a widespread fear of research concerning the measurement of one's quality of life and the use of the resultant data. There are a number of reasons for this concern or fear, including lack of knowledge, questions purpose, lack of involvement, the secretive or technical nature of some research, the ethical issues involved, past discrimination, and sometimes no agenda ("just scientists"). This concern is expressed in the context of the fundamental principle of what people want: basic human rights and basic opportunities. Often the ordinary things of everyday life are lost in research. Thus there is a real need to link quality of life research, QOL measurement, and a change agenda. This linkage and proposed applications are the focus of part 4.

PART 4

The Application of the Concept of Quality of Life

We approach the application of the concept of quality of life (QOL) from three perspectives: (a) the individual (i.e., microsystem); (b) education, health care, and social service programs (i.e., mesosystem); and (c) the larger society (i.e., macrosystem). Common to each perspective is the need to provide *evidence* demonstrating that the techniques and processes employed have actually changed or impacted the person's well-being and changed behaviors at the societal level. As discussed in the previous chapter, evidence measures can include personal appraisal (e.g., satisfaction), functional assessment (e.g., adaptive behavior level and role status), and social indicators (e.g., economic status, health and safety indicators, life expectancy, educational levels).

Three aspects of the QOL measurement model outlined in Figure 11.1 are key to its successful implementation *and* the viable application of the QOL concept to service recipients and their families. First, the techniques and processes that focus on the eight core QOL domains and the three societal levels provide information about what to do to enhance an individual's well-being. Thus, for example, at the microsystem level for emotional well-being, service providers can ask, "What can we do to ensure that the person's needs are met, that opportunities are provided to enhance the person's emotional well-being, and that obvious barriers to one's emotional well-being are addressed and reduced?"

Second, core QOL concepts are then used *as judgment criteria* to ensure that the techniques and processes: (a) reflect the QOL concepts of holism, the person's life span, choices, personal control, and empowerment; (b) are of value to the person; and (c) reflect individual variability. Thus the model should be used to guide service provision and decision making as we collaborate for change at the societal level. In that regard, the model also provides a *common language* around which public laws can be envisioned, policies and procedures developed, and evidence-gathering activities organized.

Third, at the aggregate population level, objective indicators for a defined group of interests may be compared to total population norms and ranges to establish the social equity of a group's circumstances. The distribution of a lifestyle characteristic, such as an index of health, income, or activity level, will be influenced by many factors, among them personal values and choices. The distribution, therefore, contains variance attributable to differences among individuals and the self-determination they exercise. Comparing the distribution of a salient aspect of quality of life among a representative sample of people at the margin of society against the total population distribution will reveal differences not attributable to people's personal choices. Thus, for example, the low representation of people with intellectual disabilities in the work force and their relative state of poverty may occasion social policy initiatives to develop techniques and processes that broaden the opportunity for paid work at levels of remuneration at or above the minimum wage. Similarly, the lower level of age-peer friendships in the social networks of students in special education compared to the norm may result in development of techniques and processes that facilitate enduring friendships.

This final section of the *Handbook* contains four chapters. Chapter 12 focuses on individual-referenced application of the QOL concept. The chapter begins with a discussion of nine core person-referenced themes, such as domains of well-being, personal context, life perspective, holism, and empowerment. These core QOL themes reflect the emerging framework for applying the QOL concept at the individual level, because they give us a sense of reference and guidance from the individual's perspective. They also provide the basis for the conceptualization and application principles discussed throughout the *Handbook*. After listing these nine themes, the remainder of the chapter discusses self-determination strategies and individual-referenced techniques that enhance a person's sense of self and well-being.

The focus of chapter 13 is on the organizational level and on how education, health care, and social service programs can apply the QOL construct. Although applying organization-referenced supports and program-referenced quality enhancement techniques are significant components of the chapter, the major emphasis is on a potentially more important topic: how organizations can use desired QOL-referenced outcomes to guide, monitor, and evaluate organizational change. In that regard, the chapter focuses heavily on the use of an outcomes-focused planning model whose three components include standards (performance or value), focus (organization or individual), and outcomes that are measurable and can be captured in a number of person- or organization-referenced measures.

The larger society is the focus of chapter 14, which discusses the societal-level application of the QOL concept. This chapter is divided into two sections. In the first, four societal-level action steps are proposed: (a) nations adopting the QOL concept; (b) communities implementing quality enhancement techniques; (c) consumers, policymakers, and professionals collaborating for change at the societal level; and (d) researchers and program evaluators providing information and evidence that the application of QOL-oriented policies and practices make a difference in people's well-being and perceived quality of life. As with chapter 13, the chapter focuses heavily on evaluation. In that regard, a policy evaluation model and procedural steps are introduced that incorporate the key evaluation concepts of the ecological perspective, systems-level data sets, and outcome analysis that includes personal appraisal, functional assessment, and social indicators. The chapter concludes with a discussion of a number of policy evaluation guidelines.

The text's concluding chapter summarizes the key points made throughout the *Handbook* and asks the reader to think about the future of the QOL concept and a number of contextual factors that will impact all of us. The chapter also outlines proposals that we believe are realistic and critical to the future role that the QOL concept will play in the lives of students, health care recipients, clientele within other human or social services, and families.

CHAPTER 12

Individual-Level Application of the Concept of Quality of Life

Overview

Looking at the individual level, quality of life (QOL) is a rich and varied concept that draws on the resources of both science and art and is manifested not only in research and measurement data but also in a variety of personal expressions consistent with individual being, belonging, and becoming. It follows, therefore, that most conceptions of quality of life share common features with general feelings of well-being, feelings of positive social involvement, and opportunities to achieve personal potential (Keith, 2001).

Quality of life might best be viewed as a sensitizing (rather than a definitive) concept relevant to the determination of public policy, evaluation of services, and development of innovative local, national, and international programs that will be discussed in chapters 13 and 14. However, despite the wide-ranging implications of this conceptual view of quality of life, it remains a notion rooted in individual perceptions and values and capable of contributing to the identification of necessary supports and services. In fact, individual perceptions and values — the subjective views of the person — are recognized as a key facet of quality of life by virtually all contemporary researchers. This is not to say that objective measures (e.g., economic status) are not important, but the relationship between such measures and a personal sense of well-being is modest.

The QOL concept has potential to allow a new perspective on people and to be a positive influence on those who work in the fields of education, health, and social services. It offers a new way of looking at issues addressed by the text's focus areas and is a useful paradigm that can contribute to the identification, development, and evaluation of supports, services, and policies for individuals. To that end, this chapter discusses: (a) core individual-referenced themes that are essential to understand in applying the QOL concept at the individual level, (b) a review of the critical QOL conceptualization and application principles introduced earlier in the text, (c) self-determination strategies that allow individuals to have more control over their lives, and (d) individual-referenced techniques that can be used to enhance an individual's perceived quality of life.

An ecological model is used in this and the following two chapters to guide efforts to apply the QOL concept and implement quality enhancement techniques. The model that we propose is presented in Figure 12.1. As shown in the model, the eight core QOL domains are matriced by three QOL enhancement foci: microsystem (i.e., personal growth and development opportunities) mesosystem (i.e., program or environmental-referenced quality enhancement techniques), and microsystem (i.e., social policies).

Core Person-Referenced Themes

A number of core themes have emerged in the international literature that provide an emerging framework for the individual-level application of the QOL concept (Schalock et al., in press). Chief among these are: domains of well-being; inter- and intrapersonal variability; personal context; a life-span perspective; holism; values, choices, and personal control; perception; self-image; and empowerment.

		Core QOL Domains							
		Emotional well-being	Interpersonal relations	Material well-being	Personal development	Physical well-being	Self-determination	Social inclusion	Rights
Enhancement Focus	Microsystem Personal growth and development opportunities								
	Mesosystem Program or environmantal-referenced quality enhancement techniques								
	Macrosystem Social policies								

Figure 12.1. An ecological model of quality enhancement.

Domains of Well-Being

Domains of well-being have been identified in the international QOL literature. Although the number varies slightly, the eight core domains (sometimes referred to as dimensions) key to this *Handbook* are the desired states of emotional well-being, interpersonal relations, material well-being, personal development, physical well-being, self-determination, social inclusion, and rights. Many QOL investigators suggest that the actual number of domains is perhaps less important than the recognition that any proposed structure must acknowledge (a) the need for a multi-element framework, (b) that people know what is important to them, and (c) that the essential characteristic of any set of domains is that those domains represent in aggregate the complete QOL construct.

Inter- and Intrapersonal Variability

Variability means that the domains of well-being will apply to, or be experienced variously by, different individuals and cultural groups. Thus quality of life differs for the individual over time and among individuals. It follows that "a good quality of life" may mean different things to different people.

Personal Context

People are best understood within the context of the environments that are important to them: where they live, work, and play. Environments should be viewed as changeable to accommodate the person's interests, needs, and values. An essential idea is that people, places, and surroundings can promote and enhance a good life. In turn, an individual's interests and values can emerge in part from the environment in which that person lives.

Life-Span Perspective

Quality of life involves a life-span approach that requires individuals and services to conceptualize policy and practice in terms of the cumulative effects as the individual ages. It thus involves an anticipatory process and recognizes, for example, that the nature of primary school education influences later opportunities and development in secondary school, employment, and community life.

Holism

It is also generally accepted that a QOL model should be holistic to the extent that, at any one time, different aspects or domains of the individual's life may dramatically influence other aspects or domains. This theme makes it necessary to take into account likely effects and to employ participation, activity, and motivational aspects in one area to enhance development and satisfaction in other areas. This not only has measurement and intervention implications but also requires a reexamination of service and policy development.

Values, Choices, and Personal Control

Quality of life relates to choices by individuals and, wherever possible, personal control over their interests in activities, interventions, and environments. Quality of life is thus emancipatory and recognizes different value systems. The psychological acceptance of consumer choices has major implications for self-image, motivation, self-expression, and control as well as health in its broadest sense.

Perception

It is not a question of whether, in reality, one's perceptions of these key quality of life themes are correct or incorrect, but that they are statements about what the individual perceives at any one moment in time. Such views may be stable (and often appear to be), although variation can be expected when intervention and change occur. Indeed, the greatest perceptual changes might be expected when intervention and rehabilitation are effective.

It is also necessary to take into account the suggestions, choices, and perceptions of parents, spouses, and service and support providers. However, it should be recognized that these may differ markedly and centrally from the perceptions of the individual. This multiperception aspect of quality of life provides a new challenge to the field of measurement, because many people with special needs have no or limited language. Thus multiple perceptions are central to an understanding of one's quality of life, and in many instances it may be necessary to identify personal choices using an individual's nonverbal responses, particularly when language is limited.

Self-Image

The aims of any individual-level application of the QOL concept must be to enhance the individual's self-concept and provide empowering environments. These in turn will be influenced by the values of the individual.

Empowerment

The preceding eight core themes reflect the need for individuals to have choices and personal control over their interests in activities, interventions, and environments — a form of personal empowerment that allows individual control in life and service decisions and examination of sources of control in the environment. Quality of life is thus emancipatory, accepting individual choices and recognizing personal values. This calls for a recognition that such services will be required at different times, for different durations, and at different intensities. Such services will have aspects that show major control by the service user; there will need to be a detailed examination of who, when, and how intervention takes place and who controls that environment.

Core Quality of Life Principles

The nine core QOL themes just described reflect the emerging framework for applying the QOL concept at the individual level, as they give us guidance from the individual's perspective and allow us to focus on the person and his or her environment. To that end, repeated below are the core QOL conceptualization and application principles discussed earlier in the text.

Core Conceptualization Principles
Quality of life:

1. is composed of those same factors and relationships for people with special needs that are important to everyone
2. is experienced when a person's needs are met and when one has the opportunity to pursue life enrichment in major life settings
3. has both subjective and objective components, but it is primarily the perception of the individual that reflects the quality of life he or she experiences
4. is based on individual needs, choices, and control
5. is a multidimensional construct influenced by personal and environmental factors such as intimate relationships, family life, friendships, work, neighborhood, city or town of residence, housing, education, health, standard of living, and the state of one's nation

Core Application Principles
Quality of life application should:

1. enhance a person's well-being
2. be applied in light of the individual's cultural and ethnic heritage
3. collaborate for change at the personal, program, community, and national levels
4. enhance the degree of personal control and individual opportunity exerted by the individual in relation to their activities, interventions, and environments
5. occupy a prominent role in gathering evidence, especially in identifying the significant predictors of a life of quality and the impact of targeting resources to maximize positive effects

In summary, the QOL themes and principles just reviewed have significant implications for the way we think about people and our societal and personal approaches to them. In the following two sections, we outline self-determination strategies and individual-referenced quality enhancement techniques that help to implement these themes and principles.

Self-Determination Strategies

Over the past decade self-determination has emerged as an important construct in the text's focus areas. Recently Wehmeyer and Schalock (2001) defined self-determination as "acting as the primary causal agent in one's life and making choices and decisions regarding one's quality of life free from undue external influence or interference" (p. 2). Within this framework, self-determined behavior refers to actions that are identified by four *essential characteristics:* (a) the person acts *autonomously;* (b) the action(s) is *self-regulated;* (c) the person initiates and responds to the event(s) in a *psychologically empowered* manner; and (d) the person acts in a *self-realizing* manner. These essential characteristics emerge as children, youth, and adults develop and acquire a set of *component elements* of self-determination that are summarized in Table 12.1 and discussed later in this section of the chapter.

Essential Characteristics of Self-Determined Behavior

An individual's actions must reflect, to some degree, each of the four essential characteristics just listed. Age, opportunity, capacity, and circumstances may impact the degree to which any of the essential characteristics are present and, as such, the relative self-determination expressed by an individual will likely vary, sometimes over time and other times across environments. Nonetheless, these four essential elements must be present, because each characteristic is a necessary but not a sufficient element of self-determined behavior.

Behavioral Autonomy

Sigafoos, Feinstein, Damond, and Reiss (1988) stated that "human development involves a progression from dependence on others for care and guidance to self-

TABLE 12.1
Component Elements of Self-Determined Behavior

Choice-making skills
Problem-solving skills
Decision-making skills
Goal-setting and attainment skills
Self-management skills
Self-advocacy and leadership skills
Perception of control and efficacy
Self-awareness and self-knowledge

care and self-direction" (p. 432). The outcome of this progression is autonomous functioning or, when describing the actions of individuals achieving this outcome, behavioral autonomy. Autonomous behavior should not be confused with self-centered or selfish behavior. While humans often act according to personal interests, there are occasions when they must act in ways that do not reflect self-interest. A person's preference may be to act in a manner that does not reflect directly his or her specific interests, if that is prudent or useful. In addition, most people cannot be viewed as strictly acting alone, with no external influences; interdependence is a desirable outcome, because all people are influenced on a daily basis by others, from family members to strangers. There are contextual, cultural, and social variables that will define for each person an "acceptable" level of interference and influence.

Self-Regulated Behavior
Self-regulated behaviors include self-management strategies (e.g., self-monitoring, self-instruction, self-evaluation, and self-reinforcement), goal setting and attainment, problem solving, and observational learning. Each of these permit people to become the causal agent in their lives (Agran, 1997).

Acting in a Psychologically Empowered Manner
Psychological empowerment is a term referring to the multiple dimensions of perceived control, including its cognitive (personal efficacy), personality (locus of control), and motivational domains (Zimmerman, 1990). Essentially, people acting in a psychologically empowered manner do so on the basis of a belief that they: (a) have control over circumstances that are important to them (internal locus of control), (b) possess the skills necessary to achieve desired outcomes (self-efficacy), and (c) expect that the identified outcomes will result if they choose to apply those skills.

Self-Realization
Self-determined people are self-realizing in that they use a comprehensive, and reasonably accurate, knowledge of themselves and their strengths and limitations and act to capitalize on this knowledge. This self-knowledge and understanding forms through experience with and interpretation of one's environment and is influenced by evaluations of significant others, reinforcement, and attributions of one's own behavior.

Component Elements of Self-Determined Behavior
The essential characteristics that define self-determined behavior emerge through the development and acquisition of multiple, interrelated component elements, including those listed in Table 12.1. Although not intended as an exhaustive list,

these elements are particularly important to the emergence of self-determined behavior. Each of these component elements has a unique developmental course or is acquired through specific learning experiences (Doll, Sands, Wehmeyer, & Palmer, 1996). Their development and acquisition is lifelong and begins early in life.

Given that self-determination is an important component to a life of quality, what can individuals (and indirectly programs and societies) do to achieve this outcome? The theoretical framework of self-determination described earlier suggests that self-determination emerges as individuals develop or acquire a set of component elements of self-determined behavior. Efforts to enhance these elements take three primary tracks: instruction to promote capacity (skills and knowledge), opportunities to experience control and choice, and the design of supports and accommodations. The primary role of the individual and those working with him or her in this process is in promoting capacity, although this does not mitigate the importance of providing opportunity and identifying supports and accommodations. Critical aspects of developing those component elements of self-determined behavior are discussed in some detail on subsequent pages.

Choice Making

Perhaps more emphasis has been placed on this component element as critical to a positive quality of life than on other elements. Making a choice is, quite simply, the communication of a preference, and instruction in choice making focuses on either the identification of a preference or the communication of that preference. Except in unique circumstances, there is usually no need to "teach" choice making per se, although there may be a need to enable or teach people who have problems communicating new, alternative, or even more appropriate ways to indicate their preferences. By and large, personal and program efforts should be aimed at using choice-making opportunities to provide experiences of control and to teach people that not all options are available to them and that choice options are constrained for all people. Specific suggestions for accomplishing such include (Shevin & Klein, 1984): (a) incorporating individual choice as an early step in the instructional process, (b) increasing the number of choices the person makes related to a given activity, (c) increasing the number of domains in which decisions are made and raising the significance in terms of risk and long-term consequences of the choices, and (d) communicating clearly with the person areas of possible choice and the limits within which choices can be made. Similarly, F. Brown, Appel, Corsi, and Wenig (1993) suggest seven ways to infuse choices into instructional activities: (a) choosing within an activity, (b) choosing between two or more activities, (c) deciding when to do an activity, (d) selecting the person with whom to participate in an activity, (e) deciding where to do an activity, (f) refusing to participate in a planned activity, and (g) choosing to end an activity at a self-selected time.

Problem Solving

Problem-solving skills have typically focused on problem resolution in two domains: impersonal problem solving and interpersonal or social problem solving. Social problem solving emphasizes cognitive and behavioral strategies that enable individuals to interact with one another and thus cope in an increasingly social world. Much of the focus for intervention in education and rehabilitation programs has been strictly on social skills training. Although such instruction is important, in the absence of similar emphasis on social problem-solving skills, social skills training alone is not enough to address deficits in social interactions exhibited by service recipients (Wehmeyer & Kelchner, 1994).

Instruction in problem solving typically includes three focal points: (a) problem identification, (b) problem explication and analysis, and (c) problem resolution. Instruction should occur within environments that emphasize the person's capability to solve problems, promote open inquiry and exploration, and encourage generalization. Those instructing should serve as role models by verbalizing the problem-solving steps used on a day-to-day basis and should make sure that individuals are provided adequate support and accommodations.

Decision Making

Making a decision is a process of selecting or coming to a conclusion about which set of potential solutions is the best, given one's circumstances, values, priorities, and needs. Beyth-Marom, Fischhoff, Jacobs Quadrel, and Furby (1991, p. 21) suggest that most models of decision making incorporate the following steps: (a) listing relevant action alternatives, (b) identifying possible consequences of those actions, (c) assessing the probability of each consequence occurring (if the action were undertaken), (d) establishing the relative importance (value or utility) of each consequence, and (e) integrating these values and probabilities to identify the most attractive course of action.

Be it choice making or engaging in independent living behaviors, the real barrier for many people is that the need of the caregiver for absolute assurance of safety tends to lead to the prohibition of activities that have very low level risks. Certainly behaviors that lead to a certain injury or those that have a moderate probability for harm should be cause for concern. However, most behaviors do not involve that level of risk, and individuals can be taught to assess the level of risk and weigh the consequences of action using an effective decision-making process. In addition, people can be taught safety and health-promotion skills needed to achieve independent living. These skills can include basic first aid and job safety skills, nutrition, diet and medication facts, and the prevention of abuse and disease.

Goal Setting and Attainment

To become the causal agent in his or her life, a person needs to learn the skills necessary to plan, set, and achieve goals. Goal-setting theory is built on the underlying assumption that goals are regulators of human action. This is true for personal motivation and achievement. Efforts to promote goal-setting and attainment skills should focus on the identification and enunciation of specific goals, the development of objectives and tasks to achieve these goals, and the actions necessary to achieve a desired outcome. This planning and decision-making process is an enterprise that revolves around goal setting, implementation, and evaluation. The involvement of the individual in this process is a good way to promote goal setting and attainment skills. Family members, instructors, and peers can model effective skills like identifying short- and long-term goals, describing objectives, implementing plans based on these goals and objectives and reevaluating and refining the plans.

Self Management

Self-determined behavior is primarily self-regulated. Self-regulated behavior includes managing one's own life, in terms of monitoring, direction, evaluation, instruction, and reinforcement. Self-monitoring involves assessing, observing, and recording one's own behavior. Self-monitoring strategies are most frequently used to improve work-related activities, such as attention to task, task completion, and task accuracy, and are thus important for employment-related programs. Self-evaluation activities include the use of systematic strategies to enable people to track and evaluate their progress on educational activities, including goals and objectives. This frequently involves the use of self-recording procedures in which the person graphs, charts, or otherwise documents progress toward a goal or objective. Such progress is typically determined through some form of self-observation during which the person discriminates and records that a given target behavior has occurred and then compares it with a previously determined standard or expected outcome (Agran, 1997). Individuals can be taught to score computer-based worksheets, identify the occurrence of a target behavior, track time intervals for the occurrence or nonoccurrence of a target behavior, and record this information in a graphic or chart format.

A third aspect of self-regulation is the use of self-reinforcement strategies. Agran (1997) defined self-reinforcement as the self-administration of consequences, either positive or negative, contingent on the occurrence of a target behavior, and suggested that self-reinforcement should have two functions: self-identification of reinforcers and delivery of this reinforcer. Personal involvement in the former — identification of reinforcers — can enhance the efficacy of the latter. Self-reinforcement can be more effective than having another person deliver the reinforcer, not the least because self-reinforcement can almost always be immediate.

Self-Advocacy and Leadership

To advocate means to speak up or defend a cause or person. By definition, instruction to promote self-advocacy will focus on two common themes: how to advocate and what to advocate. The strategies for the "how to advocate" side of self-advocacy include instructional emphasis on being assertive but not aggressive; how to communicate effectively in one-on-one, small-group, and large-group situations; how to negotiate, compromise, and use persuasion; how to be an effective listener; and how to navigate through systems and bureaucracies. It is evident that each of these is tied closely to the acquisition and emergence of other self-determination skills. For example, a reliable understanding of one's strengths and weaknesses is an important component if one is to use strategies like negotiation and compromise to achieve an outcome. Likewise, individuals need to be able to link such advocacy to specific goals and incorporate it into the problem-solving or decision-making process.

Perception of Control and Efficacy

The next essential element of self-determined behavior focuses not on skill development but on the attitudes that enable individuals to act in a psychologically empowered or self-realizing manner. If a person is to act in or on a given situation, it is important for her to believe that she has control over outcomes that are important to her life. People who hold such beliefs have been described as having an internal locus of control. Locus of control is the degree to which a person perceives contingency relationships between his or her actions and outcomes (Rotter, 1966). Internal locus of control has been linked to adaptive outcomes, including positive educational and achievement outcomes and increased time and attention to tasks (Lefcourt, 1976).

Promoting internal perceptions of control, as well as adaptive efficacy and outcome expectations, a positive self-awareness, and a realistic self-knowledge, is more complex than just providing adequate instructional experiences. An internal locus of control emerges as individuals make choices about things that they do daily, such as selecting clothing, and as these choices are honored and supported. Additionally, a program that emphasizes problem solving, choice- and decision-making skills and goal-setting and attainment skills using individual-directed learning activities will provide ample opportunities for people to learn that they have control over reinforcers and outcomes that are important to them.

Self-efficacy and self-efficacy expectations are constructs introduced by Bandura (1997). Self-efficacy refers to the "conviction that one can successfully execute a behavior required to produce a given outcome" (p. 193). Self-efficacy expectations refer to the individual's belief that if a specific behavior is performed, it will lead to an anticipated outcome. It should be evident that the two are individually necessary, but not sufficient, for goal-directed and self-determined actions.

Simply put, a person has to believe that (a) he or she can perform a behavior needed to achieve a desired outcome, and (b) if that behavior is performed it will result in the desired outcome. If a person does not believe that he or she can perform a given behavior (independent of the validity of that belief), he or she will not perform that action. However, a person may believe that he or she is capable of performing a given behavior, but due to past experience may not believe that a desired outcome will occur even if that behavior is exhibited, and therefore will not perform the action. For example, a person may not believe that he has the social skills necessary to initiate a conversation with peers and will refrain from initiating such actions. On the other hand, that same person may believe he has the skills, but, having been ignored in the past, may believe that he will be ignored again and, likewise, refrain from initiating the action.

Self-Awareness and Self-Knowledge
For one to act in a self-realizing manner, one must possess a basic understanding of one's strengths, weaknesses, abilities, and limitations as well as knowledge about how to use these unique attributions to beneficially influence one's quality of life. People don't learn what they can or cannot do from lectures, role playing, social skills simulations, or any other more traditional instructional activities. They learn through their own interpretation of events and experiences. This process is not one of pure introspection, however, and does not focus exclusively or even primarily on an understanding of limitations. In many cases, service recipients are quite able and more willing to identify what they do poorly than those things they do well. The specter of having a special need, as pictured in disease or deficit models, hovers over any circumstance, and individuals often dwell more on what they are unable to accomplish than what they can achieve.

In summary, from an individual perspective, self-determination involves acting as the primary causal agent in one's life and making choices and decisions regarding one's quality of life free from undue external influences or interference. Its four essential characteristics are autonomy, self-regulation, psychological empowerment, and self-realization (Wehmeyer & Sands, 1998). The component elements of self-determined behavior just discussed (and summarized in Table 12.1) are based on the assumption that people want to control their own lives and that self-determination is what life is all about. We pursue this idea further in the next section that outlines a number of individual-referenced quality enhancement techniques.

Individual-Referenced Quality Enhancement Techniques

Individuals with special needs and their families are already applying the QOL concept to their lives. Specifically, throughout the world we are seeing: (a) strong self-advocacy movements directed at increasing opportunities to participate in the mainstream of life, associated with increased inclusion, equity, and choices; (b) the provision of increased individual supports within regular environments; and (c) the participation of people with special needs and their families in major activities such as decision making, person-centered planning, and participatory action research. To this list we would add the four specific quality enhancement techniques discussed in this section. The section concludes with our integration of the component elements of self-determination and the QOL domain-specific enhancement techniques.

There is little doubt but that an enhanced quality of life is the result of a good match between a person's wants or needs and their fulfillment. Thus individuals with special needs and those with whom they associate need to develop environments that are user friendly and meet the following criteria (Ferguson, 1997): opportunity for community involvement; easy access to outdoor environment; modifications to stairs, water taps, doorknobs; safety (e.g., handrails, safety glass, nonslip walking surfaces); convenience (e.g., orientation aids such as color coding or universal pictographs); accessibility to home and community; sensory stimulation (e.g., windows, less formal furniture); prosthetics (e.g., personal computers, specialized assistive devices, and high technological environments); and opportunity for choice and control (e.g., lights, temperature, personal space, and privacy).

Domain-Specific Quality Enhancement Techniques

In addition to the person-environment matching techniques just mentioned, each core QOL domain has associated factors that the individual and those working with him or her can pursue to enhance the individual's perceived quality of life. Important examples include:

- emotional well-being: increased safety, stable and predictable environments, positive feedback
- interpersonal relations: friendships, intimacy, families
- material well-being: ownership, possessions, employment
- personal development: functional rehabilitation, application-oriented education, augmentative technology
- physical well-being: health care, mobility, wellness, nutrition
- self-determination: choices, personal control, decisions, personal goals
- social inclusion: community role, community integration, volunteerism
- rights: privacy, voting access, due process, civic responsibilities

Use of Positive Behavior Supports

Although most closely related to emotional well-being and those person-environment relationship techniques listed above, positive behavior supports are being increasingly used by instructional and rehabilitation personnel to enhance both positive behavioral change and positive outcomes. As discussed by Horner (2000), positive behavior support involves focusing on the assessment and reengineering of environments so that people "with problem behaviors experience reductions in their problem behaviors and increased social, personal, and professional quality in their lives" (p. 181). The technology of positive behavior support applies basic laws of behavior analysis to produce broad changes across environments and options available to individuals who exhibit problem behaviors. Underlying this technology are three key implementation concepts (Horner, pp. 183-184): (a) behavior support should reduce problem behaviors and affect how a person lives; (b) functional assessment is the foundation for understanding patterns of problem behavior; and (c) behavior support should be comprehensive in structure and scope.

Individuals Assessing Their Quality of Life

One of the changes over the past 20 years is the development of a strong self-advocacy movement in which individuals are advocating for increased opportunities to participate in the mainstream of life.

Participatory action research is rapidly becoming the method of choice among QOL researchers. For example, consumers are working jointly with researchers to determine the importance of the core QOL dimensions. Preliminary work suggests that for children and youth the most important dimensions may be personal development, self-determination, interpersonal relationships, and social inclusion (Schalock, 1996a; Stark & Goldsbury, 1990); for adults, the most important dimensions may be emotional well-being, material well-being, and interpersonal relations (Elorriaga et al., 2000; Verdugo, 2000); and for older people, physical well-being, interpersonal relationships, and emotional well-being (Schalock, DeVries, & Lebsack, 1999).

Consumers are also involved in assessing their own quality of life. For example, Schalock, Bonham, and Marchand (2000) have recently shown that consumers with disabilities are excellent surveyors and can assess other consumers' quality of life with highly acceptable reliability and validity. Two significant findings came of these studies.

First, among the 50 questions asked in the survey, more that three-fifths of the consumers gave the most positive response to eight questions: have transportation, feel safe in neighborhood, staff help with community integration, get needed services, help with goals, feel part of family, concern with health, and people help you learn. Seven questions received the most negative response by the majority of the respondents: what others expect, have a key to home, dating opportunities, number of groups belonged to, who decides how person spends his or her money, housemate choice, and have a job.

Second, a path analysis of the results indicated that two areas of subjective well-being contribute directly to one's satisfaction with life: the most important of the two is dignity (the more dignity with which people feel others treat them, the more satisfied they are with life); the second is their work life (the higher the quality of their work life, the more satisfied they are with life overall). The path analysis also indicated that the degree of independence people feel and their integration into the community indirectly affect satisfaction as they affect dignity and work. Further, the analysis indicated that respondents' abilities, as measured by intelligence tests, have no direct affect on life satisfaction, and characteristics such as age, communication problems, and ambulatory difficulties have no effect, either directly or indirectly, on life satisfaction.

Motivational Operators

The earlier discussion of self-determination mentioned the importance that one's internal locus of control, self-efficacy, and outcome expectancy have to one's overall motivation, including the motivation to acquire additional skills in the area of self-determination and self-advocacy. There has recently been an increased interest in the role that the QOL concept plays in end motivation (Reiss & Havercamp, 1998; Reiss, 2000; Schalock, in press). End motives are things that people enjoy for their own sake (e.g., curiosity), whereas means motives are the methods of satisfying end motives (e.g., reading books). Reiss (2000) has recently published a list of 16 end motives, some of which have direct bearing on the individual-referenced application of the QOL concept. Most of these end motives are applicable to this section of the text: independence (i.e., the desire for self-reliance), power (i.e., the desire for influence, including mastery, leadership, and dominance), honor (i.e., the desire to be loyal to one's parents, ethnic group, or heritage), order (i.e., the desire for predictable environments), status (i.e., the desire for social standing), acceptance (i.e., the desire to be included), social contact (i.e., the desire for interaction with other people), tranquillity (i.e., the desire to be free of anxiety, fear, or pain), curiosity (i.e., the desire to explore or learn), exercise (i.e., the desire to move one's muscles), and saving (i.e., the desire to collect). The close parallel between these motives and the core QOL domains is striking (see also Table 15.4).

In summary, the above discussion on self-determination strategies and individual-referenced quality enhancement techniques has suggested that the conceptions of both self-determination *and* quality of life are closely related. These constructs are often mentioned in the same context. Yet, to our knowledge, there has been no systematic treatment or exploration of the relationship between the two areas. However (and not coincidentally), the theoretical frameworks of both self-determination and quality of life described previously rely on or reference each construct as a means of defining the other. The relationship and importance of these constructs to individuals with special needs are:

- People who are self-determined make or cause things to happen in their lives; they are causal agents. However, causal agency implies more than simply making something happen; it implies that the individual who makes or causes that thing to happen does so to accomplish a specific end. These ends or changes are designed to improve or enhance the person's quality of life.

- The degree to which a person is self-determined either influences or is influenced by other core dimensions of quality of life and, in combination with these other core dimensions, influences or impacts global or overall quality of life status.

The significance of these two statements and the integration of the two concepts is shown graphically in Figure 12.2, which illustrates from a motivational perspective the relationship among the eight core QOL domains and the key role that self-determination — with its critical component elements of internal locus of control, self-efficacy, and outcome expectancy — plays in human behavior (Schalock, in press).

Conclusion

As discussed throughout the text, quality of life is a construct that attempts to define what it means to "live the good life." As such, it is an important outcome on which to focus. Perhaps a more important question is whether promoting self-determination is worth the time and effort involved. The proposition that self-determination is an important component to a life of quality is that self-determination and positive personal outcomes are causally linked (Wehmeyer & Schalock, 2001; Wehmeyer & Schwartz, 1998). For example, Wehmeyer and Schwartz empirically examined the link between self-determination and quality of life for 50 adults with mental retardation living in group homes. Controlling for level of intelligence and environmental factors contributing to a higher quality of life, they found that self-determination predicted group membership based on QOL scores; that is, a person's relative self-determination was a strong predictor of quality of life; people who were highly self-determined experienced a higher quality of life, and people who lacked self-determination experienced a less positive quality of life.

In conclusion, this chapter has focused on the individual and what might be done to work with the person to enhance quality of life. The material presented

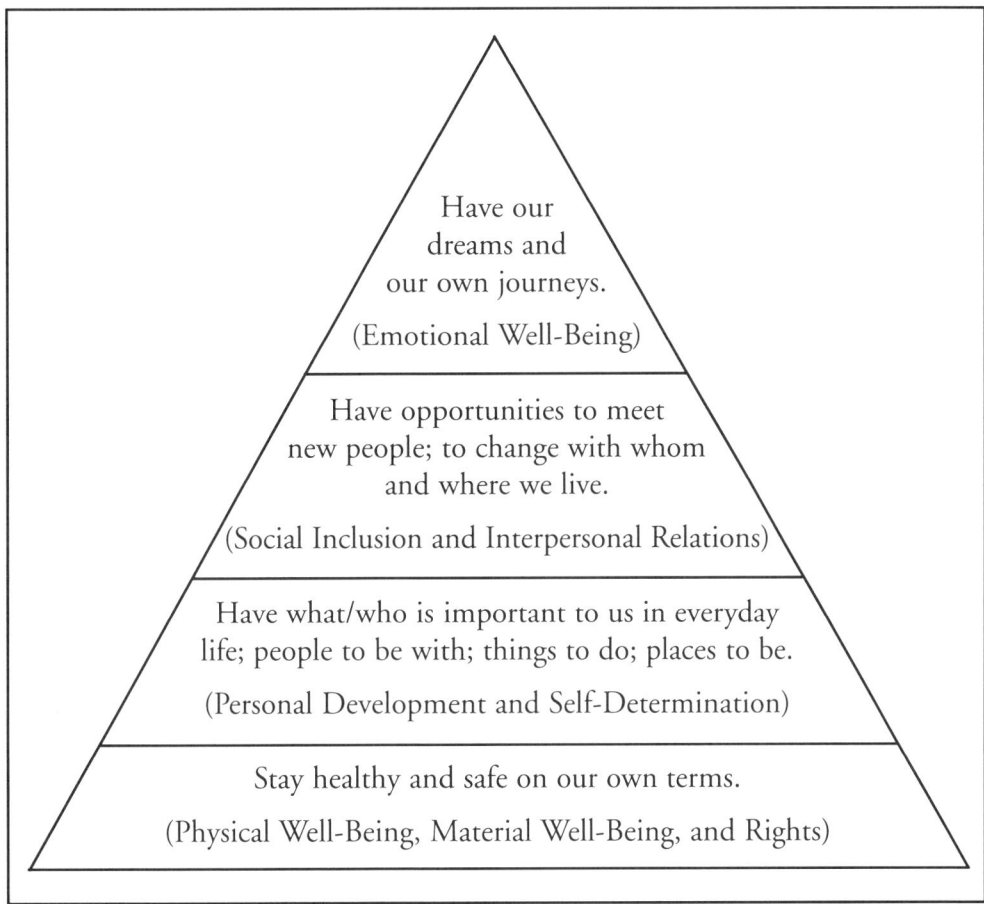

Figure 12.2. Quality of life hierarchy.

was based on core themes and principles that have emerged in the international QOL literature, and those key QOL application principles that were developed by the international work group (Schalock et al., in press). Grounded in these themes and principles, individual-referenced application suggestions were then presented based on the considerable work that has been done on self-determination and the core QOL domains.

Although the focus of the chapter was on the individual, people live in environments that also directly influence their perceived quality of life. It is to the mesosystem, composed of programs, coworkers, peers, and neighbors, that we turn next.

CHAPTER 13

Organizational-Level Application of the Concept of Quality of Life

Overview

This *Handbook* is written from an ecological perspective that stresses the impact on a person's quality of life (QOL) of the microsystem (i.e., person, family, home, peer group), mesosystem (i.e., community, programs, school, work, neighborhood, organizations), and macrosystem (i.e., society at large, economic system, governments, legislation, legal system, regulatory system). As we saw in chapter 12, a number of self-determination strategies and individual-referenced techniques can be used by the person — or encouraged by others — to enhance the individual's perceived quality of life. In this chapter we focus on the mesosystem (education, health, and social service programs) that provide the opportunities or the impediments to an enhanced quality of life. Additionally, rather than focusing only on what programs can and cannot do to enhance quality, we take a broader and more important perspective: how organizations can use desired outcomes — including QOL outcomes — to guide, monitor, and evaluate program change. We feel that this perspective will have the most impact and value to readers.

The chapter discusses ways education, health care, and social service programs can demonstrate increased QOL-referenced outcomes and accountability within the context of two powerful, potentially conflicting forces: person-centered values and economic-based restructured services. These two forces have resulted in significant changes in the way current programs operate, including:

- adopting a framework that allows for entrepreneurship, resource development, and capital formation
- creating organization-based systems involving marketing, fiscal management, clinical decision making, data-based management, and evaluation
- making total quality management and continuous improvement fundamental aspects of an organization's culture

- focusing on outcomes-based evaluation
- committing the organization to effective management, including cost-control and risk-reduction procedures
- linking outcome accountability to systems change
- shifting to results-based accountability
- defining the results that organizations expect to attain and then organizing their resources to attain these results

Despite these changes in management philosophy and techniques, increased accountability, quality outcomes, and long-lasting change have been difficult for many education, health care, and social service programs. Quality outcomes are no longer grounded in the industrial-regulatory perspective wherein quality was defined as conforming with regulations. In contrast, current definitions of quality are rooted in the postindustrial, knowledge-based society. The worldwide growth of service economies and the information revolution have elevated the importance of customer service; because this changes over time, services must be flexible to accommodate the consumer. Albrecht (1993), for example, suggests that, "quality in the 21st century must start with the customer, not with the tangible product sold or the work processes that create it. This is a profound change in focus, from activities to outcomes" (p. 54).

This chapter focuses on both activities and the evaluation of person- and organization-referenced outcomes. To that end, major sections of the chapter discuss: (a) the context of organizational-level application, (b) an outcomes-based evaluation model, (c) action steps involved in using desired outcomes to guide organizational change, (d) implementation strategies, and (e) using QOL outcomes information. The chapter concludes with a discussion of the strengths and limitations of outcome measurement and evaluation.

Organizational Context

Current education, health care, and social service programs are being significantly influenced by two phenomena: (a) the use of outcome measures to guide organizational change and (b) a changing landscape.

Use of Outcome Measures

Outcome measurement is central to efforts to gauge the quality and effectiveness of education, health care, and social service programs. The major purpose of outcomes measurement in the public sector is to enhance program accountability. For example, in an era in which revenues are growing more slowly than the demand for services, governments are forced to make tough decisions about priorities. A greater consciousness of tax burdens and policy has resulted in a desire not only to prioritize services based on need and demand but also to measure outcomes to assure that the resources put into services are used to the best advantage.

To any current service provider, there are advantages in using outcome measures. Among the more important are that outcome measurement (Mawhood, 1997; Schalock, 2001; Schorr, 1997; Wholey, 1997):

- Enhances public accountability. While publicizing outcomes evaluation information can be threatening to some, the public use of outcome data is one of the strongest benefits of a good measurement system. Reporting organizational outcomes can stimulate a much greater interest on the part of the public and can result in an even great emphasis on quality.

- Improves internal accountability. Measuring organizational outcomes gives program administrators a significant tool to achieve accountability. Administrators are accountable to upper level managers for the program's performance, and upper level managers are accountable to elected officials or boards of directors. This relationship becomes much clearer when organizational outcomes are measured by commonly accepted standards.

- Focuses on long-term goals and strategic objectives. Performance measurement involves comparing actual performance against expectations and establishing targets by which progress toward objectives can be measured. Without the ability to measure performance and progress, the process of developing strategic plans and goals is less meaningful. Thus the benefit of strategic planning and evaluation cannot be accomplished without measuring performance and achievement, that is, outcomes.

- Provides performance information to stakeholders. Outcomes data are the most effective method for communicating to legislatures, citizens, and key stakeholders the success of programs and services.

- Enhances decision making. Hierarchical structures and extensive oversight requirements can obstruct organizational effectiveness. Performance measures free senior executives for more strategic planning and management while clarifying the responsibilities and authority of managers and direct service personnel.

- Allows entities to determine effective resource use. With increasing public concern over levels of taxation and user fees, funding bodies are under pressure to justify the existence of key programs. A current trend in program evaluation is to determine if government is, in fact, the best provider of some services. Contracting services, privatizing, and abandoning some services are clearly directions for the public sector in the future. The ability to decide if a service is really making a difference in the lives of its citizens is dependent on good outcomes data. Without such data, public policymakers cannot make sound decisions.

Despite these advantages, there is a basic concern about using outcomes within the context of the strong current emphasis on accountability: we must be certain that any proposed outcomes measurement system balances measures of costs, adequacy of services, and benefits. This concern points out the importance of understanding the changing landscape of education, health care, and social service programs (discussed next) and the different perspectives on accountability that are incorporated in the outcomes-focused planning model (discussed later in the chapter).

The Changing Landscape
Education, health care, and social service programs need to respond to their competitors, who may well be aware of the significant changes in service delivery trends. One component of this change is the emergence of partnerships, which are creating new opportunities and unique challenges. Nonprofit organizations are merging into networks and cooperatives, breaking away from traditional operations and developing innovative enterprises. They frequently share a mission to conserve fiscal resources by sharing construction and operational costs, equipment, and administrative expenses. These approaches benefit from economies of scale while maintaining character, flexibility, and responsiveness.

Additionally, consumers are becoming stronger voices in the need for organizational change and increased responsiveness. Across the text's focus areas, we are seeing movements toward increased empowerment, choices, dignity, inclusion, respect, individual rights, personal goals, and self-advocacy. The net result of this movement has been an increased emphasis on measuring consumer's satisfaction and organization-referenced outcomes, such as those summarized in Table 13.1.

An Outcomes-Based Evaluation Model

One of this chapter's premises is that a missing component of successful organizational change and increased person-valued outcomes has been the minimal (or nonexistent) use of desired outcomes to guide the change process. This omission has occurred within the context of an environment that requires formative feedback (i.e., knowledge of outcomes and results) to facilitate organizational change and target resources, services, and supports. To assist organizations in responding successfully to this important omission and adapting to the two contextual factors just discussed, this section introduces an outcomes-based evaluation model that provides the framework for determining the status of desired person- and organization-referenced outcomes.

The model has three components: standards, focus, and outcomes. The model's *standard* reflect the two previously discussed perspectives on accountability, performance versus value; its *focus* reflects the current emphasis on the organization

TABLE 13.1
Consumer Satisfaction and Organization-Referenced Outcomes

Tangibles: the appearance of physical facilities, equipment, and people

Reliability: the ability to perform the promised service dependably and effectively

Responsiveness: the willingness to help consumers and provide prompt service

Assurance: the knowledge and courtesy of employees and their ability to convey trust and confidence

Empathy: the caring and individualized attention provided to consumers

Availability: the presence of needed services or interventions

Affordability: the ability to procure the services or interventions

Awareness: the degree to which the customer is aware of the potential services or interventions

Accessibility: the ability to access the services or interventions (e.g., transportation, barrier-free environments)

Extensiveness: the variety of services or interventions offered

Appropriateness: the degree of correspondence between needs of the consumer and the available services or interventions

---

(i.e., agency or service) or the individual (i.e., client, customer, or consumer); and its *outcomes* denote measurable results that are captured in a number of potential person- or organization-referenced outcome measures. As shown in Figure 13.1, some outcomes reflect performance; others, values; some focus on the organization; and others on the individual. The discerning reader will note that the eight core QOL domains are listed in cells C and D. Note also that physical and material well-being are considered "individual-performance outcomes," whereas the other six QOL domains are considered "individual-value outcomes." The assumption is that individual-performance outcomes are more likely to result in behaviors that increase the person's functioning; this means that a monetary value can more easily be assigned to performance than to value outcomes. The following are specific examples of outcomes for each matrix cell:

- *organizational-performance outcomes:* service coordination, financial stability, health and safety, program data, and staff tenure or turnover;

- *organizational-value outcomes:* access to services, consumer satisfaction, staff competencies, family or consumer supports, wrap-around services, and community supports;
- *individual-performance outcomes:* physical well-being (health status and wellness indicators) and material well-being (employment status, living status, education status);
- *individual-value outcomes:* emotional well-being, personal development, self-determination, interpersonal relations, social inclusion, and rights.

Several assumptions underlie the implementation of the outcomes-based evaluation model and its use in guiding organizational change and results-based accountability. First, new models of quality management developed from process engineering and the use of social science measurement techniques make possible objective, data-based approaches to change. These approaches include report cards, "benchmarking," quality indicators, practice guidelines, and monitoring (Jencks, 1995). Second, desired outcomes can be considered as benchmarks that allow an organization to compare its performance either to the best practices among simi-

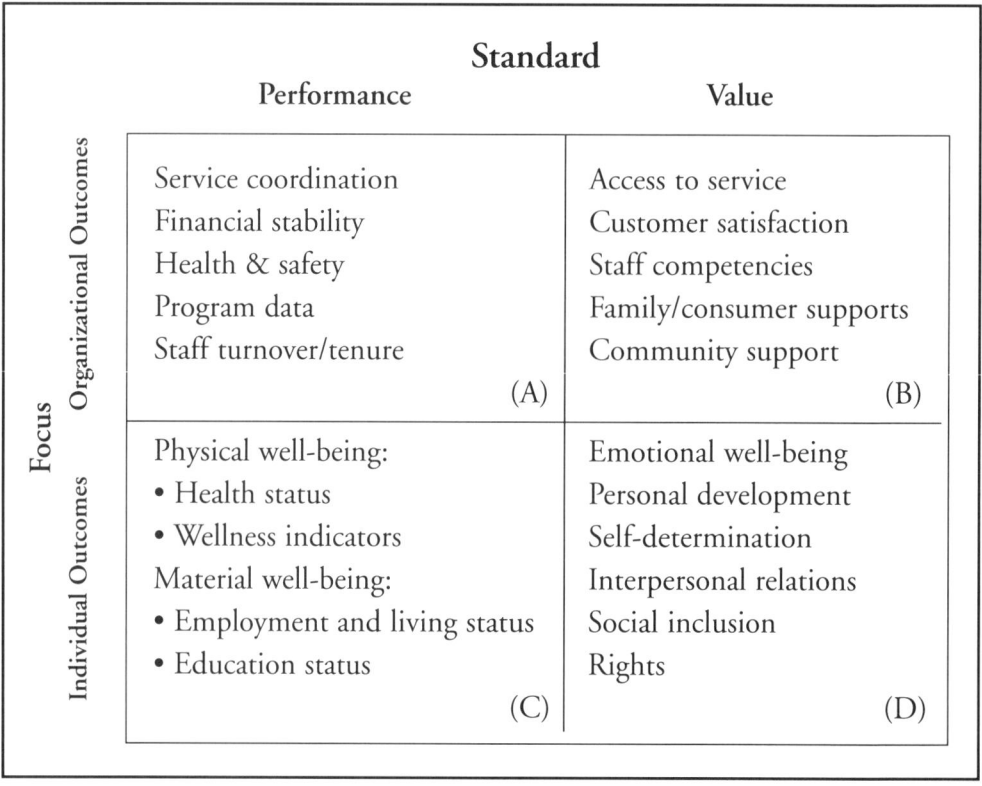

Figure 13.1. Outcomes-based evaluation model.

lar organizations or to its desired outcomes. Third, conversion planning and the targeting of resources involve a fundamental need to use multiple outcomes such as those listed in Figure 13.1. Details regarding the model's development and cross-validation can be found in Schalock (2001).

Action Steps Involved in Using Desired Outcomes to Guide Organizational Change

Four action steps are used to implement the model shown in Figure 13.1. First, a baseline of currently monitored outcomes is established. This is accomplished by completing the Outcomes Planning Inventory ("the Inventory") presented in Appendix 13.1, basing answers on outcomes on which the organization currently focuses. Second, desired outcomes are identified by organizational personnel completing the Inventory on the basis of desired outcomes that are person- and/or organization-referenced, realizing that most organizations will strive for a reasonable balance between outcomes related to performance and to value. The resulting summary indicates both the desired outcomes to guide the organization and the discrepancy between where the organization is and where it wants to go. The third step involves determining the specific outcome measures that reflect the direction of change and the basis for converting resources and targeting specific services and supports. Once these are established, they need to be measured in Step 4 via one or more techniques, such as accountability assessment, consumer appraisal, functional assessment, and personal appraisal. These four techniques will be described in more detail in a later section.

Step 1: Establish Baseline

To obtain baseline data (i.e., the outcomes currently being used), organizational personnel complete the Outcomes Planning Inventory, presented as Appendix 13.1, using the baseline instructions: "For each numbered row, circle the outcome that BEST describes your current outcome measures or evaluation focus." (The reader should note that the outcomes presented in Appendix 13.1 represent the four most commonly used exemplars for each outcome measure listed in Figure 13.1.) Although the Inventory uses a forced-choice strategy to determine one outcome per row, some practitioners may wish to use other strategies (such as the Delphi method or a Likert scale).

After the Inventory is completed (either individually or collectively), the number of circled items in each column is summed (or averaged if there are multiple respondents), resulting in a total score for each cell of the outcomes-focused model (Figure 13.1). The number of A's reflect organizational-performance outcomes; B's, organizational-value outcomes; C's, individual-performance outcomes; and D's, individual-value outcomes. An exemplary result of this baseline outcomes assessment is shown in Figure 13.2a, which indicates that this particular organization is currently emphasizing organizational-performance outcomes, with significantly less attention to the other three matrix cells.

Step 2: Determine Desired Outcomes

The second action step is to determine where the organization wants to go; that is, determine outcomes on which to base change or conversion activities and to target resources. This step involves organization staff completing the Outcomes Planning Inventory using the desired outcomes directions: "For each numbered row, circle the outcome that BEST describes the outcome your organization wants to measure or evaluate." As with Step 1, other strategies apart from the forced-choice technique can be used, as long as the number per matrix cell is obtained (as shown in Figure 13.2). Figure 13.2b indicates that the organization desires a better balance among the four outcome categories. This will require focusing more on organization and individual value outcomes than was reflected in the organization's baseline (Figure 13.2a).

a. Exemplary Baseline Outcomes

	Performance	Value
Organization	A (15)	B (1)
Individual	C (2)	D (2)

b. Exemplary Desired Outcomes

	Performance	Value
Organization	A (8)	B (6)
Individual	C (2)	D (4)

Figure 13.2. Exemplary baseline and desired outcomes.

Setting conversion goals and targeting resources depend largely upon the organization's "personality" and its strategic plan. Based on Figure 13.1, one can identify four organizational personalities:

- stability organization: focus is primarily on organizational performance outcome categories related to service coordination, financial solvency, health and safety, data systems, and/or staff turnover (cell A in Figure 13.1 and column A in Appendix 13.1)
- outreach organization: focus is primarily on outcome measures related to organization values, including access issues, consumer satisfaction, staff competencies, consumer supports, and/or community supports (cell B; column B)
- rehabilitation organization: focus is primarily on outcome categories related to the person's health status, functional status, financial status, residential status, or educational status (cell C; column C)
- advocacy organization: focus is primarily on outcome categories related to self-determination, social inclusion, social relations, rights and dignity, and personal development (cell D; column D)

Step 3: Select Specific Outcome Measures
Results from Step 2 provide the general direction for the organization's conversion and resource targeting activities. After completing Step 2, the organization will know which general outcome categories it wishes to pursue and thereby know the general direction of desired change. The third step involves selecting a few critical specific outcome measures that can be used to direct, monitor, and reinforce the change process and its effects. Five guidelines that should be used to select these specific outcome measures are summarized in Table 13.2.

Step 4: Measure Desired Outcomes
As discussed in chapters 2, 10, and 11, QOL measurement strategies have been changed, consistent with the reform movement's emphasis on accountability and quality. The term that best describes this change is *methodological pluralism,* characterized by (Schalock, 2001): (a) commitment to an epistemology of social constructionism, which assumes that there are only alternative, subjective constructions of reality produced by different individuals; (b) application of the pragmatic evaluation paradigm that emphasizes a practical, problem-solving orientation to program evaluation; (c) focus on ideographic (person-referenced) evaluation and participatory action research; (d) emphasis on decision-oriented, "human-focused" knowledge versus science-focused knowledge; (e) use of both qualitative and quantitative methods; (f) emphasis on context-specific results and knowledge versus general laws; (g) facilitation of an interpretive dialogue among a wide range of a program's stakeholders; and (h) inquiries conducted that are tailor-made to

TABLE 13.2
Important Guidelines in Selecting Outcome Measures

1. Select outcomes that are consistent with the organization's mission statement and strategic plan goals.

2. Select a minimum number of outcomes that are relevant and obtainable.

3. Select outcomes that are within the organization's evaluation (i.e., data collection and analysis) capability. Data collection and analysis take time, money, and expertise. Thus the outcomes selected should be compatible with the organization's capability to collect, store, analyze, and report the data.

4. Select outcomes that reflect age and functional level differences. Some outcomes listed in Figure 13.1 are age related; others are sensitive to individual differences in functional levels.

5. Select outcomes that the organization is committed to following over time. Outcome measurement is a dynamic, not a static, process. Outcomes for people change due to individual choice, developmental milestones, successful education or rehabilitation efforts, or the organization's services, and supports.

answer the needs of program stakeholders and fit in with the organization's culture.

In reference to the outcomes-based evaluation model presented in Figure 13.1, methodological pluralism at the individual level involves the use of functional assessment and personal appraisal; at the organizational level, it involves accountability assessment and consumer appraisal. Here is a summary of the overall measurement focus of each approach:

- *Accountability assessment* is the preferred evaluation method for measuring organizational effectiveness and efficiency. Specific methods include performance planning and reporting, performance indicators such as report cards, and financial accounting measures such as a financial audit (Schalock, 2001).

- *Consumer appraisal* is the preferred evaluation method for measuring organizational value outcomes. Specific methods include customer satisfaction surveys and measures reflecting fidelity to the service delivery model (Schalock, 2001).

- *Functional assessment* is the preferred evaluation method for measuring individual performance outcomes related to adaptive behavior and role status. Specific measures include rating scales, personal observation, objective behavioral measures, and status indicators, such as education, living, and employment status (see chap. 11).

- *Personal appraisal* is the preferred evaluation method for measuring individual value outcomes. Specific measures include QOL evaluations obtained from rating scales, attitude scales, and questionnaires (see chap. 11).

Implementation Strategies

Once the desired outcomes are selected and measured (Steps 3 & 4), one asks, "What needs to be in place for the organization to use effectively the desired outcomes for guiding organizational services and supports and thereby increasing QOL-referenced outcomes?" Five practical, possible, and applicable strategies are (a) foster a culture of change, (b) use person-centered planning, (c) build supports around the core QOL domains, (d) focus on program-referenced quality enhancement techniques, and (e) implement an outcomes-oriented monitoring system.

Foster a Culture of Change

There is considerable literature about organizational change, the concept of a culture of change, how organizational culture influences outcomes use, and the linking of outcome accountability to systems change. Although a detailed discussion of organizational change is beyond the scope of this chapter, key factors operating in change-oriented organizations include the organization's mission and its view of itself, the communication style prevailing within the organization, previous experiences with using outcome data, and the organization's relationship with regulatory bodies (Colarelli, 1998; Green & Newman, 1999).

Fostering a culture of change is inherent within the concept of total quality management (TQM). As stated by Hodges and Hernandez (1999),

> The application of TQM principles requires the systematic analysis of quantitative data with the involvement and commitment of people throughout an organization in order to concentrate organizational efforts on constantly improving quality of the goods and services it offers. The philosophy of TQM encompasses the idea of making simultaneous improvements to both quality and cost effectiveness. (p. 184)

TQM is based on five management principles that facilitate the use of desired QOL-referenced outcomes to guide organizational change and enhance an organization's accountability.

- consumer orientation: organizations must be responsive to consumer needs
- continuous improvement: an emphasis on incremental ongoing change
- data-driven decision making: an emphasis on structured problem solving based on the analysis of data

- teamwork: employees throughout an organization work together in the process of quality improvement
- focus on organization process: an emphasis on organizational processes and systems that affect the organization's clientele and/or services

Use Person-Centered Planning

Individualization is a core value of most education, health care, and social service programs, and a key principle in public or national policy as reflected in individual service plans, individual education plans, individual program plans, and individual rehabilitation plans. In recent years a variety of approaches to individualized services has been implemented, including those referred to as whole life planning, personal futures planning, essential lifestyle planning, and outcomes-based planning. These procedures have become commonly known as person-centered planning, with the following essential characteristics (Butterworth, Steere, & Whitney-Thomas, 1997):

- primary direction from the individual both in shaping the planning process and in formulating plans
- emphasis on the involvement of family members and friends in the planning process and reliance on personal social relationships as the primary source of individual supports
- a focus on the preferences, talents, and dreams of the individual rather than on needs or limitations
- a vision of the lifestyle the individual would like to have and the goals needed to achieve it, unrestricted by current resources or services
- a broad implementation approach that uses resources and supports for the individual that are local, informal, and as generic as possible

Build Supports around Core Quality of Life Domains

The supports paradigm is widely recognized as the service delivery model in social service programs and is increasingly seen in education and health care programs as well. As generally defined, supports are resources and strategies used to enhance a person's well-being and perceived quality of life. Based on a recent literature review of "supports," 100 support functions were identified. Following the identification, a group of education and disability professionals used a Q-sort technique to aggregate these supports into the eight core QOL domains. The five most common support functions aggregated into each QOL domain are listed in Table 13.3.

TABLE 13.3
Support Functions Aggregated by Quality of Life Core Domains

Domain	Support Functions
Emotional well-being	Emotional support Support groups Counseling Mental health or substance abuse Counseling appointments Treatment
Interpersonal relations	Friendship Development of networking skills Socializing Promotion of peer support groups Communication aids
Material well-being	Income support Assistance with money management Access to financial assistance Adjustment of work benefits Job creation
Personal development	Compensatory strategies (e.g., memory aids) Problem-solving strategies Adaptive behavior Self-management Transportation training strategies
Physical well-being	Provision of home health care Therapy-related activities Medical interventions Transfer and mobility Emergency procedures

(table continues)

TABLE 13.3. *(continued)*

Domain	Support Functions
Self-determination	Incorporating personal preferences into daily activities Instructing in decision making Fostering advocacy groups Making choices and taking initiatives Developing self-advocacy skills Social inclusion Community inclusion activities Providing information on community Building a sense of community at school Identifying supports in the environment Participation in preferred community activities
Rights	Protection and legal assistance Advocating for benefits Advocating for ownership and own guardianship Case management Advocacy groups

Focus on Program-Referenced Quality Enhancement Techniques

Quality enhancement techniques typically are based on input from consumers and focus on what program personnel and program services can do to enhance a person's real or perceived quality of life. A number of approaches are currently being used to enhance the quality of life of people throughout the service delivery system. Exemplary techniques are listed in Table 13.4.

TABLE 13.4
Quality of Life Enhancement Techniques

Domain	Exemplary Enhancement Technique
Emotional well-being	Increase safety Allow for spirituality Provide positive feedback Maintain as low a psychotropic medication level as possible Reduce stress Foster success Promote stable, safe, and predictable environments

(table continues)

TABLE 13.4. *(continued)*

Domain	Exemplary Enhancement Technique
Interpersonal relations	Allow intimacy Permit affection Support family Encourage interactions Foster friendships Provide supports
Material well-being	Allow ownership Advocate for financial security Ensure safe environs Support employment Encourage possessions
Personal development	Provide education and rehabilitation Teach functional skills Provide vocational and avocational activities Foster skill development Provide purposeful activity Support advancement Use augmentative technology
Physical well-being	Ensure health care Maximize mobility Support opportunities for meaningful recreation and leisure Encourage proper nutrition Support activities of daily living Promote wellness by emphasizing physical fitness, nutrition, healthy lifestyles, and stress management
Self-determination	Allow for choices Permit personal control Allow decisions Assist in developing personal goals

(table continues)

TABLE 13.4. *(continued)*

Domain	Exemplary Enhancement Technique
Social inclusion	Interface with natural support networks Promote positive role functions and lifestyles Stress normalized and integrated environments Provide opportunities for community integration and participation Support volunteerism
Rights	Assure privacy Encourage voting Reduce barriers Afford due process Encourage ownership Encourage civic responsibilities

Implement an Outcomes-Oriented Monitoring System

Many of the agencies with which the authors are familiar are data rich and information poor, due primarily to the organization not knowing for sure what data to collect, what to measure, how to measure it, or how to organize and retrieve relevant outcomes-oriented data. Part of the implementation of an outcomes-oriented monitoring system involves selecting specific outcome measures and measuring desired outcomes. Once the "what" and the "how to" are answered, the next challenge is to implement a computer-based monitoring system that can store, analyze, and report the status over time of the outcome measures selected. Key components of such a system include the use of:

- data sets that meet the following criteria: person- or organization-referenced, complete (available for all program participants or relevant program components), timely (current and cover the period in which you are interested), affordable (in terms of time, money, and expertise), and accurate (reflect actual events and characteristics)
- data collection formats that can lead directly (and electronically) to data management and entry, and data manipulation and analysis
- a data collection responsibility center that is trained in data collection strategies, data management principles, data analysis, and data reporting procedures
- data collection time lines that are consistent with the organization's strategic plan, required reporting period, and annual performance review cycle

- standardized report formats that will allow annual outcome reports (e.g., report cards) and longitudinal comparisons (e.g., benchmarks).

Using the Outcome Information

The key idea underlying this section of the chapter is to link information to action. This can be done in a number of ways, including linking outcome accountability to organization or systems change, or adopting outcome assessment strategies to provide data for programmatic improvement and management decision making. In this regard, over the years one of the authors (Schalock, 1999, 2000, 2001) has written extensively about the concept of formative feedback with multiple purposes:

- sharing outcome information with all personnel to enhance outcome use
- assuring stakeholders a strong voice in the design and management of programs
- linking both organization evaluation and program improvement to person- and organization-referenced outcomes
- allowing for the systematic evaluation and improvement of services
- identifying the potential loci for organization and program change

The use of outcomes information needs to be linked to the major changes now occurring in education, health care, and social service systems. Primary among these changes are (a) the development and evaluation of strategic plans, (b) the evaluation of outcomes in light of the reform movement, and (c) the implementation of change.

Development and Evaluation of Strategic Plans

Current accountability initiatives seek to improve management, increase efficiency and effectiveness, and improve public confidence in government. For example, reform acts throughout the world provide a legislative base for many of the most important reform efforts, asking agencies to articulate goals in their strategic plans and to report results via program performance reports.

Through *strategic planning,* an organization develops its mission statement covering the agency's major functions and operations; establishes and periodically updates long-term goals and objectives, including outcome-related goals and objectives; describes how those goals and objectives are to be achieved; describes how annual program performance goals will be related to the agency's long-term goals and objectives; and identifies key external factors (i.e., contextual variables) that can significantly affect the achievement of the long-term goals and objectives. Through *annual performance planning,* the organization prepares annual performance plans that will define performance goals for each fiscal year. These plans should include goals to be achieved by key agency programs, the resources and activities required to meet these performance goals, and the establishment of performance indicators to assess relevant program outcomes and compare actual program results with the performance goals. Through *annual program performance reports,* organizations report actual program results compared with the performance goals for that fiscal year, report actual program results for prior fiscal years, and explain why any performance goals were not met and what action is then recommended.

Evaluation of Outcomes within the Context of the Reform Movement

The current reform movement, with its dual focus of accountability and quality, has had a profound influence on outcomes measurement. Its major characteristics include (Mawhood, 1997): focusing on outputs rather than inputs; being driven by goals related to organization- and person-referenced outcomes; redefining clients as customers; decentralizing authority; using market rather than bureaucratic mechanisms; catalyzing public, private, and voluntary sectors; and empowering citizens. Current accountability initiatives are reflected in the earlier discussion of "use of outcome measures." The quality dimension of the reform movement is evolving within the context of: (a) the movement toward assessing the value and quality of respective programs on the basis of consumer satisfaction; (b) the development of new models of service delivery that reflect the devolution of government, the homogenization of services, and the community-based movement; and (c) the use of valued outcomes, including one's quality of life (Schalock, 2001).

Implementation of Change

Change is an ongoing process that is constantly evolving new forms and functions. Hence the goals, measures, and strategies established in the suggested Action Steps 2 and 3 need to be monitored to provide the formative feedback necessary both to evaluate where the organization is in the conversion process and to make the ongoing adaptations that contextual issues related to accountability and the components of change require. In that regard, Beer and his colleagues (Beer, Eisenstat, & Spector, 1990; Beer & Eisenstat, 1993) suggest six steps to effective change: (a) mobilize commitment to change through joint diagnosis of business problems; (b) develop a shared vision of how to organize and manage for competitiveness; (c) foster consensus for the new vision, competence to enact it, and cohesion to move it along; (d) spread use to all organization components without pushing it from the top; (e) institutionalize revitalization through formal policies, systems, and structures; and (f) monitor and adjust strategies based on new challenges and measured outcomes.

The critical role that each step plays in organizational change has recently been demonstrated in reference to an organization change model (Gold, Van Gelder, & Schalock, 1999). The model, and data supporting it, suggests that true, long-lasting organizational change consists of at least three components: commitment to change, producing change, and maintaining change. The key aspect of the model is that for each component there are definite outcomes that allow one to implement three important aspects of change: (a) gradual processes that produce changes in roles, responsibilities, and relationships; (b) initial structural changes that allow for formative evaluation and reinforcement; and (c) longer-term structural and policy changes that result in organizational, cultural, and attitudinal change. Central to each of these aspects is the use of desired outcomes to guide, monitor, and reinforce the change process.

Implementing change also requires understanding the psychology of personal behavioral change: change is a gradual process that is built on successive, incremental small steps (Kanfer & Goldstein, 1991; Gold, Van Gelder, & Schalock, 1999). Thus the desired direction of change should be guided by:

- the type of organization one wants to be, balancing among organizational types characterized as stable, outreach, rehabilitation, or advocacy
- the outcomes that the organization wishes to pursue, monitor, and evaluate (see Figure 13.1 and Appendix 13.1)
- the linking of these outcomes to desired change activities that target resources to change service delivery and support patterns so as to increase the probability of obtaining the desired outcomes
- the use of an "interrogatory approach to management" that relates the desired outcomes to the interrogatories (i.e., who, what, where, when, and how) that make it happen

Conclusion

A basic premise of this chapter is that the organization-based application of the concept of quality of life will require organizational change; furthermore, organizational change does not just happen. Rather, it requires a clear vision of where the organization wants to go; benchmarks related to desired outcomes that give value, direction, strategies, and reinforcement to the conversion efforts; and an interrogatory framework that directs conversion activities and provides formative feedback to all stakeholders. The outcome-based evaluation planning model discussed in this chapter helps an organization to:

- develop an appreciation and understanding of the use of desired outcomes to guide organizational change

- aid thinking about the anticipated benefits of organizational change
- implement a number of strategies to enhance person- and program-referenced desired outcomes
- enable organizational staff to work together on agreed-upon desired outcomes
- provide change strategies based on the best of management by objectives procedures and quality improvement principles
- guide the change efforts
- provide direction for obtaining both change efforts and desired outcomes

The chapter is based on the principles of outcomes research and outcomes-based evaluation, with fundamental assumptions that outcomes need to be objective and measurable, monitored, and used for multiple purposes, including organizational change. There are advantages of using desired outcomes to guide organizational change.

- Desired outcomes are complementary to the characteristics of the change process. For example, change involves an ongoing process that needs direction and monitoring toward desired outcomes.
- Change is frequently gradual and requires positive feedback to all those involved in the change process as well as communicating to those people the status of the organization's desired outcomes.
- Change also requires a commitment to objective, measurable results that are reflected in desired outcomes. Without that commitment, change is often lost in philosophy and mission statements that are less than effective without the specific indicators provided by the desired outcomes.
- Change is incremental, with results building on results: without measurable outcomes, the incremental and positive nature of change is often overlooked.

Despite potential advantages and benefits, there are also some limitations regarding outcome evaluation and the performance measurement on which it is based. This is especially true in terms of QOL application and evaluation.

- Performance measurement should be balanced with other considerations. For example, it is clear that not all outcomes can be measured quantitatively. This is especially true of subjective indicators of a person's perceived quality of life.
- Outcome measurement can have more cost than benefit. One needs to be cautious that the outcomes measurement system does not consume in resources more than its information is worth.

- The usefulness of performance measurement varies by its use. Outcome measures are useful to the management or decision-making process only to the extent that they are used and that they answer the right questions.
- Organizations are sometimes limited in their ability to influence outcomes because of significant external factors. Yet the specific program is frequently held accountable for the reported results or outcomes. Users of performance measures need to understand their limited role and recognize that a particular program does not solely determine outcomes. But these outcomes are still important, because they are indicators of whether or not one is making a difference and moving in the desired direction. If the measures are in place, one can begin to explain the relative worth of public and private programs and try to determine if the combination of efforts is accomplishing the organization's mission. As stated by Senge, "What ought to be primary are the results and accomplishments that the people in that enterprise really care about. Then the real question becomes how good you are at it and how you can do better" (quoted in Schultz, 1999, p. 88).

But one should not forget that change associated with the organizational-level application of the QOL concept is also risky and needs to be tempered with incentives and safeguards. Incentives can be in the form of obtaining desired outcomes; safeguards in the form of measurable results that can be associated with specific strategies and with accountability that comes from relating empirical change strategies to specific outcomes. Thus, using desired person- and organization-valued outcomes to guide, monitor, and evaluate organizational change will typically result in organizations being in a win-win situation. The larger, societal context of those efforts is discussed in the following chapter.

APPENDIX 13.1
Outcome Planning Inventory

Baseline Directions: For each column (A, B, C, D), circle the outcome term that BEST describes your *current outcome measures or evaluation focus*.

Desired Outcomes Directions: For each column (A, B, C, D), circle the outcome that BEST describes the outcome your organization *wishes to measure or evaluate*.

A
(Organizational Performance)

1. Interagency agreements
2. Integrated services
3. Shared services
4. Seamless services
5. Asset to liability ratio
6. Reserves to budget ratio
7. Cost data
8. Multiple revenue sources
9. Injury rates
10. Mortality rates
11. Victimization rates
12. Wellness indicators
13. Person-referenced outcomes
14. Expenditure/program data
15. Demographic data
16. Service intensity data
17. Staff tenure
18. Staff turnover rate
19. Recruitment rate
20. Managerial turnover rate

Baseline: # Circled: _____

Desired: # Circled: _____

B
(Organizational Value)

1. Flexible services/supports
2. Timely eligibility determination
3. Access to needed services
4. Telecommunication access
5. Information needs
6. Timeliness of service
7. Respect and confidentiality
8. Grievance procedure
9. Staff performance appraisal
10. Competency-based training
11. Personnel earning of credentials
12. Data utilization competencies
13. Individual family support plan
14. Adaptive equipment
15. Transition supports
16. Augmentative communication system
17. Contributed community resources
18. Media recognition
19. Services provided to community
20. Community representation on Board

Baseline: # Circled: _____

Desired: # Circled: _____

C
(Individual Performance)

1. Medical/health care utilization rate
2. Medication utilization rate
3. Recidivism rate
4. Nutritional status
5. Activities of daily living
6. Instrumental activities of daily living
7. Mobility
8. Skill development
9. Net income
10. Savings
11. Debt status
12. Employment status
13. Independent living
14. Semi-independent living
15. Supervised living
16. Incarceration rate
17. School credits
18. Postsecondary school status
19. Degrees/diplomas
20. Behavioral competencies

Baseline: # Circled: _____

Desired: # Circled: _____

D
(Individual Value)

1. Choice making
2. Personal goals
3. Personal control
4. Self-reliance
5. Community resources used
6. Community access
7. Neighborhood friendship patterns
8. Community involvement
9. Friendships
10. Family involvement
11. Intimate relations
12. Support network
13. Self-advocacy
14. Involved in individual plan
15. Receives respect and recognition
16. Voting opportunities
17. Avocational activities
18. Continuing education
19. Volunteer activities
20. Ownership

Baseline: # Circled: _____

Desired: # Circled: _____

CHAPTER 14

Societal-Level Application of the Concept of Quality of Life

Overview

The application of quality of life (QOL) to people with special needs such as those reflected in the text's focus areas requires public policies and societal actions that are consistent with the notion of quality of life. Just as we saw in the previous two chapters on bringing about change at the individual and program level, actions can also be taken at the societal level to enhance a person's subjective well-being and quality of life. How that might be done is the focus of this chapter.

The chapter begins by discussing two contextual issues that make our task challenging: the presumed cause of disability, and the scientific paradigm that is used to understand and explain disability. Then four proposed societal actions are discussed: (a) nations adopting QOL-related public policies, (b) communities implementing quality enhancement techniques, (c) citizenry collaborating for change, and (d) researchers providing information and evidence that the citizenry's well-being has been enhanced and collaboration for change has occurred. The chapter concludes with a discussion of the importance of both individual rights and a society's moral responsibility to people with special needs. Throughout the chapter, the five QOL principles summarized in Table 2.3 are used to frame the chapter's content and future public policy and evaluation efforts.

Contextual Issues

Contextualism has emerged recently as a critical concept in understanding the influence of external influences on outcomes. Contextualism has four central themes that are important for the reader to understand (Schalock, 2001). First is the appreciation of the setting or context within which societal actions occur. In that regard, the context of QOL-enhancing activities includes more than just the immediate settings we discussed in the previous two chapters; one also needs to consider the larger cultural and historical setting that allows or invites the occurrence of an event or renders it socially acceptable and timely. A second central tenant is contextualism's emphasis on reality as an active, ongoing, and changing process that involves society being transformed by its citizenry, which in turn is transformed by the society. A third theme is an assault on the division of science into "basic" and "applied" branches and an acceptance of the view that the best way to advance basic understanding is to study social reality in everyday, practical states. The fourth contextual theme is the notion that a society's citizenry plays an important role in societal development and change and that research and evaluation information can be used by various key players to bring about change. These four themes reflect both the reality and the challenges posed by the two contextual issues discussed next. As we will see, not only do these issues affect greatly the societal-level application of the QOL concept, but they are also closely related.

Presumed Cause for Disability

Evidence from a number of studies demonstrates clearly that, in the United States at least, race and poverty are not just the main impediments to societal participation and advocacy; they are also potent predictors of disability status (Fujiura, 2000; Fujiura & Yamaki, 1997, 2000). The explanation for these relations and the potential solution to overcoming the relationship among race, poverty, and disability has been discussed in detail recently by Block, Balcazar, and Keys (2001). In rethinking this relationship, Block et al. (2001) state:

> Throughout the twentieth century, theoretical models of biological and cultural pathology, such as eugenics and the culture of poverty, have presented images of race, ethnicity, and disability primarily in terms of deficiency and dependence. . . . Policies and practices based on these theories project pejorative images of low-income ethnic and racial minorities and on people with disabilities. Individuals belonging to more than one of these categories — or all three — are especially vulnerable to social stigma. (p. 18)

Although such images of biological and cultural pathology have been seriously questioned and frequently rejected, many cultures still reflect the tenets of racism, "classism," "ableism," and other forms of prejudice that create barriers resulting in social and economic marginalization for disenfranchised groups such as those reflected in the text's focus areas. If these prejudices are to be overcome, one must deal with two models of pathology — biological and cultural — and the emerging ecological model of disability.

Biological Pathology
From the time of the early eugenics movement, biological theories have always intersected theories of race, class, and disability (Block et al., 2001). Eugenics, the

science of genetic improvement of the human race, was the primary ideological framework in which policies and practices were developed to manage marginalized populations. Eugenics was used to establish race and class distinctions as natural and incontrovertible. The upper class dominated because of their superior genetic heritage; the poor remained in poverty because of their degenerate genes. Similarly, eugenicists believed that racial degeneration — or degeneration due to one's disability — would change the national character.

Although the term *eugenics* disappeared from professional discourse when it was no longer considered an effective means of program implementation, and after eugenics disappeared from official public policy, eugenicists continued to influence the social service system by advocating for the institutionalization and sterilization of people with disabilities (Schalock, 2002). Additionally, eugenics ideologies persisted through the subtle influence of cultural beliefs concerning marginalized groups, such as representations of people with disabilities in literature, film, and television as social victims or social threats. In many places people with disabilities are still portrayed as unable to control their sexuality and capable of erupting into random and unpredictable acts of violence. Thus, from this perspective, society is considered safe only when a person with disabilities (or marginalized in other ways) is deceased or locked behind the walls of an institution (Block et al., 2001).

Cultural Pathology
In the 1930s biological theories began to be replaced by the theories of culture promulgated by sociologists and anthropologists. For example, Lewis (as referenced in Block et al., 2001, p. 20) saw poverty itself as inspiring pathological forms of cultural structure. A "culture of poverty" was often characterized as some combination of the following: devaluing of education, chronic unemployment, destabilized families, dependence on social assistance, teen pregnancy, domestic and gang violence, and drug and alcohol abuse. Because of these presumed characteristics, the culture of poverty thesis often fueled the argument that there is little that government can do to break the cycle of poverty.

Whether defined as a pathological lack of culture or a culture that was pathological, the people living in poverty were considered deficient. Hunt (1969), for example, stated:

> Incompetence and poverty are interrelated. As a characteristic of individual persons, incompetence results in poverty. And, the poverty of one generation becomes, by virtue of the circumstances which hamper the development of abilities and motives, a basis for incompetence in the next generation. (p. vii)

Like the eugenics orientation, the culture of poverty thesis functioned to justify blaming the poor or persons with disabilities for their poverty and blaming social problems on innate deficiencies. Culture became an alternative to biological explanations for the inferiority, dependency, and marginalization of certain social groups such as those reflected in the text's focus areas.

Ecological Model of Disability
Theories of biological and cultural pathology are increasingly being replaced with the notion that poverty among marginalized groups and people with disabilities results from prejudice, racism, social and economic discrimination, and other environmental factors (Luckasson et al., 1992; World Health Organization, 2000b). This ecological perspective has implications for societal actions to enhance people's quality of life (Schalock, 2001), including: (a) disability is neither fixed nor dichotomized; rather, it is fluid, continuous, and changing within an evolving set of personal characteristics that depend on the services and supports available to the person; and (b) one lessens functional limitations (and hence a person's disability) by providing interventions and services or supports that focus on adaptive behavior, role or community status, and subjective well-being.

In summary, the ecological model allows one to disentangle impairments from the myth, ideology, and stigma that influence social interactions and social policy toward marginalized groups. This model can function to liberate people from long-held societal prejudices and mistaken assumptions. Disability identity can become a form of political awareness and strength as reflected currently in the self-advocacy movement. The model also provides the focus and the content of the societal-level action steps discussed later in the chapter.

Scientific Paradigm of Disability
A scientific paradigm is the way scientists think about and approach a particular phenomenon or issue. According to Kuhn (1970), science involves social collaboration among scientists who share a fundamental world view (i.e., a scientific and epistemological paradigm). This world view includes the scientists' values, beliefs, the nature of society, philosophies of truth and reality, and the best methods to arrive at truth and reality. When scientific research conflicts with and cannot be contained within the current scientific paradigm, a crisis (i.e., a "scientific revolution") occurs and the current, dominant scientific paradigm is modified to deal with new facts in order to provide a framework that can account for the identified uncharacteristic phenomena. Inevitably, a new paradigm competes with the older paradigm for adoption and acceptance as a world view.

As discussed in the previous section regarding the presumed causes of disability and marginalization, each field (focus area) reflected in the text is undergoing a "scientific revolution" or a paradigm shift, not only in reference to the presumed cause of one's disability but also in regard to how science approaches the issues of disability and disenfranchisement. Depending on the focus area, people involved are experiencing the scientific revolution and resulting paradigm somewhere along a four-stage continuum: (a) doubts and difficulties within the current (or historical) explanation or paradigm, (b) the rejection of the current paradigm, (c) the presence of a paradigm conflict, or (d) the acceptance of a new paradigm or explanation.

As discussed in detail by Rioux (1997), how disability and marginalization are perceived is related to one's assumptions about social and scientific responsibility toward such individuals. Therefore, it is important to examine the scientific conceptions of disability that underpin the various research agenda and the ways of knowing disability. In this regard, Rioux proposes four social and scientific conceptions (i.e., models) of disability: biomedical, functional, environmental, and rights-outcome.

Biomedical Model

The biomedical model conceives of disability as a result of a disease process in which the condition itself becomes the focus of attention. The goal of the professional or the researcher is to reduce the prevalence of the disorder through biological or genetic interventions or screening and also treat or cure the biological condition through medical and technological means. There is less emphasis on the role that society has in limiting and enabling people with disability. One's social responsibility is to eliminate or cure the biologically based condition.

Functional Model

This model also conceives of disability as the result of an individual pathological state. The goal of the professional or researcher is to ameliorate the condition through a variety of rehabilitative services so that the person can develop his or her potential and become as socially functional as possible. One's social responsibility is to ameliorate and provide comfort.

Both the biomedical and functional models are based on paradigms that focus on disability as a result of individual pathology that resides in the person. Both also have a number of common characteristics (Rioux, 1997), including: disability is approached as a field of professional expertise; a positivist paradigm is used; primary prevention is emphasized; disability is characterized as incapacity in relation to nondisabled people; disability is viewed as an anomaly and social burden, including costs; the inclusion of people with disabilities is seen as a private responsibility; the unit of analysis is the individual; and the point of intervention is the individual condition.

Environmental Model

The environmental model conceives that along with personal limitations, the interaction between the person and the environment can exacerbate as well as improve the impact of the condition on the individual. As we saw with the ecological model in the previous section, disabling conditions are the result of increased structural social pathology due to service arrangements and environmental factors. The model assumes further that the disability can be prevented or lessened through the elimination of social and economic physical barriers, and that one's social responsibility is to eliminate systemic barriers.

Rights-Outcome Model
This fourth model is based on the belief that disability is a function of how society is organized and the relationship of the marginalized and/or disenfranchised person to the total society that may prevent people from participating in society with equal civil and social rights. Disability issues are civil rights issues. Thus the treatment of disability is through reformulation of economic and social policy that can ameliorate the effects of the disabling condition. One's social responsibility is to advocate for and provide political and social entitlements.

The environmental and rights-outcome models are based on paradigms that focus on disability as a result of social pathology inherent to the social structure. These two models have common characteristics (Rioux, 1997), including: disability is assumed to be not inherent in the individual but dependent on the social structure; priority is given to the political, social, and current environment; secondary rather than primary prevention is emphasized; disability is recognized as difference rather than as an deficiency; disability is viewed as the interaction of the individual with society; inclusion of people with disabilities is seen as a public responsibility; the unit of analysis is the social structure; and the points of intervention are the social, environmental, and economic systems.

In conclusion, the reader will note the definite parallels between the emerging changes in the presumed cause for disability and the scientific paradigm or models of disability. Although none of the text's focus areas has accepted completely a new presumed cause of disability or marginalization or a new scientific paradigm that can be used to approach disability and disenfranchisement, the world is changing toward an ecological model of disability that explains the presumed cause of disability and toward a rights-model paradigm to study its amelioration and the enhancement of a person's subjective well-being and quality of life. How society can aid in those efforts through specific societal-level action steps is discussed next.

Societal-Level Action Steps

Based on the above discussion and our reading of the international QOL literature, we suggest four societal-level action steps that hold the most promise of enhancing the well-being of a population and thereby increasing perceived and real quality of life: (a) nations adopting QOL-related policies, (b) communities implementing quality enhancement techniques, (c) citizenry collaborating for change, and (d) researchers providing information and evidence that well-being has been enhanced and collaboration for change has occurred.

Nations Adopting Quality-of-Life-Related Policies

There are currently more than 40 worldwide treaties or conventions of human rights that address people with disabilities and other special needs. Examples include the 1971 United Nations Declaration on the Rights of Mentally Retarded Persons, the 1975 United Nations Declaration on the Rights of Disabled Persons, and the 1976 International Covenant on Civil and Political Rights. The 1990s witnessed a major initiative by the international community to increase the legal status and enhance the situation of citizens with disabilities and other special needs. Reflective of this initiative, the United Nations General Assembly adopted in 1993 the *United Nations Standard Rules on the Equalization of Opportunities for Persons with Disabilities.* Eight of the 22 rules can be considered "enabler standards" that deal with issues such as international cooperation (technical and economic), information and research, policymaking and planning, coordination of work, personnel training, and monitoring and evaluation. Significantly, the 14 "outcome standards" relate to the *Handbook's* eight core QOL domains:

- emotional well-being: reflected in the rule regarding religion
- interpersonal relations: reflected in rules relating to family life and personal integrity
- material well-being: employment, income maintenance, and social services
- personal development: education and rehabilitation
- physical well-being: medical care and recreation and sports
- self-determination: self-advocacy organizations
- social inclusion: support services
- rights: awareness raising, accessibility, equal rights to participate

An analogous initiative was the European Union's social policy about people with disabilities, which was initiated in 1974 and focused on vocational rehabilitation issues. In the 1980s there were numerous legal documents and guidelines published related to education, employment, social integration, and transport. By the end of the 1980s and in the 1990s the Program Helios and The Community Initiative Horizon facilitated development of objectives targeting people with special needs: cooperation and interchange among member states relating to economic and social integration, equality of opportunities, and independent living.

In 1996 the European Commission adopted the *Communication on Equality of Opportunity for People with Disabilities*, which defines the strategy of the European Union according to international trends. The communication proposes an approach based on ideas of equality of opportunities, nondiscrimination, rights, normalization, inclusion, and full participation, and it endorses the *United Nations Standard Rules on Equalization of Opportunities for Persons with Disabilities* (1993). Each state must draw up plans to review national policies according to these ideas, and the European Union (EU) has already started to do so. All these ideas connect EU directly with QOL concepts and domains discussed in this *Handbook*.

What principles might be used to guide nations to adopt QOL-related policies? Current work from two programs in the United States provides helpful parameters. The first is a project at the Beach Center for Families and Disabilities (Turnbull & Stowe, 2001) that has analyzed the core concepts in disability policy in the United States. These concepts, listed in Table 14.1, provide helpful guidelines for societies interested in passing legislation, implementing public policy, and creating change at the societal and community level. The second example is based on the sociopolitical perspective of self-determination and involves the National Program Office on Self-Determination at the University of New Hamp-

TABLE 14.1
Core Concepts of Disability Policy

Concept	Definition
Antidiscrimination	Generally known as/referred to as "civil rights acts."
Autonomy	Person has the right to consent, refuse consent, withdraw consent, or otherwise control or have choice over what happens to him or her.
Empowerment	Participation and involvement in decision making.
Privacy and confidentiality	Protection against unwarranted interference in decision making that affects private interests. Confidentiality refers to information concerning oneself or one's family; includes access to information, rights of correction, and control over access by others.

(table continues)

TABLE 14.1. *(continued)*

Concept	Definition
Liberty	Person has the right to be free from unwarranted physical or other confinement by a government.
Protection against harm	People have the right to live in safe and secure environments.
Individualized and appropriate services	
Productivity and contribution	Engagement in income-producing work and contributions that benefit a household or community.
Integration	The right not to be segregated, without due process, or to be barred from participation in services that serve people without special needs.
Service coordination and collaboration	
Cultural responsiveness	Services should respond to the beliefs, values, and attitudes of the person or the family's ethnic orientation.
Accountability	Achieving the specified outcomes of services and program-improvement measures.

shire (Nerney, 1998). This initiative is designed to restructure the long-term care system in the United States by moving from a facility-based, highly regulated system to individualized funding arrangements wherein people and their advocates have control over funding and services. Four principles of self-determination are being implemented: (a) the freedom to choose where and with whom to live and how to spend one's time, (b) authority to control the money needed for support with a budget that moves with the person, (c) support that is organized in highly individualized ways according to the person's needs and desires, and (d) responsibility for the wise use of public funding and for contributing to one's community. A recent independent evaluation (Nerney) of this approach found greatly enhanced quality of life among participants and reduced service costs.

Communities Implementing Quality Enhancement Techniques
The societal-level application of the QOL concept requires communities to implement quality enhancement techniques that focus on environmental factors related to a life of quality. The application of these techniques rests on the demonstration that: (a) an enhanced quality of life is the result of a good match between a person's wants or needs and their fulfillment, and reducing the barriers between a person and the environment increases the person's assessed quality of life; (b) it is possible to assess the match between people and environments; and (c) the higher the imbalance, the greater the person's support needs.

Environmentally based enhancement techniques involve designing environments that are user friendly and reduce the mismatch between individuals and their environmental requirements. Examples include: wheelchair accessible sidewalks and buildings; Braille signage in public buildings; opportunity for community involvement; easy access to outdoor environments; modifications to stairs, water taps, doorknobs; safety (e.g., handrails, safety glass, nonslip walking surfaces); convenience (e.g., orientation aids such as color coding or universal pictographs); accessibility to home and community; sensory stimulation (e.g., windows, less formal furniture); prosthetics (e.g., personal computers, specialized assistive devices, and high technological environments); and opportunity for choice and control (e.g., lights, temperature, privacy, and personal space). Additional examples include: building codes, principles of barrier-free design, adapted curricula, policy and funding commitments targeted to specific barrier resolutions.

Citizenry Collaborating for Change
The action steps related to nations adopting QOL-related policies and communities implementing quality enhancement techniques will not be taken unless citizens collaborate at the societal level. A recent history of the innovative development of community-based programs in the state of Nebraska, for example (Schalock, 2002), describes three key roles involved in significant social and organizational change: the visionary or theoretician, the organizer, and one or more promoters who implement the change. In addition, successful social and organizational change is culture-specific and directed at specific targets. Understanding each of these two concepts will assist a nation's citizenry in collaborating for change at the societal level.

Culture Specific

As reflected throughout this text, people live in a number of systems that influence the development of their values, beliefs, behavior, and attitudes. Even though different value orientations and value emphases in various cultures account for both philosophical and psychological dimensions and differences, the literature reviewed in this text indicates that many countries are currently realizing that people with disabilities and special needs can become productive members of society and live successfully within more normalized community-based environments. Past policies of segregation, isolation, and protective approaches to service provision are giving way to increased opportunities for inclusion and integration. Similarly, successful efforts to provide those opportunities and document successful efforts to enhance quality of life are appearing in the literature (Keith & Schalock, 2000). Thus one aspect of collaborating for change at the societal level is to acknowledge this universal movement and at the same time focus on culture-specific ways the changes are occurring.

Specific Targets

There is probably no end to the list of changes that readers would make in how their respective societies view people with special needs and the societal changes that need to occur for these individuals to experience an enhanced quality of life. Movements such as the inclusion of marginalized people into the mainstream of society occur within a social and cultural context that varies widely from place to place. Schalock and Kelly (1999) identified cross-culturally some of the more important contextual variables influencing the development of integrated employment and community living programs for people with disabilities. The study was influenced by the earlier work of Gaylord-Ross (1987), who identified five contextual variables that influenced the development of integrated employment in Europe: political will (as reflected in public policy), charismatic leaders, model demonstration programs, instructional technology, and the economic state of the country.

The 1999 study included 172 people working actively in the field of intellectual disabilities or mental retardation in the following countries: Canada, England, Japan, the Netherlands, Poland, the Republic of China, and the United States. Each respondent indicated the degree to which each of a number of factors contributed (positively or negatively) to the development of either integrated employment or living services and options. Across respondents and geographical regions, nine contextual variables were identified as influencing positively and significantly the development of community-based options for people. These variables and their descriptions can provide the focus and direction for citizens advocating for change at the societal level. The nine variables were (a) public policies — laws or regulations related to integration, mainstreaming, normalization, deinstitutionalization, quota systems, affirmative action; (b) funding tied to public policies — consistency between the policy and the actual money spent on policy-targeted services; (c) coalitions — business, unions, politicians, families, self-advocates, professionals; (d) technology — systematic instruction, adaptive devices, applied behavior analysis, task analysis; (e) academic or professional supports — medical and rehabilitation personnel, teachers, psychologists, social workers; (f) teaching or rehabilitation staff — direct service workers, job coaches, care providers; (g) research and development — model programs, program evaluation, association with universities and colleges; (h) political movements — trade unions, charismatic leaders, social welfare campaigns, leadership; and (i) attitudes toward people with disability — normalcy, potential, person-centered, capable, risk taking, labels, status, historical attitudes.

Researchers Providing Information and Evidence
Evaluating the impact of the three societal-level action steps discussed thus far (i.e., nations adopting QOL-related policies, communities implementing quality enhancement techniques, and citizenry collaborating for change) will not be easy without a clear focus for researchers and evaluators to provide information and evidence that societal-level actions can make a difference in the subjective well-being and quality of life of people with special needs. For example, Fujiura (2000) suggests that three features are central to the analysis of public policy and/or societal-level action steps: (a) the provision of information relevant to agenda setting, decision making, and advocacy; (b) a focus on choices in the public domain where alternatives typically represent competition of limited economic (and public) resources; and (c) the incorporation of values. In addition, there is a need to use methodological pluralism in the data gathering and analysis stages (Schalock, 2001). The following five process steps and evaluation guidelines will, we hope, allow researchers and evaluators to determine the impact of the three societal-level action steps just discussed on the lives of people reflected in the text's focus areas.

Process Steps
The first step is key: Describe the intent of the societal-level action step and its context. It is important to understand both the person- and societal-referenced goals of the policy or action step, for these goals become the basis of the information and evidence. One also needs to understand the context of the evaluation, for the context of the policy or action step will definitely affect how one approaches the evaluation.

The second step involves analyzing the anticipated outcomes of the policy or action step. This may be more difficult than it sounds, for frequently public policy and societal actions focus more on process than outcomes. Because of this, over the past 30 years there has been a series of public management reforms that have attempted to improve the outcomes of education and human service programs and thereby enhance the programs' accountability. Examples include management by objectives, zero-based budgeting, reinventing government, and, most recently, the Government Performance and Results Act (Wholey, 1997). The reform movement's impact on evaluating public policy from a QOL-outcomes perspective is just beginning to emerge (Schalock, 2001).

The third process step involves aggregating the stated goals into the respective cells of the program evaluation model presented in the previous chapter (Figure 13.1). By way of review, the model has three components: evaluation focus (the individual or the organization), evaluative standards (performance measurement or value assessment), and outcome indicators (organizational performance or value outcomes; individual performance or value outcomes). Generally, this aggregation will show that most anticipated outcomes from public policy fall into the individual performance or value cells of the model.

The fourth process step involves evaluating the status of the anticipated outcomes at either the individual or societal level. At the individual level, this step incorporates methodological pluralism and can include any of the data sets or indicators listed in Table 9.2 and measured via one or more of the techniques discussed in chapter 11: personal appraisal, functional assessment, and/or social indicators. At the societal level, data sets such as social or national indicators can be aggregated across large numbers of individuals and programs. These data sets can be obtained via a number of techniques including national surveys, national data sets, and meta-analyses.

The fifth process step involves providing formative feedback to policy stakeholders. This process step should "feed back" to influence the other steps of the public policy process: agenda building, policy formulation, policy adoption, and policy implementation. This feedback should also focus on: how well the policy and procedures are doing from the multiple perspectives identified; barriers identified from the level of the person, program, or society; potential use of the information for policy change; and the key components of a "policy system" that links three components — socioeconomic system (with its associated social and economic conditions), the political system (with its institutions, processes, and behaviors), and public policies (e.g., education, health care, and social service policies).

Evaluation Guidelines

Our collective experiences over the past two decades suggest a number of factors that explain why QOL-oriented policy evaluation is not easy and is still an "emerging science." First, the evaluation is complicated frequently by the lack of clearly stated goals and anticipated objective, person- and organization-referenced outcomes. This difficulty is currently compounded by a lack of clearly articulated QOL-oriented public policies and practices throughout the world. Second, any group of stakeholders does not just represent a heterogeneous constituency with varying goals and agenda but also frequently comes in and out of the picture in various degrees of influence. Third, any given policy or societal action is not static and varies across time in its public and political agenda, adaptation, implementation, and enforcement. Currently quality of life is popular among consumers and professionals but less evident in public-societal policies. Fourth, there is still a lack of standardized data across programs for many public policies and societal actions that makes their evaluation challenging. And fifth, evaluation potentially involves a number of key stakeholders, data sets, and evaluation techniques.

Because of these factors, we suggest five guidelines to keep in mind as we anticipate an increase in QOL-oriented public policies and societal-level actions and evaluations.

1. Evaluation should identify the values that underlie the policy being evaluated. These values can be the basis of determining the fidelity of the policy to its intended purpose and outcomes (see Table 14.1). An analogous values-analysis approach has been applied to policies and societal-level actions and their underlying values in general education, special education, human and social services, and vocational rehabilitation (Chambers, 1994). The values identified can relate to whether a policy's underlying purpose relates to human development (e.g., prevention and intervention in child maltreatment or nondiscriminatory access to health care), to bureaucratic efficiency, or to justice as street-level case managers define it. Intended outcomes can then be evaluated within this context.

2. Evaluation and evidence gathering need to move beyond a "positivist" approach, wherein one assumes that one can best comprehend and evaluate the policy or action by trying to be exclusively objective. One needs to recognize that the analyst always makes sense of the world through theories and that a theoretical or conceptual framework is essential to securing an analysis that combines scientific elegance with social policy (Schorr, 1997). Thus one needs to move to the "postpositivist" approach to evaluation and approach public policy as seeking to understand how webs of beliefs, desires, attitudes, and the histories of people who have experienced the effects of policies create a new context for the evaluation.

3. Evaluation and evidence gathering should also determine the constraints on and the resources available for meeting goals and objectives. This involves implementation research, which recognizes that policy and societal-level actions are the result of the interaction of values, the providers who implement policies, and the policy recipients. For example, policy and its implementation is affected by politics and the struggle over ideas that occurs in political communities (Stone, 1997). Thus each policy is a collection of arguments in favor of

different ways of seeing the world. Additionally, any policy and its implementation changes as street-level providers and recipients implement it.

4. No single factor influences policy or societal-level action more than any other. Some factors may be "in play" and others may not be, depending on the particular policy considered. And each in-play factor is influenced by the others. Moreover, some policies or actions that potentially affect people may or may not be funded; and still others may seem to have no clear or immediate relationship to individuals, only to become important later.

5. Significant attention needs to be devoted to the following obstacles to information and information-gathering efforts (Nagel, 1990): multiple dimensions on multiple goals, multiple missing information, multiple alternatives that preclude the determination of the effects of each one, multiple and possibly conflicting constraints, and the need for simplicity in drawing and presenting conclusions in spite of all the multiplicity. Techniques, strategies, and methods for overcoming these obstacles represent a significant 21st-century agenda for our work in the societal-level application of the QOL concept.

Conclusion

The societal-level application of the QOL concept is multifaceted. On the one hand, it builds on and is significantly impacted by factors associated with the individual- and program-referenced techniques discussed in chapters 12 and 13. It is a complex interaction among people, programs, and public policies propagated at the societal level. In addition, multicultural differences thrive within any society, which makes analysis and generalizations difficult, in large part because of the two contextual issues discussed earlier. Despite such complexity, the QOL concept is alive and well throughout the world and is reflected in (a) a vision of what constitutes the life possibility of people; (b) a new way of thinking about people that focuses on the person, the environmental variables that influence one's functioning, and the feasibility of change at both the individual and societal levels; (c) the current paradigm shift in education, health care, and social services that emphasizes inclusion, equity, empowerment, and community-based supports; (d) the quality revolution, with its emphasis on quality management and valued person-referenced outcomes; and (e) the evidence indicating that people can be more independent, productive, integrated in the community, and satisfied when education, health care, and habilitation services and supports are based on QOL-oriented policies and procedures.

Societies can do much to enhance the well-being of their citizenry. However, it is becoming increasingly apparent that rights legislation is a necessary, but not sufficient, condition for people with special needs to enjoy full acceptance by their communities (Parmenter, 2001). Reinders (2000), for example, argues that the moral language of rights is neither sufficient nor necessary to ground moral responsibility for people reflected in the text's focus areas. He suggests that to claim equal rights for the disabled and other marginalized groups makes sense only on the basis of commitments that draw on other moral sources than the sources that are intrinsic to the morality of rights. His essential argument is that the contemporary rights discourse is deficient in accounting for the moral features of caring practices — practices that are committed to the well-being of people who are dependent on the support of others. This need for each of us to foster a true sense of community is discussed in depth by Rapley (2000) and expressed well by Nirje (1985), who noted, "Laws and legislative work cannot provide total answers to problem solving and proper actions with regards to realization of human rights. These can only come into existence in the full cultural and human context. Such problems are not only practical, but also ethical" (p. 65).

In conclusion, we are seeing throughout most of the world nations adopting QOL-related policies, communities implementing quality enhancement techniques, citizenry collaborating for change at the societal level, and researchers beginning to provide information and evidence that QOL-oriented principles and practices have a positive impact on people's lives and sense of well-being. But in regard to the QOL movement, we have just begun, and the future is passing quickly. So we conclude the text with a chapter that reflects our best hopes and anticipated outcomes for the future that the Spanish philosopher Gasset reminds us is the preoccupation of all humans.

CHAPTER 15

Putting It All Together and Moving Ahead

A *Handbook on Quality of Life for Human Service Practitioners* should be useful to a wide range of constituents. This "heterogeneous constituency" includes consumers, advocates, educators, practitioners, program administrators, policymakers, and researchers. Our intent throughout this text has been to provide concepts, ideas, and information that will be of value to all of these constituencies. Now it is time to "put it all together and move ahead." We have three primary goals in this final chapter: first, to summarize and integrate the literature reviewed along with the principles, models, and application strategies discussed throughout the text so the reader will have a "handbook" that is truly usable, viable, and helpful; second, to discuss a number of challenges and opportunities for the field; and third, to outline a future quality of life (QOL) agenda.

Putting It All Together

Throughout the text we have summarized considerable literature regarding the concept of quality of life and have presented principles, models, and QOL-referenced themes related to the text's focus areas: education and special education, physical health, mental and behavioral health, mental retardation and intellectual disabilities, aging, and families. We hope that the reader has been impressed with the considerable international work that has been done regarding the QOL concept. Although our full understanding of the concept and its implementation is still in its infancy, we now understand better its conceptualization, measurement, and application. This section of the chapter summarizes those QOL-referenced principles, core domains and indicators, and models presented throughout the text.

Core Principles

Throughout the text, reference has been made to a series of principles developed by the IASSID Special Interest Research Group on Quality of Life (Schalock et al., in press) regarding the conceptualization, measurement, and application of the QOL concept. These principles, summarized in Table 15.1, have been developed with significant input from the international community and reflect our best conceptualization of quality of life and the best practices regarding its measurement and application.

TABLE 15.1
Quality of Life Conceptualization, Measurement, and Application Principles

Conceptualization Principles

Quality of life:

1. is composed of the same factors and relationships for all people
2. is experienced when a person's needs are met and when one has the opportunity to pursue life enrichment in major life settings
3. has both subjective and objective components; but it is primarily the perception of the individual that reflects the quality of life he or she experiences
4. is based on individual needs, choices, and control
5. is a multidimensional construct, influenced by individual and environmental or contextual factors

Measurement Principles

Quality of life measurement:

1. assesses the degree to which people have meaningful life experiences that they value
2. enables people to move toward a meaningful life they enjoy and value
3. assesses the degree to which life's domains contribute to a full and interconnected life
4. is undertaken within the context of environments that are important to people: where they live, work, and play
5. is based on both common human experiences and unique, individual life experiences

(table continues)

TABLE 15.1. *(continued)*

Application Principles

Quality of life application should:

1. enhance a person's well-being
2. be applied in light of the individual's cultural and ethnic heritage
3. collaborate for change at the personal, program, community, and national levels
4. enhance the degree of personal control and individual opportunity exerted by the individual in relation to their activities, interventions, and environments
5. occupy a prominent role in gathering evidence, especially in identifying the significant predictors of a life of quality and the impact of targeting resources to maximize positive effects

Core Quality of Life Domains and Indicators

The eight core QOL domains used as an organizing framework for the text were developed originally on the basis of the extensive literature reviews and meta-analyses conducted by Hughes and Hwang (1996) and Schalock (1996b). These eight domains were generally confirmed in the extensive international QOL literature reviewed in chapters 3 through 7. A significant contribution of that review of the literature from 1985 to 1999 was the identification of core indicators for all eight domains for all the text's focus areas (see Table 9.1).

Two aspects of the synthesis reported in chapter 9 are important to repeat here. The first relates to the relative importance given in the literature to the eight domains. As discussed in chapter 9, an average ranking was obtained for each domain, collapsing across the focus area, with a smaller mean ranking corresponding to higher number of references in the literature reviewed. Independent of focus area, mean rankings are summarized in Table 15.2. Note that these rankings are based on the 1985 the 1999 published literature, and they may change as we see more emphasis being devoted to domains such as self-determination and rights. The second important aspect of the synthesis relates to the most commonly referenced indicators for each core domain. Again, collapsing across the text's focus areas, the three most common indicators mentioned in the literature for the eight core domains are summarized in Table 15.3.

Conceptualization, Measurement, and Application Models

Throughout the text we have provided models that both integrate what we currently know about various aspects of the QOL concept and provide heuristic models for future research, application, and evaluation. Here we summarize

TABLE 15.2
Core Quality of Life Domain Average (Mean) Rankings

Domain	M
Physical well-being	2.6
Emotional well-being	2.8
Interpersonal relations	3.0
Social inclusion	3.4
Personal development	4.2
Material well-being	5.8
Self-determination	6.6
Rights	7.6

Note. Ranked from most (1) to least (8) frequently found in the literature.

briefly the nine models previously presented and discussed.

- *An ecological approach to the analysis of QOL indicators* (see Figure 2.1). This model allows one to determine and/or measure core indicators for each core QOL domain and for each systems level of analysis. For the microsystem, we suggest personal appraisal as the best approach to measurement; for the mesosystem, functional assessment; and for the macrosystem, social indicators.

- *Heuristic model: QOL measurement, application, and evaluation* (see Figure 2.2). Our generic QOL model integrates the eight core domains with the systems perspective (micro, meso, and macro) and the measurement, application, and evaluation of one's perceived quality of life.

- *Comparison of person- and family-centered QOL domains* (see Figure 8.1) and *an individual and family outcomes-focused evaluation model* (see Figure 8.2). These two models summarize our current understanding of and approach to family-centered quality of life and the potential integration of the areas of person-centered and family-centered quality of life.

- *Generic approach to QOL measurement* (see Figure 11.1) and *QOL measurement model* (see Figure 11.2). These two models help the reader better understand our suggested approach to the measurement of the QOL construct. Specifically, the approach we suggest is that objective indicators be identified for each core domain across each systems level (i.e., micro, meso, and macro), and then one or more measurement techniques (i.e., personal appraisal, functional assessment, and/or social indicators) be used to assess each core QOL domain.

- *An ecological model of quality enhancement* (see Figure 12.1). This heuristic model matrices generic quality enhancement techniques to each of the eight core QOL domains. It suggests that at the microsystem level, the focus should be on personal growth and development opportunities; at the mesosystem, program or environmental-referenced quality enhancement techniques; and at the macrosystem level, social policies.
- *Quality of life hierarchy* (see Figure 12.2). This figure shows from a motivational perspective the potential relationship among the eight core QOL domains and the key roles played in human behavior by self-determination, locus of control, self-efficacy, and outcome expectancy.
- *Outcome-based evaluation model* (see Figure 13.1). This model was developed and validated to address the increasing need that education, health care, and social service programs are experiencing in their evaluation of both person-referenced value outcomes and a program or service's effectiveness and efficiency (i.e., accountability). This response to the reform movement's accountability and value dimensions allows researchers and evaluators to focus on either person- or program-referenced performance and value outcomes.

TABLE 15.3
Most Commonly Used Core Indicators per Core Quality of Life Domain

Domain	Indicators
1. Physical well-being	Health status Activities of daily living Leisure
2. Emotional well-being	Contentment Self-concept Freedom from stress
3. Interpersonal relations	Interactions Relationships Supports
4. Social Inclusion	Community integration and participation Community roles Social supports

(table continues)

TABLE 15.3. *(continued)*

Domain	Indicators
5. Personal development	Education Personal competence Performance
6. Material well-being	Financial status Employment Housing
7. Self-determination	Autonomy/personal control Goals and personal values Choices
8. Rights	Human (respect, dignity, equality) Legal (citizenship, access, due process)

General Statements about the Literature Reviewed

As discussed previously, we found 20,900 articles and book chapters published between 1985 and December 1999 with the term *quality of life* in their titles. Of that number, 9,749 abstracts were obtained and read, with 2,455 full articles or book chapters selected and read that met four criteria: (a) there were multiple references in the text; (b) the text was empirically based, employing a reasonable number of participants; (c) the text related to the conceptualization, measurement, or application of the QOL concept; and (d) the text related to one or more of the focus areas of this handbook. Of these 2,455 articles or book chapters, only 897 were used as the basis for the literature reviewed in chapters 3 through 7 and synthesized in chapter 9, because only these texts specified particular QOL domains and/or indicators. Three general statements can be made about the QOL literature reviewed in these articles: (a) there is very little reference to the rights domain; (b) there is currently little emphasis in education (including special education) on the QOL concept; and (c) there is a lack of family-centered QOL literature. A discussion of these observations follows.

Little Reference to Rights

Reference to rights of service recipients is found mainly in the literature on mental retardation and intellectual disabilities and on aging. Our belief is that two reasons might account for the lack of attention to this domain in the text's other focus areas. First, there is a "professional culture" in many countries wherein researchers do not identify rights with behavior, while in education, mental health, and health, the person is placed into a passive role of "student or patient" whose welfare is controlled by professionals or educators. Second, throughout much of the world there is a "social perception" that suggests that rights are less important than curriculum or treatment.

As one looks at the more recent literature, however, change is occurring. Specifically, we are beginning to see (a) the passage of public laws addressing the rights of people and reflected in civil rights and antidiscrimination movements throughout the world; (b) the emergence of self-advocacy movements in mental and behavioral health and in physical health that focus on self-determination, self-efficacy, and patients' rights; and (c) the use of the ecological (person and environment) perspective in diagnosis, terminology, and classification systems.

Little Emphasis on Quality of Life in Education

In addition to the "professional culture" mentioned above in which the student's role is viewed as passive in the educational process, there is also currently a strong emphasis on reforms that elevate curriculum issues to the main focus of one's educational experience (Hegarty, 1994). When quality is incorporated into education, it has generally been related to the evaluation of the objective work of the schools, the educational system, and/or students' performance, but not the student's quality of life. Thus students today are caught between a "quality education culture" and an "accountability education culture." We suggest the need to balance performance and value outcomes for students in education and special education and to focus on individual value outcomes such as those shown in cell D of Figure 13.1: emotional well-being, personal development, self-determination, interpersonal relations, social inclusion, and rights. In addition, there is an urgent need to work on conceptualizing the QOL construct in the areas of infancy and early childhood.

This need is reflected in the recent paradigm shift in education to equity, inclusive education, the transition services requirements by Individuals with Disabilities Education Act (IDEA) in the United States, as well as the current literature on "best practices," especially in the fields of mental retardation and severe disabilities. These shifts reflect an increased effort in program planning based on the QOL concept as exemplified in (a) leisure education programs for youth with mental retardation (Dattilo & Hope, 1999); (b) the Choosing Options and Accommodations for Children (COACH) system developed by Giangreco, Cloninger, and Iverson (1993), which identifies "valued life outcomes" and includes family members, professionals, and students with disabilities to assess and plan a student's individualized educational program; (c) the positive behavioral support approach suggested by Janney and Snell (2000), which is a team approach that targets not only increasing a student's behavior and social-communication skills but also the student's overall quality of life, including relationships, health, and autonomy; and (d) the emphasis in recent textbooks on the need to include "quality enhancers" in students' individual educational programs (Snell & Brown, 2000; Westling & Fox, 2000).

Lack of Family-Centered Quality of Life Research
Historically families of people with special needs have been seen as service recipients and part of the "social services system." They have traditionally played a very passive and powerless role, and in most countries have been seen as — and expected to be — appreciative of any supports or services they received. Two additional phenomena might well account for this lack of family-centered research on family quality of life. First, there has been in many countries a perception that has led to an attribution of "social guilt," as if somehow the family is bad or less because of the disabled child or family member. Second, even in the emerging parent or family rights movement, the focus is frequently on asking for help for the child or family member, with the corresponding belief that if the person's (i.e., patient's) condition can be cured, the problem will go away. Again, the focus is frequently on care, treatment, and the fulfillment of basic needs.

We are beginning to see change as reflected in the literature summarized in chapter 8 on family-centered quality of life and the emergence of a strong family advocacy movement in which families are asking for services, opportunities, and respect (Blacher, 2001; Magana, 2000). In reference to Figure 13.1, the historical emphasis with families has been on cell C (physical and material well-being); now the emphasis is beginning to shift to cell D, with a focus on family-value outcomes. It is also important to point out that the current family advocacy movement has strong parallels with the movements of the 1960s and 1970s in the areas of mental retardation and intellectual disabilities and special education as well as the 1980s and 1990s in the areas of mental and behavioral health and aging.

Challenges and Opportunities

No one group owns the concept of quality of life. Whether it is viewed as a sensitizing notion, social construct, or unifying theme, the concept is affecting thinking and service delivery across the world. The intent of this section of the chapter is to respond to the needs of the heterogeneous constituency, including consumers, advocates, educators, practitioners, program administrators, policymakers, and researchers or evaluators, by discussing four challenges and opportunities that collectively we face to (a) integrate the emerging areas of self-determination and self-advocacy, subjective well-being, self-efficacy and intrinsic motivation, and positive psychology into the QOL field; (b) apply the QOL concept to nondeveloped countries; (c) use the QOL concept as a tool for organization and systems change; and (d) embrace a holistic approach to QOL research.

Integrate Emerging Areas into the Quality of Life Field
Recent work in four social science areas has the potential to merge with the larger QOL movement: self-determination and self-advocacy; subjective well-being; self-efficacy and intrinsic motivation; and positive psychology. Common themes among these areas are person-centeredness, the positive potential of people, and the need to focus on and support personal competence and psychological well-being across the life span. As described by Ryan and Deci (2000):

> The fullest representations of humanity show people to be curious, vital, and self-motivated. At their best, they are agentic and inspired, striving to learn; extend themselves; master new skills; and apply their talents responsibly. That most people show considerable effort, agency, and commitment in their lives appears, in fact, to be more normative than exceptional, suggesting some very positive and persistent features of human nature. (p. 68)

The QOL concept is very consistent with this notion and can thereby provide the overarching and integration principle to foster positive human potential through the organizational change strategies and holistic approach to QOL research discussed in subsequent sections. Before addressing those suggested strategies and approaches, however, we give a brief overview of current research and application efforts in the areas of self-determination and self-advocacy, subjective well-being, self-efficacy and intrinsic motivation, and positive psychology.

Self-Determination and Self-Advocacy
Research guided by self-determination theory has focused on the personal and sociocultural conditions that facilitate the natural processes of self-motivation and enhanced intrinsic motivation, self-regulation, and well-being. This research has produced three significant results: (a) the successful satisfaction of an individual's competence, autonomy, and relatedness motives yield enhanced self-motivation, constructive social development, and personal well-being (Ryan & Deci, 2000); (b) there is a positive and significant correlation between assessed levels of self-determination and quality of life (Wehmeyer & Schalock, 2001); (c) self-determination is not the same as personal control.

Self-determined behavior refers to actions that are identified by four essential characteristics: (a) the person acts autonomously; (b) the action(s) was self-regulated; (c) the person initiated and responded to the event in a "psychologically empowered manner" reflective of personal efficacy and internal locus of control; and (d) the person acted in a self-realizing manner. However, a full understanding of self-determination involves more than just these components; rather one must explore individuals' self-determination and those aspects of the environment that support or act as barriers to personal control. According to Stancliffe, Abery, and Smith (2000), *self-determination* involves a person having the degree of control over his life that he desires in those areas that he values and over which he wishes to exercise control, whereas *personal control* refers to the absolute levels of that individual's exercise over what happens to him in his life, when and where it occurs, and with whom it takes place. Through a series of studies Stancliffe et al. (Stancliffe, Abery, & Smith, 2000; Stancliffe, Abery, Springborg, & Elkin, 2000) have found that increased personal control is related to:

- measured self-determination skills (e.g., choice making, goal setting, problem solving, self-regulation, personal advocacy, social and communication skills, and core living skills)
- measured self-determination knowledge (e.g., resources and the system, laws, rights and responsibilities, perceived options, and self-awareness)
- measured self-determination attitudes and beliefs (e.g., locus of control, self-esteem, self-acceptance, self-confidence or self-efficacy, self-determination, and being valued by others)
- policies and practices that support autonomy
- individualization in programming and supports
- money for discretionary spending
- own guardianship

Subjective Well-Being
Subjective well-being refers to people's evaluation of their lives and includes evaluations that are both affective and cognitive. Four separable components of subjective well-being have been identified (Diener, 2000): life satisfaction (i.e., global judgments of one's life), satisfaction with important domains (e.g., work satisfaction), positive affect (i.e., experiencing many pleasant emotions and moods), and low levels of negative affect (i.e., experiencing few unpleasant emotions and moods).

Considerable research involving the predictors of subjective well-being has been spearheaded and integrated by Myers and others (Myers, 2000; Myers & Diener, 1996). These researchers have aggregated data from 916 surveys of 1.1 million people in 45 nations, calibrating subjective well-being on a 0-to-10 scale (where 0 is the low extreme, such as very unhappy or completely dissatisfied with life; 5 is neutral; 10 the high extreme). Across these 1.1 million respondents, the average response was 6.75 (Myers & Diener, 1996). Major generalizations from the survey findings include:

- People are happier than one might expect, and happiness does not appear to depend significantly on external circumstances, since happiness cuts across almost all demographic classifications of age, economic class, race, and education level.
- Predictors of subjective well-being include a combination of personal characteristics and social-cultural factors such as extroversion, meeting intellectual challenges, social belonging and social support, health, religiosity, personal freedom, and being reasonably affluent (although in most nations, the correlation between income and happiness is negligible).

Two concepts are embedded in the research on subjective well-being: happiness and satisfaction. Although these concepts are closely related, the following distinction can be made: Happiness represents one component of satisfaction, and reflects the positive and negative affects of positive or negative emotions and moods. Happiness tends to be more transitory than satisfaction (Helm, 2000). Satisfaction represents the global judgments about one's life, including subdomains such as work or health status. Satisfaction demonstrates a trait-like stability over time (Diener, 2000; Edgerton, 1996).

Self-Efficacy and Intrinsic Motivation

There is an emerging research and application area related to personality and motivation processes and their relationship to quality of life. Three assumptions underlie this work (Schalock, in press): (a) the end states represented by each QOL domain represent desired human conditions and therefore result in incentives that underlie the motivational process; (b) the person-centered nature of the QOL concept and its application promotes an increase in one's internal locus of control, self-regulation, autonomy, self-determination, personal control, and expectancy of success; (c) the ecological nature of QOL enhancement techniques augments the positive effects of mediated learning experiences, thereby increasing one's intrinsic motivation.

The concept of mastery (effectance) motivation suggests that everyone has an intrinsic need to feel competent, which is associated with internal reinforcement, exploration, play, curiosity, and mastery of the environment. Over the years research in this area has helped us understand better the following concepts integral to the motivational aspects of the core QOL domains.

- *self-regulation,* with the associated principles of (a) self-efficacy (i.e., beliefs concerning one's capabilities to organize and implement actions necessary to attain designated levels of performance); and (b) goal setting and values as reasons for task engagement

- *autonomy and self-determination,* which leads to an internal locus of control, increased intrinsic motivation, a sense of competence, and enhanced decision making
- *knowledge acquisition strategies* that involve mediational learning experiences and active problem-solving processes
- *personality traits* in people with mental retardation suggesting that these individuals have (a) lower levels of expectancy of success and mastery motivation than those of normal intellect; (b) higher levels of dependency on a supportive adult, with initial wariness when interacting with strange adults; (c) higher levels of outer-directedness and looking to others for solutions of difficult or ambiguous problems; and (d) higher levels of extrinsic motivation orientation and learned helplessness (Zigler & Bennett-Gates, 1999)

The relationships among each person-centered core QOL domain and potential motivational states are summarized in Table 15.4. As shown and discussed more fully in Schalock (in press), each core QOL domain is associated with a number of motivation constructs currently found in the literature.

Positive Psychology

In a recent special issue of the *American Psychologist* on positive psychology, Seligman and Csikszentmihalyi (2000) state that "a science of positive subjective experience, positive individual traits, and positive institution's promises to improve quality of life and prevent the pathologies that arise when life is barren and meaningless" (p. 5). In a series of articles in that volume, numerous researchers discuss the components of positive psychology: (a) positive experiences as defined by subjective well-being, optimism, happiness, and self-determination; (b) positive personality characteristics such as self-organizing, self-directed, adaptive, and creative; and (c) an ecological perspective that recognizes that people and experiences are embedded in a social context (Seligman & Csikszentmihalyi). Note the significant fact that most of these components are the same as those just discussed regarding self-determination and self-advocacy, subjective well-being, self-efficacy, and intrinsic motivation.

Although still an emerging discipline, positive psychology has a number of objectives that include an increased emphasis on building positive qualities in people; making the lives of all people more productive and fulfilling; identifying and nurturing high talent; adapting what is best in the scientific method to the unique problems that human behavior presents to those who wish to understand it in all its complexity; discovering how to develop buffers against negative events through courage, future-mindedness, optimism, interpersonal skills, faith, work ethic, hope, honesty, perseverance, and the capacity for flow and insight; and emphasiz-

TABLE 15.4
Core Quality of Life Domains and Potential Motivation States

Domain	Motivation State
Emotional well-being	Esteem Honor Tranquillity Order
Interpersonal relations	Relatedness Social contact Family Romance
Material well-being	Status Savings Achievement
Personal development	Competence Goal setting and values Self-actualization Curiosity
Physical well-being	Physiological Exercise
Self-determination	Autonomy Self-actualization Intrinsic motivation Self-efficacy Independence Power
Social inclusion	Love and belonging Idealism Acceptance
Rights	Safety

ing aesthetics that focus on building those factors that allow individuals, communities, and societies to flourish and to live a life more worth living.

Summary

It is interesting that all four areas just discussed started from very different roots and have very different histories. Yet they seem to be moving in the same direction with a focus on positive human potential, positive experiences and behavioral supports, holism, and quality of life. So how might we integrate self-determination and self-advocacy, subjective well-being, self-efficacy and intrinsic motivation, and positive psychology into the QOL field? The model in Figure 15.1 might assist our thinking. As shown, the lowest level of the triangle is the suggested primary focus of the macrosystem, including policymakers and national policy initiatives. The middle level and upper levels concern the mesosystem and microsystem — that is, education and human service programs, and the individual. Methodological considerations regarding the area of quality of life and the field of positive psychology are discussed in a later section.

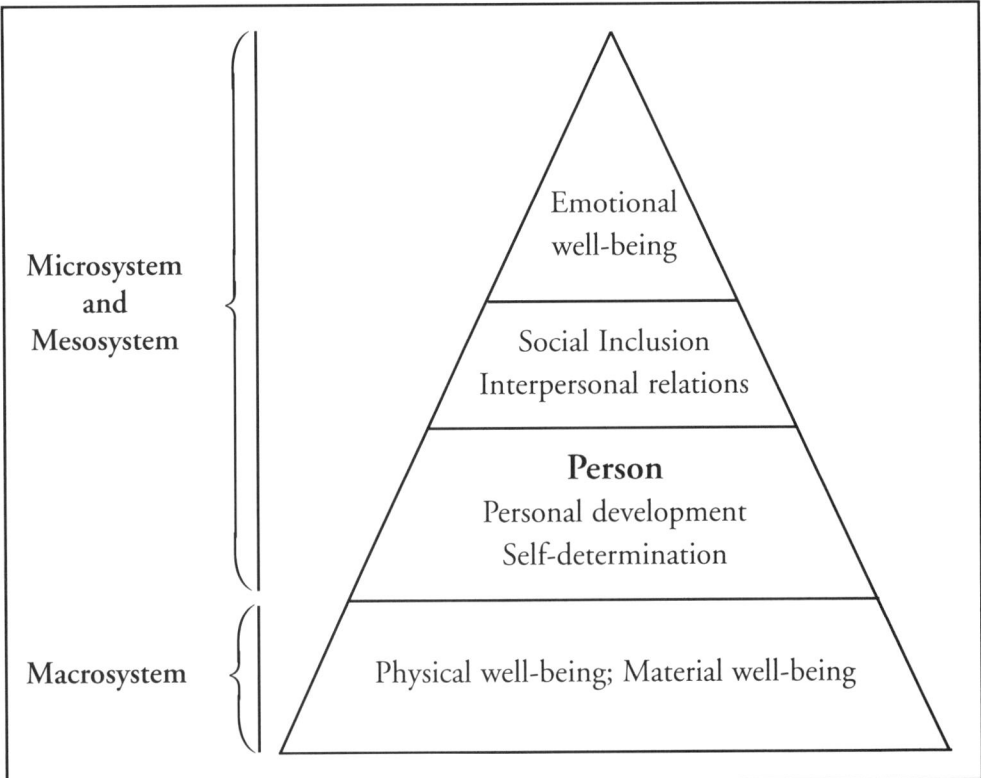

Figure 15.1. A quality of life integration model.

Apply the Quality of Life Concept to Nondeveloped Countries

A quick review of the text's reference section indicates clearly that there has been little published work from nondeveloped countries on quality of life. Although many countries are still focusing on fulfilling the basic human needs of their citizens, the QOL concept is beginning to emerge in these countries as people think beyond the physical necessities of everyday life to the importance of human rights, human growth and development opportunities, and psychological well-being (Keith & Schalock, 2000). The current situation can be explained well in reference to the bottom two cells of Figure 13.1. Although the historical approach in nondeveloped and developing countries is to focus on physical and material well-being (cell C in Figure 13.1), we are beginning to see an emphasis on individual-referenced, value outcomes that involve emotional well-being, personal development, self-determination, interpersonal relations, social inclusion, and rights (cell D).

It is our firm belief that quality of life is very important in all countries. As a social construct and overarching principle, it can be used as a basis for the systems-level action steps summarized in Table 15.5.

TABLE 15.5
Suggested Action Steps for Countries to Apply the Quality of Life Concept

Microsystem	• Encourage and facilitate self-determination.
	• Focus rehabilitation efforts on adaptive behaviors and activities of daily living.
	• Increase a person's valued role status and visibility by providing integrated schools, integrated employment, and community-based living programs.
Mesosystem	• Incorporate quality enhancement techniques into education, health care, and rehabilitation programs.
	• Develop professional and teacher education programs that include a QOL focus and orientation.
	• Evaluate quality outcomes.
Macrosystem	• Implement QOL-oriented policies and national priorities.
	• Evaluate person-referenced QOL outcomes that are that are valued by the individual.

In addition to the action steps suggested in Table 15.5, as we approach the second challenge and opportunity, it is essential that we embark on cross-cultural research in developed and nondeveloped countries to answer a number of questions, including:

- What is the relative importance of each core quality of life domain and core indicator summarized in Table 15.3 within different countries and cultures?
- What is the degree to which each domain and core indicator (Table 15.3) is either used by service providers or experienced by service recipients?
- Why does the QOL concept "play out" better in some countries than in others? Is it an issue of the "haves" versus the "have nots"; of collectivism versus independence; or a different emphasis on autonomy and individual liberty versus liberty, fraternity, or equality?
- What are the cultural adaptations of the QOL concept? For example, some language-based cross-cultural studies have confirmed the factor structure of the Quality of Life Questionnaire (Kober & Eggelton, 2000; Rapley & Lobley, 1995; Schalock & Keith, 1993), but some have found difficulty with the community integration or satisfaction subscales (Kober & Eggelton, 2002; Verdugo, Caballo, Pelaez, & Prieto, in press).
- Which cultural factors facilitate the application of the QOL concept, and which factor(s) inhibit or preclude its cultural acceptance and inclusion?

The action steps summarized in Table 15.5 and the five cross-cultural research areas just suggested represent a large future agenda. Completing that agenda is not impossible if we consider the success of the Genome Project to identify the human genetic structure and the Global Action Plan to eradicate iodine deficiency. If we begin to consider the area and suggested approach to quality of life as an "action science," its potential can be seen to: assess and appreciate human variability; reflect on how we view and deal with people; provide a vehicle for improving the human condition; and encourage the gathering of evidence demonstrating that quality-of-life-oriented policies and procedures can indeed improve the human condition.

Use the Quality of Life Concept as a Tool for Change
Chapters 12 to 14 outlined procedures and strategies that can be used at the micro-, meso-, and macrosystem levels to bring about personal, organizational, and societal changes to enhance people's quality of life. As discussed throughout the three chapters, these efforts should stress a comprehensive view of the person and be directed at both individuals and their families. It is our strong belief that the QOL concept has moved beyond a theoretical construct and is quickly emerg-

ing as an instrument or tool to guide and produce change as proposed in the following systems-perspective strategies that encompass our third challenge and opportunity.

Consumers and Advocates

These individuals are in the best position to suggest the components of quality services and outcomes that impact positively their sense of well-being and perceived quality of life. Change efforts should focus on (a) self-efficacy, (b) internal locus of control and self-determination, (c) empowerment so that individuals can define and achieve their own goals, and (d) self-advocacy.

Educators and Practitioners

These individuals are in a prime position to affect attitudes of others toward people with special needs and provide opportunities for personal growth and development. Change efforts should focus on (a) person-centered planning, (b) personal development (i.e., empowerment and self-determination), (c) user-friendly and person-first language, and (d) prosthetics and technology.

Program Administrators

These individuals are in a prime position to advocate for change at the program and societal levels and to collaborate for change. Change efforts should focus on (a) dimensions of service quality (see Table 13.1; reliability, responsiveness, empathy, extensiveness, appropriateness), (b) quality enhancement techniques, (c) collaboration, and (d) evaluation of outcomes that reflect both person- and organization-referenced outcomes.

Policymakers

These individuals need to be very sensitive to the fact that all people want a life of quality as reflected in the eight core QOL domains and core indicators. Change efforts should focus on (a) listening to consumers and advocates (e.g., agenda building, policy formulation, policy adoption, policy implementation), (b) incorporating key QOL concepts and principles into public policy, (c) funding research and demonstration projects to develop culturally sensitive QOL models and data sets, and (d) evaluating the effects and impacts of QOL-oriented policies and procedures.

Researchers and Evaluators

These individuals are in an excellent position to further the "QOL movement" by fostering QOL as a "discovery science" that (a) gives access to human variability, (b) refashions how we view people, (c) provides a vehicle for improving the human condition, and (d) encourages the gathering of evidence demonstrating that QOL principles and procedures can improve the human condition. Change efforts should focus on: (a) providing the scientific basis for what could become "a discovery science," (b) fostering the use of a holistic approach to QOL research (see next section), (c) incorporating the use of participatory action research into all research and evaluation activities, (d) conducting cross-cultural research into the etic and emic properties of the QOL concept.

Embrace a Holistic Approach to Quality of Life Research
The QOL literature reviewed in chapters 3 through 8 and the analysis of the research and evaluation strategies currently being used (chap. 10) suggest a "mixed bag" that we need to address as our fourth challenge and opportunity. For example, in the mental retardation and intellectual disabilities field, we found that most models are multidimensional, focusing frequently on five to eight of the core domains used throughout the text. However, this was not the case in physical health, where literature focused primarily on the health domain or investigators used a disease-specific (e.g., cancer) approach to assessing the patient's quality of life. The other focus areas were less clear. In addition, we found very few qualitative approaches reported in the literature, in part because of either the perceived difficulty in establishing "acceptable" reliability and validity in qualitative research or the fact that few of the journals reviewed publish qualitative research results.

It is our opinion that the QOL field is now ready to embrace a holistic approach that includes both the "what" and the "how" interrogatories. The "what" includes the core QOL domains and the systems perspective; the "how" includes methodological pluralism and multivariate research designs. Integral to both the "what" and "how" are the acceptable approaches summarized in Table 15.6 to establishing reliability and validity in a holistic approach to QOL research (Guba & Lincoln, 1989; Lincoln, 1995; Schalock, 2001).

The specifics of the "what" and "how" interrogatories reflect the emerging best practices in QOL measurement. The five key measurement principles underlying this effort were summarized in Table 15.1. The four elements of our proposed holistic approach to QOL research are summarized briefly below. A more detailed discussion of each can be found in chapter 11.

Multidimensional
The focus should be on the eight core QOL domains and those core indicators listed in Tables 9.1 and 15.3.

Systems Perspective
Consistent with the text's systems perspective, the conceptualization, measurement, and application of quality of life needs to address and incorporate the microsystem (person, family, close friends), mesosystem (community and educa-

tion, rehabilitation, and human service programs), and macrosystem (society and the larger culture, including government and media).

Methodological Pluralism

The history of QOL measurement has focused on *either* subjective evaluation *or* objective life conditions. As we have proposed throughout the text (and especially in chap. 10 on measurement), we suggest the use of *both* subjective and objective research and evaluation methods, focusing on evaluating the core indicators for each QOL domain. We have proposed further that these components of methodological pluralism include personal appraisal, functional assessment, and social indicators.

Multivariate Research Design

The research design that QOL investigators are using is also changing. Historically, a between-groups design was used in which different groups of people (or nations) were compared on either subjective QOL indicators or, more likely, social indicators. More recently we have seen a multivariate research design being used that incorporates personal and contextual variables as predictors of assessed QOL scores. In addition, statistically we are seeing the rapid emergence of multiple regression and hierarchical regression analyses of quality of life and program evaluation data (Schalock, 2001).

TABLE 15.6
Approaches to Establishing Reliability and Validity

| **Quantitative Methodologies** | Reliability | • Test-retest: Administer the measure to the same individual at Time 1 and Time 2.
• Split-half: Correlate the total score on the first half of a measure with the total score on the second half.
• Odd-even: Correlate the total score of the odd-numbered items of a measure with the total score on the even-numbered items.
• Item-total: Average the correlations of the score on each item of a measure with the total score on the measure.
• Inter-rater: Correlate ratings made by one observer of behavior with ratings made by a second observer. |
|---|---|---|

(table continues)

TABLE 15.6. *(continued)*

Quantitative Methodologies *(continued)*	Validity	• Content: The items measure what the test or measure purports to measure. • Construct: The items measure the underlying construct being studied. • Predictive: The person's test results actually predict future performance or role status. • Concurrent: The current results are consistent with a second, independent measure of the behavior or output under consideration.
Qualitative Methodologies	Credibility	Parallels internal validity in quantitative research and refers to the manner in which the researcher represents the realities of the participants. Techniques include triangulation, peer debriefing, and member checking.
	Transferability	Parallels external validity in quantitative research and refers to the extent to which particular findings can be applied to other contexts and other participants. Techniques include describing the methodology and results in considerable detail ("think description") and purposive sampling.
	Dependability	Parallels reliability in quantitative research. The major technique involves a dependaability audit — an external check documenting the processes by which the research was conducted.
	Confirmability	Concerned with objectivity or neutrality. The major emphasis is on whether someone else looking at the data could trace the conclusions back to the data; the logic used to assemble the interpretations into structured coherent and corroborating results is both explicit and implicit.

In summary, a clearer understanding of the QOL concept and its impact on people with special needs rests heavily on the approach we use in research and evaluation. To that end, we suggest strongly the use of a holistic approach whose "what" is the multiple domains and core indicators and the systems perspective, and whose "how" is the use of methodological pluralism and multivariate research designs. As we continue to embrace a holistic research approach to quality of life, we also need to:

- Develop more qualitative methods, especially in regard to people with severe functional limitations.
- Focus more on a broader concept of behavior that stresses adaptive behavior and a person's role status within the community, not just symptom reduction.
- Rethink what are social indicators. At the individual level, social indicators currently focus primarily on physical and material well-being (cell C of Figure 13.1). A comprehensive view of the person requires that we expand the concept and measurement of social indicators to include those other QOL domains: emotional well-being, personal development, self-direction, interpersonal relations, social inclusion, and rights (cell D in Figure 13.1).

Moving Ahead: The Future Agenda

The past two decades have seen considerable progress in understanding the significant role and the impact that the concept of quality of life has had on people throughout education, health care, and social service programs, and on the systems that affect those lives. During this time we have seen the concept emerge from its diffuse nature of the 1980s, to its operationalization via core domains and core indicators in the 1990s, to its use as a tool for social change in the first decade of the 21st century. Indeed, the QOL concept has extended beyond the person and has now influenced an entire service delivery system because of its power as a sensitizing notion, social construct, and unifying principle. At its core the QOL concept gives a sense of reference and guidance from the individual's perspective, an overriding principle to enhance an individual's well-being and collaboration for change at the societal level, and a common language and systematic framework to guide our current and future endeavors.

The integration of the literature reviewed and synthesized for this text suggests a future agenda, including applying the core QOL domains and indicators; increasing the focus on rights and self-determination; employing the QOL concept more in education, rehabilitation and in health care policies and programs; embracing family-centered quality of life; integrating the emerging areas of self-determination, motivation, and positive psychology into the QOL field; applying the QOL concept to nondeveloped countries; using the concept as a tool for change; and embracing a holistic approach to QOL research.

But there is more that needs to be done regarding our future agenda. The future requires more than "putting it all together" and outlining challenges and opportunities. As William James reminds us, "the only meaning of ideas is found in terms of their possible consequences." So what are the consequences to the field of human services of their adopting more fully the concept of quality of life?

Thus far quality of life has been used as a sensitizing notion, a social construct, and a unifying framework for it conceptualization, measurement, and application. In addition, the concept has also become a social movement whose purposes are similar to earlier efforts related to civil rights, deinstitutionalization, normalization, mainstreaming, and inclusion. At the heart of each of these movements has been the goal of equality and communitarianism. If quality of life is to continue to be a viable social construct and a unifying framework to guide our efforts, human services will need to address three additional key issues.

The first key issue is how to integrate the concept of quality of life into the major social forces impacting human behavior. Figure 15.2 depicts four major forces: the reform movement, social Darwinism, the quality revolution, and the human rights movement. In a general sense these four forces represent a dialectic, with the "thesis" being the emphasis on quantitative issues and foci, and the "antithesis" being the emphasis on qualitative issues and values. It is apparent to us that the QOL concept has the potential to balance or synthesize these two major forces — that is, to strive for a balance between the quantitative and qualitative.

The second issue involves answering the question "What is the proper use of the concept of quality of life?" Should it be used only as a sensitizing notion, a social construct, and/or an overarching principle for public policy, human service programs, and program or policy evaluation? Might it also be used as a criterion for "the good life," guarding against its potential down-side and improper use. Or should the concept be used as a multidimensional outcome measure that assesses change in people's lives based on their personal appraisal, functional assessment, or social status? As T. S. Eliot reminds us, "looking into our hearts is not enough; we must also look into the cerebral cortex." Thus we need to continue to debate the concept and evaluate its use, misuse, and potential.

The third key issue is perhaps the ultimate challenge: to answer the question "so what?" Does the QOL concept make a difference in people's lives? Has it contributed to improving the welfare and psychological well-being of consumers interacting with the "systems" reflected in the text's focus areas? It is probably too soon to tell, and certainly this is an issue that is not easy to resolve. But we must continue to ask "Does it make a difference?" and embark on serious program and policy outcome evaluations that will allow us to answer the "so what?" question. Fortunately, because of the literature synthesized in this text and the concepts presented throughout the book, we are increasingly in a good position to address

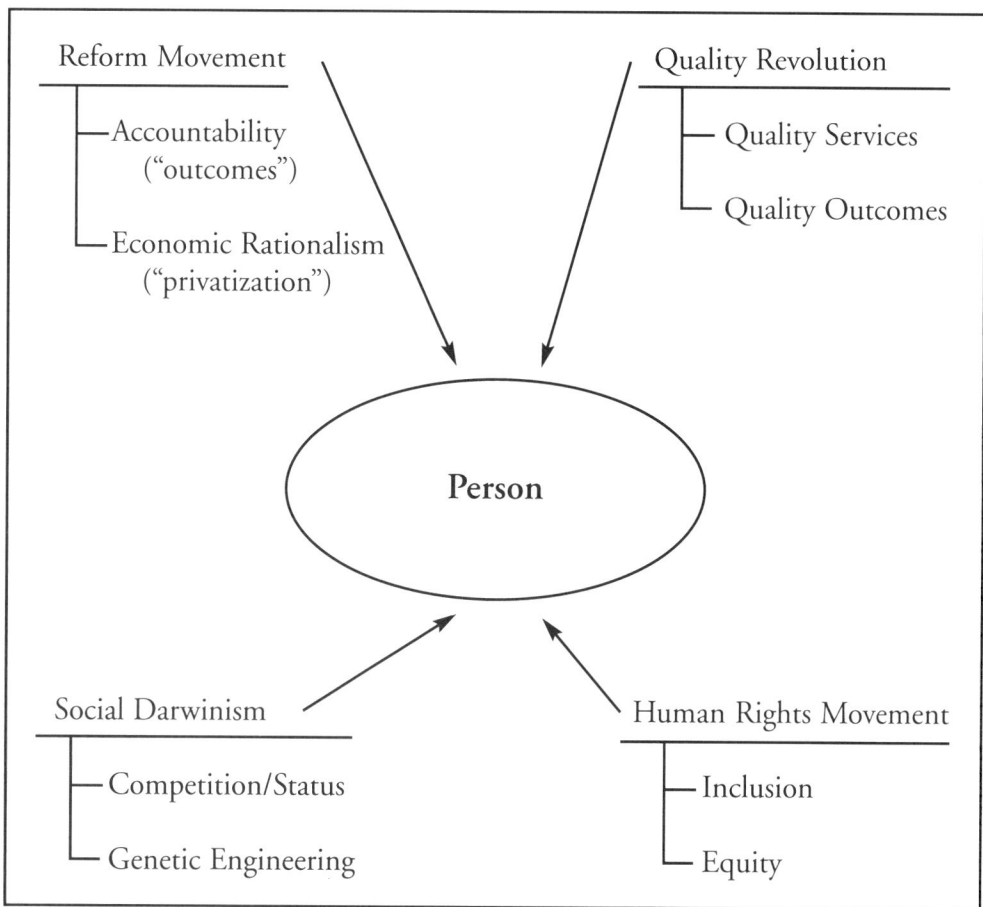

Figure 15.2. Major societal forces impacting a person.

these issues and answer related questions, for we now understand the core domains and indicators of a life of quality and the components of the holistic research approach required to demonstrate its efficacy and effectiveness.

When we embarked on "quality of life" research in the mid-1980s, we had no idea that in 2002 we would be writing the concluding paragraph to a *Handbook on Quality of Life for Human Service Practitioners*. It has been quite a journey for us. It has been a journey of discovery and cautious optimism. In our studies to date, we have discovered much about the quality of our own lives and those of others; we have learned that ideas are important and their consequences real, and that the experiencing and expression of human life is complex. We have also realized that science and social philosophy are not incompatible and that enhancing a life of quality for each person is both our scientific responsibility and our moral obligation.

References

Aaronson, N. K. (1987). *European Organization for Research and Treatment of Cancer (EORTC) protocol 15861: Development of a core quality of life questionnaire for use in cancer clinical trials.* Brussels: EORTC Data Center.

Aaronson, N. K. (1991). Methodologic issues in assessing the quality of life of cancer patients. *Cancer, 67*(3), 844–850.

Abbott, J., & Gee, L. (1998). Contemporary psychosocial issues in cystic fibrosis: Treatment adherence and quality of life. *Disability and Rehabilitation, 20*(6–7), 262–271.

Achat, H., Kawachi, I., Levine, S., Berkey, C., Coakley, E., & Colditz, G. (1998). Social networks, stress, and health-related quality of life. *Quality of Life Research, 7*(8), 735–750.

Adelman, H. S., Taylor, L., & Nelson, P. (1989). Minors' dissatisfaction with their life circumstances. *Child Psychiatry and Human Development, 20,* 135–147.

Affleck, J. W., & McGuire, R. J. (1984). The measurement of psychiatric rehabilitation status: A review of the needs and a new scale. *British Journal of Psychiatry, 145,* 517–525.

Agosti, V., Stewart, J. W., & Beattie, L. (1991). Depression in dementia: Its impact on functioning in chronic depression: Effect of acute treatment with antidepressants. *Journal of Affective Disorders, 23,* 35–41.

Agran, M. (1997). *Student-directed learning: Teaching self-determination skills.* Pacific Grove, CA: Brooks/Cole.

Ainscow, M. (1999). Tendiéndoles la mano a todos los estudiantes: algunos retos y oportunidades. In M. A. Verdugo and F. B. Jordán de Urries (Eds.), *Hacia una nueva concepción de la discapacidad* (pp. 15–37). Salamanca: Amarú.

Albin, J. M. (1992). Quality improvement in employment and other human services. *Managing for quality through change.* Baltimore: Paul H. Brookes.

Albrecht, G. L., & Fitzpatrick, R. (1994). A sociological perspective on health-related quality of life research. In G. L. Albrecht & R. Fitzpatrick (Eds.), *Advances in medical sociology: Vol. 5. Quality of life in health care* (pp. 1–21). London: Jai Press.

Albrecht, K. (1993). *The only thing that matters: Bringing the power of the customer into the center of your business.* New York: Harper Business.

Allen, D. (1989). The effects of deinstitutionalisation on people with mental handicaps: A review. *Mental Handicap Research, 2,* 18–37

Alpiner, J. (1982). Evaluation of communication function. In J. Alpiner (Ed.), *Handbook of adult rehabilitative audiology* (pp. 18–78). Baltimore: Williams & Wilkins.

Álvarez Pérez, L. (1995). Alumnos con necesidades educativas especiales. *Aula Abierta,* no. 65, 75–100.

Anderson, J. A., Rivera, V. R., & Kutash, K. (1998). Measuring consumer satisfaction with children's mental health services. In M. E. Kutash & A. Duchnowski (Eds.), *Outcomes for children and youth with emotional behavioral disorders and their families: Programs and evaluation best practices* (pp. 455–482). Austin, TX: Pro-Ed.

Andreasen, N. C. (1983). *The scale for the assessment of negative symptoms.* Iowa City, IA: The University of Iowa.

Andreasen, N. C. (1984). *The scale for the assessment of positive symptoms.* Iowa City, IA: The University of Iowa.

Andrews, F. M. (1974). Social indicators of perceived quality of life. *Social Indicators Research, 1,* 279–299.

Andrews, F. M., & Whithey, S. B. (1974). Developing measures of perceived life quality: Results from several national surveys. *Social Indicators Research, 1,* 1–26.

Andrews, F. M., & Whithey, S. B. (1976). *Social indicators of well-being. Americans' perceptions of life quality.* New York: Plenum Press.

Angermeyer, M. C., & Katschnig, H. (1997). Psychotropic medication and quality of life: A conceptual framework for assessing their relationship. In H. Katschnig, H. Freeman, & N. Sartorius (Eds.), *Quality of life in mental disorders* (pp. 215–225). Chichester, England: John Wiley.

Antaki, C., & Rapley, M. (1996). Questions and answers to psychological assessment schedules: Hidden troubles in quality of life interviews. *Journal of Intellectual Disability Research, 40*(5), 421–437.

Apajasalo, M., Sintonen, H., Rautonen, J., & Kaitila, I. (1998). Health-related quality of life of patients with genetic skeletal dysplasias. *European Journal of Pediatrics, 157,* 114–121.

Apgar, D., Cook, S., & Lerman, P. (1998). *Life after Johnstone: Impacts on consumer competencies, behaviors, and quality of life.* Research report. New Jersey Institute of Technology.

Aronson, K. J. (1997). Quality of life among multiple sclerosis patients and their caregivers. *Neurology, 48,* 74–80.

Atkinson., M. J., Coia, D. A., Harper, W., & Harper, J. P. (1996). The impact of education groups for people with schizophrenia on social functioning and quality of life. *British Journal of Psychiatry, 168,* 199–204.

Atkinson, M. J., Zibin, S., & Chuang, H. (1997). Characterizing quality of life among patients with chronic mental illness: A critical examination of the self-report methodology. *American Journal of Psychiatry, 154*(1), 99–105.

Awad, A. G. (1992). Quality of life of schizophrenic patients on medications and implications for new drug trials. *Hospital and Community Psychiatry, 43,* 262–265.

Awad, A. G., Voruganti, L. N. P., & Heslegrave, R. J. (1997). A conceptual model of quality of life in schizophrenia: Description and preliminary clinical validation. *Quality of Life Research, 6,* 21–26.

Bailey, D. B., McWilliam, R. A., Darkes, L. A., Hebbeler, K., Simeonsson, R. J., Spiker, D., & Wagner, M. (1998). Family outcomes in early intervention: A framework for program evaluation and efficacy research. *Exceptional Children, 64,* 313–328.

Baker, F., & Intagliata, J. (1982). Quality of life in the evaluation of community support systems. *Evaluation and Program Planning, 5,* 69–79.

Bandura, A. (1997). *Self-efficacy.* New York: W. H. Freeman.

Bánfalvy, C. (1996). The paradox of the quality of life of adults with learning difficulties. *Disability & Society, 11*(4), 569–577.

Barcia, D., Ayuso, J. L., Herraiz, M. L., & Fernández, A. (1996). Quality of life of patients treated with Risperidone. *Anales de Psiquiatría, 12,* 134–141.

Barcia, D., Morcillo, L., & Borgoñós, E. (1995). Esquizofrenia, calidad de vida, y formas clínicas. *Anales de Psiquiatría, 11,* 81–87.

Bautista, R. (1991). *Necesidades educativas especiales. Manual teórico práctico* [Special education needs. A practical theoretical handbook]. Málaga: Aljibe.

Bech, P. (1994). The PCASEE model: An approach to subjective well-being. In J. Orley & Kuypen (Eds.), *Quality of assessment: International perspectives* (pp. 75–79). Berlin: Springer-Verlag.

Bech, P. (1996). Quality of life measurements in major depression. *European Psychiatry, 11,* 123–126.

Bech, P., & Angst, J. (1996). Quality of life in anxiety and social phobia. *International Clinical Psychopharmacology, 11*(3), 97–100.

Beck, A. T., Ward, C. H., & Mendelson, M. (1961). An inventory for measuring depression. *Archives of General Psychiatry, 4,* 561–571.

Becker, M., Diamond, R., & Sainfort, F. (1993). A new patient-focused index for measuring quality of life in persons with severe and persistent mental illness. *Quality of Life Research, 2,* 239–251.

Beer, M., Eisenstat, R., & Spector, B. (1990). Why change programs don't produce change. *Harvard Business Review,* 158–166.

Beer, M., & Eisenstat, R. (1993). Organizational diagnosis: Its role in organizational learning. *Journal of Counseling and Development, 71,* 642–650.

Bellamy, G. T., Newton, J. S., LeBaron, N. M., & Horner, R. H. (1990). Quality of life and lifestyle outcomes: A challenge for residential programs. In R. Schalock (Ed.), *Quality of life: Perspectives and issues* (pp. 127–137). Washington, DC: American Association on Mental Retardation.

Bengtsson-Tops, A., & Hansson, L. (1999). Subjective quality of life in schizophrenic patients living in the community: Relationship to clinical and social characteristics. *European Psychiatry, 14,* 256–263.

Bergner, M., Bobbit, R., Carter, W., & Gilson, B. (1981). The sickness impact profile: Development and final revision of a health status measure. *Medical Care, 19,* 787–805.

Beyth-Marom, R., Fischhoff, B., Jacobs Quadrel, M., & Furby, L. (1991). Teaching decision-making to adolescents: A critical review. In J. Baron & R. V. Brown (Eds.), *Teaching decision making to adolescents.* Hillsdale, NJ: Lawrence Erlbaum.

Bickman, L., Guthrie, P. R., Foster, E. W., & Lambert, E. W. (1995). *Evaluating managed mental health services: The Fort Bragg experiment.* New York: Plenum.

Bigelow, D., Brodsky, G., Steward, L., & Olson, M. (1982). The concept and measurement of quality of life as a dependent variable in evaluation of mental health services. In G. J. Stahler & W. R. Tash (Eds.), *Innovative approaches to mental health evaluation* (pp. 345–366). New York: Academic Press.

Bigelow, D. A., Gareau, M. J., & Young, D. J. (1990). A quality of life interview. *Psychosocial Rehabilitation Journal, 14,* 94–98.

Birch, J. W. (1974). *Mainstreaming: Educable mentally retarded children in regular classes.* Reston, VA: Council for Exceptional Children.

Blacher, J. (2001). Transition to adulthood: Mental retardation, families, and culture. *American Journal on Mental Retardation, 106*(2), 173–188.

Block, P., Balcazar, F., & Keys, C. (2001). From pathology to power: Rethinking race, poverty, and disability. *Journal of Disability Policy Studies, 12*(1), 18–27, 39.

Blumenschein, K., & Johannesson, M. (1998). Relationship between quality of life instruments, health state utilities, and willingness to pay in patients with asthma. *Annals of Allergy, Asthma & Immunology, 80,* 189–194.

Blumer, H. (1969). *Symbolic interactionism: Perspective and method.* Englewood Cliffs, NJ: Prentice-Hall.

Bobes, J. (1998). How is recovery from social anxiety disorder defined? *Journal of Clinical Psychiatry, 59,* 12–16.

Bobes, J., & González, M. P. (1997). Quality of life in schizophrenia. In H. Katschnig, H. Freeman & N. Sartorius (Eds.), *Quality of life in mental disorders* (pp. 165–178). Chichester, England: John Wiley.

Bobes, J., González, M., Bousoño-García, M., Muñoz, L., G-Quiros, M., & Wallace, D. (1996). Quality of life in schizophrenic outpatients. In American Psychiatric Association (Ed.), *Annual Meeting — New Research Program and Abstracts* (p. 223). Washington, DC: Editor.

Bobes, J., González, M. P., Bousoño, M., & Sáiz, P. A. (1997). *Calidad de vida y salud mental.* Madrid: Aula Médica.

Borthwick-Duffy, S. A. (1992). Quality of life and quality of care in mental retardation. In L. Rowitz (Ed.), *Mental retardation in the year 2000* (pp. 52–66). New York: Springer-Verlag.

Børup, C., & Undén, M. (1994). Combined fluoxetine and disulfiram treatment of alcoholism with comorbid affective disorders. *European Psychiatry, 9,* 83–90.

Bouvenot, G. (1993). Evaluation de la qualité de vie des patients. Evolution des idées. In C. Hérisson & L. Simon (Dir.), *Evaluation de la qualité de vie* (pp. 8–10). Paris: Masson.

Bradburn, N. H. (1969). *The structure of psychological well-being.* Chicago: Aldine.

Brent, D. A., Poling, K., McKain, B., & Baugher, M. (1993). A psychoeducational program for families of affectively ill children and adolescents. *Journal of the American Academy of Child and Adolescent Psychiatry, 32,* 770–774.

Bronfenbrenner, U. (1979). *The ecology of human development.* Cambridge, MA: Harvard Unversity Press.

Brotherson, M. J., Cook, C. C., & Cunconan-Lahr, R. (1995). Policy supporting self-determination in the environments of children with disabilities. *Education and Training in Mental Retardation and Developmental Disabilities, 30,* 3–14.

Brown, F., Appel, C., Corsi, L., & Wenig, B. (1993). Choice diversity for people with severe disabilities. *Education and Training in Mental Retardation, 28,* 318–326.

Brown, F., & Lehr, D. (1993). Making activities meaningful for students with severe multiple disabilities. *Teaching Exceptional Children, 26,* 12–16.

Brown, I., Renwick, R., & Nagler, M. (1996). The centrality of quality of life in health promotion and rehabilitation. In R. Renwick, I. Brown, & M. Nagler (Eds), *Quality of life in health promotion and rehabilitation* (pp. 3–13). Newbury Park, CA: Sage.

Brown, R. I. (Ed.). (1988). *Quality of life for handicapped people.* London: Croom Helm.

Brown, R. I. (Ed.). (1997). *Quality of life for people with disabilities: Models, research, and practice* (2nd ed.). Cheltenham, England: Stanley Thornes.

Brown, R. I. (2000a). Learning from quality of life models. In M. P. Janicki & E. F. Ansello (Eds.), *Community supports for aging adults with lifelong disabilities* (pp. 19–38). Baltimore: Brookes.

Brown, R. I. (2000b). Quality of life: Challenges and confrontation. In K. D. Keith & R. L. Schalock (Eds.), *Cross-cultural perspectives on quality of life* (pp. 347–362). Washington, DC: American Association on Mental Retardation.

Brown, R. I., & Shearer, J. (1999). Quality of life: Some implication for the process of inclusion. *Exceptionality Education Canada, 9,* 83–103.

Browne, S., Garavan, J., Gervin, M., Roe, M., Larkin, C., & O'Callaghan, E. (1998). Quality of life in schizophrenia: Insight and subjective response to neuroleptics. *Journal of Nervous Mental Disorders, 186*(2), 74–78.

Browne, S., Roe, M., Lane, A., Gervin, M., Morris, M., Kinsella, A., Larkin, C., & O'Callaghan, E. (1996). Quality of life in schizophrenia: Relationship to sociodemographic factors, symtomatology, and tardive dyskinesia. *Acta Psychiatrica Scandinavica, 94,* 118–124.

Bucquet, D. (1993). Qualité de vie, santé perceptuelle. Définition, concept, évaluation. In C. Hérisson and L. Simon (Eds.), *Evaluation de la qualité de vie* (pp. 1–7). Paris: Masson.

Bullinger, M. (1994). KINDL — A questionnaire for health-related quality of life assessment in children. *Zeitschrift fur Gesundheitspsychologie, 1,* 64–77.

Bullinger, M. (1995). German translation and psychometric testing of the SF-36 health survey: Preliminary results from the IQOLA project. *Social Science and Medicine, 41,* 1359–1366.

Bullinger, M. (1997). Generic quality of life assessment in psychiatry: Potentials and limitations. *European Psychiatry, 12,* 203–209.

Bullinger, M., Anderson, R., Aaronson, N., & Cella, D. (1995). Developing and evaluating cross-cultural instruments from minimum requirements to optimal models. In S. Schumaker & R. Beron (Eds.), *The international assessment of health-related quality of life: Theory, translation, measurement, & analysis* (pp. 83–91). Oxford, England: Oxford Rapid Communications.

Bullinger, M., & Ravens-Sieberer, U. (1995). Health-related quality of life assessment in children: A review of the literature. *Revue Européenne de Psychologie Appliquée, 45*(4), 245–254.

Burchard, S., Hasazi, J., Gordon, L., & Yoe, J. (1991). An examination of lifestyle and adjustment in three community residential alternatives. *Research in Developmental Disabilities, 12,* 127–142.

Burleigh, S. A., Farber, R. S., & Gillard, M. (1998). Community integration and life satifaction after traumatic brain injury: Long-term findings. *American Journal of Occupational Therapy, 52*(1), 45–52.

Butterworth, J., Hagner, D., Kiernan, W., & Schalock, R. (1996). Natural supports in the workplace: Defining an agenda for research and practice. *Journal of The Association for Persons with Severe Handicaps, 21*(3), 103–113.

Butterworth, J., Steere, D. E., & Whitney-Thomas, J. (1997). Using person-centered planning to address personal quality of life. In R. L. Schalock (Ed.), *Quality of life: Vol. 2. Application to persons with disabilities* (pp. 5–24). Washington, DC: American Association on Mental Retardation.

Campbell, A., Converse, P. E., & Rodgers, W. L. (1976). *The quality of American life: Perceptions, evaluations, and satisfactions.* New York: Russell Sage.

Campbell, A. G. M., & McHaffie, H. E. (1995). Prolonging life and allowing death: Infants. *Journal of Medical Ethics, 21,* 339–344.

Campbell, J., & Schraiber, R. (1989). *The well-being project: Mental health clients speak for themselves.* Sacramento: California Network of Mental Health Clients.

Campo, S., Sharpton, W., Thompson, B., & Sexton, D. (1996). Measurement characteristics of the quality of life index when used with adults who have severe mental retardation. *American Journal on Mental Retardation, 100*(5), 546–550.

Cantril, H. (1965). *The pattern of human concerns.* New Brunswick, NJ: Rutgers University Press.

Cardol, M., Elvers, J. W. H., Ostendorp, R. A. B., Brandsma, J. W., & Groot, I. J. M. (1996). Quality of life in patients with amyotrophic lateral sclerosis. *Journal of Rehabilitation Sciences, 9*(4), 99–103.

Carling, P. J. (1993). Housing and support for persons with mental illness: Emerging approaches to research and practice. *Hospital and Community Psychiatry, 44*(5), 439–449.

Carver, C. S. (1997). You want to measure coping but your protocol's too long: Consider the Brief COPE. *International Journal of Behavioral Medicine, 4,* 92–100.

Carver, C. S., Scheier, M. F., & Weintraub, J. K. (1989). Assessing coping strategies: A theoretically based approach. *Journal of Personality and Social Psychology, 56,* 267–283.

Casas, F. (1992). Las representaciones sociales de las necesidades de niños y niñas, y su calidad de vida. *Anuario de Psicología, 52,* 27–45.

Cass, A. R., Volk, R. J., & Nease. D. E. (1999). Health-related quality of life in primary care patients with recognized and unrecognized mood and anxiety disorders. *International Journal of Psychiatry in Medicine, 29*(3), 293–309.

Castanon, D. G., & Bujan, M. G. (2000). The rights and social inclusion of people with mental retardation in Argentina. In K. D. Keith & R. L. Schalock (Eds.), *Cross-cultural perspectives on quality of life* (pp. 301–310). Washington, DC: American Association on Mental Retardation.

Cella, D. F., Diennen, K., Arnason, B., Reder, A., Webster, M., Karabastos, B., Chang, C., Lloyd, S., Mo, F., Stewart, J., & Stefoski, D. (1999). Validation of the functional assessment of multiple sclerosis quality of life instrument. *American Academy of Neurology, 47,* 129–139.

Chambers, F. (1994). Removing confusion about formative and summative evaluation: Purpose versus time. *Evaluation and Program Planning, 17,* 9–12.

Che, T. H., Bruininks, R., Lakin, K., & Hayden, M. (1993). Personal competencies and community participation in small community residential programs: A multiple discriminant analysis. *American Journal on Mental Retardation, 98*(3), 390–399.

Chubon, R. A., Clayton, K. S., & Vandergriff, D. V. (1995). An exploratory study comparing the quality of life of South Carolinians with mental retardation and spinal cord injury. *Rehabilitation Counseling Bulletin, 39*(2), 107–118.

Chwalow, J. (1993). Méthodologie de l'évaluation de la qualité de vie dans les essais cliniques. In C. Hérisson and L. Simon (Eds.), *Evaluation de la qualité de vie* (pp. 22–32). Paris: Masson.

Clark, P. G. (1991). Ethical dimensions of quality of life in aging: Autonomy vs. collectivism in the United States and Canada. *The Gerontologist, 31*(5), 631–639.

Clark, P. G. (1995). Quality of life, values, and teamwork in geriatric care: Do we communicate what we mean? *The Gerontologist, 35*(3), 402–411.

Clark, R. E., Teague, G. B., Ricketts, S. K., Bush, P. W., Keller, A. M., Zubkoff, M., & Drake, R. E. (1994). Measuring resource use in economic evaluations: Determining the social costs of mental illness. *Journal of Mental Health Administration, 21*(1), 32–41.

Cohen, J. (1996). Preferences, needs, and QALYs. *Journal of Medical Ethics, 22*, 267–272.

Cohi, A. (1990). Estudio comparativo de la calidad de vida en pacientes esquizofrénicos según la condición de tratamiento [Comparative studies of the quality of life in schizophrenic patients according to treatment conditions]. *Revista de Psiquiatría, 17*(5), 201–218.

Colarelli, S. M. (1998). Psychological interventions in organizations. *American Psychologist, 53*(9), 1044–1056.

Cole, S., Horvath, B., Sprague, J., Wilcox, B., & Pratt, C. (1999). *Quality indicators for inclusive schools: A template for including all students.* Bloomington, IN: Center on Education and Lifelong Learning, Institute for the Study of Developmental Disabilities.

Conliffe, C., & Walsh, P. N. (1999). An international perspective on quality of life: Prospects for older people with disabilities. In S. J. Herr and G. Weber (Eds.), *Aging, rights, and quality of life: Prospects for older people with developmental disabilities* (pp. 237–252). Baltimore: Brookes.

Conroy, J. (1996). The small icf/mr program: Dimensions of quality and cost. *Mental Retardation, 34*(1), 13–26.

Cordoba, M. J., Andrykowski, M. A., Kenady, D. E., McGrath, P. C., Sloan, D. A., & Redd, W. H. (1995). Frequency and correlates of posttraumatic-stress-disorder-like symptoms after treatment for breast cancer. *Journal of Consulting and Clinical Psychology, 63*(6), 981–986.

Cornes, J. M., & Arrojo, M. (1999). Calidad de vida y enfermedad mental [Quality of life and mental illness]. *Revista de Psiquiatría, 26*(1), 9–17.

Cortina, A., Gómez, M., & Guell, M. (1998). Retraso mental. Integración laboral y calidad de vida. *Revista de Servicios Sociales y Política Social, 42,* 41–61.

Coyle, C. P., Lesnik-Emas, S., & Kinney, W. B. (1994). Predicting life satisfaction among adults with spinal cord injuries. *Rehabilitation Psychology, 39*(2), 95–112.

Cragg, R., & Harrison, J. (1986). *Living in a supervised home: A questionnaire on quality of life.* Birmingham: Campaign for People with a Mental Handicap.

Craig, R., & Harrison, J. (1984). *Living in a supervised home. A questionnaire for quality of life.* Manchester, England: West Midlands Campaign for People with Mental Handicap.

Cronin, M. (1996). Life skills curricula for students with learning disabilities: A review of the literature. *Journal of Learning Disabilities, 29*(1), 53–68.

Cullen, C. (1999). Contextualism in intellectual disability research: The case of choice behaviour. *Journal of Intellectual Disability Research, 43*(6), 437–444.

Cummins, R. A. (1991). The comprehensive quality of life scale — intellectual disability: An initial report. *Australia and New Zealand Journal of Developmental Disabilities, 17*(2), 259–264.

Cummins, R. A. (1993). *Comprehensive quality of life scale — intellectual disability* (4th ed.). Melbourne, Australia: Psychology Research Centre.

Cummins, R. A. (1996). The domains of life satisfaction: An attempt to order chaos. *Social Indicators Research, 38,* 303–328.

Cummins, R. A. (1997a). Assessing quality of life for people with disabilities. In R. I. Brown (Ed.), *Quality of life for people with disabilities: Models, research, and practice* (2nd ed., pp. 116–150). Cheltenham, England: Stanley Thornes.

Cummins, R. A. (1997b). Self-rated quality of life scales for people with an intellectual disability: A review. *Journal of Applied Research in Intellectual Disabilities, 10,* 199–216.

Curtis, J. L., Millman, E. J., Struening, E., & Dércole, A. (1992). Effect of case management on rehospitalisation and utilisation of ambulatory care services. *Hospital and Community Psychiatry, 43*(9), 895–899.

Czyzewski, D. I., Mariotto, M. J., Bartholomew, L. K., LeCompte, S. H., & Sockrider, M. M. (1992). *Measurement of quality of well being in a child and adolescent cystic fibrosis population.* Paper presented at the sixth annual North American Cystic Fibrosis Conference, Washington, DC.

Dagnan, D., Look, R., Ruddick, L., & Jones, J. (1995). Changes in the quality of life of people with learning disabilities who moved from hospital to live in community-based homes. *International Journal of Rehabilitation Research, 18,* 115–122.

Dagnan, D., Ruddick, L., & Jones, J. (1998). A longitudinal study of the quality of life of older people with intellectual disability after leaving hospital. *Journal of Intellectual Disability Research, 42*(2), 112–121.

Dahlöf, C. G. H., & Dimenas, E. (1995). Migraine patients experience poorer subjective well-being/quality of life even between attacks. *Cephalalgia, 15,* 31–36.

Dahlöf, C. G. H., & Solomon, G. D. (1998). The burden of migraine to the individual sufferer: A review. *European Journal of Neurology, 5*(6), 525–533.

Dalton, A. J., & Janicki, M. P. (1999). Aging and dementia. In M. P. Janicki and A. J. Dalton (Eds.), *Dementia, aging, and intellectual disabilities: A handbook* (pp. 5–31). Philadelphia, PA: Brunner Mazel.

Daniels, H., & Hogg, B. (1991). An intercultural comparison of the quality of life of children and youth with handicaps in Denmark, Italy, the United Kingdom, and Germany. *Educational and Child Psychology, 8*(4), 74–83.

Dattilo, J., & Hope, G. (1999). Aspects of leisure education program on youth with mental retardation. *Education and Training in Mental Retardation and Developmental Disabilities, 34*(1), 20–34.

Davies, C. (1996). Prohibiting and taxing everyday pleasures. In D. M. Warburton & N. Sherwood (Eds.), *Pleasure and quality of life* (pp. 199–207). Chichester, England: John Wiley.

Davis, H., Zeiss, A., Shea, E., & Tinklenberg, J. R. (1998). Sexuality and intimacy in Alzheimer's patients and their partners. *Sexuality and Disability, 16*(3), 193–203.

Dayson, D., Gooch, C., & Thornicroft, G. (1992). The TAPS project: 16. Difficult to place, long-term psychiatric patients: Risk factors for failure to resettle long-stay patients in community facilities. *British Medical Journal, 305,* 993–995.

Dazord, A., Augier, F., Guisti, P., & Frot, E. (1996). Quality of life and socio-professional rehabilitation: Study on patients with chronic mental diseases. *European Psychiatry, 11,* 277–293.

DeJong, A., Giel, R., & Sloof, C. J. (1985). Social disability and outcome in schizophrenia patients. *British Journal of Psychiatry, 147,* 631–636.

De Leo, M., René, F., & Diekstra, P. (1998). LEIPAD. An internationally applicable instrument to assess quality of life in the elderly. *Behavioral Medicine, 24,* 17–27.

Dennis, R. E., Williams, W., Giangreco, M. F., & Cloninger, C. (1993). Quality of life as context for planning and evaluation of services for people with disabilities. *Exceptional Children, 59*(6), 499–512.

Diener, E. (2000). Subjective well-being: The science of happiness and a proposal for a national index. *American Psychologist, 55*(1), 34–43.

Doll, B., Sands, D. J., Wehmeyer, M. L., & Palmer, S. (1996). Promoting the development and acquisition of self-determined behavior. In D. J. Sands & M. L. Wehmeyer (Eds.), *Self-determination across the life span: Independence and choice for people with disabilities* (pp. 63–88). Baltimore: Paul H. Brookes.

Dossetor, D., & Nicol, R. (1990). Community care for adolescents with developmental retardation: Problems and proposals. *Health Trends, 22*(4), 148–151.

Dropsy, R. (1993). Qualité de vie. Le point de vue de l'industriel du médicament. In C. Hérisson & L. Simon (Eds.), *Evaluation de la qualité de vie* (pp. 49–58). Paris: Masson.

Dunn, M., O'Driscoll, C., Dayson, D., Wills, W., & Leff, J. (1990). The TAPS project: 4. An observational study of the social life of long-stay patients. *British Journal of Psychiatry, 157,* 842–848.

Ebrahim, S. (1995). Clinical and public health perspectives and applications of health-related quality of life measurement. *Social Science and Medicine, 41*(10), 1383–1394.

Echeita, G. (1997). *Necesidades especiales en el aula. Evaluación de un proyecto internacional de la UNESCO para la formación del profesorado.* In M. A. Verdugo and F. B. Jordan de Urries (Eds.), Hacia una nueva concepcion de la Discapacidad (pp. 25-46). Salamanca: Amaru.

Echeita, G. (1999). *Necesidades especiales en el aula. Evaluación de un proyecto internacional de la UNESCO para la formación del profesorado* [Unpublished manuscript]. Salamanca, Spain: University of Salamanca, Dept. of Psychology.

Edgerton, R. B. (1990). Quality of life from a longitudinal research perspective. In R. L. Schalock (Ed.), *Quality of life: Perspectives and issues* (pp. 149–160). Washington, DC: American Association on Mental Retardation.

Edgerton, R. B. (1996). A longitudinal-ethnographic research perspective on quality of life. In R. L. Schalock (Ed.), *Quality of life: Vol. 1. Conceptualization and measurement* (pp. 83–90). Washington, DC: American Association on Mental Retardation.

Edgerton, R. B., & Gaston, M. A. (Eds.). (1991). *"I've seen it all."* Baltimore: Paul H. Brookes.

Eggelton, I., Robertson, S., Ryan, J., & Kober, R. (1999). The impact of employment in the quality of life of people with intellectual disability. *Journal of Vocational Rehabilitation, 13,* 95–107.

Eiser, C. (1997). Need for a distinctive child quality of life measure. In E. W. Gerharz (Ed.), *Quality of life research in children: Fashion or future? Dialogues in Pediatric Urology, 20,* 1–2.

Elias, M. J., & Clabby, J. F. (1989). *Social decision-making skills: A curriculum guide for elementary grades.* Rockville, MD: Aspen.

Elorriaga, J., Garcia, L., Martinez, J., & Unamunzaga, E. (2000). Quality of life of persons with mental retardation in Spain. In K. D. Keith & R. L. Schalock (Eds.), *Cross-cultural perspectives on quality of life* (pp. 113–124). Washington, DC: American Association on Mental Retardation.

Emerson, E., & Hatton, C. (1996). Deinstitutionalization in the UK and Ireland: Outcome for service users. *Journal of Intellectual and Developmental Disability, 21*(1), 17–37.

Epstein, R. S., & Lydick, E. (1995). Quality of life assessment: A pharmaceutical industry perspective. In J. E. Dimsdale & A. Baum (Ed.), *Quality of life in behavioral medicine research* (pp. 57–68). Hillsdale, NJ: Lawrence Erlbaum.

European Commission (1996). *Communication on equality of opportunity for people with disabilities.* Brussels: Author.

European Organization for Research and Treatment of Cancer Study Group on Quality of Life. (1993). The European Organization for Research and Treatment of Cancer QLQ-C30: A quality-of-life instrument for use in international clinical trials in oncology. *Journal of the Netherlands Cancer Institute, 85,* 365–376.

Evans, R., Dingus, M., & Haselkorn, J. (1993). Living with a disability: A synthesis and critique of the literature on quality of life, 1985–1989. *Psychological Reports, 72,* 771–777.

Evenhuis, H., Henderson, C. M., Beange, H., Lennox, N., Chicoine, B., & Working Group. (2000). *Healthy aging — adults with intellectual disabilities: Physical health issues.* Geneva, Switzerland: World Health Organization.

Fabian, E. (1991). Supported employment and the quality of life: Does a job make a difference? *Rehabilitation Counseling Bulletin, 36*(2), 84–97.

Fallowfield, L. (1993). *The quality of life: The missing measurement in health care* (3rd ed.). London: WBC Bridgend.

Farré, R., Frasque, P., & Romá, R. (1999). Estado de salud y calidad de vida de un colectivo de ancianos institucionalizados. *Revista Especial de Geriatría y Gerontología, 34*(1), 25–33.

FEAPS (2000). *Educación para personas con retraso mental. Orientaciones para la calidad.* Madrid: Author, Col. Manuales de Buena Práctica.

Felce, D. (1997). Defining and applying the concept of quality of life. *Journal of Intellectual Disability Research, 41*(2), 126–135.

Felce, D. (2000). Engagement in activity as an indicator of quality of life in British research. In K. D. Keith & R. L. Schalock (Eds.), *Cross-cultural perspectives on quality of life* (pp. 173–190). Washington, DC: American Association on Mental Retardation.

Felce, D., & Perry, J. (1995). Quality of life: Its definition and measurement. *Research in Developmental Disabilities, 16,* 51–74.

Felce, D., & Perry, J. (1996). Assessment of quality of life. In R. L. Schalock (Ed.), *Quality of life: Vol. 1. Conceptualization and measurement* (pp. 63–72). Washington, DC: American Association on Mental Retardation.

Felce, D., & Perry, J. (1997). Quality of life: The scope of the term and its breadth of measurement. In R. I. Brown (Ed.), *Quality of life for people with disabilities: Models, research, and practice* (2nd ed., pp. 56–71). Cheltenham, England: Stanley Thornes.

Felce, D., Lowe, K., & de Paiva, S. (1994). Ordinary housing for people with severe learning disabilities and challenging behaviours. In E. Emerson, P. McGill, & J. Mansell (Eds.), *Severe learning disabilities and challenging behaviours* (pp. 97–118). London: Chapman & Hall.

Felton, C. J., Stastny, P., Shern, D. L., Blanck, A., Donahue, S. A., Knight, E., & Brown, C. (1995). Consumers as peer specialists on intensive case management teams: Impact on client outcomes. *Psychiatric Services, 46,* 1037–1044.

Ferguson, R. V. (1997). Environmental design and quality of life. In R. I. Brown (Ed.), *Quality of life for people with disabilities: Models, research, and practice* (pp. 56–70). Cheltenham, England: Stanley Thornes.

Fernández-Ballesteros, R., & Maciá, A. (1993). Calidad de vida en la vejez. *Intervención Social, 5,* 77–94.

Fernández-Ballesteros, R., Zamarrón, M.D., & Maciá, A. (1996). *Calidad de vida en la vejez en distintos contextos.* Madrid: Ministerio de Trabajo y Asuntos Exteriores, Instituto Nacional de Servicios Sociales.

Fillenbaum, G. G. (1988). *Multidimensional functional assessment of older adults: The Duke older American resources and service procedures.* Hillsdale, NJ: Lawrence Erlbaum.

Finzen, A., & Hoffmann-Richter, U. (1997). Stigma and quality of life in mental disorders. In H. Katschnig, H. Freeman, & N. Sartorius (Eds.), *Quality of life in mental disorders* (pp. 69–76). Chichester, England: John Wiley.

Fitzgerald, F. (1996). Choosing how to live. In D. M. Warburton & N. Sherwood (Eds.), *Pleasure and quality of life* (pp. 183–188). Chichester, England: John Wiley.

Fitzpatrick, R. (1995). [Review of the book, *The international assessment of health-related quality of life: Theory translation, measurement, and analysis.*] *Book Reviews,* 248–249.

Flanagan, J. C. (1976). A research approach to improving our quality of life. *American Psychologist, 33,* 138–147.

Flanagan, J. C. (1982). Measurement of quality of life: Current state of the art. *Archives of Physical Medicine and Rehabilitation, 63,* 56–59.

Fleming, I., & Stenfert, B. (1990). Evaluation of a community care project for people with learning difficulties. *Journal of Mental Deficiency Research, 34,* 451–464.

Flynt, S. W., & Wood, T. A. (1989). Stress and coping of mothers of children with moderate mental retardation. *American Journal on Mental Retardation, 94*(4), 278–283.

Ford, J. D., & Kidd, P. (1998). Early childhood trauma and disorders of extreme stress as predictors of treatment outcome with chronic posttraumatic stress disorder. *Journal of Traumatic Stress, 11*(4), 743–761.

Ford, J., Young, D., Perez, B. C., Obermeyer, R. L., & Rohner, D. G. (1992). Needs assessment for persons with severe mental illness: What services are needed for successful community living? *Community Mental Health Journal, 28*(6), 491–503.

Fox-Rushby, J., & Parker, M. (1995). Culture and the measurement of health. *Revue Européenne de Psychologie Appliquée, 45*(4), 257–263.

Freeman, R. A. (1995). A commentary on the pharmaceutical industry's sponsorship of health-related quality of life research. In J. E. Dimsdale & A. Baum (Eds.), *Quality of life in behavioral medicine research* (pp. 69–76). Hillsdale, NJ: Lawrence Erlbaum.

Frey, K. S., Greenberg, M. T., & Fewell, R. R. (1989). Stress and coping among parents of handicapped children: A multidimensional approach. *American Journal on Mental Retardation, 94*, 240–249.

Frisch, M. B. (1994). *The happiness handbook: A tool kit for life based on quality of life therapy.* Waco, TX: Author.

Frisch, M., Cornell, J., Vilanueva, M., & Retzlaff, P. (1992). Clinical validation of the quality of life inventory: A measure of life satisfaction for use in treatment planning and outcome assessment. *Psychological Assessment, 4*(1), 92–101.

Fristad, M. A., Gavazzi, S. M., & Soldado, K. W. (1998). Multi-family psychoeducation groups for childhood mood disorders: A program description and preliminary efficacy data. *Family Therapy, 20*(3), 385–402.

Fristad, M. A., Stephens, M., Gavazzi, S. M., & Soldado, K. W. (1996). Psychoeducation: A promising intervention strategy for families of children and adolescents with mood disorders. *Family Therapy, 18*(3), 371–383.

Fromm, K., Andrykowski, M. A., & Hunt, J. (1996). Positive and negative psychosocial sequelae of bone marrow transplantation: Implications for quality of life assessment. *Journal of Behavioral Medicine, 19*(3), 221–240.

Fuhred, M., Rintala, D., Hart, K., Clearman, R., & Young, M. (1992). Relationship of life satisfaction to impairment, disability, and handicap among persons with spinal cord injury living in the community. *Archives of Physical Medical Rehabilitation, 73,* 552–557.

Fujiura, G. T. (1998). Demography of family households. *American Journal on Mental Retardation, 103*(3), 225–235.

Fujiura, G. T. (2000). The implications of emerging demographics: A commentary on the meaning of race and income inequity to disability policy. *Journal of Disability Policy Studies, 11*(2), 66–75.

Fujiura, G. T., & Yamaki, K. (1997). An analysis of ethnic variations in developmental disabilities: Prevalence and household economic status. *Mental Retardation, 35,* 286–294.

Fujiura, G. T., & Yamaki, K. (2000). Trends in demography of childhood poverty and disability. *Exceptional Children, 66,* 187–199.

Ganz, P. A., & Coscarelli, A. (1995). Quality of life after breast cancer: A decade of research. In J. E. Dimsdale & A. Baum (Eds.), *Quality of life in behavioral medicine research* (pp. 97–113). Hillsdale, NJ: Lawrence Erlbaum.

Gardner, J. F. (1999). Quality services. In J. F. Gardner & S. Nudler (Eds.), *Quality performance in human services: Leadership, values, and vision* (pp. 3–19). Baltimore: Paul H. Brookes.

Gardner, J. F., & Nudler, S. (1997). Beyond compliance to responsiveness: Accreditation reconsidered. In R. L. Schalock (Ed.), *Quality of life: Vol. 2. Application to persons with disabilities* (pp. 135–148). Washington, DC: American Association on Mental Retardation.

Garg, N., Yates, W. R., Jones, R., Zhou, M., & Williams, B. A. (1999). Effect of gender, treatment site, and psychiatric comorbidity on quality of life outcome in substance dependence. *American Journal on Addictions, 8,* 44–54.

Garralda, M. E. (1994). Chronic physical illness and emotional disorder in childhood. *British Journal of Psychiatry, 164,* 8–10.

Gavazzi, S. M., Fristad, M. A., & Law, J. (1997). The understanding mood disorders questionnaire. *Psychological Reports, 81,* 172–174.

Gavino, A. (1991). Las variables del proceso terapéutico. In V. E. Caballo (Ed.). *Manual de técnicas de terapia y modificación de conducta.* Madrid: Siglo Veintiuno.

Gaylord-Ross, R. (1987). Vocational integration for persons with mental handicaps: A cross-cultural perspective. *Research in Developmental Disabilities, 8,* 532–548.

Gerber, G. J., Coleman, G. E., Johnston, L., & Lafave, H. G. (1994). Quality of life of people with psychiatric disabilities 1 and 3 years after discharge from hospital. *Quality of Life Research, 3,* 379–383.

Gerharz, E. W. (1997). Quality of life research in children: Fashion or future? *Dialogues in Pediatric Urology, 20,* 1–2.

Gettings, R. M., & Bradley, V. J. (1997). *Core indicator project.* Alexandria, VA: National Association of State Directors of Developmental Disabilities Programs.

Giangreco, M. F., Cloninger, C. J., & Iverson, V. S. (1993). *Choosing options and accommodations for children: A guide to planning inclusive education.* Baltimore: Paul H. Brookes.

Giangreco, M. F., Cloninger, C. J., Mueller, P. H., Yuan, S., & Ashworth, S. (1991). Perspectives of parents whose children have dual sensory impairments. *Journal of the Association for Persons with Severe Handicaps, 16*(1), 14–24.

Giangreco, M., Edelman, S., Dennis, R., & Cloninger, C. (1995). Use and Impact of COACH with students who are deaf-blind. *Journal of The Association for Persons with Severe Handicaps, 20*(2), 121–135.

Gjaerum, B., & Heyerdahl, S. (1998). Assessment of the mental state in medically ill children and adolescents. *Current Opinion in Psychiatry, 11,* 635–641.

Goel, S. B. (2000). Improved quality of life in India: Challenges and emerging concerns. In K. D. Keith & R. L. Schalock (Eds.), *Cross-cultural perspectives on quality of life* (pp. 231–240). Washington, DC: American Association on Mental Retardation.

Gold, M., Van Gelder, M., & Schalock, R. L. (1999). A behavioral approach to understanding and managing organizational change: Moving from workshop to community employment. *Journal of Rehabilitation Administration, 22*(3), 191–207.

Goldberg, D. (1978). *Manual of the general health questionnaire.* Windsor, England: NFER-Nelson Publishing.

Goldstrom, I. D., & Manderscheid, R. W. (1982). The chronically mentally ill: A descriptive analysis from the uniform client data instrument. *Community Support Service Journal, 2,* 4–9.

Goode, D. A. (1988). *Quality of life: A review and synthesis of the literature.* Valhalla, NY: The Mental Retardation Institute.

Goode, D. A. (1989). Quality of life and quality or work life. In W. E. Kiernan & R. L. Schalock (Eds.), *Economics, industry, and disability: A look ahead* (pp. 337–349). Baltimore: Paul H. Brookes.

Goode, D. A. (1990). Thinking about and discussing quality of life. In R. L. Schalock (Ed.), *Quality of life: Perspectives and issues* (pp. 41–58). Washington, DC: American Association on Mental Retardation.

Goode, D. A. (Ed.). (1994). *Quality of life for persons with disabilities: International perspectives and issues.* Cambridge, MA: Brookline.

Goode, D. A. (1997a). Assessing the quality of life of adults with profound disabilities. In R. I. Brown (Ed.), *Quality of life for people with disabilities: Models, research, and practice* (2nd ed., pp. 56–70). Cheltenham, England: Stanley Thornes.

Goode, D. A. (1997b). Quality of life as international disability policy: Implications for international research. In R. L. Schalock (Ed.), *Quality of life: Vol. 2. Application to persons with disabilities* (pp. 211–222). Washington, DC: American Association on Mental Retardation.

Goodman, M., Hull, J. W., Terkelsen, K. G., Smith, T. E., & Anthony, D. (1997). Factor structure of quality of life: The Lehman interview. *Evaluation and Program Planning, 20*(4), 477–480.

Grant, G. M., Salcedo, V., Hynan, L., Frisch, M. B., & Puster, K. (1995). Effectiveness of quality of life therapy for depression. *Psychological Reports, 76,* 1203–1208.

Green, R. S., & Newman, F. L. (1999). Total quality management principles promote increased utilization of client outcome data in behavioral health care. *Evaluation and Program Planning, 22,* 179–182.

Greenbaum, B., Graham, S., & Scales, W. (1996). Adults with learning disabilities: Occupational and social status after college. *Journal of Learning Disabilities, 29*(2), 167–173.

Grégoire, J. (1995). L´évaluation de la qualité de vie. *Revue Européenne de Psychologie Appliquée, 4,* 243–244.

Gritti, A., Vajro, P., Di Sarno, A. M., Comito, M., & De Vicenzo, A. (1998). Le conseguenze psicologique e psicopatologique del trapianto epatico in etá evolutiva. Revisione critica della letteratura. [The psychological and psychopathological consequences of an hepatic transplant and the process of development. Critical review of the literature]. *Rivista Italiana di Pediatria, 1,* 923–927.

Groulx, R., Dore, R., & Dore, L. (2000). My quality of life as I see it. In K. D. Keith & R. L. Schalock (Eds.), *Cross-cultural perspectives on quality of life* (pp. 23–28). Washington, DC: American Association on Mental Retardation.

Guba, E. G., & Lincoln, Y. S. (1989). *Fourth-generation evaluation.* Newbury Park, CA: Sage.

Gudex, C. (1986). *QALYs and their use by the health service.* York, Great Britain: University of York, Centre for Health Economics (Discussion Paper No. 20).

Guillemin, F. (1993). Mesures de qualité de vie génériques ou spécifiques: Quel instrument choisir? In C. Hérisson and L. Simon (Eds.), *Evaluation de la qualité de vie* (pp. 16–21). Paris: Masson.

Guyatt, G. H., Juniper, E. F., Griffith, L. E., Feeny, D. H., & Ferrie, P. (1997). Children and adult perceptions of childhood asthma. *Pediatrics, 99,* 165–168.

Halpern, A. (1993). Quality of life as a conceptual framework for evaluating transition outcomes. *Exceptional Children, 59*(6), 486–498.

Hamilton, M. (1967). Development of a rating scale for primary depressive illness. *British Journal of Social and Clinical Psychology, 6,* 278–296.

Harju, B., & Bolen, L. (1998). The effects of optimism on coping and perceived quality of life of college students. *Journal of Social Behavior and Personality, 13*(2), 185–192.

Harner, C. J., & Heal, L. W. (1993). The multifaceted lifestyle satisfaction scale (MLSS): Psychometric properties of an interview schedule for assessing personal satisfaction of adults with limited intelligence. *Research in Developmental Disabilities, 14,* 221–236.

Hatton, C. (1998). Whose quality of life is it anyway? Some problems with the emerging quality of life consensus. *Mental Retardation, 36,* 104–115.

Hatton, C., Emerson, E., Roberston, J., Henderson, D., & Cooper, J. (1995). The quality and cost of residential services for adults with multiple disabilities: A comparative evaluation. *Research in Developmental Disabilities, 16*(6), 439–460.

Hawkins, B. (1997). Health, fitness, and quality of life for older adults with developmental disabilities and leisure. *Activities, Adaptation, & Aging, 21*(3), 29–35.

Hawkins, B. (1999). Rights, place of residence, and retirement: Lessons from case studies on aging. In S. S. Herr & G. Weber (Eds.), *Aging, rights, and quality of life. Prospects for older people with developmental disabilities* (pp. 93–107). Baltimore: Paul H. Brookes.

Hayes, R. L., Halford, W. K., & Varghese, F. T. (1995). Social skills training with chronic schizophrenic patients: Effects on negative symptoms and community functioning. *Behavior Therapy, 26,* 433–449.

Heal, L. W. (1996). [Review of the book *Quality of life for persons with disabilities: International perspectives and issues*]. *American Journal on Mental Retardation, 100*(6), 557–560.

Heal, L. W., Borthwick-Duffy, S. A., & Saunders, R. R. (1996). Assessment of quality of life. In J. W. Jacobson & J. A. Mulick (Eds.), *Manual of diagnosis and professional practice in mental retardation* (pp. 199–209). Washington, DC: American Psychological Association.

Heal, L. W., & Chadsey-Rusch, J. (1985). The lifestyle satisfaction scale (LSS): Assessing individuals' satisfaction with residence, community setting, and associated services. *Applied Research in Mental Retardation, 6,* 475–490.

Heal, L. W., Khoju, M., & Rusch, F. R. (1997). Predicting quality of life of youth after they leave special education high school programs. *Journal of Special Education, 31*(3), 279–299.

Heal, L. W., Khoju, M., Rusch, F. R., & Harnisch, D. L. (1999). Predicting quality of life of students who have left special education high school programs. *American Journal of Mental Retardation, 104*(4), 305–319.

Heal, L. W., Rubin, S. S., & Park, W. (1995). *Lifestyle satisfaction scale.* Champaign-Urbana: University of Illinois, Transition Research Institute.

Heal, L. W., & Sigelman, C. (1996). Methodological issues in quality of life measurement. In R. L. Schalock (Ed.), *Quality of life: Vol. 1. Conceptualization and measurement* (pp. 91–104). Washington, DC: American Association on Mental Retardation.

Hegarty, S. (1994). Quality of life at school. In D. Goode (Ed.), *Quality of life for persons with disabilities: International perspectives and issues.* Cambridge, MA: Brookline.

Heller, T., Pederson, E. L., & Miller, A. B. (1996). Guidelines from the consumer: Improving consumer involvement in research and training for persons with mental retardation. *Mental Retardation, 34*(3), 141–148.

Helm, D. T. (2000). The measurement of happiness. *American Journal on Mental Retardation, 105*(5), 326–335.

Heinrichs, D., Hanlon, T., & Carpenter, W. (1984). The quality of life scale: An instrument for rating the schizophrenic deficit syndrome. *Schizophrenia Bulletin, 10,* 388–398.

Henderson, C., & Davidson, P. (2000). Comprehensive adult and geriatric assessment. In M. Janicki & E. Ansello (Eds.), *Community supports for aging adults with lifelong disabilities* (pp. 373–386). Baltimore: Paul H. Brookes.

Herr, S. S., & Weber G. (1999). Aging and developmental disabilities: Concepts and global perspectives. In S. S. Herr & G. Weber (Eds.), *Aging, rights, and quality of life: Prospects for older people with developmental disabilities* (pp. 1–16). Baltimore: Paul H. Brookes.

Hirschfeld, R., Russell, J. M., Delgado, P. L., Fawcett, J., Friedman, R. A., Harrison, W. M., Koran, L. M., Thase, M. E., Howland, R. H., Connolly, M. A., & Miceli, R. J. (1998). Predictors of response to acute treatment of chronic and double depression with sertraline or imipramine. *Journal of Clinical Psychiatry, 59*(12), 669–675.

Hodges, S. P., & Hernandez, M. (1999). How organizational culture influences outcome information utilization. *Evaluation and Program Planning, 22,* 183–197.

Hoffman, F. L., Leckman, E., Russo, N., & Knauf, R. (1999). In it for the long haul: The integration of outcomes assessment, clinical services, and management decision-making. *Evaluation and Program Planning, 22,* 211–219.

Hogg, J., Lucchino, R., Wang, K., Janicki, M. P., & Working Group (2000). *Health of aging adults with intellectual disabilities: Aging & social policy.* Geneva, Switzerland: World Health Organization.

Horner, R. H. (2000). Positive behavior supports. In M. Wehmeyer & J. R. Patton (Eds.), *Mental retardation in the 21st century* (pp. 181–196). Austin, TX: Pro-Ed.

Howe, J., Horner, R. H., & Newton J. S. (1998). Comparison of supported living and traditional residential services in the state of Oregon. *Mental Retardation, 36*(1), 1–11.

Huber, L., & Edelberg, B. (1993). A community integration model of head injury rehabilitation. *Journal of Cognitive Rehabilitation, 11,* 22–26.

Huebner, E. S. (1991). Initial development of the student's life satisfaction scale. *School Psychology International, 12,* 231–240.

Huebner, E. S. (1994). Preliminary development and validation of a multidimensional life satisfaction scale for children. *Psychological Assessment, 6,* 149–158.

Hughes, C., & Hwang, B. (1996). Attempts to conceptualize and measure quality of life. In R. L. Schalock (Ed.), *Quality of life: Vol. 1. Conceptualization and measurement* (pp. 51–62). Washington, DC: American Association on Mental Retardation.

Hunt, J. M. (1969). *The challenge of incompetence: Papers on the role of early education.* Urbana: University of Illinois Press.

Hunt, S. M., & McEwen, J. (1980). The development of a subjective health indicator. *Sociology of Health and Illness, 2*(3), 231–246.

Hunt, S. M., & McKenna, S. P. (1993). Measuring quality of life in psychiatry. In S. R. Walker & R. M. Rosser (Eds.), *Quality of life assessment: Key issues in the 1990s.* Dordrecht, The Netherlands: Kluwer Academic.

Ineichen, B., & Rohde, J. (1994). Leaving special schools. Are school-leavers with severe learning disabilities getting enough help? *British Journal of Learning Disabilities, 22,* 113–115.

Ionescu, S. (1995). La recherche dans le domaine de la qualité de vie des personnes présentant une déficience intellectuelle. *Revue Francophone de la Déficience Intellectuelle, 8*(1), 5–17.

Iso, A., Seppo, E., & Park, C. J. (1996). Leisure-related social support and self-determination as buffers of stress-illness relationship. *Journal of Leisure Research, 28,* 169–187.

Jacobson, A. M., Groot, M., & Samson, J. (1995). Quality of life research in patients with diabetes mellitus. In J. E. Dimsdale & A. Baum (Eds.), *Quality of life in behavioral medicine research* (pp. 241–262). Hillsdale, NJ: Lawrence Erlbaum.

Janicki, M. (1996). Quality of life for older persons with mental retardation. In R. L. Schalock (Ed.), *Quality of life: Vol. 2. Application to persons with disabilities* (pp. 105–115). Washington, DC: American Association on Mental Retardation.

Janikowski, T., Bordieri, J., & Musgrave, J. (1991). Dimensions of client satisfaction with vocational evaluation services. *Vocational Evaluation and Work Adjustment Bulletin, 9,* 43–48.

Janney, R., & Snell, M. E. (2000). *Behavior support.* Baltimore: Paul H. Brookes.

Jencks, S. F. (1995). Measuring quality of care under Medicare and Medicaid. *Health Care Financing Review, 16*(4), 39–54.

Jenkinson, C., & Wright, L. (1993). The SF-36 health survey questionnaire. *Auditorium, 2,* 7–12.

Jones, V. F., & Jones, L. S. (1995). *Comprehensive classroom management: Creating positive learning environments for all students.* Boston: Allyn & Bacon.

Jones, K., Robinson, M., & Golightley, M. (1986). Long-term psychiatric patients in the community. *British Journal of Psychiatry, 149,* 537–540.

Jonsson, A., Dock, J., & Ravnborg, M. H. (1996). Quality of life as a measure of rehabilitation outcome in patients with multiple sclerosis. *Acta Psychiatrica Scandinavica, 93,* 229–235.

Juniper, E. F., Guyatt, G. H., & Epstein, R. S. (1992). Evaluation of impairment of health-related quality of life in asthma: Development of a questionnaire for use in clinical trials. *Thorax, 47,* 76–83.

Juniper, E. F., Guyatt, G. H., Feeny, D. H., Griffith, L. E., & Ferrie, P. J. (1997). Minimum skills required by children to complete health-related quality of life instruments for asthma: Comparison of measurement properties. *European Respiratory Journal, 10,* 2285–2294.

Juniper, E. F., Guyatt, G. H., & Jaeschke, R. (1995). How to develop and validate a new quality of life instrument. In B. Spilker (Ed.), *Quality of life and pharmacoeconomics in clinical trials* (2nd ed., pp. 49–56). New York: Raven Press.

Kanfer, F. H., & Goldstein, A. P. (1991). *Helping people change: A textbook of methods* (4th ed.). New York: Pergamon.

Kaplan, M. K. (1995). Quality of life, resource allocation, and the U.S. healthcare crisis. In J. E. Dimsdale & A. Baum (Eds.), *Quality of life in behavioral medicine research* (pp. 3–30). Hillsdale, NJ: Lawrence Erlbaum.

Katschnig, H. (1997). How useful is the concept of quality of life in psychiatry? In H. Katschnig, H. Freeman, & N. Sartorius (Eds.), *Quality of life in mental disorders* (pp. 3–16). Chichester, England: John Wiley.

Katschnig, H., & Angermeyer, M. C. (1997). Quality of life in depression. In H. Katschnig, H. Freeman, & N. Sartorius (Eds.), *Quality of life in mental disorders* (pp. 137–147). Chichester, England: John Wiley.

Katz, J. N., Larson, M. G., & Phillips, C. B. (1992). Comparative measurements sensitivity of short and longer health status instruments. *Medical Care, 30,* 917–926.

Katz, S. C., Ford, A. B., & Moskowitz, R. W. (1963). Studies of illness in the aged: The index of ADL: A standardized measure of biological and psychological function. *Journal of the American Medical Association, 185*(8), 914–919.

Keith, K. D. (1996). Measuring quality of life across cultures: Issues and challenges. In R. L. Schalock (Ed.), *Quality of life: Vol. 1. Conceptualization and measurement* (pp. 73–82). Washington, DC: American Association on Mental Retardation.

Keith, K. D. (2001). International quality of life: Current conceptual, measurement, and implementation issues. *International Review of Research in Mental Retardation, 24,* 49–74.

Keith, K. D., & Schalock, R. L. (1995). *Quality of student life questionnaire.* Worthington, OH: IDS Publishing.

Keith, K. D., & Schalock, R. L. (Eds). (2000). *Cross-cultural perspectives on quality of life.* Washington, DC: American Association on Mental Retardation.

Keith, K. D., Heal, L. W., & Schalock, R. L. (1996). Cross-cultural measurement of critical quality of life concepts. *Journal of Intellectual and Developmental Disability, 21,* 273–293.

Keith, K. D., Schalock, R. L., & Hoffman, K. (1986). *Quality of life: Measurement and programmatic implications.* Lincoln: Nebraska Region V Mental Retardation Services.

Keith, K. D., Yamamoto, M., Okita, N., & Schalock, R. L. (1995). Cross-cultural quality of life: Japanese and American college students. *Social Behavior and Personality, 23,* 163–170.

Kempen, G., Jelicic, M., & Ormel, J. (1997). Personality, chronic medical morbidity, and health-related quality of life among older persons. *Health Psychology, 16*(6), 539–546.

Kennedy, C., Horner, R., Newton, J., & Kanda, E. (1990). Measuring the activity patterns of adults with severe disabilities using the resident lifestyle inventory. *Journal of The Association for Persons with Severe Handicaps, 15*(2), 79–85.

Keogh, B. K., Bernheimer, L. P., Gallimore, R., & Weisner, T. S. (1998). Child and family outcomes over time: A longitudinal perspective on developmental delays. In M. Lewis & C. Feiring (Eds.), *Families, risk, and competence* (pp. 269–287). Mahwah, NJ: Lawrence Erlbaum.

Kiernan, W. E., & Schalock, R. L. (1997). *Integrated employment. Current status and future directions.* Washington, DC: American Association on Mental Retardation.

Kiernan, W. E., Sanchez, R., & Schalock, R. L. (1989). Epilogue: Economics, industry, and disability in the future. In W. E. Kiernan & R. L. Schalock (Eds.), *Economics, industry, and disability: A look ahead* (pp. 365–374). Baltimore: Paul H. Brookes.

Kiernan, W. E., Schalock, R. L., Butterworth, J., & Mank, D. (1997). The next steps. In W. Kiernan & R. L. Schalock (Eds.), *Integrated employment: Current status and future directions* (pp. 133–144). Washington, DC: American Association on Mental Retardation.

Kober, R., & Eggleton, I. R. C. (2002). Factor stability of the Schalock and Keith (1993). *Quality of life questionnaire. Mental Retardation, 40*(2), 157–165.

Koegel, L. K., Stiebal, D., & Koegel, R. L. (1998). Reducing agression in children with autism toward infant or toddler siblings. *Journal of the Association for Persons with Severe Handicaps, 23*(3), 111–118.

Koran, L. M., Thieneman, M. L., & Davenport, R. (1996). Quality of life for patients with obsessive-compulsive disorder. *American Journal of Psychiatry, 153*(6), 783–788.

Kramer, M. (1992). Barriers to the primary prevention of mental, neurological, and psychosocial disorders of children: A global perspective. *Improving Children's Lives, 3*–36.

Kuehn, M. L., & McClainm, J. W. (1994). Quality of life in the United States: A multicultural context. In D. A. Goode (Ed.), *Quality of life for persons with disabilities: International perspectives and issues* (pp. 185–193). Boston: Brookline.

Kuhn, R. S. (1970). *The structure of scientific revolutions* (2nd ed.). Chicago: University of Chicago Press.

Kuyken, W. (1995). The World Health Organization quality of life assessment (WHOQOL): Position paper from the World Health Organization. *Social Science and Medicine, 41*(10), 1403–1409.

Lafave, H. G., de Souza, H. R., Prince, P. N., Atchison, K. E., & Gerber, G. J. (1995). Partnerships for people with serious mental illness who live below the poverty line. *Psychiatric Services, 46*(10), 1071–1073.

Lamb, H. R. (1993). Lessons learned from desinstitutionalisation in the U.S. *British Journal of Psychiatry, 162,* 587–592.

Land, K., & Spilerman, S. (Eds.). (1975). *Social indicator models.* New York: Russell Sage.

Lawton, M. P., & Brody, E. M. (1969). Assessment of older people: Self-maintaining and instrumental activities of daily living. *Gerontologist, 9,* 176–186.

Lawton, M. P., Moss, M., Fulcomer, M., & Kleban, M. H. (1982). A research and service orientated multilevel assessment instrument. *Journal of Gerontology, 37,* 91–99.

Le Bidois, J., Vouhe, P., Tamisier, D., Sidi, D., & Cachaner, J. (1998). Transplantation cardiaque de l'enfant. Indications et résultats. *Annales de Pediatrie, 45,* 673–676.

Lefcourt, H. M. (1976). *Locus of control.* Hillsdale, NJ: Lawrence Erlbaum.

Leff, J. P. (1997). Whose life is it anyway? Quality of life for long-stay patients discharged from psychiatric hospitals. In H. Katschnig, H. Freeman, & N. Sartorius (Eds.), *Quality of life in mental disorders* (pp. 241–260). Chichester, England: John Wiley.

Leff, J. P., O'Driscoll, C., Dayson, D., Wills, W., & Anderson, J. (1990). The TAPS project: 5. The structure of social-network data obtained from long-stay patients. *British Journal of Psychiatry, 157,* 848–852.

Lehman, A. F. (1983). The well-being of chronic mental patients: Assessing their quality of life. *Archives of General Psychiatry, 40,* 369–373.

Lehman, A. F. (1988). A quality of life interview for the chronically mentally ill (QOLI). *Evaluation and Program Planning, 11,* 51–62.

Lehman, A. F. (1993). The effects of psychiatric symptoms on quality of life assessments among the chronically mentally ill. *Evaluation and Program Planning, 6,* 143-151.

Lehman, A. F. (1997). Instruments for measuring quality of life in mental illnesses. In H. Katschning, H. Freeman, & N. Sartorius (Eds.), *Quality of life in mental disorders* (pp. 79–94). Chichester, England: John Wiley.

Lehman, A. F., Possidente, S., & Hawker, F. (1986). The quality of life of chronic patients in a state hospital and in community residences. *Hospital and Community Psychiatry, 37*(9), 901–907.

Lehman, A., Postrado, L., & Rachuba, L. (1993). Convergent validation of quality of life assessments for persons with severe mental illnesses. *Quality of Life Research, 2,* 327–333.

Lehman, A. F., Rachuba, L. T., & Postrado, L. T. (1995). Demographic influences on quality of life among persons with chronic mental illnesses. *Evaluation and Program Planning, 18*(2), 155–164.

Lehman, A. F., Ward, N. C., & Linn, L. S. (1982). Chronic mental patients: The quality of life issue. *American Journal of Psychiatry, 139*(10), 1271–1276.

Lenz, G., & Demal, U. (1997). Psychotherapy and quality of life. In H. Katschnig, H. Freeman, & N. Sartorius (Eds.), *Quality of life in mental disorders* (pp. 227–239). Chichester, England: John Wiley.

Leval, N. (1995). Scales of depression, ill-being, and the quality of life: Is there any difference? An essay in taxonomy. *Quality of Life Research, 4,* 259–269.

Liebowitz, M. R., Gorman, J. M., Fyer, A. J., & Klein, D. F. (1985). Social phobia: Review of a neglected anxiety disorder. *Archives of General Psychiatry, 42,* 729–736.

Lieu, A. T., & Newton, T. B. (1998). Issues in studying the effectiveness of health services for children. *Health Services Research, 33,* 1041–1048.

Lin, H. C. (2000). Quality of life of individuals with disabilities in Taiwan. In K. D. Keith & R. L. Schalock (Eds.), *Cross-cultural perspectives on quality of life* (pp. 205–218). Washington, DC: American Association on Mental Retardation.

Lincoln, Y. (1995). Emerging criteria for quality in qualitative and interpretive research. *Qualitative Inquiry, 1*(3), 275–289.

Lindstrom, B. (1992). Quality of life: A model for evaluating health for all. *Soz Praventivmed, 37,* 301–306.

Linhorst, D. M. (1988). The development of a program evaluation system for psychosocial rehabilitation centers. *Psychosocial Rehabilitation Journal, 12,* 35–43.

Linn, M. W. & Linn, B. S. (1984). Self-evaluation of life function scale: A short comprehensive self-report of health for elderly adults. *Journal of Gerontology, 39,* 603–612.

Lipsey, M. W., & Pollard, J. A. (1989). Driving toward theory in program evaluation: More models to choose from. *Evaluation and Program Planning, 12,* 317–328.

Litwins, N. M., & Rodriguez. J. R. (1994). Quality of life in adult recipients of bone marrow transplantation. *Psychological Reports, 75,* 323–328.

Liu, B. C. (1976). *Quality of life indicators in U.S. metropolitan areas: A statistical analysis.* New York: Praeger.

Llamas, R., Pattison, E. M., & Hunt, G. (1981). Social networks: A link between psychiatric epidemiology and community mental health. *International Journal of Family Therapy, 3,* 180–192.

Logan, S. (1999). Evaluation of services for children with disabilities and their families. *Child Care, Health and Development, 25,* 81–83.

Long, J. S. (1983). *Confirmatory factor analysis.* Beverly Hills, CA.: Sage.

López, A. E. (1994). *Valoración de los efectos de la rehabilitación psicosocial.* Unpublished doctoral dissertation, Universidad de Málaga, Málaga, Spain.

Lord, J., & Pedlar, A. (1991). Life in the community: Four years after the closure of an institution. *Mental Retardation, 29*(4), 213–221.

Lowe, G. (1996). Pleasure, relaxation, and unwinding. In D. M. Warburton & N. Sherwood (Eds.), *Pleasure and quality of life* (pp. 67–77). Chichester, England: John Wiley.

Luckasson, R. (1990). A lawyer's perspective on quality of life. In R. L. Schalock (Ed.), *Quality of life: Perspectives and issues* (pp. 211–214). Washington, DC: American Association on Mental Retardation.

Luckasson, R. (1997). Foreword. In R. L. Schalock (Ed.), *Quality of life: Vol. 2: Application to persons with disabilities* (pp. vii–x). Washington, DC: American Association on Mental Retardation.

Luckasson, R., Coulter, D. L., Polloway, E. A., Reiss, S., Schalock, R. L., Snell, M. E., Spitalnik, D. M., & Stark, J. A. (1992). *Mental retardation: Definition, classification, and systems of supports.* Washington, DC: American Association on Mental Retardation.

Lukoff, D., Liberman, R. P., & Nuechterlein, K. H. (1986). Symptom monitoring in the rehabilitation of schizophrenic patients. *Schizophrenia Bulletin, 12,* 578–602.

Lutgendorf, S., Antoni, M. H., Shneiderman, N., & Ironson, G. (1995). Psychosocial interventions and quality of life changes across the HIV spectrum. In J. E. Dimsdale & A. Baum (Eds.), *Quality of life in behavioral medicine research* (pp. 205–240). Hillsdale, NJ: Lawrence Erlbaum.

MacCraughrin, W. B., Ellis, W. K., Rusch, F. R., & Heal, L. W. (1993). Cost-effectiveness of supported employment. *Mental Retardation, 31*(1), 41–48.

MacNeil, R. D., & Anderson, S. C. (1999). Leisure and persons with developmental disabilities: Empowering self-determination through inclusion. In P. Retish & S. Reiter (Eds.), *Adults with disabilities: International perspectives in the community* (pp. 125–143). Mahwah, NJ: Lawrence Erlbaum.

MacPhee, M., Hoffenberg, E. J., & Feranchak, A. (1998). Quality of life factors in adolescent inflammatory bowel disease. *Medline, 4,* 6–11.

MacPhillamy, D. J., & Lewinsohn, P. M. (1982). The pleasant events schedule: Studies on reliability, validity, and scale inter-correlation. *Journal of Consulting and Clinical Psychology, 50,* 363–380.

Magana, S. M. (2000). Mental retardation research methods in Latino communities. *Mental Retardation, 38*(4), 303–315.

Magee, W. J., Eaton, W. W., Wittchen, H. U., McGonagle, K. A., & Kessler, R. C. (1996). Agoraphobia, simple phobia, and social phobia in the national comorbidity survey. *Archives of General Psychiatry, 53,* 159–168.

Mangione-Smith, R., & McGlynn, A. (1998). Assessing the quality of health care provided to children. *Health Services Research, 33,* 1059–1090.

Manificat, S., & Dazord, A. (1997). Evaluation de la qualité de vie de l'enfant: Validation d'un questionnaire, premiers résultats. *Neuropsychiatrie de l'Enfance et de l'Adolescence, 45*(3), 106–114.

Manificat, S., Dazord, A., Cochat, P., & Nicolas, J. (1997). Evaluation de la qualité de vie en pédiatrie: Comment receuillir le point de vue de l'enfant. *Archives Françaises de Pediatrie, 4,* 1238–1246.

Mank, D. (1996). Natural supports research project takes shape. *TASH Newsletter, 22*(6), 22–23.

Mank, D., Cioffi, A., & Yovanoff, P. (1997). Analysis of the typicalness of supported employment jobs, natural supports and wage and integration outcomes. *Mental Retardation, 35*(3), 185–197.

Mank, D. (1997). Systems change strategies for integrated employment: A blueprint for the future. In W. E. Kiernan & R. L. Schalock (Eds.), *Integrated employment: Current status and future directions* (pp. 107–119). Washington, DC: American Association on Mental Retardation.

Mank, D., & Buckley, J. (1989). Strategies for integrated employment. In W. E. Kiernan & R. L. Schalock (Eds.), *Economics, industry, and disability: A look ahead* (pp. 319–335). Baltimore: Paul H. Brookes.

Mank, D., Cioffi, A., & Yovanoff, P. (2000). Direct support in supported employment and its relation to job typicalness, coworker involvement, and employment outcomes. *Mental Retardation, 38,* 506–516.

Mansell, J. (1994). Specialized group homes for persons with severe or profound mental retardation and serious problem behaviour in England. *Research in Developmental Disabilities, 15*(5), 371–388.

Markowitz, J. S., Weissman, M. M., Quellette, R., Lish, J., & Klerman, G. L. (1989). Quality of life in panic disorders. *Archives of General Psychiatry, 46,* 984–992.

Markus, H., & Kitayama, S. (1991). Culture and the self: Implications for cognition, emotion, and motivation. *Psychological Review, 98,* 224–253.

Marsh, H. W. (1990). *The self-description questionnaire-II.* San Antonio, TX: Psychological Corporation.

Masera, G., Spinetta, J. J., Jancovic, M., Ablin, A. R., D'Angio, G. J., Van Dongen-Melman, J., Eden, T., Martins, A. G., Mulhern, R. K., Oppenheim, D., Topf, R., & Chesler, M. A. (1999). Guidelines for assistance to terminally ill children with cancer: A report of the SIOP working committee on psychosocial issues in pediatric oncology. *Medical and Pediatric Oncology, 32,* 44–48.

Massion, A. O., Warshaw, M. G., & Keller, M. B. (1993). Quality of life and psychiatric morbidity in panic disorder and generalized anxiety disorder. *American Journal of Psychiatry, 150*(91), 600–607.

Mawhood, C. (1997). Performance measurement in the United Kingdom (1985-1995). In E. Chelimsky & W. R. Shadish (Eds.), *Evaluation for the 21st century: A handbook* (pp. 134–144). Thousand Oaks, CA: Sage.

McCabe, S., & Unzicker, R. (1995). Changing roles of consumer/survivors in natural mental health systems. *New Directions in Mental Health Services, 66,* 61–73.

McClary, S., Lubin, B., Evans, C., Watt, B., & Lebedun, M. (1989). Evaluation of a community treatment program for young adult schizophrenics. *Journal of Clinical Psychology, 45,* 806–808.

McConkey, R., & O'Toole, B. (2000). Improving the quality of life of people with disabilities in least affluent countries: Insights from Guyana. In K. D. Keith & R. L. Schalock (Eds.), *Cross-cultural perspectives on quality of life* (pp. 281–290). Washington, DC: American Association on Mental Retardation.

McGill, P., Emerson, E., & Mansell, J. (1994). Individually designed residential provision for people with seriously challenging behaviours. In E. Emerson, P. McGill, & J. Mansell (Eds.), *Severe learning disabilities and challenging behaviours* (pp. 119–156). London: Chapman & Hall.

McKenna, S. P. (1997). Measuring quality of life in schizophrenia. *European Psychiatry, 12*(3), 267–274.

McLenan, A. (1995). Empowerment and the psychiatric consumer ex-patient movement in the United States: Contradictions, crisis, and change. *Social Science & Medicine, 40,* 1053–1071.

Meltzer, H. Y., Burnett, S., Bastani, B., & Ramirez, L. F. (1990). Effects of six months of clozapine treatment on the quality of life of chronic schizophrenic patients. *Hospital and Community Psychiatry, 150,* 1630–1638.

Mendoza, R., Batista-Foguet, J. M., & Oliva, A. (1994). Lifestyles of European school-children: Findings of the WHO cross-national study on health-related behaviour. In J. P. Dauwalder (Ed.), *Psychology and promotion of health* (pp. 9–19). Bern, Switzerland: Hogrefe & Huber.

Mercier, C. (1989). Conditions de vie et lieux de résidence. *Sante Mentale au Quebec, XIV,* 158–171.

Mercier, M., & Schraub, S. (1993). Appréciation de la souffrance psychosociale. Application en cancérologie. In C. Hérisson & L. Simon (Eds.), *Evaluation de la qualité de vie* (pp. 65–69). Paris: Masson.

Mercier, C., Tempier, R., & Renaud, C. (1992). Services communautaires et qualité de la vie: Une étude d'impact en région éloignée. *Canadian Journal of Psychiatry/Revue Canadienne de Psychiatrie, 37,* 553–563.

Michalos, A. C. (1985). Multiple discrepancy theory (MDT). *Social Indicators Research, 16,* 347–413.

Milbrath, L. W. (1979). Policy relevant quality of life research. *Annals of the American Academy of Political and Social Science, 444,* 33–45.

Miller, L. (1992). Back to the future: Legal, vocational, and quality-of-life issues in the long-term adjustment of the brain-injured patient. *Journal of Cognitive Rehabilitation, 10,* 14–20.

Mitchell, D., & Winslade, J. (1997). Developmental systems and narrative approaches to working with families of persons with disabilities. In R. I. Brown (Ed.), *Quality of life for people with disabilities* (2nd ed., pp. 151–182). Cheltenham, England: Stanley Thornes.

Moinpour, C. M., Savage, M., Hayden, K. A., Sawyers, J., & Upchurch, C. (1995). Quality of life assessment in cancer clinical trials. In J. E. Dimsdale & A. Baum (Eds.), *Quality of life in behavioral medicine research* (pp. 79–96). Hillsdale, NJ: Lawrence Erlbaum.

Montazeri, A., Gillis, C. R., & Mc Ewen, J. (1998). Quality of life in patients with lung cancer: A review of literature from 1970 to 1995. *Chest, 113,* 467–481.

Montoro, J. (1999). Factores determinantes de la calidad del cuidado asistencial institucional a personas mayores y/o con discapacidad. *Papers, 57,* 89–112.

Moorcroft, A. J., Dodd, M. E., & Webb, A. K. (1998). Exercise limitations and training for patients with cystic fibrosis. *Disability and Rehabilitation, 20,* 247–253.

Moos, S. (1999). Mental health issues of access and quality of life. In S. J. Herr and G. Weber (Eds.), *Aging, rights, and quality of life: Prospects for older people with disabilities* (pp. 167–187). Baltimore: Brookes.

Morcillo, L., Barcia, D., & Borgoñós, E. (1995). Esquizofrenia. Calidad de vida y años de evolución. *Actas Luso-Españolas de Neurología Psiquiatrica, 23,* 293–298.

Moreno, B., & Ximénez, C. (1996). Evaluación de la calidad de vida. In G. Buela-Casal, V. E. Caballo & C. J. Sierra (Eds.), *Manual de Evaluación en Psicología Clínica y de la Salud* (pp. 1045–1070). Madrid: Siglo Veintiuno.

Morris, M. H., & Lewis, P. S. (1991). Entrepreneurship as a significant factor in societal quality of life. *Journal of Business Research, 23,* 21–36.

Muijen, M., Marks, I., Connolly, J., & Audini, B. (1992). Home-based care and standard hospital care for patients with severe mental illness: A randomised control trials. *British Medical Journal, 304,* 749–754.

Mulkern, V. M., & Manderscheid, R. W. (1984). Characteristics of community support program clients in 1980 and 1984. *Hospital and Community Psychiatry, 40,* 165–172.

Murrell, S. A., & Norris, F. H. (1983). Quality of life as the criterion for need assessment and community psychology. *Journal of Community Psychology, 11,* 88–97.

Myers, D. G. (2000). The funds, friends, and faith of happy people. *American Psychologist, 55*(1), 56–67.

Myers, D. G., & Diener, E. (1996). The pursuit of happiness: New research uncovers some anti-intuitive insights into how many people are happy and why. *Scientific American,* 70–72.

Naber, D. (1995). A self-rating to measure subjective effects of neuroleptic drugs, relationships to objective psychopathology, quality of life, compliance, and other clinical variables. *International Clinical Psychopharmacology, 10,* 133–138.

Nagel, S. (1990). Bridging theory and practice in policy and program evaluation. *Evaluation and Program Planning, 13,* 275–283.

Nerney, T. (1998). Self-determination for people with developmental disabilities. Doing more with less. Rethinking long-term care. *AAMR News and Notes, 11*(6), 10–12.

Neugarten, B. L., Havighurst, R. J., & Tobin, S. S. (1961). The measurement of life satisfaction. *Journal of Gerontology, 16,* 134–143.

Newport, C. P. (1996). *So what is a QALY?* [On-line]. Available: www.ebando.com/band24/b24-7.html (Consulted February 25, 2000).

Newsom, J. T., & Schutz, R. (1996). Social support as a mediator in the relation between functional status and quality of life in older adults. *Psychology and Aging, 111*(1), 34–44.

Nicolas, J., Dazord, A., & Manificat, S. (1996). Evaluation of life quality for children infected by HIV: Validation of a method and preliminary results. *Pediatric AIDS and HIV Infection: Fetus to Adolescent, 7,* 254–260.

Nihira, K., Foster, R., Shellhaas, M., & Leland, H. (1975). *AAMD Adaptive Behavior Scale.* Washington, DC: American Association on Mental Deficiency.

Nikkel, R. E., Smith, G., & Edwards, P. (1992). A consumer operated case management project. *Hospital and Community Psychiatry, 43,* 577–579.

Nirje, B. (1985). The basis and logic of the normalization principle. *Australia and New Zealand Journal of Developmental Disabilities, 11,* 65–68.

Nisbet, J. (Ed.). (1992). *Natural supports in school, at work, and in the community for people with severe disabilities.* Baltimore: Paul H. Brookes.

Nisbet, J., & Hagner, D. (1988). Natural supports in the workplace: A reexamination of supported employment. *Journal of The Association for Persons with Severe Handicaps, 13*(41), 260–267.

Nowicki, S., & Strickland, B. (1973). Locus of control scale for children. *Journal of Consulting and Clinical Psychology, 40,* 148–154.

Obuchowska, I., & Obuchowski, M. (1992). Quality of life in families with mentally retarded children: Promoting independence and acceptance. In G. W. Albee, L. A. Bond, & T. V. Cook Monsey (Eds.), *Improving children's lives* (pp. 254–251). Newbury Park, CA: Sage.

O'Donnell, M., Parker, G., Proberts, M., Matthews, R., Fisher, D., Johnson, B., & Hadzi-Pavlovic, D. (1999). A study of client-focused case management and consumer advocacy: The community and consumer service project. *Australia and New Zealand Journal of Psychiatry, 33,* 684–693.

Oliver, J. P. J. (1991). The social care directive: Development of a quality of life profile for use in community services for the mentally ill. *Social Work and Social Sciences Review, 3*(1), 5–45.

Oliver, J., & Mohamad, H. (1992). The quality of life of chronically mentally ill: A comparison of public, private, and voluntary residential provisions. *British Journal of Social Work, 22,* 391–404.

Oliver, J., Huxley, P., Bridges, K., & Mohamad, H. (1996). *Quality of life and mental health services.* London: Routledge.

O' Mahony, P. G., Rodgers, H., Thomson, R. G., Dobson, R., & James, O. F. W. (1998). Is the SF-36 suitable for assessing health status of older stroke patients? *Age and Aging, 27,* 19–22.

Ormel, J., Kempen, G. I., Steverink, B., van Eijk, L. M., Brilman, E. I., Wolfensberger, E. W., & Meyboom-de Jong, B. (1992). *The Groningen longitudinal aging study on functional status and need for care: Outline of a NESTOR research program.* Gronigen, The Netherlands: University of Groningen, Northern Centre for Healthcare Research.

Ors, A., & Laguna, A. (1997). Reflexiones sobre el envejecimiento y la calidad de vida. *Cultura de los Cuidados, 1*(2), 60–63.

Osgood, C. E., May, W. H., & Miron, M. S. (1975). *Cross cultural universals of affective meaning.* Urbana: University of Illinois Press.

Osher, T. W. (1998). Outcomes and accountability from a family perspective. *Journal of Behavioral Health Services and Research, 25*(2), 230–232.

Overall, J. E., & Gorham, D. R. (1962). The brief psychiatric rating scale. *Psychological Reports, 10,* 799–812.

Parmenter, T. R. (1994). Quality of life as a concept and measurable entity. *Social Indicators Research, 33,* 9–46.

Parmenter, T. R. (1996). The use of quality of life as a construct for social and health policy development. In R. B. Renwick, I. Brown, & M. Nagler (Eds.), *Quality of life in health promotion and rehabilitation: Conceptual approaches, issues, and applications* (pp. 89-103). Newbury Park, CA: Sage.

Parmenter, T. R. (2001). The contribution of science in facilitating the inclusion of people with intellectual disabilities into the community. *Journal of Intellectual Disabilities Research, 45*(3), 183–193.

Parmenter, T., & Donelly, M. (1997). An analysis of the dimensions of quality of life. In R. I. Brown (Ed.), *Quality of life for people with disabilities: Models, research, and practice* (2nd ed., pp. 91–114). Cheltenham, England: Stanley Thornes.

Patrick, D. L., Bush, J. W., & Chen, M. M. (1973). Toward an operational definition of health. *Journal of Health and Social Behavior, 14,* 6–23.

Patrick, D. L., & Erickson, P. (1988). Assessing health-related quality of life for clinical decision making. In R. S. Walker & R. M. Rosser (Eds.), *Quality of life: Assessment and application* (pp. 9–50). London: MTP Press.

Patterson, T., Kaplan, R. M., Grant, I., Semple, S. J., Moscona, S., Koch, W. L., Harris, M. J., & Jeste, D. V. (1996). Quality of well being in late life psychosis. *Psychiatry Research, 63,* 169–181.

Pattison, E. M., Difrancisco, D., Wood, P. Frazier, H., & Crowder, J. A. (1975). A psychological kinship model for family therapy. *American Journal of Psychiatry, 132,* 1246–1251.

Pattison, E. M., & Pattison, M. L. (1981). Analysis of a schizophrenic psychosocial network. *Schizophrenia Bulletin, 7,* 135–142.

Pengra, L. M. (2000). Lakota quality of life: Mitakuye oyasin. In K. D. Keith & R. L. Schalock (Eds.), *Cross-cultural perspectives on quality of life* (pp. 191–204). Washington, DC: American Association on Mental Retardation.

Pfeiffer, E. (1975a). A short portable mental status questionnaire for the assessment of organic brain deficit in the elderly patients. *Journal of the American Geriatrics Society, 23*(10), 433–441.

Pfeiffer, E. (1975b). *Multidimensional functional assessment: The OARS methodology, a manual* (1st ed.). Durham, NC: Duke University Center for the Study of Aging and Human Development.

Pickney, A. A., Gerber, G. J., & Lafave, H. G. (1991). Quality of life after psychiatric rehabilitation: The clients' perspective. *Acta Psychiatrica Scandinavica, 83,* 86–91.

Quine, L., & Pahl, J. (1989). *Stress and coping in families caring for a child with severe mental handicap: A longitudinal study.* Canterbury, England: University of Kent.

Raphael, D. (1996). Defining quality of life: Debates concerning its measurement. In R. Renwick, I. Brown, & M. Nagler (Eds.), *Quality of life in health promotion and rehabilitation: Conceptual approaches, issues, and applications* (pp. 146–165). Thousand Oaks, CA: Sage.

Raphael, D. (1999). The quality of life of exceptional adolescents: Implications for educators. *Exceptionality Education Canada, 9,* 157–171.

Rapley, M. (2000). The social construction of "quality of life": The interpersonal production of well-being revisited. In K. D. Keith & R. L. Schalock (Eds.), *Cross-cultural perspectives on quality of life* (pp. 15–172). Washington, DC: American Association on Mental Retardation.

Rapley, M., & Hopgood, L. (1997). Quality of life in a community-based service in rural Australia. *Journal of Intellectual & Developmental Disabilities, 22*(2), 125–141.

Rapley, M., & Lobley, J. (1995). Factor analysis of the Schalock & Keith (1993) quality of life questionnaire: A replication. *Mental Handicap Research, 8*(3), 194–202.

Rapley, M., Lobley, J., & Bozatzis, N. (1993). *Preliminary validation of the Schalock & Keith (1994) quality of life questionnaire with a British population.* Lancaster, England: Lancaster University, Department of Psychology.

Ravens-Sieberer, U., & Bullinger, M. (1998). Assessing health-related quality of life in chronically ill children with the German KINDL: First psychometric and content analytical results. *Quality of Life Research, 7,* 339–407.

Read, J. L. (1988). The new era of quality of life assessment. In S. R. Walker & R. M. Rosser (Eds.), *Quality of life: Assessment and application* (pp. 1-8). London: MTP Press.

Regier, D. A., Narrow, W., & Rae, D. S. (1990). The epidemiologic catchment area (ECA) experience. *Journal of Psychiatric Research, 24,* 3–14.

Reid, D. T., & Renwick, R. M. (1994). Preliminary validation of a new instrument to measure life satisfaction in adolescents with neuromuscular disorders. *International Journal of Rehabilitation Research, 17,* 184–188.

Reinders, H. S. (2000). *The future of the disabled in liberal society: An ethical analysis.* Notre Dame, IN: University of Notre Dame Press.

Reiss, S. (2000). A mindful approach to mental retardation. *Journal of Social Issues, 56*(1), 65–80.

Reiss, S., & Havercamp, S. H. (1998). Toward a comprehensive assessment of fundamental motivation. Factor structure of the Reiss profiles. *Psychological Assessment, 10,* 97–106.

Reiter, S., & Bendov, D. (1996). The self-concept and quality of life of two groups of learning-disabled adults living at home and in group homes. *British Journal of Developmental Disabilities, 42,* 97–111.

Renwick, R., & Brown, I. (1996). The Centre for Health Promotion's conceptual approach to quality of life. In R. Renwick, I. Brown, & M. Nagler (Eds.), *Quality of life in health promotion and rehabilitation: Conceptual approaches, issues, and applications* (pp. 75–86). Thousand Oaks, CA: Sage.

Renwick, R., Brown, I., & Raphael, D. (2000). Person-centered quality of life: Contributions from Canada to an international understanding. In K. D. Keith & R. L. Schalock, *Cross-cultural perspectives on quality of life* (pp. 5–21). Washington, DC: American Association on Mental Retardation.

Revicki, D. A., Simon, G. E., Chan, K., Katon, W., & Heiligenstein, J. (1998). Depression, health-related quality of life, and medical cost outcomes of receiving recommended levels of antidepressant treatment. *Journal of Family Practice, 47*(2), 446–452.

Reynolds, D. (1992). Escolarización eficaz de niños con necesidades educativas especiales. La investigación y sus implicaciones. *Siglo Cero, 143,* 24–32.

Rioux, M. H. (1997). Disability: The place of judgment in a world of fact. *Journal of International Disability Research, 41*(2), 102–111.

Roberts, L., & Clifton, R. (1992a). Measuring the affective quality of life of university students: The validation of an instrument. *Social Indicators Research, 27,* 113–137.

Roberts, L., & Clifton, C. (1992b). Measuring the cognitive domain of the quality of life: An instrument for faculties of education. *Canadian Journal of Education, 17*(2), 176–191.

Robine, J. M., Mathers, C. D., & Bucquet, D. (1993). Distinguishing health expectancies and health-adjusted life expectancies from quality-adjusted life years. *American Journal of Public Health, 83*(9), 797–798.

Rodríguez, A., Jarne, A., Soler, R., Miarons, R., & Grau, A. (1995). Estudio factorial y adaptación de la escala de calidad de vida en la esquizofrenia (QLS). *Revista de Psicología General y Aplicada, 48*(3), 353–364.

Roessler, W., Salize, H. J., Cucchiaro, G., Reinhard, I., & Kernig, C. (1999). Does the place of treatment influence the quality of life of schizophrenics? *Acta Psychiatrica Scandinavica, 100,* 142–148.

Rosen, M., Simon, E. W., & McKinsey, L. (1995). Subjective measure of quality of life. *Mental Retardation, 33*(1), 31–34.

Rosen, R. C., & Kostis J. B. (1995). Antihypertensive therapy and quality of life: Effects of drug and nondrug interventions on sleep, mood state, and sexual functioning. In J. E. Dimsdale & A. Baum (Eds.), *Quality of life in behavioral medicine research* (pp. 145–160). Hillsdale, NJ: Lawrence Erlbaum.

Rosenberg, M. (1965). *Society and the adolescent self-image.* Princeton, NJ: Princeton University Press.

Rosenfield, S. (1992). Factors contributing to the quality of life of the chronic mentally ill. *Journal of Health and Social Behavior, 33,* 229–315.

Rosenfield, S. (1997). Labeling mental illness: The effects of received services and perceived stigma on life satisfaction. *American Sociological Review, 62*(4), 660–672.

Rosenfield, S., & Neese-Todd, S. (1993). Why model programs work: Factors predicting the subjective quality of life of the chronic mentally ill. *Hospital and Community Psychiatry, 44,* 76–78.

Ross, J. (1993). Social phobia: The consumer's perspective. *Journal of Clinical Psychiatry, 54*(Suppl. 12), 5–9.

Rotter, J. B. (1966). Generalized expectancies for internal versus external control of reinforcement. *Psychological Monographs, 80,* 60–69.

Russo-Watson, S. M. (2000). Themes affecting social inclusion of individuals with disabilities in Brazil. In K. D. Keith & R. L. Schalock (Eds.), *Cross-cultural perspectives on quality of life* (pp. 241–255). Washington, DC: American Association on Mental Retardation.

Ryan, R. M., & Deci, E. L. (2000). Self-determination theory and the facilitation of intrinsic motivation, social development, and well-being. *American Psychologist, 55*(1), 68–78.

Sainfort, F., Becker, M., & Diamond, R. (1996). Judgments of quality of life of individuals with severe mental disorders: Patient self-report versus provider perspectives. *American Journal of Psychiatry, 153*(7), 497–502.

Salamanca Statement. (1994). *Salamanca statement and framework for action on special needs education.* Salamanca, Spain: University of Salamanca Department of Psychology.

Salend, S. J. (1998). *Effective mainstreaming. Creating inclusive classrooms* (3rd ed.). Newark, NJ: Merrill.

Sayce, L., Craig, T. K. J., & Boardman, A. P. (1991). The development of community mental health centres in the UK. *Social Psychiatry and Psychiatric Epidemiology, 26*(1), 18–20.

Schalock, R. L. (Ed.). (1990). *Quality of life: Perspectives and issues.* Washington, DC: American Association on Mental Retardation.

Schalock, R. L. (1994). Quality of life, quality enhancement, and quality assurance: Implications for program planning and evaluation in the field of mental retardation and developmental disabilities. *Evaluation and Program Planning, 17*(2), 121–131.

Schalock, R. L. (1996a). The quality of children's lives. In A. H. Fine & N. M. Fine (Eds.), *Therapeutic recreation for exceptional children: Let me in, I want to play* (2nd ed., pp. 83–94). Springfield, IL: Charles C. Thomas.

Schalock, R. L. (1996b). Reconsidering the conceptualization and measurement of quality of life. In R. L. Schalock (Ed.), *Quality of life: Vol. 1. Conceptualization and measurement* (pp. 123–139). Washington, DC: American Association on Mental Retardation.

Schalock, R. L. (Ed.). (1997). *Quality of life: Vol. 2. Application for persons with disabilities.* Washington, DC: American Association on Mental Retardation.

Schalock, R. L. (1999). A quest for quality: Achieving organizational outputs and personal outcomes. In J. Gardner & S. Nudler (Eds.), *Quality performance in human services* (pp. 55–80). Baltimore: Paul H. Brookes.

Schalock, R. L. (2000). Three decades of quality of life. In M. L. Wehmeyer & J. R. Patton (Eds.), *Mental retardation in the 21st Century* (pp. 335–358). Austin, TX: Pro-Ed.

Schalock, R. L. (2001). *Outcome-based evaluation* (2nd ed.). New York: Kluwer Academic/Plenum.

Schalock, R. L. (Ed.). (2002). *Out of the darkness and into the light: Nebraska's experience with mental retardation.* Washington, DC: American Association on Mental Retardation.

Schalock, R. L. (in press). Quality of life from a motivational perspective. In H. Switzky (Ed.), *International review of research in mental retardation: Current perspectives on individual differences in personality and motivation in persons with mental retardation and other developmental disabilities.* New York: Lawrence Erlbaum.

Schalock, R. L., Bartnik, E., Wu, F., Konig, A., Lee, C. S., & Reiter, S. (1990, May). *An international perspective in quality of life: Measurement and use.* Paper presented at the annual meeting of the American Association on Mental Retardation, Atlanta, GA.

Schalock, R. L., Bonham, G., & Marchand, C. (2000). Consumer-based quality of life assessment: A path model of perceived satisfaction. *Evaluation and Program Planning, 23,* 77–87.

Schalock, R. L., Brown, I., Brown, R., Cummins, R. A., Felce, D., Matikka, L., Keith, K. D., & Parmenter, T. (in press). Quality of life: Its conceptualization, measurement, and application: Results of an international consensus process. *Mental Retardation.*

Schalock, R. L., DeVries, D., & Lebsack, J. (1999). Rights, quality measures, and program changes. In S. S. Herr & G. Weber (Eds.), *Aging, rights, and quality of life: Prospects for older persons with developmental disabilities* (pp. 81–92). Baltimore: Paul H. Brookes.

Schalock, R. L., & Faulkner, E. H. (1997). Cross-validation of a contextual model of quality of life. *European Journal on Mental Disability, 4*(14), 18–27.

Schalock, R. L., & Genung, L. T. (1993). Placement from a community-based mental retardation program: A 15-year follow-up. *American Journal on Mental Retardation, 98*(3), 400–407.

Schalock, R. L., & Jensen, M. (1986). Assessing the goodness-of-fit between persons and their environments. *Journal of The Association for Persons with Severe Handicaps, 11*(2), 103–109.

Schalock, R. L., Keith, K. D., Hoffman, K., & Karan, O. C. (1989). Quality of life: Its measurement and use. *Mental Retardation, 27*(1), 25–31.

Schalock, R. L., & Keith, K. D. (1990). *The quality of life questionnaire.* Lincoln, NE: Nebraska Region III Mental Retardation Services.

Schalock, R. L., & Keith, K. D. (1993). *Quality of life questionnaire.* Worthington, OH: IDS Publishing.

Schalock, R. L., & Kelly, C. (1999). Sociocultural factors influencing social and vocational inclusion of persons with mental retardation: A cross-cultural study. In P. Retish & S. Reiter (Eds.), *Adults with disabilities: International perspectives in the community* (pp. 309–324). New York: Lawrence Erlbaum.

Schalock, R. L., Lemanowicz, J. A., Conroy, J. W., & Feinstein, C. S. (1994). A multivariate investigative study of the correlates of quality of life. *Journal on Developmental Disabilities, 3*(2), 59–73.

Schalock, R. L., Nelson, G., Sutton, S., Holtan, S., & Sheehan, M. (1997). Evaluación multidimensional del estado actual y la calidad de vida de los receptores de servicios de salud mental. *Siglo Cero, 28*(4), 5–12.

Scheier, M. F., Carver, C. S., & Bridges, M. W. (1994). Distinguishing optimism from neuroticism (and trait anxiety, self-mastery, and self-esteem). A reevaluation of the life orientation test. *Journal of Personality and Social Psychology, 67*(6), 1063–1078.

Scherer, M. J. (1996). Outcome of assistive technology use on quality of life. *Disability and Rehabilitation, 18*(9), 439–448.

Schipper, H., Clinch, J., & Powell, V. (1990). Definitions and conceptual issues. In B. Spilker (Ed.), *Quality of life assessments in clinical trials* (pp. 11–24). New York: Raven.

Schneier, F. R. (1994). Functional impairment in social phobia. *Journal of Clinical Psychiatry, 55,* 322–331.

Schneier, F. R., Johnson, J., Hornig, C. D., Liebowitz, M. R., & Weissman, M. M. (1992). Social phobia: Comorbidity and morbidity in an epidemiologic sample. *Archives of General Psychiatry, 49,* 282–288.

Schorr, L. B. (1997). *Common purpose: Strengthening families and neighborhoods to rebuild America.* New York: Anchor Books, Doubleday.

Schultz, J. R. (1999). Peter Senge: Master of change. *Executive Update,* 85–88.

Schutt, R., & Goldfinger, S. (1996). Housing preferences and perceptions of health and functioning among homeless mentally ill persons. *Psychiatric Services, 47*(4), 381–386.

Schuttinga, J. A. (1995). Quality of life from a federal regulatory perspective. In J. E. Dimsdale & A. Baum (Eds.), *Quality of life in behavioral medicine research* (pp. 31–42). Hillsdale, NJ: Lawrence Erlbaum.

Seaman, B., Roberts, P., Gilewski, M., & Nagai, J. (1993). Clinic to the real world: Community reintegration of head injured patients. *Journal of Cognitive Rehabilitation, 11,* 6–17.

Seligman, M. E. P., & Csikszentmihalyi, M. (2000). Positive psychology: An introduction. *American Psychologist, 55*(1), 5–14.

Seltzer, M. M., Wyngaarden Krauss, M., Hong, J., & Orsmond, G. I. (2001). Continuity or discontinuity of family involvement following residential transitions of adults who have mental retardation. *Mental Retardation, 39*(3), 181–194.

Shadish, W. R., Cook, T. D., & Leviton, L. C. (1991). *Foundations of program evaluation: Theories of practice.* Newbury Park, CA: Sage.

Shapiro, D., Hui, K. K., Oakley, M. E., Jagoda, P., & Jammer, L. D. (1995). Effectiveness of a combined behavioral-drug intervention for hypertension: Drug, personality, and quality of life effects. In J. E. Dimsdale & A. Baum (Eds.), *Quality of life in behavioral medicine research* (pp. 171–190). Hillsdale, NJ: Lawrence Erlbaum.

Shatahmasebi, S. M., Davies, R. P., & Wenger, G. (1992). A longitudinal analysis of factors related to survival in old age. *The Gerontologist, 32*(3), 404–413.

Sheikh, J. I., & Yesavage, J. A. (1986). Geriatric depression scale (GDS): Recent evidence and development of a shorter version. In T. L. Brink (Ed.), *Clinical gerontology: A guide to assessment and intervention.* New York: Haworth Press.

Sherbourne, C. D., Wells, K. B., & Judd, L. (1996). Functioning and well-being of patients with panic disorder. *American Journal of Psychiatry, 153*(2), 213–218.

Sherwood, N. (1996). Pleasure, choice, and the quality of everyday life. In D. M. Warburton & N. Sherwood (Eds.), *Pleasure and quality of life* (pp. 275–280). Chichester, England: John Wiley.

Shevin, M., & Klein, N. K. (1984). The importance of choice-making skills for students with severe disabilities. *Journal of The Association for Persons with Severe Handicaps, 9,* 159–166.

Shinn, C., Ahn, C., Kim, K., & Lee, H. (1992). Perceptions of quality of life in an industrializing country: The case of Korea. *Social Indicators Research, 10,* 475–492.

Shtasel, P. L., Gur, R. E., Gallacher, F., Heimberg, C., & Gur, R. (1992). Gender differences in the clinical expression of schizophrenia. *Schizophrenia Research, 7,* 225–231.

Shug, S. H. (1996). *Choosing a health outcome measurement instrument.* [On-line]. Available: www.meb.uni-bonn.de/standards/ERGHO/ERGHO_Instruments.html (Consulted March 4, 1999).

Siffert, M., Atoui, N., & Reynes, J. (1993). Retentissement de l'infection par le HIV sur la qualité de vie. In C. Hérisson & L. Simon (Eds.), *Evaluation de la qualité de vie* (pp. 224–250). Paris: Masson.

Sigafoos, A. D., Feinstein, C. B., Damond, M., & Reiss, D. (1988). The measurement of behavioral autonomy in adolescence: The autonomous functioning checklist. In C. B. Feinstein, A. Esman, J. Looney, G. Orvin, J. Schimel, A. Schwartzberg, A. Sorsky, & M. Sugar (Eds.), *Adolescent psychiatry: Vol. 15* (pp. 423–462). Chicago: University of Chicago Press.

Simpson, C. J., Hyde, C. E., & Faragher, E. B. (1989). The chronically mentally ill in community facilities. A study of quality of life. *British Journal of Psychiatry, 154,* 77–82.

Sinnott-Oswald, M., Gliner, J. A., & Spencer, K. C. (1991). Supported and sheltered employment: Quality of life issues among workers with disabilities. *Education and Training in Mental Retardation, 26*(4), 388–397.

Skantze, K. (1998). Subjective quality of life and standard of living: A 10-year follow-up of outpatients with schizophrenia. *Acta Psychiatrica Scandinavica, 98,* 390–399.

Skantze, K., & Malm, U. (1994). A new approach to facilitation of working alliances based on patients' quality-of-life goals. *Nordic Journal of Psychiatry, 1,* 37–55.

Skantze, K., Malm, U., Dencker, S. J., May, P. R. A., & Corrigan, P. (1992). Comparison of quality of life with standard of living in schizophrenic outpatients. *British Journal of Psychiatry, 161,* 797–801.

Skrtic, T. M. (1991). Students with special education needs: Artifacts of the traditional curriculum. In M. Ainscow (Ed.), *Effective schools for all.* London: Fulton.

Slade, M., Leesea, M., Taylor, R., & Thornicroft, G. (1999). The association between needs and quality of life in an epidemiologically representative sample of people with psychosis. *Acta Psychiatrica Scandinavica, 100*(2), 149–157.

Sloper, P. (1998). Models of service support for parents of disabled children. What do we know? What do we need to know? *Child Care, Health, and Development, 25,* 85–99.

Smith, D. C., Adelman, H. S., Nelson, P., Taylor, L., & Phares, V. (1987). Students' perceptions of control at school and problem behavior and attitudes. *Journal of School Psychology, 25,* 167–176.

Smith-Davis, J. (2000). People with disabilities in Russia: Progress and prospects. In K. D. Keith & R. L. Schalock (Eds.), *Cross-cultural perspectives on quality of life* (pp. 219–230). Washington, DC: American Association on Mental Retardation.

Snell, M., & Vogtle, L. (1997). Facilitating relationships of children with mental retardation in schools. In R. L. Schalock (Ed.), *Quality of life: Vol. 2. Application to persons with disabilities* (pp. 43–61). Washington, DC: American Association on Mental Retardation.

Snell, M. E., & Brown, F. (2000). *Instruction of students with severe disabilities* (5th ed.). Upper Saddle River, NJ: Prentice Hall.

Solomon, G. D. (1997). Evolution of the measurement of quality of life in migraine. *Neurology, 48,* 10–15.

Sommer, B., & Sommer, R. (1997). *A practical guide to behavioral research: Tools and techniques* (4th ed.). New York: Oxford University Press.

Spitzer, W. O., & Dobson, A. J. (1981). Measuring the quality of life of cancer patients. *Journal of Chronic Diseases, 34,* 585–597.

Stambrook, M., Peters, L. C., & Moore, A. D. (1989). Issues in the rehabilitation of severe traumatic brain injury: A focus on the neuropsychologist's role. *Canadian Journal of Rehabilitation Réadaptation, 3,* 87–98.

Stancliffe, R. (2000). Proxy respondents and quality of life. *Evaluation and Program Planning, 23,* 89–93.

Stancliffe, R. J., Abery, B. H., & Smith, J. (2000). Personal control and the ecology of community living settings: Beyond living-unit size and type. *American Journal on Mental Retardation, 105*(6), 431–454.

Stancliffe, R. J., Abery, B. H., Springborg, H., & Elkin, S. (2000). Substitute decision-making and personal control: Implications for self-determination. *Mental Retardation, 38*(5), 407–421.

Stark, J. A., & Goldsbury, T. (1990). Quality of life from childhood to adulthood. In R. L. Schalock (Ed.), *Quality of life: Perspectives and issues* (pp. 71–84). Washington, DC: American Association on Mental Retardation.

Stastny, P., & Amering, M. (1997). Integrating consumer perspectives on quality of life in research and service planning. In H. Katschnig, H. Freeman, & N. Sartorius (Eds.), *Quality of life in mental disorders* (pp. 261–269). Chichester, England: John Wiley.

Stewart, J. W., Quitkin, F. M., McGrath, P. J., Rabkin, J. G., Markowitz, J. S., Tricamo, E., & Klein, D. F. (1988). Social functioning in chronic depression: Effect of 6 weeks of antidepressant treatment. *Psychiatric Research, 25,* 213–222.

Stone, D. (1997). *Policy paradox: The art of political decision making.* New York: Norton.

Sturt, E., & Wykes, T. (1986). The social behaviour schedule: A validity and reliability study. *British Journal of Psychiatry, 148,* 1–11.

Sudman, S., & Bradburn, N. M. (1982). *Asking questions: A practical guide to questionnaire design.* San Francisco: Jossey-Bass.

Sullivan, G. S., Wells, K. B., & Leake, B. (1992). Clinical factors associated with better quality of life in a seriously mentally ill population. *Hospital and Community Psychiatry, 4,* 752–755.

Sullivan, M., Karlsson, J., & Ware, J. E. (1994). The Swedish SF-36 health survey: Evaluation of data quality, scaling assumptions, reliability, and construct validity across several populations. *Social Science and Medicine, 41,* 1349–1358.

Tamburini, M. (1998). *Quality of life assessment in medicine* [CD-Rom]. Milano, Italy: Glamm Interactive.

Taylor, S. J. (1994). In support of research on quality of life, but against QOL. In D. Goode (Ed.), *Quality of life for persons with disabilities: International perspectives and issues* (pp. 260–265). Cambridge, MA: Brookline.

Taylor, S. J., & Bogdan, R. (1996). Quality of life and the individual's perspective. In R. L. Schalock (Ed.), *Quality of life: Vol. 1. Conceptualization and measurement* (pp. 11–22). Washington, DC: American Association on Mental Retardation.

Telch, M. J., Schmidt, N., Jaimez, T. L., Jacquin, K., & Harrington, P. (1995). Impact of cognitive-behavioral treatment on quality of life in panic disorder patients. *Journal of Consulting and Clinical Psychology, 63*(5), 823–830.

Temple University (1988). *A national survey of consumers of services for individuals with developmental disabilities: Final survey instrument.* Washington, DC: National Developmental Disabilities Planning Council.

Tempier, R., Caron, J., Mercier, C., & Leouffre, M. (1998). Quality of life of severely mentally ill individuals: A comparative study. *Community Mental Health Journal, 34*(5), 477–485.

Test, D. W. (1994). Supported employment and social validity. *Journal of The Association for Persons with Severe Handicaps, 19*(2), 116–129.

Thompson, L., Powers, G., & Houchard, B. (1992). The wage effects of supported employment. *Journal of The Association for Persons with Severe Handicaps, 17*(21), 87–94.

Thomson, D. A. (1992). New direction. *Psychosocial Rehabilitation Journal, 15,* 105–109.

Thorndike, E. L. (1939). *Your city.* New York: Harcourt Brace.

Thorpe, L., Davidson, P., & Janicki, M. P. (2000). *Healthy aging — adults with intellectual disabilities: Biobehavioural issues.* Geneva, Switzerland: World Health Organization.

Thunedborg, K., Black, C., & Bech, P. (1995). Beyond the Hamilton depression scores in long-term treatment of manic-melancholic patients: Predictor of recurrence of depression by quality of life measurements. *Psychotherapy Psychosomatic, 64,* 131–140.

Timmons, V. (1993). *Quality of life of teenagers with special needs.* Unpublished doctoral dissertation, University of Calgary, Alberta, Canada.

Timmons, V., & Brown, R. (1997). Quality of life: Issues for children with handicaps. In R. I. Brown (Ed.), *Quality of life for people with disabilities: Models, research, and practice.* Cheltenham, England: Stanley Thornes.

Todd, S. (1991). Into adulthood: The vocational situation of young people with severe learning difficulties. *British Journal of Mental Subnormality, 37,* 5–16.

Townsend, M., Feeny, D. H., Guyatt, G. H., Furlong, W. J., Seip, A. E., & Dolovich, J. (1991). Evaluation of the burden of illness for pediatric asthmatic patients and their parents. *Annals Allergy, 67,* 403–408.

Trueman, P., & Duthie, T. (1998). Use of the hospital anxiety and depression scale (HADS) in a large general population study of epilepsy. *News Quality of Life Letter, 19,* 9–10.

Turnbull, A., Poston, D., Park, J., Mannan, H., & Marquis, J. (in press). Family quality of life outcomes. *Mental Retardation.*

Turnbull, A., Turnbull, R., & Brown, I. (Eds.). (in press). *Disability and the family: An international perspective on family quality of life.* Washington, DC: American Association on Mental Retardation.

Turnbull, H. R. III, & Brunk, G. L. (1997). Quality of life and public policy. In R L. Schalock (Ed.), *Quality of life: Vol. 2. Application to persons with disabilities* (pp. 201–209). Washington, DC: American Association on Mental Retardation.

Turnbull, H. R. III, & Stowe, M. J. (2001). A taxonomy for organizing the core concepts according to their underlying principles. *Journal of Disability Policy Studies, 12*(3), 177–197.

Turnbull, H. R. III, Wilcox, B. L., Stowe, M. J., & Umbarger, S. T. III. (2001). Matrix of federal statutes and federal and state court decisions reflecting the core concepts of disability policy. *Journal of Disabilty Policy Studies, 12*(3), 144–176.

Tuynman-Qua, H., De Jonghe, F., McKenna, S., & Hunt, S. (1992). *Quality of life depression rating scale.* Houston: Ibero.

UNESCO project for the training of teachers. In M. A. Verdugo & F. B. Jordán de Urríes (Eds.), *Hacia una nueva concepción de la discapacidad.* Salamanca: Amarú.

United Nations. (1989). *The convention on the rights of the child.* New York: Author.

United Nations. (1993). *United Nations standard rules on the equalization of opportunities for persons with disabilities.* New York: Author.

Urciuoli, O., Dello Buono, M., Padoani, W., & De Leo, D. (1998). Assessment of quality of life in the oldest-olds living in nursing homes and at home. *Archives of Gerontology and Geriatrics, 6,* 507–514.

Varni, J. W., Katz, E. R., Seid, M., Quiggins, D. J., Friedman-Bender, A., & Castro, C. M. (1998). *The pediatric cancer quality of life inventory* (PCQL). I. Instrument development, descriptive statistics, and cross-informant variance. *Journal of Behavioral Medicine, 21*(2), 179–199.

Varni, J. W., Seid, M., & Rode, C. A. (1999). The PedsQL: Measurement model for the pediatric quality of life inventory. *Medical Care, 37*(2), 126–139.

Veach, R. (1993). Utilization of community resources in a community-based rehabilitation program for mild to mild-moderate brain-injured survivors. *Journal of Cognitive Rehabilitation, 11,* 18–20.

Velde, B. P. (1997). Quality of life through personally meaningful activity. In R. I. Brown (Ed.), *Quality of life for handicapped people* (2nd ed., pp. 12–26). Cheltenham, England: Stanley Thornes.

Ventry, I. M., & Weinstein, B. E. (1982). The hearing handicap inventory for the elderly: A new tool. *Ear Hear, 3*(3), 128–134.

Verdugo, M. A. (1995). Calidad de vida y educación especial. Aportaciones de la nueva definición de retraso mental de la AAMR (1992). *Aula de Innovación Educativa, 45,* 11–14.

Verdugo, M. A. (1989a). *La integración personal, social, y vocacional de los deficientes psíquicos adolescentes.* Madrid: Ministerio de Educación y Ciencia, Centro de Investigación y Documentación Educativa.

Verdugo, M. A. (1989b). *Programas conductuales alternativos: 1. Habilidades sociales.* Madrid: MEPSA.

Verdugo, M. A. (1997). *Programa de habilidades sociales. Programas conductuales alternativos.* Salamanca: Amarú Ediciones. Colección Psicología, 1997.

Verdugo, M. A. (2000). Quality of life for persons with mental retardation and developmental disabilities in Spain: The present zeitgeist. In K. D. Keith & R. L. Schalock (Eds.), *Cross-cultural perspectives on quality of life* (pp. 263–280). Washington, DC: American Association on Mental Retardation.

Verdugo, M. A., Caballo, C., Pelaez, A., & Prieto, G. (in press). Evaluación de la calidad de vida de adultos con deficiencia visual y ceguera. *Integración.*

Verdugo, M. A., Caballo, C., Prieto, G., & Peláez, A. (2000). *Calidad de vida en personas ciegas y con deficiencia visual.* Salamanca, Spain: University of Salamanca, Instituto de Integración en la Comunidad, Organización Nacional de Ciegos de España.

Verdugo, M. A., Canal, R., & Gutierrez, B. G. (1997, May). *Enhancing residential services for persons with mental retardation and extensive support needs.* Paper presented at the 121st annual meeting of the American Association on Mental Retardation, New York.

Verdugo, M. A., & Gómez-Vela, M. (2000). *Evaluación de la calidad de vida de alumnos con discapacidad escolarizados en centros de integración.* Technical report. Salamanca, Spain: University of Salamanca, Instituto de Integración en la Comunidad.

Verdugo, M. A., & Sabeh, E. (2000). Quality of life assessment in children. *Psico Therma, 14,* 10–21.

Verri, A., Cummins, R. A., Petito, F., Vallero, E., Monteath, S., Gerosa, E., & Nappi, G. (1999). An Italian-Australian comparison of quality of life among people with intellectual disability living in the community. *Journal of Intellectual Disability Research, 43*(6), 513–522.

Vreeke, G. J., Janssen, C. G. C., Resnick, S., & Stolk, J. (1997). The quality of life of people with mental retardation: In search of an adequate approach. *International Journal of Rehabilitation Research, 20,* 289–301.

Wacker, H. R., Müllejans, R., Klein, K. H., & Battegay, R. (1992). Identification of cases of anxiety disorders and affective disorders in the community according to ICD-10 and DSM-III-R by using the Composite International Diagnostic Interview (CIDI). *International Journal of Methods of Psychiatric Research, 2,* 91–100.

Walsh, P. N. (2000). Quality of life and social inclusion. In K. D. Keith & R. L. Schalock (Eds.), *Cross-cultural perspectives on quality of life* (pp. 315–326). Washington, DC: American Association on Mental Retardation.

Wang, M. C. (1995). *Atención a la diversidad del alumnado.* Madrid: Narcea.

Warburton, D. M., & Suiter, J. I. (1996). The costs of job dissatisfaction. In D. M. Warburton & N. Sherwood (Eds.), *Pleasure and quality of life* (pp. 13–28). Chichester, England: John Wiley.

Warnock, H. M. (1978). *Report of the committee of enquiry into the education of handicapped children and young people.* London: Her Majesty's Stationery Office.

Ward, N. (2000). The universal power of speaking for oneself. In K. D. Keith & R. L. Schalock (Eds.), *Cross-cultural perspectives on quality of life* (pp. 33–36). Washington, DC: American Association on Mental Retardation.

Ware, J. E. (1991). Conceptualizing and measuring generic health outcomes. *Cancer, 67*(3), 774–779.

Ware, J. E., Keller, S., Bentler, P. M., Sullivan, M., Brazier, J., & Gandek, B. (1994). Comparison of health status measurement models and the validity of SF-36 in Great Britain, Sweden, and the USA. *Quality of Life Research, 3,* 68.

Ware, J. E., Snow, K., Kosinski, M., & Gandek, B. (1993). *SF-36 health survey: Manual and interpretation guide.* Boston: New England Medical Center.

Warner, R. (1999). Environmental interventions in schizophrenia: 1. The individual and the domestic levels. In M. Wasov (Ed.), *Speculative innovations for helping people with serious mental illness: New directions for mental health services* (pp. 61–70). San Francisco: Jossey-Bass.

Warshaw, M., Fierman, E., Pratt, L., Hunt, M., Yonkers, K. A., Massion, A. O., & Keller, M. (1993). Quality of life and dissociation in anxiety disorder patients with histories of trauma or PTSD. *American Journal of Psychiatry, 150*(10), 1512–1516.

Wehmeyer, M. L. (1994). Employment status and perception. *Research in Developmental Disabilities, 15*(2), 119–131.

Wehmeyer, M. L., & Kelchner, K. (1994). Interpersonal cognitive problem-solving skills in individuals with mental retardation. *Education and Training in Mental Retardation, 29,* 265–278.

Wehmeyer, M. L., & Sands, D. J. (1998). *Making it happen: Student involvement in education planning, decision-making, and implementation.* Baltimore: Paul H. Brookes.

Wehmeyer, M. L., & Schalock, R. L. (2001). Self-determination and quality of life: Implications for special education services and supports. *Focus on Exceptional Children, 33*(8), 1–16.

Wehmeyer, M. L., & Schwartz, M. (1998). The relationship between self-determination, quality of life, and life satisfaction for adults with mental retardation. *Education and Training in Mental Retardation and Developmental Disabilities, 33,* 3–12.

Weinstein, B. E. (1986). Validity of a screening protocol: Identifying elderly people with hearing problems. *American Speech-Language-Hearing Association, 28,* 41–45.

Weinstein, B. E., Spitzer, J. B., & Ventry, I. M. (1986). Test-retest reliability of the hearing handicap inventory for the elderly. *Ear Hear, 7*(5), 295–299.

Wells, K. B., Katon, W., Rogers, B., & Camp, P. (1994). Use of minor tranquilizers and antidepressant medications by depressed outpatients: Results from the Medical Outcomes Study. *American Journal of Psychiatry, 151*(7), 694–700.

Wesley, P. W. (1994). Innovative practices: Providing on-site consultation to promote quality in integrated child care programs. *Journal of Early Intervention, 18,* 391–402.

Westling, D. L., & Fox, L. (2000). *Teaching students with severe disabilities* (2nd ed.). Upper Saddle River, NJ: Prentice-Hall.

Whitney-Thomas, J. (1997). Participatory action research as an approach to enhancing quality of life for individuals with disabilities. In R. L. Schalock (Ed.), *Quality of life: Vol. 2. Application to persons with disabilities* (pp. 181–198). Washington, DC: American Association on Mental Retardation.

Wholey, J. S. (1997). Trends in performance measurement. In E. Chelimsky & W. R. Shadish (Eds.), *Evaluation for the 21st century: A handbook* (pp. 124–133). Thousand Oaks, CA: Sage.

Williams, A. H. (1985). Economics of coronary artery bypass grafting. *British Medical Journal, 291,* 326–329.

Williams, T., & Batten, M. (1981). *The quality of school life* (ACER Research Monograph No. 12). Hawthorn, Victoria: The Australian Council for Educational Research.

Williamson, G. M., & Walters, A. S. (1996). Perceived impact of limb amputation on sexual activity: A study of adult amputees. *Journal of Sex Research, 33,* 221–230.

Wilson, P. M. (1985). *The adapted pleasant events schedule.* Unpublished questionnaire. Sydney, Australia: University of Sydney.

Wittchen, H. U., & Beloch, E. (1996). The impact of social phobia on quality of life. *International Clinical Psychopharmacology, 11*(3), 15–23.

Wolfensberger, W. (1975). *Program analysis of service systems (PASS): Handbook and field manual* (3rd ed.). Toronto: National Institute on Mental Retardation.

Wolfensberger, W. (1994). Let's hang up 'quality of life' as a hopeless term. In D. A. Goode (Ed.), *Quality of life for persons with disabilities: International perspectives and issues* (pp. 450–465). Cambridge, MA: Brookline Books.

Wolfensberger, W. (1975). *PASS (Program Analysis of Service Systems): Handbook and field manual* (3rd edition). Toronto: National Institute on Mental Retardation.

Wolfensberger, W., & Glenn, L. (1983). *PASSING (program analysis of service systems' implementation of normalization goals): Normalization criteria and ratings manual.* Toronto: National Institute on Mental Retardation.

Wolfensberger, W., & Thomas, S. (1983). *Program analysis of service systems' implementation of normalization goals (PASSING): Normalization criteria and ratings manual* (2nd ed.). Toronto: National Institute on Mental Retardation.

Wolkenstein, A., & Butler, D. (1992). Quality of life among the elderly: Self-perspectives of some healthy elderly. *Gerontology and Geriatrics Education, 12*(4), 59–69.

Woodend, A. K., Nair, R. C., & Tang, S. L. (1997). Definition of life quality from a patient versus health care professional perspective. *International Journal of Rehabilitation Research, 20,* 71–80.

World Health Organization (1997). *Measuring quality of life: The World Health Organization quality of life instruments.* Geneva, Switzerland: Author.

World Health Organization (2000). *Aging and intellectual disabilities. Improving longevity and promoting healthy aging: Summative report.* Geneva, Switzerland: Author.

World Health Organization (2001). *International classification of functioning, disability, and health.* Geneva, Switzerland: Author.

World Health Organization Quality of Life Group (1993). Study protocol for the World Health Organization project to develop a quality of life assessment instrument (WHOQOL). *Quality of Life Research, 2,* 153, 159.

World Health Organization Quality of Life Group (1995a). The World Health Organization quality of life assessment (WHOQOL): Position paper from the World Health Organization. *Social Science and Medicine, 41* [Special issue on health-related quality of life: What is it? And how should we measure it?], 1403–1409.

World Health Organization Quality of Life Group (1995b). *Field trial WHO-QOL-100 February 1995: Facet definitions and questions.* Geneva, Switzerland: WHO (MNH/PSF 95.1.b).

Wright, R. G., Heiman, J. R., Shupe, J., & Olvera, G. (1989). Defining and measuring stabilization of patients during four years of intensive community support. *American Journal of Psychiatry, 146*(10), 1293–1298.

Wright, S. J. (1994). Health-related quality of life: A critical review of the concept and its measurement. In J. P. Dauwalder (Ed.), *Psychology and promotion of health* (pp. 163–169). Bern, Switzerland: Hogrefe & Huber.

Wykes, T. (1982). A hostel ward for "new" long-stay patients: An evaluation study of "a ward in a house." In J.K. Wing (Ed.), *Long-term community care: Experience in a London borough* (pp. 55–97). London: Psychological Medicine Monographs.

Yesavage, J. A., & Brink, T. L. (1983). Development and validation of a geriatric depression screening scale: A preliminary report. *Journal of Psychiatric Research, 17,* 37–49.

Zhu, D. T., Jin, L. J., Xie, G. J., & Xiao, B. (1998). Quality of life and personality in adults with epilepsy. *Epilepsia, 39*(11), 1208–1212.

Zigler, E., & Bennett-Gates, D. (1999). *Personality development in individuals with mental retardation.* Cambridge: Cambridge University Press.

Zimmerman, M. A. (1990). Toward a theory of learned hopelessness: A structural model analysis of participation and empowerment. *Journal of Research in Personality, 24,* 71–86.

Subject Index

Accountability
    reform movement, 22
    initiatives, 22
Aging
    and intellectual disability, 146–148
    QOL domains, 150–154
    QOL indicators, 150–154
    Rights, 148–149
    variables influencing quality of life, 144–146
Application of the QOL concept
    See Individual-level application; Organization-level application; QOL application; Societal-level application
Assessment
    See QOL measurement; Functional assessment; Personal appraisal; Social Indicators
Attitude scales
    See QOL measurement measurement strategies

Behavioral health
    See Mental health and behavioral health

Contextual factors, 33
    aging, 7
    education/special education, 7
    families, 7
    mental health and behavioral health, 7
    mental retardation/intellectual disabilities, 7
    physical health, 7

Cross-culture
    methodological issues, 284
    studies, 5–6

Disability
    changing conception of, 2, 13
    core concepts of disability policy, 338–339
    presumed causes of, 332–334
    scientific paradigms of, 334–336
    See also Ecological perspective
Diseases
    brain injury, 57–58
    cancer, 56–57
    cardiovascular, 59
    epilepsy, 60
    HIV, 57
    multiple sclerosis, 58–59
    spinal cord injury, 60

Ecological perspective, 6–7, 15
    See also Macrosystem; Microsystem; Mesosystem
Education/special education
    education resources, 38–39
    evaluation of consumer satisfaction, 39–40
    normalization and inclusion, 36
    QOL concept in schools, 38
    QOL domains, 41–45
    QOL indicators, 41–45
    themes and research issues, 36–38
Evaluation theory, 26
    See also Methodological pluralism; Functional Assessment; Personal Appraisal; Social Indicators

Family-centered QOL
    conceptual and measurement approaches, 166–167
    future research approaches, 169–176
    measurement and application principles, 176
    overview, 167–168
    outcome-focused evaluation model, 175
    QOL domains, 168, 170–171
    QOL indicators, 171
    vs. Individual QOL, 170–171
Families as Caregivers, 177
    caregiver guidelines, 178–179
Functional assessment, 27–28
    See also QOL measurement: measurement strategies
Future
    agendas, 367–370
    challenges and opportunities, 354–367

Handbook goals, 1–4
Health
    See Physical health

Individual-level application of QOL concept
    core person-referenced themes, 292–294
    core QOL application and conceptualization principles, 295
    ecological model of quality enhancement, 292
    person-centered planning, 320
    QOL hierarchy, 307
    self-determination strategies, 296–302
    quality enhancement techniques, 303–306

Inclusion, 36
Infancy
    health and QOL in, 61–62
Intellectual disabilities
    See Mental Retardation/Intellectual Disabilities
International covenants, 281–282

Macrosystem, 7, 15, 21–22
Mental health and behavioral health
    concepts, 77
    deinstitutionalization and community integration, 78–80
    QOL domains, 88–102
    QOL indicators, 88–102
    self-determination, 79–80
    social support, 80–81
    See also Mental Disorders
Mental Disorders
    anxiety, 86–87
    depression, 85–86
    schizophrenia, 82–85
Mental Retardation/Intellectual Disabilities
    concepts, 117–119, 134–135
    community integration and deinstitutionalization, 119–123
    employment, 123–125
    QOL domains, 126–134
    QOL indicators, 126–134
Mesosystem, 7, 15, 20–21
Methodological pluralism, 26
    See also QOL research
Microsystem, 6, 15, 20–21

Normalization, 36

Organizational change
    action steps, 315–319
    implementation of change, 326–327

Subject Index

outcomes planning inventory, 315–316, 330
Organization-level application of QOL concept
    implementation strategies, 319–325
    overview, 309–310
    organizational context, 310–312
    organization culture, 319
    person-centered planning, 320
    supports, 320–322
    quality enhancement techniques and QOL domains, 322–324
    total quality management, 319–320
    Outcomes-based evaluation model
    using desired outcomes to guide organization change, 319
    See also Organizational change; Outcomes-based evaluation; Quality enhancement techniques
Outcome measures
    advantages to using, 311
    consumer satisfaction measures, 313
    individual-referenced outcomes, 314
    organization-referenced outcomes, 313–314
    selection criteria, 318
    use of, 310–311
    See also Outcomes-based evaluation
Outcomes-based evaluation
    advantages and limitations, 328–329
    evaluation model, 314, 327–328
    measurement foci, 318–319
    monitoring system, 324–325
    using outcome information, 325–327

Personal appraisal, 27
    See also QOL measurement: measurement strategies
Personal well-being
    See QOL domains; QOL indicators
Person-centered planning, 320
Person-referenced outcomes, 23
Physical health
    concepts and measures, 53–54, 68–69
    health-related QOL (HRQOL), 52–55, 68
    quality adjusted life years, 55–56
    QOL domains, 63–69
    QOL indicators, 63–69
    See also Diseases; Infancy
Positive psychology, 358–360

Quality enhancement techniques
    domain specific, 303–306
    individual referenced, 303
    organization referenced, 322–324
    societal referenced, 336–345, 361–362
QOL application
    overview, 287–289
    See also Individual-level application; Organizational-level application; Societal-level application
QOL Assessment
    See QOL measurement
QOL Concept
    as a tool for change, 362–364
    discourses about, 12

implementation of
See Individual-level application, Organizational-level application; Societal-level application
importance of, 4–5, 19–22
meaning of, 1, 6, 11–13

QOL Domains
average rankings (literature-referenced frequency), 350
core indicators per domain, 184–187
definition of, 14
domain hierarchy model, 307
exemplary domains, 16, 18
history of, 14–15
list of, 24
rank ordering of (literature based), 182–183
relation to motivational states, 359
See also QOL literature; QOL measurement

QOL Indicators
aging, 150–153, 183
core indicators per QOL domain, 184–187, 351
definition of, 14, 25, 272
education/special education, 41–45, 182
family-centered, 171
guidelines, 188
mental health and behavioral health, 88–101, 183
mental retardation/intellectual disabilities, 126–133, 183
physical health, 63–67, 182
rank ordering of (literature based), 182–183
selection criteria, 25, 272
See also QOL literature; QOL measurement

QOL literature
critique of, 352–354
extensiveness, 4, 32
review criteria, 31–32
synthesis of QOL domains and indicators, 181–187

QOL measurement: current techniques (instruments) by QOL domain
aging, 224–229
education/special education, 196–201
mental health and behavioral health, 210–217
mental retardation/intellectual disabilities, 218–223
physical health, 202–209

QOL measurement: domain and system-levels indicators, 274–277

QOL measurement: historical approaches
behavioral measures, 191–192
discrepancy analysis, 191
ethnographic approaches, 190
multidimensional scales, 189–190
self-assessment, 192–193
social indicators, 192

QOL measurement: measurement issues
cross-cultural issues, 284
factors affecting responses, 230
interpretation guidelines, 283–284
measurement guidelines, 283
methodological decisions, 229–230
role of personal values, 230
use of proxies, 230–231
viability of measurement, 229

QOL measurement: measurement
  model, 268, 270
QOL measurement: measurement
  principles, 231–232, 269–272
QOL measurement: measurement
  strategies
    attitude scales, 277–278
    functional assessment/measures,
      279–280
    personal appraisal, 273
    questionnaires, 278–279
    rating scales, 189–190
    social indicators, 280–281
QOL measurement: step-wise
  procedures, 282–283
QOL model
    heuristic model, 24
    integration model, 360
    relation to quality and reform
      movements, 22–23
QOL principles
    application, 20, 195, 349
    conceptualization, 19, 295, 348
    measurement, 231–232,
      269–272, 349
QOL research
    holistic approach to, 364–367
    qualitative methodologies, 366
    quantitative methodologies, 365
    See also QOL literature; QOL
      measurement: current tech-
      niques; QOL measurement:
      domain and system-level indi-
      cators; QOL measurement:
      measurement issues: QOL
      measurement: measurement
      strategies
Quality revolution, 17, 23
Questionnaires, 278–279
    See also QOL measurement:
      measurement strategies

Rating scales, 189–190
    See also QOL measurement;
      measurement strategies
Reform movement, 326
    accountability dimension, 22
    quality dimension, 22

Satisfaction
    consumer satisfaction, 23
    See also Personal appraisal
Scientific paradigms of disability
    See Disability
Self-assessment
    See Personal appraisal
Self-determination
    characteristics, 296
    component elements, 296–302,
      355–356
Self-efficacy, 357–358
Social indicators, 28, 192
Social well-being research, 281
Social system perspective, 25
Societal-level application of QOL
  concept
    action steps, 336–345. 361–362
    contextual issues, 331–332
    guidelines for evaluating,
      344–345
    societal forces impacting a per-
      son, 369
Strategic plans, 325–326
Subjective well-being, 356–357
    See also Personal well-being
Supports
    support functions and QOL do-
      mains, 321–322
Systems perspective, 25
    See also Macrosystem; Mesosys-
      tem; Microsystem

Total quality management, 319–320